NETWORKS OF INTERNATIONAL TRADE AND INVESTMENT

Understanding globalisation through the lens of network analysis

Sara Gorgoni
University of Greenwich

Alessia Amighini
University of Eastern Piedmont, Italy

Matthew Smith
University of Greenwich

Series in Economics

VERNON PRESS

www.vernonpress.com

In the Americas:
Vernon Press
1000 N West Street,
Suite 1200, Wilmington,
Delaware 19801
United States

In the rest of the world:
Vernon Press
C/Sancti Espiritu 17,
Malaga, 29006
Spain

Series in Economics

Library of Congress Control Number: 2018942478

ISBN: 978-1-62273-065-0

Notice:
Color images of figures can be downloaded at the book's page
[URL: https://vernonpress.com/book/96]

Table of Contents

Preface

> "Ithaka gave you the marvelous journey.
> Without her you would not have set out [...]
> And if you find her poor, Ithaka won't have fooled you.
> Wise as you will have become, so full of experience,
> you will have understood by then what these Ithakas mean."
> (C.P. Cavafy, *Collected Poems.* Translated by Edmund Keeley and Philip Sherrard. Edited by George Savidis. Revised Edition. Princeton University Press, 1992)

The roots of this book are to be traced back to the autumn of 2009 when Alessia Amighini and I were at the University of Eastern Piedmont in Italy. I was then a post-doctoral fellow on a project aimed at applying Network Analysis (NA) to the study of foreign direct investment of multinationals from emerging economies and she was an already established researcher in the area of international trade. Over a few informal lunches, we had grown quickly fascinated with the idea of using NA to map and analyse - rather than just conceptualise – the complex network of international trade, and we started working on some research questions in international trade in the automotive sector which culminated on our first publication in this area.

In September 2010 I was hired by the University of Greenwich and became part of the Centre for Business Network Analysis (CBNA). The University of Greenwich had a long tradition in the area of Social Network Analysis (SNA) thanks to Prof. Martin Everett, and was the birthplace of UCINET, one of the most widely used software in SNA. The CBNA provided me with the support an inspiration needed to carry out further research in this area.

In October 2013 Alessia and I attended an executive training seminar on Global Value Chains: Policy Implications and Opportunities by the Academy of Global Governance at the European Institute in Florence. The seminar brought together representatives from the major international organisations and renowned international professors to discuss, among other things, methodological issues related to the study of the international fragmentation of production. To us, the most relevant outcome of the three days seminar was the shared view across all participants about the limitations of the current international datasets to quantitatively map and analyse Global Value Chains (GVCs). More specifically, it was clear that there was a gap in the possibility of linking micro (firm level) strategies to macro (trade-level) flows. Timely enough, in January of that same year Prof. Bruce Cronin and I were awarded a

University of Greenwich Vice-Chancellor scholarship on a research project on Corporate Networks of International Investment and Trade, which gave us the opportunity to support for three years a PhD student to work on linking firm-level and country-level data in order to better understand the international fragmentation of production and its trade implications. Matthew Smith was selected among many talented applicants to embark with us in this adventure. During the following years Alessia, Matthew and I worked jointly and separately to better understand today's complex international organisation of production. During that time, we attended several conferences and workshops, where we increasingly saw works applying network analysis to the study of international trade. In 2015 and 2016 together with Prof. Raja Kali we also organised a special session on Networks of International Trade and Investment in the International (Sunbelt) Conference organised by the International Network for Social Network Analysis (INSNA). The experience of presenting all over the world and the submissions we received to the special sessions organised on this topic made it clear that this had become a very fertile area of research. There are scholars in different parts of the world who work on related topics and address similar challenges, yet they come from a variety of disciplines and network approaches, which makes it sometimes challenging for someone coming to this research area for the first time to make sense of the rich yet fragmented literature.

The aim of this book is therefore to provide a starting point, state of the art, and examples that will aid interested readers in the exploration of this literature and help them make sense of the inter-disciplinary nature of the work that applies network analysis to international trade and investment in the hope that this will facilitate navigation in these deep waters and push research forward towards unexplored shores.

Sara Gorgoni

Acknowledgements

We thank our chapter contributors for their knowledge, dedication and patience in producing this book. We also thank our colleagues who provided advice, comments and invaluable feedback on the individual chapters. In particular, Prof. Bruce Cronin, Dr. Nicola Perra, Dr. Riccardo de Vita, Dr. Athina Piterou, Prof. Silvia Nenci, Dr. Paola Zappa, Dr. Gabriella Cagliesi and Dr. Cornell Jackson.

List of Tables

List of Figures

List of Acronyms

BRIC	Brazil, Russia, India and China
COW	Correlates of War Project
EMNE	Emerging (economy) Multinational Enterprise
ERGM	Exponential Random Graph Model
FDI	Foreign Direct Investment
GDP	Gross Domestic Product
GPN	Global Production Network
GVC	Global Value Chain
GVT	Global Value Tree
HTI	Historical Trade Index
ICIO	Inter-Country Input-Output
IMF	International Monetary Fund
IMN	International Migration Network
ITN	International Trade Network
MNE	Multinational Enterprise
NA	Network Analysis
NS	Network Science
OECD	Organisation for Economic Co-operation and Development
PTA	Preferential Trade Agreement
RTA	Regional Trade Agreement
SAOM	Stochastic Actor Oriented Model
SNA	Social Network Analysis
UN	United Nations
WION	World Input-Output Network
WTM	World Trade Map
WTN	World Trade Network
WTW	World Trade Web

Author Biographies

Antoine Allard received a Ph.D. in theoretical physics from Université Laval in Québec, Canada, in 2014. He then worked as an FRQ-NT postdoctoral fellow at the Departament de Física Fonamental of the Universitat de Barcelona and then as a senior research fellow at the Centre de Recerca Matemàtica in Bellaterra, Spain. He came back to the Universitat de Barcelona in January 2018 as a Juan de la Cierva postdoctoral fellow and will start as an assistant professor at the Département de physique, de génie physique et d'optique at Université Laval in August 2018. His research interests include the modeling of complex networks, the application of network science to neuroscience, and the mathematical modeling of the propagation of emergent infectious diseases.

Alessia Amighini is Co-Head of Asia Centre and Senior Associate Research Fellow at ISPI. She is Associate Professor of Economics at the Department of Economic and Business Studies (DiSEI) at the University of Piemonte Orientale (Novara, Italy), and Adjunct Professor of International Economics at the Catholic University (Milan, Italy). Amighini previously worked as an Associate Economist at the United Nations Conference on Trade and Development (UNCTAD, Geneva, Switzerland). Alessia holds a PhD in Development Economics from the University of Florence (Italy) and a Master in Economics as well as a BA in Economics from Bocconi University (Milan, Italy). She has published in many international peer-reviewed journals such as China Economic Review, World Development, The World Economy, International Economics, China and the World Economy. Alessia also published chapters in several books for Edwar Elgar, Harvard University Press, Oxford University Press, Palgrave, Routledge; she coauthored 'L'economia della Cina' (Carocci, 2007) and Macroeconomics: A European Perspective (Pearson, 2010 and 2013). She has contributed to several international research projects sponsored by Central Bank of Sweden, Inter-American Development Bank and UNU-WIDER.

Marián Boguñá Espinal is an associate professor and ICREA Academia researcher at the Departament de Física de la Matèria Condensada of the Universitat de Barcelona. He graduated in Physics in 1994 and obtained his Ph.D. also in Physics in 1998. In 1999, he moved to the USA to do a postdoctoral stay at the National Institutes of Health, Washington DC. After this period, he moved back to Barcelona where, in 2003, he was awarded a Ramón y Cajal fellowship. He got the tenure position at the end of 2008. During this period, he has also spent several months in the USA as an invited guest scientist at Indiana University. M. Boguñá has written over 80 publications in major peer-reviewed international scientific journals. Among those, Nature, Nature Physics, Nature Communications, Proceedings of the National Academy of Sciences US, Physical Review Letters, and Physical Review X. Since January 2013 he serves as an editorial board member for Scientific Reports.

Bruce Cronin is a Professor at the University of Greenwich. He specialises in the role of business networks in strategy and innovation within and across organisational and national boundaries. He is Director of Research for the University of Greenwich Business School and Director of the University's Centre for Business Network Analysis since its establishment. His corporate clients have included Unilever, The Pensions Regulator, Defra, Nesta, NHS, The Work Foundation, The Institute of Management Consultants, Universities UK and the London Knowledge Network.

Luca De Benedictis is a Professor in Economics. He teaches International Economics at the University of Macerata and at Luiss, Rome, Italy. He serves as the Secretary General of the Italian Economic Association and as Editor in chief of the Italian Economic Journal, associate editor of the International Journal for Re-Views in Empirical Economics, and of the Journal of Historical Network Research. His research focuses on the empirics of international trade and migration. His ongoing research deals with network theory and applied network analysis, on causal models with interference, on historical trade and trade policy and on the theory and application of gravity models to international trade and migration issues.

Giulia De Masi is a Ph.D. in Physics and Visiting Professor in the Canadian University in Dubai. In her research, she applies methods from Statistical Physics and Machine Learning to several topics in Economics, including interbank market, credit market, and foreign direct investments. As a Post-Doctoral Researcher in the Polytechnic University of Marche and Visiting Researcher at Hitachi Research Laboratory in Nara, Japan, she conducted research on Italian and Japanese Credit Networks. She also leads Data Science-based Projects at the industry level. Her current research interests are the analysis of statistical properties and modelling of Complex Networks, Economic Networks, particularly Foreign Direct Investment networks, Machine Learning methods for forecasting and decision making.

Guillermo García-Pérez is a Ph.D. student in Physics at the Departament de Física de la Matèria Condensada of the Universitat de Barcelona. He graduated in Physics in 2014 and obtained his MSc with honours in Advanced Physics in 2015. Currently, his research focuses on geometric models able to explain the universal features exhibited by complex networks from many different domains. He is also interested in science outreach; he is a cofounder of the non-profit organisation "Quadrívium per la divulgació," which has delivered more than 100 talks in schools and public libraries across Catalunya.

Sara Gorgoni is a Ph.D. in Development Economics and Senior Lecturer at the Department of International Business and Economics at the University of Greenwich Business School, where she is Programme Leader for the BA Hons Business Economics. She is part of the Centre for Business Network Analysis at the same university, and her current research activity relates to the application of network analysis to international trade and investment to investigate the international fragmentation of production. She has conducted research on foreign direct investments of multinationals from emerging economies and on innovation and upgrading in Global Value Chains. Dr. Gorgoni has worked as a consultant for the private sector and international organisations including the Food and Agriculture Organisation, the World Bank and the United Nations Economic Commission for Latin America and the Caribbean.

Raja Kali is Professor in Economics and the ConocoPhillips Chair in International Economics & Business. He received his Ph.D. and MA from the University of Maryland at College Park. His major areas of research include networks in trade and finance, industrial organization, development economics, and economics & finance of emerging markets. He has published his work in journals including Journal of Economics and Management Strategy, the Review of Social Economy, the Journal of Economic Geography, Economics and Sociology, the Journal of Interdisciplinary Economics, the Journal of Development Economics, the Journal of Comparative Economics, the Journal of Banking and Finance, the Economic Inquiry, the Journal of International Business Studies, and the Journal of International Trade and Economic Development.

Massimo Riccaboni (PhD) Full Professor of Economics, Director of AXES research unit at IMT Lucca. He is visiting professor at the Dept. of Managerial Economics, Strategy and Innovation at K.U.Leuven. He has published, among the others, in Science, PNAS, Nature Reviews, Journal of the European Economic Association, Management Science, Research Policy, Economic Letters, International Journal of Industrial Organization, World Economy R&D Management, Health Affairs, Marketing Letters, Health Policy, Small Business Economics, Scientometrics, Physical Review E, New Journal of Physics, Journal of Economic Dynamics and Control, Nature Scientific Data, Nature Scientific Reports, Europhysics Letters. His current research focuses on industrial organization, innovation, trade and production networks and the economics of science, with particular reference to the life sciences.

Giorgio Ricchiuti is an Associate Professor at the Department of Economics and Management of the University of Florence (Italy), instructor of Macroeconomics at New York University in Florence and, since the beginning of 2016, fellow of the Complexity Lab in Economics (CLE) at Catholic University in Milan.
His research is focused on both empirical and theoretical analysis in International and Industrial Economics. His empirical research focuses on how different modes of internationalization - mainly FDI - affect productivity, sales and firms' survival probability. His theoretical analysis focuses on dynamic models with heterogeneous agents and bounded rationality in financial markets, on the market structure when the demand is unknown, and new sources of heterogeneity among firms with different modes of internationalization.

Stijn Ronsse is visiting professor in the Economics Department at Ghent University. Stijn completed his undergraduate studies in history and economics and his Ph.D. in applied economics (2015) at the same university. His research interests lie in the area of cliometrics and quantitative economic history, ranging from international trade to industrialisation. He has collaborated actively with researchers in other disciplines, combining economics, history, and physics.

Valerio Leone Sciabolazza is a Postdoc Associate at the University of Florida (UF). He is an applied economist and his research interests center on spatial econometrics, the econometrics of networks, and the new science of networks. He received a Ph.D. in International Economics and Finance from Sapienza University in 2016. Before joining UF, he was a Postdoc Associate at the Swedish Institute for Social Studies (SOFI). He is part of the UF Network Science Program, where he conducts research on the determinants and constraints that shape professional collaborations among scientists. He also works on two different sets of topics, namely migrant networks and their impact on labor market outcomes; and the causal effect of political networks on legislative success.

M. Ángeles Serrano obtained her Ph.D. in Physics at the Universitat de Barcelona in 1999. One year later, she also received her Master in Mathematics for Finance from the Centre de Recerca Matemàtica. After four years in the private sector as IT consultant and mutual fund manager, she returned to academia in 2004 to work in the field of Network Science. She completed her postdoctoral research at Indiana University (USA), the École Polytechnique Fédérale de Lausanne (Switzerland) and IFISC Institute (Spain). She came back to Barcelona in 2009 when she was awarded a Ramón y Cajal Fellowship at UB. In February 2009, she obtained the Outstanding Referee award of the

American Physical Society. She is a Founder Member of Complexitat, the Catalan Network for the study of Complex Systems, and a Promoter Member of UBICS, the Universitat de Barcelona Institute of Complex Systems. M. Ángeles Serrano is ICREA Research Professor at the Universitat de Barcelona from October 2015.

Matthew Smith is a postdoctoral researcher at the University of Oxford. Dr Smith completed his PhD in international business and economics at the University of Greenwich in 2016, where he made use of advanced social network analysis techniques to inform on the organisation of production in the global economy. Broadly, his research interests focus on social network analysis, more specifically, the application of Exponential Random Graph Models (ERGMs) to explain how observed network structures emerge, and multilevel network analysis. Currently, Dr Smith is working on a project that aims at testing hypotheses derived from theoretical models of cultural evolution to shed light on the diffusion of innovations in a small scale society.

Silvia Sopranzetti is research fellow at LUISS University and Adjunct Professor in International Economics at the University of Roma Tor Vergata. She holds a Ph.D. from the University of Roma Tor Vergata. Her main areas of research are international trade, global and European integration of production and value added flows and social network analysis.

Samuel Standaert postdoctoral researcher at Ghent University, visiting associate professor at Clemson University and is a FWO [PEGASUS]^2 Marie Skłodowska-Curie research fellow. His research can be situated in the confluence of applied econometrics, international trade, and development economics. Examples include the study of the effects and determinants of trade agreements, gravity models, as well as how to measure corruption, migration policy and inclusive and sustainable structural transformation.

Lucia Tajoli is Professor of Economics at the Department of Economics, Management, and Industrial Engineering at Politecnico di Milano, Italy, where she teaches Economics, International Economics and Economic Policy. She is also Senior Research Fellow at the Italian Institute for International Political Studies (ISPI) in Milan, and member of the Scientific Committee of the Italian Trade Agency, the Italian Trade Study Group, and the European Trade Study Group. Her research activity deals with theoretical and empirical issues related to international trade and economic integration among countries, currently with a special focus on international fragmentation of production, and with applications of network analysis.

Ekaterina Turkina holds a Ph.D. in Public and International Affairs from the University of Pittsburgh, USA. She is associate professor at HEC Montreal and a holder of Professorship in International Business Networks. Ekaterina is also an associate editor of Journal of Small Business and Entrepreneurship, as well as a member of International Advisory Board of International Journal of Productivity Management and Assessment Technologies. Her main research areas are social network analysis, innovation and inter-firm networks, industrial clustering, international business and international entrepreneurship. She has published in Journal of Business Venturing, Economic Geography Journal, Journal of Common Market Studies, Journal of Business Research, Physica A: Statistical Mechanics and its Applications, International Journal of Computer Science and Network and other journals. She has written four books and was a recipient of several awards, including the Highly Commended Paper Award from the Journal of Enterprising Communities, Best Paper from the European Community Studies Association.

Ari Van Assche is Associate Professor and chair of the International Business department at HEC Montreal, as well as research fellow at the research centers CIRANO and IRPP. He is deputy editor of the Journal of International Business Policy. He holds a BA and an MA in Chinese Studies from the Katholieke Universiteit Leuven and a Ph.D. in Economics from the University of Hawaii at Manoa. His research focuses on the organization of global value chains and their implication for trade and industrial cluster policy. In 2017, he co-edited the book Redesigning Canadian Trade Policy for New Global Realities.

Benjamin Vandermarliere holds an interdisciplinary Ph.D. in Physics and applied economics from Ghent University where he is currently working as a postdoc. His focus lies on the empirical analysis of economic interactions between individuals, companies, or countries. To this end, he combines tools from econometrics, machine learning, and network theory. He has published on payment networks, interbank lending, and international trade. Currently, he is working on a project concerning the drivers of social mobility.

Zhen Zhu is a Lecturer in Network Science jointly affiliated with the Centre for Business Network Analysis and the Department of International Business and Economics of the University of Greenwich. He obtained a PhD in Economics from the Sam M. Walton College of Business of the University of Arkansas in the United States in 2013. His work on trade and production networks has appeared or is forthcoming in Journal of Complex Networks, Journal of Public Economic Theory, Network Science, PLOS ONE, and The World Economy.

Introduction

The international economy in recent decades has witnessed fundamental changes in the way manufacturing is organised: production processes are often split across a number of stages located in countries that are frequently far apart from each other. Multinational enterprises (MNEs) play a focal role in this reorganisation of production, as they spread out their manufacturing and supply chain activities globally, through international investment and intra firm trade. Our ability to understand the global economy, therefore, requires understanding the interdependencies between entities involved in such fragmented production.

Traditional methods and statistical approaches are insufficient to address this challenge. Global Value Chain (GVC) analysis, the leading theoretical approach trying to make sense of these changes suffers from several limitations, most prominently the difficulty of aggregating from firm-level observations to national-level implications. As production is more and more fragmented across borders, countries are increasingly integrated through international investment and trade, channels and vehicles of a more interconnected world economy. Therefore, a useful approach would be one that allows encompassing the overall networks of investment and trade across countries, not just among firms spreading their activities across countries.

The most promising approach so far is network analysis. Among the benefits of using a network analysis over standard statistical techniques, is the fact that it assumes dependency of observations, and therefore represents a more realistic approach to analyse the interdependence that characterises investment, production, and trade today. Traditional approaches used to analyse international trade (most notably, gravity models) consider only the bilateral relationships, meaning that in analysing trade between countries *i* and *j*, it assumes that this is independent from any other relationship *i* and *j* establish with other countries. This, however, is too strong an assumption, especially given that most of today's trade is a reflection of production fragmentation among different locations, which imposes the necessity to consider that the choice for a firm to source/export from/to country *i* and country *j* depends from the possibility of also sourcing/exporting from/to other locations. Network analysis allows to specifically model the interdependencies amongst actors, and when applied to international trade and investment data it can provide new insight.

This edited book makes a case for network analysis to be used alongside existing techniques in answering challenging questions in the areas of international business and economics, such as whether trade has become more global or regional, to what extent emerging economies challenge the role of traditional producers in specific industries. The book looks at how the approach and methodologies of network analysis can contribute in explaining international business and economics phenomena, in particular, related to international trade and investment. It provides a comprehensive but accessible explanation of network analysis' applications and some of the most recent methodological advances that can contribute to research in the area of international trade and investment.

In this book we bring together research originating from both network science (see the chapter by Serrano et al.; Tajoli and De Benedictis, etc.) – the majority - and social network analysis (see chapter by Smith et al.), with the aim of providing a comprehensive account of the fertile field that applies network analysis to international trade and investment. Chapter 1 by Sara Gorgoni and Matthew Smith describes the origins of social network analysis and network science – the two main approaches taken in this book - and the differences between the two. It introduces briefly to the theory and methods of network analysis and provides an overview of the most recent methodological developments and how these can be applied to push further our understanding of complex contemporary economic phenomena. It introduces the reader to what a network is, by defining key terms such as nodes and ties, and by applying these to the context of international trade in particular in order to describe the International Trade Network (ITN). It also provides an introduction to network measures that are commonly used in describing the structure of a network, and in particular, the ITN, as well as of more advanced statistical models applied to international trade and investments.

Chapter 2 by Matthew Smith and Sara Gorgoni offers a comprehensive literature review that surveys applications of network analysis to international trade and investment data and discusses how this approach and methodology can complement statistical techniques that have traditionally been used in the empirical literature. The chapter identifies five key themes in this literature: International trade; Foreign Direct Investments; The international fragmentation of production; Regionalisation and globalisation; and, finally, Multinational Enterprises (MNEs). For each of these research areas, traditional approaches will first be examined, followed by a discussion of how network analysis can contribute answering the research questions those methods have left partly unanswered.

Chapters 3-8 of the book are devoted to the application of network techniques to the analysis of a number of broad research questions in international trade. Chapter 3 by Benjamin Vandermarliere, Samuel Standaert, and Stijn Ronsse studies the structure and the evolution of the world's historical trade patterns from the 1880s to the late 1980s, with the aim to identify which specific pattern of international integration prevailed. Three patterns are tested: globalisation (a geographically neutral world is one where all countries trade with each other, irrespective of their distance or other geographical concerns); regionalisation (a situation where the trade network is organized into a few regions containing countries that trade intensively with each other, but where inter-regional links are sparse); and core-periphery (a world where there is a small core of very densely connected countries surrounded by a large peripheral group of countries that trades mostly with the core and not among themselves). Using the historical trade integration index that measures the relative importance of trade flows for countries around the world from as early as the 1880s, the total time-period under study is split up into three sub-periods: the first globalisation wave (1880-1913), the Interbellum, i.e. a period of de-globalisation (1919-1939) and the second globalisation wave until the fall of the Berlin wall (1946-1989). The authors find evidence of a very strong core-periphery structure during the first globalisation wave, where the core is made up of countries like the USA and Great Britain, the semi-periphery by India and China, and the periphery by Chile and Peru. However, this structure is progressively dismantled over the next two periods, when an increasing number of countries started forming their own blocks and the core itself is no longer the same homogenous group it was during the first interbellum. This is when we start seeing signs of increasing regionalisation, together with strong links with countries in the core group. Most regional blocks also start forming links with blocks other than the core (a sign of globalisation), but these links remain relatively weak. Finally, the start of the second globalisation wave is not marked by either globalisation, regionalisation or core-periphery, but rather a hub-and-spoke pattern where strong regional clusters are linked to a central hub.

In a nice match with Chapter 3, Chapter 4 by Guillermo García Pérez, Marian Bogugñá, Antoine Allard, and Maria Ángeles Serrano offers a complementary analysis of the historical evolution of the world trade network to understand the long-term evolution of international economic integration. The authors apply a new approach to the study of international trade taken from network geometry, i.e., the so-called World Trade Atlas, a collection of fourteen decades of maps of the world trade network since 1870. Beyond the obvious advantages of visualization, the World Trade Atlas increases significantly our understanding of the long-run evolution of the international trade system and helps us to address a number of important and challenging questions. In particular, which is the role of distance in trade - not merely in geographical terms - and how far or close have countries been through recent history? The answers lead to a clear picture in which the evolution of the international trade system has been shaped by three simultaneous forces: globalisation, hierarchisation, and localisation. The authors find that the international trade system is becoming more heterogeneous and hierarchical than ever before and, at the same time, more interconnected and clustered into natural trade communities not fully consistent with Preferential Trade Agreements. Two waves of globalisation are identified in recent history. The first wave goes from 1870 until the beginning of World War I and results from decreasing costs for transportation of materials and goods triggered by the Industrial Revolution, with steam power encouraging the expansion of railroad networks and oceanic routes and the telegraph connecting the two sides of the Atlantic. The second wave, from 1960 to the present is intimately related to the ease of the exchange of information and ideas facilitated by the Information Technology Revolution, which is causing communications costs to drop dramatically at the same time that information management capabilities are exploding. As a result, the large-scale organization of the world economies nowadays exhibits a high level of local heterogeneity and of global interdependence at the same time. The world is not flat. Instead, the authors claim it is hyperbolic. In contrast to the widespread perception that globalisation has led to a decrease in the importance of distance, countries preferentially select their significant trade partners from geographically close neighbours. According to the World Trade Atlas 1870-2013, the role of trade distance has not decreased but increased over time over the last 14 decades. Interestingly, this trend seems to have been reverted since 2009, maybe because of a fast-rising China as a new commercial power and due to the effects of the economic crisis. The World Trade Atlas approach also helps to shed light on a further issue that has long challenged scholars and policymakers alike, i.e., whether the proliferation of PTAs has effectively reduced barriers to trade between their members. The authors find only a moderate overlap of PTAs with natural communities, meaning that PTAs have not necessarily reduced barriers to trade between their members, but they may serve purposes other than trade in economics or politics since their ambiguous consequences on the creation or steering of trade depend upon several other conditions.

Chapter 5 by Luca De Benedictis and Lucia Tajoli explores the issue of emerging countries' role in the international trade network in order to assess whether they are standing out from the rest of developing countries in relation to the central position they occupy and their effect on the overall connectivity of the network. The authors use local and global centrality measures and find that the overall structure of the international trade network changed significantly over the past decades shifting the relative position of many countries. The authors observe an international trade network composed by a system of hubs and satellites, with emerging countries occupying different positions in this structure. The results from this chapter provide a nice complement to some of the results in Chapter 3, which also detected a hub and spoke structure as a pattern of the international integration that describes today's global economy. The authors identify a heterogeneous group of emerging countries scattered across all continents, different in economic size and population, with different levels of development and models of specialization and uneven growth paths. Among them, they focus on two cases, China and Mexico, which followed different trajectories that are quite paradigmatic in interpreting the role of emerging countries in world trade. On the one hand, China rises to a hub position at the regional level for some specific manufacturing sectors, but also globally to a certain extent. On the other hand, Mexico became the satellite of the US economy. In addition to the descriptive analysis based on centrality measures, the authors test the conditional correlation between the centrality indices discussed in the first part of the chapter with other economic variables to assess how relevant the position of the emerging countries in the international trade network is in affecting their economic performance. The analysis reveals the crucial role of trade links for emerging economies.

Chapter 6 by Massimo Riccaboni and Zhen Zhu explores the issue of the international integration of countries through trade by analysing the World Input-Output Network (WION), i.e. the complex web of trade relations that link together countries that participate in Global Value Chains (GVCs), where the nodes are the individual sectors in different countries and the links are the input-output relationships between them. The chapter takes a network approach to investigate the GVCs at the macroeconomic level by relying on a specific national accounting framework, the input-output tables, more specifically the World Input-Output Database (WIOD) 2016 release, which covers 43 major countries in the world for the period from 2000 to 2014. The authors apply a community detection method to visually detect the presence and significance of GVCs for the years 2000 and 2014 and decomposing the final demand of each sector into the value-added contributions from all over the world. They find that the sectors belonging to the same country tend to cluster together, which suggests that most transactions still happen domestically. Moreover, some cross-country communities - such as the NAFTA (North American Free Trade Agreement) - are detected for the years examined. Perhaps the chapter's most interesting contribution is that the method exposed allows them to detect the presence and significance of GVCs at the sectoral level in a clear way. The authors use a network pruning algorithm to reveal the essential value-added relationships for a selected root country. The resulted sub-network is called Global Value Tree (GVT). GVTs can be generated for each sector in the world and for each year there is data available. This allows the authors to trace the evolution of the GVTs for a given sector or compare the GVTs across countries and sectors over time.

Chapter 7 by Raja Kali, Ekaterina Turkina and Ari Van Assche focuses on a specific industry case – the aerospace – to answer the question of whether changes in the structure of the global aerospace cluster network have allowed it to become an increasingly "small world", i.e. a network which combines high clustering among nodes with short average distance across nodes (which can be considered an "efficient" configuration of the network). The chapter builds on previous research by the authors showing that cluster firm connections have become less agglomerated within the geographical boundaries of clusters, and more clustered within value chain boundaries that cross multiple locations. Such a transformation is because industrial clusters in the aerospace industry are gradually moving from sectoral to functional specialization, where they are now positioning in finer sliced value chain stages. The authors find that changes in the configuration of trans-local and local linkages are transforming the topology of the overall network into a "small-world," as the growth in trans-local linkages has reduced average distance in the network while the persistence of many local linkages has maintained a high level of clustering in the network. They also find important regional trends: traditional clusters in developed countries are reorienting their supply chains and investments towards emerging industrial clusters in Eastern Europe and Mexico, while trans-local partnership linkages develop mainly between clusters specialized in similar value chain stages. Taken together, the chapter suggests that the organization of the network of global linkages across industrial clusters is becoming more efficient over time.

Chapter 8 by Matthew Smith, Sara Gorgoni, and Bruce Cronin presents a strategy for combining firm and country-level data to overcome the fictitious separation between the micro and the macro level. Studies generally examine international trade in isolation of Foreign Direct Investment (FDI) decisions, yet this is clearly not a realistic assumption in a world where production is a globally fragmented process, with many multinational and corporate groups utilising FDI and locational assets in their manufacturing activities to retain competitive advantages. Studies that make use of FDI stock and flow statistics only illustrate overall country patterns. This approach elides the fact that FDI stock and flow data are an aggregation of the international investment activity of individual firms and that therefore trade and investment flows are ultimately dependent on corporate networks. The authors argue that in order to better understand the complex nature of production as it is today, there is a need for this complexity to be reflected in the datasets used, capturing the increasing importance of MNEs and intra-firm trade. The rise of GVCs requires the creation of new datasets that can be used in quantitative studies; a factor also recognised by international economic organisations. The chapter examines the challenges of building a multilevel relational dataset using firm ownership data from Orbis and country-level international trade data from UN Comtrade. They then propose a multilevel network model that could be used with such data to investigate the micro determinants of ties observed at the macro-level. Finally, they consider potential challenges and propose solutions to such a modelling approach.

The rest of the book includes a set of applications of network techniques and methods to selected non-trade issues in international economics. Chapter 9 by Giulia De Masi and Giorgio Ricchiuti explores the network of European outward foreign direct investments using network analysis, with the main aim to reveal the existence of heterogeneity between and within sectors and/or the possible presence of common behaviour among firms. This chapter is inspired by the rich theoretical and empirical literature on firm productivity and competitiveness in international markets. The authors reconstruct the network of the European (EU28) firms investing abroad based on the database 'fDi markets,' a rich global, detailed database developed by the Financial Times. They look separately at the years 2003 and 2015, in order to compare the structural change on the longest available period and try to identify changes before and after the recent financial crisis. The network they analyse is a bipartite graph, where the nodes are both investors and host countries, and a link is drawn if a parent company invests in a certain host country. The authors detect the presence of subnets and main hubs (countries/firms) within three selected sectors (Coal, Machinery, and Textile). Overall, across all the three sectors taken together, there is evidence of a structural change from 2003 to 2015 in the direction of formation of sub-networks or clusters. This is particularly evident in the Machinery sector, which experienced near-shoring of manufactures and for Coal, where there is evidence of both merging and near-shoring phenomena after the crisis. The opposite behaviour is observed for the Textile sector, which can be explained by the increasing tendency to invest not only in manufacture but more and more in retail.

In Chapter 10, Silvia Sopranzetti applies network analysis to one of the more recent and understudied topics in international economics, namely the proliferation of free trade agreements all over the world over the last twenty years. The author explores the relative position of the individual countries in the global FTA network from 1960 to 2016 (nearly 75% of all trade agreements in force in 2017 are FTA). The chapter shows how accounting for the network structure of FTAs helps to explain some aspects of FTA formations that would not otherwise be explained by countries' economic characteristics. The chapter considers how multiple FTAs interact and evolve over time. Additionally, the author looks at the role of geographical proximity as a condition affecting the probability of two countries signing an FTA. Results show clear signs of preferential attachment process and a semi-globalised structure in which FTA agreements are mainly inside countries' region, while only a few countries chose partners outside their region. More recently, however, geographical proximity seems to be losing importance. In this new scenario, new countries are emerging as key players. Differently from the past, not only are the European countries to be deeply involved in FTAs formation, but also some middle-income countries, which are emerging as regional leaders in this process and are signing new agreements with partners outside their geographical region.

In Chapter 11, Valerio Leone Sciabolazza outlines a set of methods and visualization strategies to explore, describe and synthesize migratory processes from a network standpoint. The study of international migration is a natural field of application for network analysis. In fact, the set of interpersonal ties that connect migrants in origin and destination areas generate a network where each node indicates a place, and one edge connecting two nodes registers the number of people moving from one place to another. Three are the contributions of this chapter. First, it presents a number of analytical tools provided by network analysis that are particularly suited to explore the externalities generated by the interconnected nature of migration flows. Second, it provides an empirical framework to confirm and further extend our knowledge of the factors determining a decision to move from one place (push factors) to another (pull factors). Third, it shows how the level of embeddedness of one country in the international migration network (IMN) represents a powerful source of information on local processes of migrants' sorting and self-selection. Consistent with extant literature, the main result is that geography matters also from a network perspective. The probability of observing the creation of a human corridor in the IMN decreases when considering larger distance radius. In addition to that, the analysis suggests that within the set of destinations available within a certain space, migrants do not choose at random: they prefer moving to countries sharing their linguistic-colonial heritage and with higher welfare. Moreover, comparing the GDP of the topmost sender and receiving countries at various distances, the author finds that the out-degree of one country might proxy the skill composition of its labour force: while unskilled workers from developing countries move in large numbers through few human corridors, skilled migrants from developed nations are sparsely located in a higher number of links. Finally, comparing the results over time, there is evidence of an increase in the number of topmost destinations in the IMN, largely resulting from an involvement of developing countries increasingly assimilated into the globalisation process. However, the analysis shows that the major modifications of the IMN occurred in the intensive margin of the network, meaning that the architecture of international migration has remained stable.

Whilst each of the chapters contributes to improving our understanding of current international economics' issues by applying network techniques and approaches; there are still some limitations that should be tackled in future research, as summarised in the concluding remarks.

1.

An introduction to network analysis

Matthew Smith and Sara Gorgoni

"Network analysis provides a versatile framework for modelling complex systems and because of its universal applicability it has been invented and rediscovered in many disciplines" (Zweig, 2016: 23).

1.1 Introduction

This chapter will introduce the main perspectives of the fields that are at the core of network analysis and its application to the study of international trade and investments: graph theory, sociology, and physics. Each of these disciplines enriches the field by providing its own approach and method. As more effectively stated by Zweig (2016), however, their different perspective, the way they do science and their publication strategies make it more difficult to develop a literacy of the set of methods than in other fields.

As the application of these perspectives to the area of international trade and investments has significantly grown over the past decade, becoming a research area in its own right, it is more important than ever to understand the differences in the underlying approaches and language, and consider the extent to which these can be reconciled into a unitary framework.

Section 1.2 will discuss the origins of social network analysis and network science – the two main approaches followed in this book - and the differences between the two. Section 1.3 will explain what a network is, by defining key terms such as *nodes* and *ties*, and by applying these to the context of international trade (the field in international economics that has been more extensively explored through the application of network techniques), more specifically to describe the International Trade Network (ITN). The section will also provide an introduction to network measures that are commonly used in describing the structure of a network, and in particular the ITN. An examination of more advanced statistical models from social network analysis and network science and their application to international trade and investments is included in Section 1.4, which closes the chapter. An appendix at the end of the chapter contains a table with a summary of the different models from social network analysis and network science that have been or could potentially be applied to analyse international trade and investment networks. The table provides a description of each model, the data requirements, and key references.

1.2 Graph theory, social network analysis and network science

Getting into the field of Network Analysis is challenging as there are many different terms for it: social network analysis, complex network analysis, network science, and network theory. In this chapter, we focus on *Network Science* (NS) and *Social Network Analysis* (SNA) and we will try to clarify the differences and similarities between these two fields. Both SNA and NS have a shared history in graph theory, but these two fields have distinct applications and approaches.

Social Network Analysis originated from sociology. Many see the origins of the field in the 1932 book by Jacob Moreno *Who Shall Survive* (Freeman, 2011; O'Malley and Onnela, 2014). According to Scott and Carrington (2011), SNA is more of a paradigm rather than a theory or a method, concerned chiefly with understanding complex phenomena in various social systems, by examining the structure of a single, small to medium network with respect to some sociological theory. More specifically, SNA focuses on (i) how variation in structure across different social groups or contexts leads to different global outcomes (for example, teams with the same composition of member skills can perform very differently depending on the patterns of relationships among the members); (ii) how the position of a node in a network is correlated to a personal attribute of the node (for example, the wealth or power of a person can be correlated to its position in the network); (iii) the identification of nodes that have a similar role in the network (based on a sociological theory that persons in a social context take on different roles that determine part of their connections to others) (Borgatti et al., 2009).

Network Science emerged during the 1990s, with the landmark publications of Watts and Strogatz (1998) on small world networks and Barabási and Albert (1999) that present random graph models, and is mainly concerned with identifying universal structural features across different complex (non-random) networks from real-world data, such as the property of having scale-free distributions. NS is a truly inter-disciplinary field, which draws chiefly on the work of physicists and computer scientists and was made possible by the digital revolution and consequent data availability that enabled to collect, assemble, share and analyse data from real networks in disciplines as diverse as biochemistry, sociology and brain science. Thanks to the data availability it was possible to draw detailed maps of these networks, and these maps allowed network scientists to identify universal properties of various network characteristics. "A key discovery of network science is that the architectures of networks emerging in various domains in science, nature, and technology are similar to each other, a consequence of being governed by the same organising principles. Consequently, we can use a common set of mathematical tools to explore these systems" (Barabási, 2016: 27).

Zweig (2016) explains the key differences between SNA and NS as rooted in the differences between sociology and physics. The main motivation of sociology is to understand human behaviour and social structures through psychological and sociological theories, models of human behaviour (weak ties, structural holes, etc.) and models to explain individual data (e.g., exponential random graphs). Instead, the main goal of physics is to understand self-organisation in complex systems based on principles in statistical mechanics and using mathematical models for interaction structures. While in sociology, theory comes first, leading to hypothesis formulation, network generation and analysis, in physics analyses are data-driven, as data reveal patterns leading to hypothesis formulation to explain those patterns and then generating models for those patterns (Zweig, 2016).

Thus, the most important difference between SNA and NS is that the former typically promotes a hypothesis-driven approach, making use of relational techniques to test specific hypothesis. Instead, the NS approach can be characterised as being largely context-free and data-driven, as a large enough number of interactions and possibly complex networks of the same kind are needed to make statistically valid statements (Hidalgo, 2016). Watts (2017) argues that there is a need to move away from theory-based approaches in the social sciences, to take a solution-oriented approach, i.e., to address a practical problem and subsequently identify a theory and computational methods to address it. He suggests that NS (and associated fields) could be a potentially insightful framework when employing a solution-oriented approach.

The very different approaches by sociologists and physicists have led to some tensions between the two fields, which have been extensively discussed by Bonacich (2004), Freeman (2011) and Scott (2011), and still today, the two academic communities tend not to cite each other's papers. This is also reflected in the two sets of conferences organised by the two (somehow parallel and competing) fields, with Sunbelt and EUSN in *Social Network Analysis* and NetSci and Complex Networks in *Network Science.*

These tensions result in the works of SNA and NS publishing in different outlets, whilst not referring to each other. As a result, most non-sociologists doing network analysis today are not inspired by the rich social network analysis research (as seen in the Social Networks journal), and they cite papers from prestigious journals such as Nature, Science and the Proceedings of the National Academy of the Sciences (PNAS) written mainly by physicists

(Bonacich, 2004). This is also seen in the analysis of other economic networks, not just the international trade network. For instance, in a special issue of Social Networks (SNA journal) on international migration (Bilecen, Gamper and Lubbers, 2018), there is only one paper (Danchev and Porter, 2018) that cites the existing work in network science by Giorgio Fagiolo on the international migration network (Fagiolo and Mastrorillo, 2013, 2014).

The first applications of network analysis to international trade data originated in economic sociology and political science with the application of SNA as a tool to quantitatively test for "world system" or "dependency" theories (see for example the seminal paper by Snyder and Kick 1979 and the work by Nemeth and Smith,1985; Sacks et al., 2001; Breiger,1981; Smith and White,1992; and more recently Kim and Shin, 2002 and Mahutga, 2006).

More recently, a whole new strand of literature has emerged which applies complex network analysis to economic networks, including the international trade network. This empirical literature has attracted however some criticism, chiefly regarding theoretical frameworks used to explain empirical phenomena, where they do not fully connect with theories in economics (Gallegati et al., 2006; Carbone et al., 2007; Ormerod, 2016), suggesting that the application of NS becomes especially problematic when complex network analytical measures are used to learn something about the individual network and the complex system it represents, rather than to identify universal structural features across different complex networks.

The huge popularity recently gained by network analysis, with applications in a plurality of scholarly areas, has also led to the implementation of many of its methods in a variety of software widely used packages such as R and Python, along with the development of specialised software to implement analysis and network visualisation procedures.

The next section will introduce the reader to some basic network concepts used by the chapters in this book, using the context of international trade to illustrate how these concepts can be applied to an economic network.

1.3 Networks as a description

A *network* is based on two sets – set of *nodes* (vertices or points), that represent the selected *units*, such as for example people, organisations or countries; and the set of *links* (lines), that represent *ties* between units. Together they determine a *graph* or a *network*. The International Trade Network (ITN), also frequently referred to as the World Trade Web (WTW) or the World Trade Network (WTN), is a graph representing bilateral trade flows among world countries at a given time.

A link in a network can be *directed* (an *arc*) or *undirected* (an *edge*). The ITN is *de facto* a directed graph, where *directed* means that trade flows are not necessarily symmetric (if country *i* exports to country *j*, *j* does not necessarily export to *i*). The ITN is also a *weighted* graph, meaning that trade flows differ in terms of intensity. Despite these inherent characteristics of the ITN, depending on the specific research questions, any given weighted directed ITN can be analysed disregarding either the weighted or directed nature of trade links (or both). For example, if only the existence/absence of trade links is of interest, the ITN can be transformed into a binary network by replacing all existing link weights with 1. This operation generates binary directed graphs, where a link from country *i* to country *j* is present only if *i* exports to *j*. Likewise, when asymmetries between exports from *i* to *j* and imports of *i* from *j* are not of interest, one might consider symmetrising the networks by replacing real values with the arithmetic average of imports and exports (Fagiolo, 2017).

Empirical data for the ITN over time are easily available both at an aggregate and commodity-specific level based on various classifications (e.g., Harmonised System – HS – or Standard International Trade Classification - SITC). Due to a lack of comprehensive data on service trade, however, most of the studies applying network analysis to international trade deal only with the trade of goods and commodities (De Benedictis et al., 2014).

Network analysis provides a valuable tool to map and describe the complex web of trade relationships among countries. Descriptive network analysis can be used to investigate with whom countries trade; how important (or central) they are in the ITN; whether they trade with countries that in turn trade a lot, or trade with pairs of countries that are themselves trade partners; if they are embedded in tightly connected groups (or communities) of countries, relatively disconnected to others; and so on (Fagiolo, 2017).

Among the most common and widespread network measures that have been applied to international trade data, an important metric to describe network connectivity is *density*; density is the proportion of observed ties to all possible ties in the network (Robins, 2013). In addition to density, there are a number of fundamental measures to describe a network structure, with a focus on the distribution of ties in the network. A number of studies focus on explaining the *degree distribution* of a network. The *degree* refers to the number of ties a node has, and for directed networks, this can be split into the *out-degree* (sending ties) and *in-degree* (receiving ties). Explaining the degree distribution is an important step in describing the network structure. For instance, in work examining the ITN, the degree distribution allows for an examination of import and export ties, which are highly heterogeneous (Fagiolo, 2017).

Weighted variants of these degree measures are also available, which not only account for the number of links a node has but also the strength of the interaction. In the case of the ITN, this allows not only to examine the number of trade partners a country has but for example also the value of imports and exports. In the literature applying network analysis to international trade weighted out (in) degree is often used a measure to examine the number of trade partners a country exports to (from) and the contribution of these export (import) ties to the total world trade in the network.

Examining whether a network is characterised by a core-periphery structure is often a key aspect of describing a network. Core-periphery analysis captures whether a network is characterised by a dense core, consisting of a few nodes that account for the majority of ties in the network, with the remainder of the nodes in the disconnected periphery (Borgatti and Everett, 2000). This approach is frequently applied to the ITN, where a core-periphery structure indicates that trade is characterised by a tightly connected group of countries accounting for most trade, while countries in the periphery show a lower number of trading relationships, mainly with core countries.

An additional concept to explain the unequal distribution of ties, and hierarchical structures in a network, often seen in economic networks (such as the ITN) is the notion of assortativity. The assortativity metric allows us examining whether there a tendency of nodes with similar degree scores (number of ties) to connect to each other, or instead, whether large-degree nodes are chiefly connected to low-degree nodes (Newman, 2002). The latter is referred to as disassortativity. The degree assortativity score can range for 1 to -1, where a positive score would indicate actors of similar degree connect to each other, and a negative score indicates that large-degree nodes tend to attach to low degree nodes. Assortativity chiefly refers to node degree yet it can also be implemented for other nodal attributes. For instance, in the context of the international trade network, regional assortativity can be calculated, which would allow for the examination of whether there is a tendency for countries to trade with those in their region. In sociology and social network analysis, the idea of assortativity, and especially assortativity based on a nodal attribute, would be widely referred to as homophily. Where homophily captures the tendency of similar individuals (nodes) with a shared characteristic to associate or connect (McPherson et al., 2001).

Substantial research has been undertaken to examine whether networks are characterised by a community structure. Several community detection algorithms have been developed to examine whether there are areas of the network that are denser than other, i.e. communities (Newman and Girvan, 2004; Newman, 2006; Fortunato, 2010). Community detection is a useful technique in economic settings, for instance when applied to the ITN, it allows detecting whether regionalisation governs the emergence of community structure (see Zhu et al., 2014 for an example of this).

Another important aspect of networks is how tightly clustered they are. For example, the extent to which my friends are friends with one another captures one aspect of this clustering. With respect to the ITN this translates into whether the trading partners of two countries that trade, also trade. There are a variety of concepts that measure how cohesive a network is (such as transitivity and the clustering coefficient – see Wasserman and Faust, 1994 for a detailed overview of these measures).

This section has presented some of the key concepts in network analysis that are often utilised and applied to analyse the ITN. However, it is beyond the scope of this book to provide a comprehensive explanation of all concepts and measures in network analysis. Whenever necessary, the chapters in this book introduce the reader to key network concepts. For a more comprehensive explanation of network concepts and measures, however, we refer the reader to other books in SNA and NS such as Scott (2012), Wassermann and Faust (1994), Newman (2010), and Borgatti et al. (2013).

1.4. More advanced network models

The field of network analysis is a relatively young and dynamic one. Statistical network models have experienced rapid development and attention in recent years. Whilst descriptive analysis provides a useful contribution, allowing active and important players to be identified in the network (for example using centrality measures), statistical models allow for a deeper understanding of network formation and evolution. These models can constitute an improvement on standard statistical techniques (e.g., gravity models) in addressing research questions related to international trade and investments, as they take into account interdependencies and allow for the full network structure as well as individual actor attributes to be explained.

1.4.1 Complex Network Analysis

Econophysicists[1] from the field of Network Science have championed complex network analysis to examine economic networks and have presented a number of more advanced network models to better explain features of the global economy, often with a focus on explaining the topology of economic networks.

---

[1] Econophysics refer to the field of work that use methods and approaches developed in physics to address research problems in economics

Network Science research is grounded in generative random graph modelling, where these approaches emerged from the work of Erdös and Rényi (1959). They proposed a probability model for network analysis, where all nodes in the network have the same probability of connecting to each other, independent from other connections in the network. This basic model has been expanded, where advanced variants have been developed to better explain complex network topologies (Fienberg, 2012).

There have been substantial applications of this approach to explain the degree distribution of real-world networks, as not all nodes in a network have the same number of edges (Albert and Barabási, 2002). There has been a high level of interest into whether real-world networks are *scale free*, that is the degree distribution follows a *power law* distribution. The power law degree distribution is a specific functional form of heavy tailed degree distribution.

One of the most influential approaches to identify and explain the emergence of scale free networks is the Barabási-Albert (BA) model. This can be thought of as a variant of the Erdös – Rényi (ER) model to explain the process of preferential attachment that drives the emergence of power law degree distribution in a network. *Preferential attachment* is a process by which the "rich get richer," that is high degree nodes attract further ties and partners. In the context of the trade network, this suggests that countries at the core with a high level of trade ties are more likely to attract further trade ties. Barabási and Albert (1999) present a formal model of preferential attachment; network growth is driven by the tendency of connecting to highly connected nodes.

A variant of the preferential attachment model is the fitness model, unlike the preferential attachment model, the fitness model suggests that the "fit get richer." This is where nodes with a high fitness (a nodal attribute) are more likely to attract ties (Pham et al., 2016). Garlaschelli et al. (2007) and Garlaschelli and Loffredo (2004) apply fitness models to the trade network, to demonstrate countries with a higher GDP (node fitness) are more likely to attract trade ties.

A further approach to explain network topology, especially the topology of complex economic systems, is the null network model. This approach is based on generating a network based on a statistical model – the null model – that preserves some characteristic of the observed, empirical network and all other features are purely random (Fagiolo, 2017). These preserved features are often referred to as constraints and range from preserving only the density of the network to preserving the full binary network structure. A comparison of the simulated and observed networks allows the researcher to identify what topological features are different from the null model, and therefore are not generated by a random process. Squartini et al. (2011) apply this to the ITN, preserving the degree distribution (the number of trade ties each country has). They find that the null model is able to sufficiently reproduce the disassortativity property of the ITN, yet cannot explain the exact distribution of weights in the network, so the intensity of trade between countries. Fagiolo et al. (2013) emphasise a strength of this approach, which can act as a sieve to identify the interesting and insightful features of an observed network.

A further complex network analysis approach that has been proposed to better inform on features of the modern global economy is *multiplex* (or *multi-layer*) network analysis. A multiplex network consists of a fixed set of nodes which are connected by several different types of ties; each tie can represent a different layer in the network (Kivelä et al., 2013).

Multiplex analysis is popular amongst physicists applying advanced statistical models to complex economic systems. For instance, Barigozzi et al. (2010) consider the international trade system as a set of multi-networks, one for each commodity group. Other multiplex analysis includes Zhang et al. (2016), where they provide a comparison of the topological features of a two-layer network of international trade and portfolio investments. Giorgio Fagiolo argues for a multiplex approach to examine economic networks and to inform on macroeconomic topics, emphasising that examining the position of a country in multiple networks would allow one to dig deeper into the relationship between the role of a country in the network and its economic performance (Fagiolo, 2017, 2016).

1.4.2 Exponential Random Graph Models (ERGMs)

Exponential Random Graph Models (ERGMs) are a family of statistical models representing a probability distribution of all possible graphs on a fixed node set; and the probability of observing a graph is dependent on the local network configurations defined in the model (Robins et al., 2007). ERGMs can test the hypothesis at the very local level, where the model is able to identify micro configurations that represent a theoretical process, and then calculates whether this process is seen in the network more than a researcher would expect by chance. For example, a very simple micro configuration is *reciprocity*, yet *higher order configurations* are also available, such as *transitive, cyclical* and *open triads* which can be used to capture clustering patterns in the network. In the context of the ITN reciprocity refers to the case in which two nations both import and export from one another; the ERGM would provide a count of observed trading relationships, and would assess whether there is a higher tendency for reciprocal trade relationships in the observed network than would be expected by chance (Borgatti et al., 2013). The application of ERGMs to international trade or investment data is relatively limited, with a notable exception being Chu-Shore (2010) with a study on the homogenizing effect of trade on cultural goods.

The limited application of standard ERGMs may be explained by the fact that until recently they could only deal with cross-sectional binary data. However, in recent years a number of extensions have overcome these limits. Longitudinal ERGMs have been developed, specifically Separable Temporal ERGMs (STERGMs) introduced and developed by Krivitsky and Handcock (2014), which not only allow for a longitudinal analysis to explain the duration of ties but also enable to distinguish the factors explaining the formation of ties in a network from those explaining their dissolution. Application of these models appears particularly promising in the areas of foreign direct investments (FDI) and trade agreements.

The fact that the standard ERGMs (and some of the other extensions) can only deal with binary ties has been another important reason explaining their limited application to international trade, as it can lead to a number of biases and to a loss of important information (see Thomas and Blitzstein, 2011 for a discussion of dichotomising ties). ERGMs have however been extended to be used with valued network data (Desmarais and Cranmer, 2012; Krivitsky, 2012; Wilson et al., 2017).

Recent advances in ERGMs have also led to new ways of modelling spatial effects in a network, providing a framework to better assess the "puzzle" of distance in international trade. Daraganova et al. (2012) develop an ERGM which is able to capture the spatial embeddedness of network ties; they do this by specifying a distance interaction function. The model allows considering whether spatial processes are able to explain other network structures such as the propensity for triads in the network. Koskinen and Lomi (2013) and Koskinen et al. (2015) make use of this approach in considering spatial distance when modelling longitudinal FDI flows, in which they demonstrate that spatial embeddedness and endogenous network effects both drive the dynamics of FDI flows over time. However, it must be noted that the aims of these works are chiefly methodological, with the aim of developing improved longitudinal ERGMs, rather than explaining the economic phenomenon per se. Sohn et al. (2013) investigate the influence of geographic context on the formation of policy networks through an ERGM. Their approach is somewhat different from Daraganova et al. (2012) and Koskinen and Lomi (2013), as they consider both distance and the presence of territorial borders in their modelling specification, thereby going beyond the typical approaches in considering spatial effects.

These studies illustrate the scope to further consider the effect of distance when considering international trade and investment and to investigate the interaction between spatial proximity and higher order network patterns (or trading patterns). However, it must be noted that the geographic implementation of ERGMs is not readily available in many SNA packages, and is yet to be implemented for a number of the other ERGM extensions (such as the valued and multilevel case).

In addition to the longitudinal and valued extensions, there has been a more substantial extension to ERGMs, which has a large scope in terms of its application to international trade and investment; this is the multilevel ERGM developed by Wang et al. (2013). This model applies an ERGM to a multilevel network, which is defined as a network with two node sets (A and B), and multiple linkages. The multilevel network is constituted by three networks: (1) network A, and the ties between actors in this network (the macro level); (2) network B, and the ties between the actors in this network (the micro level); (3) network X, containing the actors from networks A and B, and the ties linking the actors across these two networks (the meso level). These three networks combined form the full multilevel network. This model can be used to determine whether the structure at one level – for example, ownership ties between firms in different locations – determines the structure at another level, such as the ITN. This multilevel network analysis would allow for an identification of the local patterns and empirical regularities of trading and investment patterns within the sector under investigation, such as examining the tendency for intra-firm trade.

1.4.3 Latent Space Models for Network Analysis

A further set of models which can be applied to relational international trade data are latent space models introduced by Hoff et al. (2002). In this class of models, the probability of a relation between actors depends on the positions of individuals in an unobserved "social space." Latent space models assume that each node in the network has some unknown position in the Euclidean latent space. Where the probability of a link forming between two nodes depends on the distance between their positions in the latent space, and between their observed characteristics. The closer two nodes are in the latent space,, the more likely it is for a link to be established between them. The authors make inference for the social space within maximum likelihood and Bayesian frameworks and propose Markov chain Monte Carlo procedures for making inference on latent positions and the effects of observed covariates.

The model was then extended by Handcock et al. (2007), to model the clustering of latent space positions of actors, identifying groupings of nodes. Krivitsky et al. (2009) then built on this to construct a latent cluster random effects model, which is able to explicitly model homophily, clustering and degree heterogeneity of actors. The latent space model captures higher order network effects naturally (rather than directly modelling them). For instance, in the case of transitivity, this is captured by the model, as two actors with a third actor in common are assumed to be relatively close to each other in the latent space, therefore making connected triangles in the network more likely (Rastelli et al., 2015).

One set of latent space models which have received attention are the General Bilinear Mixed Effects (GBME) models (Hoff, 2005). In demonstrating the value and applicability of these models, authors often make use of international trade data, as in the longitudinal extension developed by Westveld and Hoff (2011). Ward et al. (2013) develop a GBME model to account for both valued and longitudinal data, applying it to international trade data to theoretically extend the gravity model with relational effects. They identify the presence of higher order effects, and that the inclusion of these relational effects outperforms standard specifications that ignore the interdependencies in international trade data.

Latent space models are primarily designed to analyse clustering patterns and the positions and behaviour of groups of actors. Whilst latent space models and ERGMs both represent advanced statistical models to analyse network data, they take very different approaches and address different research questions. The research questions which these latent space models are able to answer include whether there are cohesive groups of actors in the network, and how individual actors are positioned in these groupings. ERGMs on the other hand, test for the propensity for local substructures, and whilst there is some overlap between the two, (for instance, they are both capable of examining patterns of structural equivalence in the network), they are primarily distinctive approaches.

When comparing ERGMs with latent space models, there is not one modelling approach that is better than another, rather that these models are equipped to answer different research questions, especially when considering the more recent extensions to ERGMs (such as the multilevel case). Latent space models still hold a number of advantages in considering longitudinal and valued data, along with their ability to identify clustering patterns. When applied to international trade, the research area where latent space models could contribute most to is the mapping of specific groups of economies over time, such as emerging countries; one such case is the BRIC's group[2]. Do these nations hold similar positions? Do patterns of regional clustering emerge? If so, what are the positions of individual nations in these clusters? Have emerging economies moved into positions previously held by industrialised nations? Latent space models go beyond merely descriptive analysis to address these questions; rather they allow for statistical inferences to be made regarding clustering and the evolution of the position of nodes in a network.

---

[2] Brazil, Russia, India and China

The best approach depends on the problem and research questions, with the main distinction that latent space models are better at answering questions regarding clustering, while ERGMs allow for a better consideration of topics in which dependence is at the heart of the research problem. Whilst complex network analysis may also be able to address some of these research questions through null models; these would focus on whether clustering of trade can be explained by preserving some other feature of the trading system. Whereas latent space models allow for a focus on the individuals involved in clustering and how these patterns have evolved over time.

1.5 Summary

In the first part of this chapter, we try to clarify the differences and similarities between *Network Science* (NS) and *Social Network Analysis* (SNA) – the two main approaches taken in this book. While both have a shared history in graph theory, these two fields have distinct applications and approaches. The second part of the chapter introduces key concepts in network analysis. It introduces the reader to what a network is in general, by defining key terms such as nodes and ties, and by applying these to the context of international trade to describe the International Trade Network (ITN). It also provides an introduction to key descriptive network measures that are commonly used in describing the structure of the ITN. It introduces the reader to what a network is in general, by defining key terms such as nodes and ties, and by applying these to the context of international trade in particular in order to describe the International Trade Network (ITN). It also provides an introduction to key descriptive network measures that are commonly used in describing the structure of the ITN. Whilst descriptive analysis provides a useful contribution, allowing important players to be identified in the network, statistical models allow for a deeper understanding of network formation and evolution. These models can constitute an improvement on standard statistical techniques (e.g., gravity models) in addressing research questions related to international trade and investments, as they take into account interdependencies and allow for the full network structure as well as individual actor attributes to be explained. The final part of this chapter then examines how statistical models in NS and SNA can be applied to the study of international trade and investments to further move forward our understanding of complex contemporary economic issues. An appendix at the end of the chapter contains a table which summarises the different models from social network analysis and network science which have been used or could potentially be used to analyse international trade and investment networks. The table provides a description of each model, the data requirements, and key references.

1.6 Appendix

Table 1.1: SNA software to implement models and methods

Model	Software	Description/Application	C	L	V	B	D	U	Key References
ERGM	PNet R – ergm	Exponential Random Graph models (ERGMs) are generative models that treat network topology (local network substructures) as the response variable. This makes them ideal to inform on how and why economic ties occur.	X			X	X	X	Lusher, D., Koskinen, J. and Robins, G. (2013) *Exponential random graph models for social networks: theory, methods, and applications.*
Temporal ERGMs	R – tergm, stergm, xergm	Temporal extension of the ERGM. The stergm allows to model in parallel the mechanisms behind both the formation and dissolution of ties over time.		X		X	X	X	Krivitsky, P. N. and Handcock, M. S. (2014) A separable model for dynamic networks, *Journal of the Royal Statistical Society: Series B (Statistical Methodology)*, 76(1), pp. 29–46.
Multilevel ERGM	MPNet	Multilevel extension of the ERGM, allowing the researcher to examine how the network structure at one level (micro or macro) shapes the network topology at another. Capturing the level of interdependencies	X			X	X	X	Wang, P., Robins, G., Pattison, P. and Lazega, E. (2013) Exponential random graph models for multilevel networks, *Social Networks*, 35(1), pp. 96–115.
Valued ERGM	R – GERGM	An ERGM that is able to account for the weighted ties.	X		X		X	X	Wilson, J. D., Denny, M. J., Bhamidi, S., Cranmer, S. J. and Desmarais, B. A. (2017) Stochastic weighted graphs: Flexible model specification and simulation, *Social Networks*, 49, pp. 37–47.
Bivariate ERGM	XPNet	This is an extension of the ERGM and involves two one mode network. This model allows to look at the association between two networks structures. For instance, is there an association between sending/receiving ties in one network with sending/receiving ties in another one?	X			X	X	X	Simpson, C. R. (2015) Multiplexity and strategic alliances: The relational embeddedness of coalitions in social movement organisational fields, *Social Networks*, 42, pp. 42–59.

Key: C – Cross Sectional, L – Longitudinal, V – Valued, B – Binary, D – Directed, U – Undirected

Model	Software	Description/Application	C	L	V	B	D	U	Key References
ALAAM	MPNet	Part of the ERGM family of models, instead of modelling network topology, the actor attribute is the response variable. The ALAAM models an actor's (binary or auto logistic) attribute as a function of exogenous tie variables and other exogenous attributes.	X			X	X	X	Daraganova, G. and Robins, G. (2013) Autologistic actor attribute models, *Exponential random graph models for social networks: Theory, methods and applications*, pp. 102–114.
Latent Space Model	R – Latentnet	Latent space models assume that each node has an unknown position in the unobserved "social space", and that the distance between two nodes decreases as their characteristics become more similar. They then model the probability of a connection between two nodes as a function of the distance between their latent space positions, i.e. their positions in the social space of characteristics. Consequently, nodes are conditionally independent given their positions in the social space.	X	X	X		X	X	Krivitsky, P. N. and Handcock, M. S. (2008) Fitting position latent cluster models for social networks with latentnet, *Journal of Statistical Software*, 24
Preferential Attachment & Fitness Model	R - PAFit	These frameworks allow to test the extent to which the network is characterised by preferential attachment or fitness processes. The preferential attachment is a process by which the "rich get richer", that is high degree nodes attract further ties and partners. Whereas the fitness model suggests that the "fit get richer" that a node with a particular attribute attracts ties.	X	X		X	X	X	
Power Law	R – igraph, PoweRlaw	Identifying whether a network is characterised by the power law (or is scale free) is an important research question in network science. The power law suggests that the degree distribution is emerges as a result of a preferential attachment mechanisms, leading to a heavy tailed degree distribution.	X	X		X	X	X	Serrano, M. A. and Boguná, M. (2003) Topology of the world trade web, *Physical Review E*, 68(1), p. 015101.

Key: C – Cross Sectional, L – Longitudinal, V – Valued, B – Binary, D – Directed, U – Undirected

Model	Software	Description/Application	C	L	V	B	D	U	Key References
Multiplex Network Analysis	MuxViz R – Multinet, Multiplex Python – multiNetX, Pymnet	This framework allows to analyse multiplex (or multi-layered) network. These are networks that consist of the same set of nodes, but with multiple ties linking these nodes. These software package allow to analyse where community emerge in this multiplex system, and the level of overlap in the various layers. Multiplex networks may also refer to temporal network, where each layer is a realisation of the network at a different timepoint.	X	X	X	X	X	X	De Domenico, M., Porter, M. A. and Arenas, A. (2015) MuxViz: a tool for multilayer analysis and visualization of networks, *Journal of Complex Networks*, 3(2), pp. 159–176.
Stochastic Actor Oriented Models (SAOM)	R – Rsiena	SAOMs are actor based models designed to model transitions in networks between discrete time points. These are highly flexible models that allow the researcher to inform on the coevolution of network ties and behaviour (or an actor characteristic). This allows to examine how network ties influence behaviour and in turn how behaviour shapes network ties. In terms of valued ties – however, this is only in terms of ordinal ties.		X	X		X	X	Snijders, T. A. B., van de Bunt, G. G. and Steglich, C. E. G. (2010) Introduction to stochastic actor-based models for network dynamics, *Social Networks*, 32(1), pp. 44–60.
Multiple regression quadratic assignment procedure	UCINET R – qaptest (part of sna package), asnipe	Multiples regression quadratic assignment procedure (MRQAP) is a permutation based approach to examine the complex dependencies between matrices/networks.	X			X	X	X	Dekker, D., Krackhardt, D. and Snijders, T. A. B. (2007) Sensitivity of MRQAP Tests to Collinearity and Autocorrelation Conditions, *Psychometrika*, 72(4), pp. 563–581.

Key: C – Cross Sectional, L – Longitudinal, V – Valued, B – Binary, D – Directed, U – Undirected

Model	Software	Description/ Application	C	L	V	B	D	U	Key References
Block-models	Pajek R – block-model (part of sna package), block-modeling, ITNr Python – graph-tool	This approach allows us to identify the extent of which the network is organised into blocks of structurally equivalent actors in the network. When two actors are structurally equivalent in the network, they have identical ties to all others in the network. A more relaxed version of structural equivalence is regular equivalence, which instead captures the extent to which two actors hold the same position in the network, that is they have identical ties to equivalent actors in the network							Doreian, P., Batagelj, V. and Ferligoj, A. (2004) *Generalized Blockmodeling*, Cambridge University Press.
Community Detection	UCINET R – igraph	This approach detects whether the network is characterised by separate communities, that is areas of the network more densely connected between themselves than other. This is a useful technique in the analysis of the international trade network, where is can be used to examine whether the network is organised into communities characterised by regional partitions.							Newman, M. E. and Girvan, M. (2004) Finding and evaluating community structure in networks, *Physical review E*, 69(2), p. 026113.

Key: C – Cross Sectional, L – Longitudinal, V – Valued, B – Binary, D – Directed, U – Undirected

Model	Software	Description/Application	C	L	V	B	D	U	Key References
Network Auto-correlation Models	R – lnam function (part of the sna package), TNAM (part of xergm package, can implement longitudinal analysis)	Network autocorrelation model are a flexible framework to assess the extent to which the behaviour of an alter impacts the behaviour of an ego within a network This modelling approach allows for an investigation into the extent to which an actor's attribute is constrained by its position in the network and the attribute of its connections. This is a similar modelling approach the ALAAM, yet it can model both continuous and binary outcome attributes, not restricted to the binary/auto logistic attribute of the ALAAM. However, in the network autocorrelation model, dependency must be defined by user and its goodness-of-fit cannot be tested.	X	X	X	X	X	X	Leenders, R. T. A. J. (2002) Modeling social influence through network autocorrelation: constructing the weight matrix, *Social Networks*, 24(1), pp. 21–47.
Small World Analysis	UCINET R – igraph, Statnet	Research has often examined how an actor's position in a small world network influences actor outcome, where small world are frequently described as "efficient" networks. A small world network is described as one with a short path length (the maximum number of intermediaries an actor would have to go through to reach any other in the network) and high clustering (local density of ties around a specific actor).	X			X	X	X	Watts, D. J. and Strogatz, S. H. (1998) Collective dynamics of 'small-world'networks, *nature*, 393(6684), p. 440.

Key: C – Cross Sectional, L – Longitudinal, V – Valued, B – Binary, D – Directed, U – Undirected

Model	Software	Description/Application	C	L	V	B	D	U	Key References
Network Visualisation	Visone, Pajek, Netdraw, Gephi,	Network visualisation can reveal key insights from the data and can aid in addressing a range of research problems. For instance, a visualisation of the international trade network can allow to identify whether trade is organised according to regional partitions, along with finding the key players in the network.	X	X	X	X	X	X	Whilst there is not a single reference for network visualisation, we would like to refer the reader to the journal, IEEE Transactions on Visualization and Computer Graphics. Along with the following book, which provides a foundation reference for ggplot approaches implemented in R (ggnet and ggnetwork):
	R - igraph, Statnet, ITNr, ggnet, ggnetwork Python	Network animations can be constructed to examine longitudinal networks.							Wilkinson, L. (2011) *The Grammar of Graphics*, 2nd ed. 2005 edition, New York, NY, Springer

Key: C – Cross Sectional, L – Longitudinal, V – Valued, B – Binary, D – Directed, U – Undirected

Bespoke null models to analyse complex systems (including the international trade network) in network science are often implemented using a python framework.

A detailed tutorial on network analysis of the international trade network in R can be found at: https://rpubs.com/matt_smith/ITNr. This outlines how several of the methods and models above can be implemented in R, along with a range of further analysis that can be applied to the international trade network.

1.7 References

Albert, R. and Barabási, A.-L. (2002) Statistical mechanics of complex networks, *Reviews of modern physics*, 74(1), p. 47.

Barabási, A.-L. (2016) *Network Science*. Cambridge University Press.

Barabási, A.-L. and Albert, R. (1999) Emergence of scaling in random networks, *science*, 286(5439), pp. 509–512.

Barigozzi, M., Fagiolo, G. and Garlaschelli, D. (2010) Multinetwork of international trade: A commodity-specific analysis, *Physical Review E*, 81(4), p. 046104.

Bilecen, B., Gamper, M. and Lubbers, M. J. (2018) The missing link: Social network analysis in migration and transnationalism, *Social Networks, The missing link: Social network analysis in migration and transnationalism*, 53, pp. 1–3.

Bonacich, P. (2004) The Invasion of the Physicists, *Social Networks*, 26(3), pp. 285–288.

Borgatti, S. P. and Everett, M. G. (2000) Models of core/periphery structures, *Social networks*, 21(4), pp. 375–395.

Borgatti, S. P., Everett, M. G. and Johnson, J. C. (2013) *Analyzing Social Networks*, SAGE.

Borgatti, S. P., Mehra, A., Brass, D. J. and Labianca, G. (2009) Network Analysis in the Social Sciences, *Science*, 323(5916), pp. 892–895.

Carbone, A., Kaniadakis, G. and Scarfone, A. M. (2007) Where do we stand on econophysics?, *Physica A: Statistical Mechanics and its Applications, Applications of Physics in Financial Analysis*, 382(1), pp. xi–xiv.

Chu-Shore, J. (2010) Homogenization and Specialization Effects of International Trade: Are Cultural Goods Exceptional?, *World Development*, 38(1), pp. 37–47.

Danchev, V. and Porter, M. A. (2018) Neither global nor local: Heterogeneous connectivity in spatial network structures of world migration, *Social Networks, The missing link: Social network analysis in migration and transnationalism*, 53, pp. 4–19.

Daraganova, G., Pattison, P., Koskinen, J., Mitchell, B., Bill, A., Watts, M. and Baum, S. (2012) Networks and geography: Modelling community network structures as the outcome of both spatial and network processes, *Social Networks, Capturing Context: Integrating Spatial and Social Network Analyses*, 34(1), pp. 6–17.

De Benedictis, L., Nenci, S., Santoni, G., Tajoli, L. and Vicarelli, C. (2014) Network Analysis of World Trade using the BACI-CEPII dataset, *Global Economy Journal*, 14(3–4), pp. 287–343.

Desmarais, B. A. and Cranmer, S. J. (2012) Statistical Inference for Valued-Edge Networks: The Generalized Exponential Random Graph Model, *PLoS ONE*, 7(1), p. e30136.

Erdös, P. and Rényi, A. (1959) On random graphs, I, *Publicationes Mathematicae (Debrecen)*, 6, pp. 290–297.

Fagiolo, G. (2017), "The International Trade Network: Empirics and Modeling", in Jennifer Nicoll Victor, Alexander H. Montgomery, and Mark Lubell (Eds.), The Oxford Handbook of Political Networks, Oxford University Press, Oxford.

Fagiolo, G. (2016), "The Empirics of Macroeconomic Networks: A Critical Review", in P. Commendatore, M. Matilla-García, L. M. Varela and J.S. Cánovas (Eds.), Complex Networks and Nonlinear Dynamics: Social and Economic Interactions, Springer, Berlin.

Fagiolo, G. and Mastrorillo, M. (2014) Does human migration affect international trade? A complex-network perspective, *PloS one*, 9(5), p. e97331.

Fagiolo, G. and Mastrorillo, M. (2013) International migration network: Topology and modeling, *Physical Review E*, 88(1), p. 012812.

Fagiolo, G., Squartini, T. and Garlaschelli, D. (2013) Null models of economic networks: the case of the world trade web, *Journal of Economic Interaction and Coordination*, 8(1), pp. 75–107.

Fienberg, S. E. (2012) A brief history of statistical models for network analysis and open challenges, *Journal of Computational and Graphical Statistics*, 21(4), pp. 825–839.

Fortunato, S. (2010) Community detection in graphs, *Physics Reports*, 486(3–5), pp. 75–174.

Freeman, L. C. (2011) The Development of Social Network Analysis–with an Emphasis on Recent Events, *The SAGE Handbook of Social Network Analysis*, pp. 26–39.

Gallegati, M., Keen, S., Lux, T. and Ormerod, P. (2006) Worrying trends in econophysics, *Physica A: Statistical Mechanics and its Applications*, 370(1), pp. 1–6.

Garlaschelli, D. and Loffredo, M. I. (2004) Fitness-Dependent Topological Properties of the World Trade Web, *Physical Review Letters*, 93(18), p. 188701.

Garlaschelli, D., Matteo, T. D., Aste, T., Caldarelli, G. and Loffredo, M. I. (2007) Interplay between topology and dynamics in the World Trade Web, *The European Physical Journal B*, 57(2), pp. 159–164.

Handcock, M. S., Raftery, A. E. and Tantrum, J. M. (2007) Model-based clustering for social networks, *Journal of the Royal Statistical Society: Series A (Statistics in Society)*, 170(2), pp. 301–354.

Hidalgo, C. A. (2016) Disconnected, fragmented, or united? a transdisciplinary review of network science, *Applied Network Science*, 1(1), p. 6.

Hoff, P. D. (2005) Bilinear Mixed-Effects Models for Dyadic Data, *Journal of the American Statistical Association*, 100(469), pp. 286–295.

Hoff, P. D., Raftery, A. E. and Handcock, M. S. (2002) Latent Space Approaches to Social Network Analysis, *Journal of the American Statistical Association*, 97(460), pp. 1090–1098.

Kivelä, M., Arenas, A., Barthelemy, M., Gleeson, J. P., Moreno, Y. and Porter, M. A. (2013) *Multilayer Networks*, arXiv e-print, Available at: http://arxiv.org/abs/1309.7233.

Koskinen, J., Caimo, A. and Lomi, A. (2015) Simultaneous modeling of initial conditions and time heterogeneity in dynamic networks: An application to Foreign Direct Investments, *Network Science*, pp. 1–20.

Koskinen, J. and Lomi, A. (2013) The Local Structure of Globalisation, *Journal of Statistical Physics*, 151(3–4), pp. 523–548.

Krivitsky, P. N. (2012) Exponential-family random graph models for valued networks, *Electronic journal of statistics*, 6, pp. 1100–1128.

Krivitsky, P. N. and Handcock, M. S. (2014) A separable model for dynamic networks, *Journal of the Royal Statistical Society: Series B (Statistical Methodology)*, 76(1), pp. 29–46.

Krivitsky, P. N., Handcock, M. S., Raftery, A. E. and Hoff, P. D. (2009) Representing degree distributions, clustering, and homophily in social networks with latent cluster random effects models, *Social Networks*, 31(3), pp. 204–213.

Newman, M. E. (2002) Assortative mixing in networks, *Physical review letters*, 89(20), p. 208701.

Newman, M. E. (2006) Modularity and community structure in networks, *Proceedings of the national academy of sciences*, 103(23), pp. 8577–8582.

Newman, M. (2010) *Networks: an introduction*, Oxford university press.

Newman, M. E. and Girvan, M. (2004) Finding and evaluating community structure in networks, *Physical review E*, 69(2), p. 026113.

O'Malley, A. J. and Onnela, J.-P. (2014) Topics in social network analysis and network science, *arXiv:1404.0067 [physics]*, Available at: http://arxiv.org/abs/1404.0067.

Ormerod, P. (2016) Ten years after 'Worrying trends in econophysics': developments and current challenges, *The European Physical Journal Special Topics*, 225(17–18), pp. 3281–3291.

Pham, T., Sheridan, P. and Shimodaira, H. (2016) Joint estimation of preferential attachment and node fitness in growing complex networks, *Scientific Reports*, 6, p. 32558.

Rastelli, R., Friel, N. and Raftery, A. E. (2015) Properties of Latent Variable Network Models, *arXiv preprint arXiv:1506.07806*, Available at: http://arxiv.org/abs/1506.07806.

Robins, G. (2013) A tutorial on methods for the modeling and analysis of social network data, *Journal of Mathematical Psychology*, 57(6), pp. 261–274.

Robins, G., Pattison, P., Kalish, Y. and Lusher, D. (2007) An introduction to exponential random graph (p*) models for social networks, *Social Networks*, 29(2), pp. 173–191.

Scott, J. (2011) Social network analysis: developments, advances, and prospects, *Social Network Analysis and Mining*, 1(1), pp. 21–26.

Scott, J. (2012) *Social network analysis*, SAGE Publications Limited.

Sohn, C., Christopoulos, D. and Koskinen, J. H. (2013) Geography and Social Networks. Modelling the Effects of Territorial on Policy Networks, Available at: http://papers.ssrn.com/sol3/papers.cfm?abstract_id=2491736.

Squartini, T., Fagiolo, G. and Garlaschelli, D. (2011) Randomizing world trade. I. A binary network analysis, *Physical Review E*, 84(4), p. 046117.

Thomas, A. C. and Blitzstein, J. K. (2011) Valued Ties Tell Fewer Lies: Why Not To Dichotomize Network Edges With Thresholds, *arXiv:1101.0788 [physics, stat]*, Available at: http://arxiv.org/abs/1101.0788.

Wang, P., Robins, G., Pattison, P. and Lazega, E. (2013) Exponential random graph models for multilevel networks, *Social Networks*, 35(1), pp. 96–115.

Ward, M. D., Ahlquist, J. S. and Rozenas, A. (2013) Gravity's Rainbow: A dynamic latent space model for the world trade network, *Network Science*, 1(01), pp. 95–118.

Wasserman, S. and Faust, K. (1994) *Social network analysis: methods and applications*, Cambridge; New York, Cambridge University Press.

Watts, D. J. (2017) Should social science be more solution-oriented?, *Nature Human Behaviour*, 1(1), p. 0015.

Watts, D. J. and Strogatz, S. H. (1998) Collective dynamics of 'small-world'networks, *nature*, 393(6684), pp. 440–442.

Westveld, A. H. and Hoff, P. D. (2011) A mixed effects model for longitudinal relational and network data, with applications to international trade and conflict, *The Annals of Applied Statistics*, 5(2A), pp. 843–872.

Wilson, J. D., Denny, M. J., Bhamidi, S., Cranmer, S. J. and Desmarais, B. A. (2017) Stochastic weighted graphs: Flexible model specification and simulation, *Social Networks*, 49, pp. 37–47.

Zhang, S., Wang, L., Liu, Z. and Wang, X. (2016) Evolution of international trade and investment networks, *Physica A: Statistical Mechanics and its Applications*, 462, pp. 752–763.

Zhu, Z., Cerina, F., Chessa, A., Caldarelli, G. and Riccaboni, M. (2014) The Rise of China in the International Trade Network: A Community Core Detection Approach, *PLOS ONE*, 9(8), p. e105496.

Zweig, K. A. (2016) Graph Theory, Social Network Analysis, and Network Science, In *Network Analysis Literacy*, Springer, pp. 23–55.

2.

Network Analysis and the study of international trade and investment

Matthew Smith and Sara Gorgoni

2.1 Introduction

Over the last fifty years, the volume and value of international trade in goods and services have boomed and the share of world trade to GDP has more than doubled. Such a spectacular trend has been achieved not only intensively (i.e., through increases of trade flows between countries already trading in the past), but also extensively (i.e., via newly created trade relationships) (Fagiolo, 2017). The result has been an intricate web of trade linkages, which connects the great majority of world countries, channels huge economic value, and facilitates cross-border technological diffusion (Keller, 2004) and global human mobility (Egger et al., 2012). Empirical evidence supports that in order to fully understand international trade and its macroeconomic implications, countries need to be analysed in a systemic fashion, looking at how embedded they are in the complex web of trade relationships, as it is not sufficient to look at each country in isolation or only at their bilateral trade relationships. While bilateral relationships are important channels of interaction between countries (Krugman, 1995), recent studies have emphasised the importance of indirect relationships, suggesting that bilateral trade linkages can only explain a small fraction of the impact that an economic shock originating in a given country can have on another one with which they don't trade (Abeysinghe and Forbes, 2005). Moreover, bilateral trade relationship may play an important role in linking groups of countries that would have been otherwise disconnected (Fagiolo, 2017).

The conceptualisation of international trade as a network is not new (see Fagiolo, 2017 and De Benedictis and Tajoli, 2011 for a discussion). In economic sociology and political science Social Network Analysis (SNA) has been applied for nearly forty years to international trade data, mainly to quantitatively test for "world system" or "dependency" theories (see for example the seminal paper by Snyder and Kick 1979 and the work by Nemeth and

Smith,1985; Sacks et al., 2001; Breiger,1981; Smith and White,1992; and more recently Kim and Shin, 2002 and Mahutga, 2006).

It is only recently, however, that international trade and economics scholars have also started to apply network analysis and complex network models mostly rooted in Network Science to international trade data to quantitatively understand the structure of the international trade network (ITN), as well as its socio-economic, political and geographical determinants. A parallel strand of literature has also revealed how the structure of the ITN helps explain the spreading of international crises and the transmission of economic shocks (Helliwell and Padmore, 1985; Artis et al., 2003). Alongside this macroeconomic approaches, scholars in the area of international business and economic geography have also started to use network analysis to explain the microeconomic determinants of trade, by looking at foreign direct investments at the firm level, and at corporate ownership networks.

This chapter critically reviews the literature that applies network analysis to international trade and investments data. The chapter identifies five key themes in this literature: International trade; Foreign Direct Investments; The international fragmentation of production; Regionalisation and globalisation; and, finally, the role of Multinational Enterprises (MNEs). For each of these research areas, traditional approaches will first be examined, followed by a discussion of how network analysis can add value.

2.2a International Trade: Traditional Approaches

Over the past few decades, a number of trade studies have emphasised the use of the gravity model, which is often considered the standard bearer in the analysis of international trade; Ward et al. (2013: 95) state that it has long been the "empirical workhorse for modelling international trade" and that it is a very successful empirical model in predicting bilateral trade flows. The model has been extended and altered to answer a number of specific questions within the discipline, including the modelling of intermediate inputs and intra-firm trade (Bardhan and Jaffee, 2004). The gravity model is an econometric model reminiscent of Newton's law of universal gravitation; where the volume of trade between two nations is positively related to their economic size, and negatively to their distance (Anderson, 2010). While its virtue is parsimoniousness, perhaps the most serious disadvantage of the gravity model is that it assumes that dyadic trade is independent, ignoring multilateral dependencies. With products no longer being manufactured in a single location and increasingly made of parts produced in multiple nations, the independence assumption becomes too strong (Ward et al., 2013).

Anderson and van Wincoop (2004) recognise that the gravity model only captures bilateral trade in a multilateral world and attempt to compensate for this by introducing a multilateral resistance term. Multilateral resistance is where the economic distance between two nations is not only based on the bilateral distance but also the weighted average of economic distance to all other trading partners. Despite the fact that the gravity model has been extended to account for this limitation through the use of multilateral resistance it still fails to capture different aspects and effects of these interdependencies (Kareem et al., 2014) and does not capture the full interdependence of trade in the global economy as indicated by trade theory (Koch and LeSage, 2015).

Bernard et al. (2006) acknowledge that in the analysis of international trade, the role of firms, and in particular MNEs, is often omitted. In line with New Trade Theory, within economic models of international trade, the roles of firms are primarily addressed through the use of heterogeneous firm models. These models explain the interaction between firm heterogeneity, trade and the productivity advantage of exporters. This allows the models to capture the uneven distribution of trade, and that trade is concentrated within a small number of firms. Although these theories explain patterns of productivity growth and trade through their inclusion of heterogeneous firms, much remains unexplained, such as an explicit consideration of the boundaries of firms, including their production decisions.

The next section reviews extant studies to show how methodologies that analyse international trade as a complex network can complement existing techniques to capture the interdependencies characterising the global economy.

2.2b International Trade: Network Approaches

The international trade network (ITN) is a network of nations linked by trade ties, directed from the exporter nation to the importer.

The literature that applies network analysis to international trade crosses a number of disciplines, ranging from statistical approaches to the theoretical use of the net. One stream of literature focuses on making use of network science to complement gravity equation models, and to assess how well the gravity model is able to predict topological properties of the ITN (Dueñas and Fagiolo, 2014). For example, Fagiolo (2010) simulates a network based on the gravity model and compares this with the empirical ITN. This comparison leads to the construction of two networks; one generated by the gravity model specifications and another network, which contains the network characteristics and topology not explained by the gravity model. Fagiolo (2010) refer to this as the residual model, as it contains the variance that remains unexplained by the gravity model. The primary property which cannot be explained by the gravity specifications, (a characteristic of the residual network), is the power law distribution, reflecting the skewed distribution of trade ties within the network. This suggests that the gravity model is unable to capture the preferential attachment process occurring in international trade, that countries with high levels of trade ties are more likely to attract trade ties in the future.

Magerman et al. (2013) recognise the need to include third country effects, rather than only considering the bilateral effect (that only involve two countries) within the gravity model specification, including a number of network measures to represent concepts such as international competitiveness (out-degree), import openness (in-degree) and potential competition effects (clustering coefficient). From the gravity model analysis, they note that countries that are highly clustered are subject to intense international competition, identifying that regular determinants of international trade remain important and that network effects are more important for larger nations.

An area of early application of network analysis to international trade as a tool for economic analysis is that of World Systems Theory, which conceptualises national economic development and trade within a core-periphery structure (Wallerstein, 1987). Snyder and Kick (1979) applied formal blockmodelling techniques to empirically classify countries within the world systems core-periphery concept.[1] Smith and White (1992) then built upon the work of Snyder and Kick, making use of different block-modelling techniques to reassess the empirical status of the world system; identifying the rise of exporters from newly industrialised economies.

Positional analysis, utilising structural equivalence and blockmodelling techniques, has been used to analyse trade in specific sectors. For example, Cassi et al. (2012) apply a blockmodelling approach to investigate how globalisation has affected the wine sector and to examine the role of emerging economies in wine production. Anderson et al. (2016) provide additional analysis of the wine sector, examining patterns of intra-industry trade in the "world wide web." They provide further evidence of emerging countries becoming increasingly important in the sector, entering the core of the trade network (yet not necessarily displacing original members). This suggests that a positional analysis of the ITN can be utilised to inform on whether in terms of trade, these emerging economies are moving into trading positions previously strongly held by Western nations, and how this differs across sectors.

---

1 Blockmodelling involves identifying structurally equivalent positions, where two actors have identical ties to all other actors in the network. A more relaxed version of structural equivalence is regular equivalence, which instead captures the extent to which two actors hold the similar position in the network, that is they have identical ties to equivalent actors in the network (Wasserman & Faust, 1994).

This positional analysis approach could be utilised to consider issues pertaining to macroeconomic phenomena, for instance, analysing the major changes in countries' trade and integration patterns. Reyes et al. (2008, 2010) make use of network analysis to provide an alternative to the trade to GDP ratio to investigate trade openness. They specifically analyse the integration of East Asian and Latin American nations, concluding that the high performance of Asian economies is associated with increased economic integration. Further macroeconomics topics addressed through the use of network analysis include an investigation of how trade enhances the growth of a country in relation to its position in the ITN (Kali et al., 2007) and the examination of the spread of shock originating from financial crisis within the ITN (Kali and Reyes, 2010).

Another research area still underexplored and where network analysis could further contribute is the one aiming to explore how trade patterns and the role of nations differ across industries, given the increasing empirical evidence pointing in this direction (as exemplified by De Benedictis and Tajoli, 2011; De Benedictis et al., 2014).

2.3 Foreign Direct Investments (FDIs)

FDI is a key focus within the field of international business, which focuses on the topic from the firm level perspective. Yet the majority of available data on the topic is limited to the country level. Blonigen and Piger (2011) note a lack of consensus on how to model bilateral FDI flows. In terms of standard approaches, empirical studies include the gravity model and MNE general equilibrium models, such as those introduced by Helpman (1984). Early MNE general equilibrium theory suggested that FDIs were motivated by either horizontal or vertical growth considerations. Since then, much work has been undertaken to reveal more complex motivations for FDI, such as the part they play in the international fragmentation of the production process. Blonigen (2005) highlights a key weakness of the MNE general equilibrium theory, specifically that it assumes the bilateral relationship of a parent investing in a foreign affiliate is independent of the parents' other investments (and bilateral ties).

The limitations of the gravity model in the case of FDIs is even more apparent than in the context of international trade, as a firm's investment decisions are not made in isolation of each other, rather they are highly interdependent, forming part of a long-term business strategy (Baltagi et al., 2008).

Chen and Chen (1998) suggest that a network perspective represents a different way of considering FDI and business group activities. They provide an early example of conceptualising FDI flows as a network, noting that the network linkages of a business or multinational group (both internal and external) drive and facilitate the locational decisions of FDI.

Although network analysis provides a natural way to examine FDI, there are relatively few studies examining it with a network analysis framework, and even fewer are those oriented toward explaining the network structure of FDI flows and their drivers. For instance, Koskinen and Lomi (2013) make use of FDI data, using this network to test a variant of the longitudinal exponential random graph model that they have developed, focusing more on the statistical side of the model, rather than on the outcomes in terms of explaining the dynamics of FDI. A further study considering a network of FDI is that of De Masi et al. (2013) based on a relational dataset of Italian firms linked to countries where they provide an analysis of firm-to-firm and country-to-country networks. More recently, Metulini et al. (2017) made use of corporate data (from the Orbis database) to examine the indirect impacts of FDI on international trade. They construct a country level network of cross-country ownership, where the network indicates a pair of countries and the number of control links present between them. They refer to these networks as Corporate Control Networks (CCNs), which they use as a measure of stock FDI. They make use of a gravity model, including network metrics of the CCN in the specification to test for the indirect effects of FDI on international trade.

One particular explanation for the lack of network studies examining research areas pertaining to FDI is the lack of appropriate data; unlike international trade, reliable FDI data is unavailable for many nations. There is a lack of complete cross-country datasets, especially when compared to the case of international trade, where there is extensive coverage over several decades and highly disaggregated, which is presented in a format that can be easily converted into relational data.

However, as more extensive and reliable data becomes increasingly available, there is much scope for the use of network analysis in order to capture the interdependent nature of FDI. An area of study which seems particularly promising – but also very challenging in terms of data requirements – is one attempting to explain FDI through firm-level data, rather than country-level data. For instance, the fDi Markets database provides the opportunity to examine various cross border investments, providing both firm and country-level data, which can be utilised to map sectoral and national investment networks. FDi Markets provides detailed geographic data, where investments can be tracked to the city level, therefore, this database can be used to analyse a city investment network, not only country level investment patterns. This is demonstrated by Crescenzi et al. (2017) in their examination of MNEs investment in European cities.

2.4a Fragmentation of Production: Traditional Approaches

GVCs provide one of the fundamental approaches in considering research questions pertaining to the international fragmentation of production (Sturgeon, 2008; Gereffi, 2001; OECD, 2012). The GVC framework considers the linear sequence of activities that bring a product from its conception to end use and beyond, acknowledging that these activities may be spread across a wide geographic space (Gereffi et al., 2005).

Whilst GVCs are clearly a useful analytical tool in the investigation of the organisation of production across borders, the majority of the empirical studies utilise case studies, (such as Linden et al., 2009; Dedrick et al., 2010), rather than quantitative methods, so the conclusions which can be made are often case-specific rather than relating to the overall patterns of production and trade (Fine, 2013). Also, within the literature utilising the GVC framework, the role of FDI is often omitted, along with the nature of parent-subsidiary relationships; as there is often a focus on inter-firm trade and transactions rather than intra-firm (Sturgeon, 2000). Despite these shortcomings, the GVC framework remains a valuable and prominent tool in the study of the international fragmentation of production, with its use well documented in the study of the electronics (Sturgeon and Kawakami, 2010), automotive (Sturgeon et al., 2009; Sturgeon and Biesebroeck, 2011) and apparel industries (Gereffi and Frederick, 2010).

More recently there have been several attempts to explain GVC patterns, and to address questions in terms of value added in a more quantitative manner. For instance, a collaboration between the OECD and the World Trade Organisation (WTO) has resulted in the development of the Trade in Value Added (TiVA) dataset (OECD, 2013). In addition to this there have been a number of efforts to improve input-output datasets, which can be used to map production chains; one is World Input–Output Database (see Dietzenbacher et al., 2013 for details). Baldwin and Lopez-Gonzalez (2015) acknowledge the value of these datasets and recognise that they have been underutilised. However, the limits of these databases must be noted, in terms of industry and country coverage, when compared to that of standard international trade databases.

A further analytical tool available in the study of the disintegration of production is that of Global Production Networks (GPNs), which runs parallel to the GVC concept, sharing many elements, such as, the idea that production is split into interrelated operations. However, the key difference between these two frameworks is that whilst GVCs are sequential linear structures with a focus on governance, GPNs attempt to encompass a wider range of network possibilities, and various other actors in the network, not just firms. Coe et al. (2008) note that whilst the GPN concept contains a number of insights from the GVC concept, it provides a multi-actor analysis which reveals a range of characteristics about transnational production. It must also be noted that within this framework, the term network is a metaphor and much of the research on GPNs takes a conceptual approach rather than an empirical. Whilst GVC and GPN are considered separate (yet related) frameworks, the production process is often a combination of the two, with some elements taking on a linear sequence, and others a network (Baldwin and Venables, 2013).

A number of other distinct approaches exist to map the fragmentation of production. One of the most widely applied is the use of highly disaggregated international trade data of intermediate goods. This approach was first conducted by Yeats (2001) and Ng and Yeats (1999) and has been utilised in a number of empirical studies (such as Athukorala and Yamashita, 2006).

2.4b Fragmentation of Production: Where can network analysis contribute?

The GVC and GPN approaches emphasise a paradigm shift in the way in which production is organised, with products no longer manufactured in their entirety in a single location. This structural change has strongly increased the economic interdependence amongst countries and has led policy-makers to reconsider areas such as macroeconomics and competitiveness (Amador and Cabral, 2016a). Network analysis provides a way in which to investigate this fragmented organisation of production, capturing interdependences empirically; however, there have been a relatively small number of studies which have considered the fragmentation of production through a network analysis framework. Srholec (2006) takes a network approach to consider the topic of fragmentation, constructing a trade network of intermediate inputs. Yet the network analysis here is a rather broad, narrative approach, concluding that this intermediate input network is characterised by a core-periphery structure, and that determinants of trade differ between the core and the periphery. Where at the densely connected core of the network, trade is not related to cross-country differences in productivity, technology or skills. However, these cross-country differences are noted to play an important role in determining trade between the nations belonging to the core and those in the periphery, along with intra-periphery trade. Cingolani et al. (2017) provide a more detailed network analysis of trade in intermediate and final goods. They make use of network metrics (clustering, assortativity, and centralisation) to describe the topology of global and regional value chains. They note that the process of preferential attachment plays an important role in the formation of trade ties (and often occurs at the regional level), in particular for intermediate goods (when compared to final goods). Amighini and Gorgoni (2014) examine the reorganisation of production within the automotive industry. They use network visualisation tools and apply network analysis measures to highly disaggregated, directed and valued trade data, in order to examine the structure of the trade network for individual component categories. They highlight that within the automotive sector, the participation and changing role of emerging economies in production activities, (primarily as key suppliers), has caused a shift in the way production is organised. Their study highlights the value of considering a high level of disaggregation and examining components rather than final products trade to make sense of the fragmentation of production and current patterns of international trade. Their work provides a clear example of how the structure of international trade can differ not only across industries but also at the component level. In addition, their analysis of brokerage provides insights on the degree of power that actors may possess in the network despite not being at the core. In fact, consideration of the structural position countries occupy in the network allows the notion of power to expand beyond that of individual attributes (such as GDP) and onto one which is relational.

Blázquez and González-Díaz (2015) provide an empirical network analysis of the automotive sector in a similar way, examining a trade network of parts and components and a network of final goods. They undertake a descriptive analysis of the networks for 1996 - 2009, where they note consistent patterns between the structure of parts and components and final goods networks.

A different strand of research which aims at investigating the structure of production with network analysis is one that uses industry input-output tables. These datasets have become more widely available in recent years, which has resulted in increased interest in attempts to map and analyse this data with a network analysis perspective (Amador and Cabral, 2016b; Maluck and Donner, 2015; Tsekeris, 2017; H. Xiao et al., 2017; W. Xiao et al., 2017). The input-output tables map supply and use between industries in a number of nations. This suggests that in network terms, the nodes need to capture both the industry and the nation; this would be represented by a set of nodes, in which each entity would represent industry *i* in country *j*, where the link between nodes would reflect the flow of goods between sectors (either domestic or foreign). A number of scholars have analysed the structure of input-output networks; one of the main reasons for this is to develop a set of statistical measures to analyse the unique and complex structure of these networks. These networks are characterised by a high density and a strong tendency for self-loops, in which goods from a sub-sector of industry *i* in country *j* flow to another sub-sector of industry *i*, and still in country *j*. This is a result of the data used to construct the network, as input-output data is often defined at the macro sector level, therefore, the self-loops reflects the flow of goods within the broad industrial classification, within the same nation (Cerina et al., 2015; Zhu et al., 2015).

The research questions that are addressed through the analysis of these input-output networks do not primarily deal with explaining economic phenomena, such as the organisation of production. For instance, McNerney et al. (2013) focus on testing statistical physics models on the network, applying community detection techniques to identify groupings in this unique network. Along similar lines, Blöchl et al. (2011) present an assessment of centrality measures in a network characterised by self-loops, rather than examining economic phenomena.

To conclude, network analysis seems particularly valuable in identifying patterns and trends in the international organisation of production, assessing the rise of certain nations, changes in the overall structure, and capturing the interdependencies that characterise production today.

2.5a The regionalisation versus globalisation debate: traditional approaches

Alongside research on the fragmentation of production, another area which has attracted a high level of scholarly interest from a range of disciplines and with a number of significant policy implications, is the issue of whether production and trade today are regional or a truly global phenomena (Los et al., 2015). The economist Richard Baldwin has contributed significantly to this debate, in which he strongly argues that production is a regional phenomenon characterised by regional production blocs (Baldwin, 2006). He goes on to suggest that production is characterised by a number of regional factories, such as Factory Asia and Factory Europe, which depend on a headquarter economy, such as Japan or Germany (Baldwin, 2012). Baldwin and Lopez-Gonzalez (2015: 1695) go a step further and clearly state that "supply chain trade is not global, it's regional."

Lejour et al. (2014) make use of a *hubs* and *spokes* concept in order to examine global production networks. They find (in line with the work of Baldwin, 2012) that production networks are actually characterised by regionalisation; mainly located in North America, Europe, and South East Asia; however, the sub regions of these areas play different roles within production as either a hub or a spoke. Lejour et al. (2014) define hubs as regions or nations which import a large portion of value added inputs to use in the output for final use in foreign markets. Whereas spokes are defined as regions or nations which are important suppliers of intermediate inputs to the hubs. For instance, in the European regional production bloc (or Factory Europe), Germany acts as the hub.

In contrast, Los et al. (2014) model the input - output structure of the world economy and note that GVCs are converging towards being truly global. They suggest that the support for regionalisation by Baldwin and Lopez-Gonzalez (2015) is a result of double counting in their data, which they suggest is a result of focusing on intermediate inputs, rather than mapping value added.

2.5b The regionalisation versus globalisation debate: a network perspective

A number of scholars have approached the regionalisation versus globalisation debate making use of network analysis techniques; one frequently used approach is to apply descriptive statistics to evaluate the overall connectivity of the network, and the extent to which nations are integrated according to region in the ITN (amongst them Kim and Shin, 2002; Kastelle et al., 2006; Duernecker et al., 2012; Iapadre and Tajoli, 2014). Along similar lines to traditional approaches, there is somewhat mixed support, with Kim and Shin (2002) noting that globalisation and regionalisation are not necessarily contradictory processes.

Amighini and Gorgoni (2014) apply an alternative network technique to consider whether production in the automotive industry is more regional or global. They make use of an E-I (External – Internal) index, which assesses the number of internal and external ties in a regional partition (see Krackhardt and Stern, 1988 for an overview of this method). This method assesses the extent to which trade in each partition is regional, and presents an overall score, which indicates whether overall trade is more regional or global.

Basile et al. (2017) apply a triad census to the ITN to assess the level of connectivity within regional partitions. A triad census provides a method to detect substructures in a network, more specifically the tendency for certain types of triadic ties. There are 16 different realisations of directed triadic configurations (the various directed ties possible between three nodes – where ties can be mutual, asymmetric or missing), the triadic census provides a count of how many of these configurations are present in the network (Wasserman and Faust, 1994). Basile et al. (2017) use this approach to assess connectivity in the ITN at the regional level (i.e., are there closed or open triads within regional partitions). They find the ITN is characterised by a large number of empty graphs and mutual edge configurations; they suggest that this points towards an ITN consisting of highly connected regions, whilst others have far lower levels of connectivity.

A further method applied to assess whether trade is regional or global is community detection (Gomez et al., 2013), capturing whether trade is organised into blocks characterised by a geographic partition. The method of community detection is often applied by network analysts across a number of disciplines, where a community refers to an area of the network which is denser than other regions (Robins, 2013). Community detection goes further than descriptive measures or the E-I measures based on counts of ties, as it provides a tool to expose significant internal network structure, detecting a special relationship between nodes that may have otherwise gone unnoticed through the use of descriptive metrics alone. Furthermore, advancements in community detection algorithms allow for the modelling of longitudinal data, which in turn allows for commentary on how the community structure influences dynamic network processes (Yang, Algesheimer, and Tessone, 2016). Zhu et al. (2014) provide an empirical example of this, utilising community detection to examine the interplay between globalisation and regionalisation. They note that global dynamics (capturing the disappearance and re-emergence of communities) and regional dynamics (changes in members of the core in regional communities) are highly related and both contribute in explaining network formation patterns in the ITN.

Community detection can also be applied to assess the impact Regional Trade Agreements have on patterns of international trade (see Reyes et al., 2014 for an empirical application).

Typical methodologies attempt to detect regionalisation of trade patterns through a variety of techniques, such as considering it within the gravity model and examining intensity indices (Iapadre and Plummer, 2011). Whereas trade intensity measures and gravity models focus on the dyadic perspective, a network perspective can examine higher order effects and is able to capture the impact that local trade ties have on the overall network structure of international trade (Piccardi and Tajoli, 2012). This suggests that network analysis can complement these typical measures and provide a further contribution in considering the regionalisation versus globalisation debate. Additionally, network analysis allows for a detailed examination of local structures, considering whether a nation acts like a hub in the system at the regional level. Descriptive network measures provide a way in which to evaluate the importance of a nation in the network, both at the regional level and in the entire ITN (Iapadre and Tajoli, 2014).

2.6a Multinational Enterprises: Traditional Approaches

The globalisation of industries in recent decades has led to a number of fundamental changes in the patterns which characterise the world economy as it is today. A key driver of these changes is an increase in the activity and operations of Multinational Enterprises (MNEs), with international trade and investment patterns closely linked to the organisational form and strategies of MNEs (UNCTAD, 2013)

As noted by Helpman (2006: 626) the organisational change of MNEs has driven the "transformation of the world economy." These changes include a reorganisation of their production activities; no longer manufacturing a product in a single location, rather having a disintegrated production process, making use of international sourcing strategies (including both offshoring and outsourcing) in order to coordinate their global supply chain.

Therefore, the nature, organisation, and behaviour of Multinational Enterprises (MNEs) and their relationship to value chain activities is an area of fundamental importance to understand the international reorganisation of production.

There is a vast stream of literature surrounding MNE activity and their internationalisation strategies, along with their place in the production process. The most extensive theory on MNE activity is the eclectic paradigm as introduced by Dunning (2013), and has been altered and extended in a number of ways since its original introduction. One of the fundamental questions is why a firm would choose to serve a foreign market through an affiliate, rather than exports? This question has primarily been answered through the examination of a firm's intangible assets, making use of the Ownership-Location-Internationalisation (OLI) paradigm.[2]

Along with a change in the international activity and organisational form of MNEs, a new breed of MNE has also arisen in recent years: emerging market MNEs (EMNEs). The rise of these EMNEs is one of the more recent and important aspects of globalisation, with an increasing economic significance, contributing to a high level of FDI activity (Amighini, Sanfilippo and Rabellotti, 2009; Hoskisson et al., 2013). The rise of these EMNEs has generated a debate into whether the typical OLI framework can help explain the behaviour and characteristics of these multinationals (Mathews, 2006b; Guillén and García-Canal, 2009; Narula, 2012; Cuervo-Cazurra, 2012) and a rich strand of literature has developed, which investigates the behaviour of Emerging Multinational Enterprises (EMNEs), and their FDI patterns (see Amighini et al., 2009 for a review of this literature).

In terms of how multinational enterprises organise their supply chain activities, a useful approach is the one that considers MNEs as "business groups," making use of the definition provided by Altomonte and Rungi (2013: 1). The authors define business groups as "network-like forms of hierarchical organi-

[2] The ownership advantage refers to the extent to which an enterprise owns or possesses assets which foreign firms do not have access to. The location specific asset determines the extent to which a firm can locate its production facilities outside of the home nation. The internationalisation specific advantage assesses whether an enterprise should internationalise or licence a foreign enterprise.

zation between legally autonomous firms spanning both within and across national borders." According to this definition, MNEs can be classified as business groups because their subsidiaries are legally separate and yet are managed by a common parent firm. This approach suggests that an analysis of an ownership network can prove to be useful in an investigation of the behaviour of MNEs.

Amighini et al. (2014) make use of the business group framework to explain EMNE behaviour. They acknowledge that investment decisions of EMNEs are not made in isolation of other firms belonging to the multinational or business group, whereas standard approaches only consider the perspective of the investing firm from emerging markets, neglecting the behaviour of the remainder of the group. Amighini et al. (2014) further note that the business group framework can be utilised to consider three research areas; Firstly, capturing and assessing the complexity of business group structure; Secondly, to account for how group level structure is connected to value chain activities; Finally, how business group strategy and organisation affect performance and productivity.

2.6b Multinational Enterprise: How can network analysis contribute?

As a business group can be easily conceptualised as a network, addressing MNE behaviour in terms of network analysis appears natural. Scholars have previously conceptualised an MNE as a network of firms; an early instance is that of Ghoshal and Bartlett (1990) who conceptualised a multinational enterprise as an inter-organisational network. They suggest that the configuration of these enterprises goes beyond the simple dyadic relationship of parent and affiliate and should be considered at the group level. These early attempts to approach MNEs from a network perspective, however, only use the network as a metaphorical concept, and do not apply network analysis to capture the interdependencies characterising these networks.

When considering EMNEs, a network approach provides scope to better explain their investment decisions and behaviour. Mathews (2006a) introduces an alternative theoretical approach to analyse EMNEs, which considers the global economy as a web of inter-firm linkages. He presents a framework consisting of three components: linkage, leverage and learning (LLL). The linkages element captures an EMNE's ability to identify and compensate for gaps (or limited ownership assets) via an extensive network. Leverage refers to the EMNEs ability to exploit unique comparative advantages. The third, and perhaps most novel aspect, with respect to EMNEs, is the learning element, capturing whether an EMNE's investment is motivated by a need to learn and strengthen capabilities (Peng, 2012). Therefore, an empirical network analysis of emerging multinational groups can contribute in operationalising and extending this theoretical framework. The alternative approach of the LLL framework has generated some debate in international business over its validity, along with whether it is in a direct contest with the OLI paradigm (Narula, 2006). However, many recognise that the LLL paradigm simply complements the OLI, providing another tool to consider the patterns of firms from emerging markets (Dunning, 2006; Mathews, 2006b).

Network analysis provides a way to represent business groups, expressing MNEs as a network of firms linked by ownership. Ownership networks reflect the close, persistent relationships between legally separate entities which characterise a business group. Network analysis of firms tied by ownership links is not new, and a range of studies have approached research questions using ownership networks, primarily addressing issues such as corporate control and how the network structure can influence corporate governance and behaviour (Piccardi et al., 2010; Kogut, 2012; Vitali et al., 2011).

The research questions dealt with by the literature on ownership networks, however, differ from those considered by standard MNE and business group literature. For instance, the literature examining business groups focuses on examining the presence of business groups in emerging economies (Carney et al., 2011; Cuervo-Cazurra, 2006), along with a debate in regards to whether these business groups are paragons or parasites (Khanna and Yafeh, 2007).

Corporate firm-level data has also been used to construct unique networks to inform on a number of research areas. For instance, Dueñas et al. (2017), construct an international merger and acquisition (M&A) network, where they aggregated firm level M&A data to the country level to construct a network of countries, where a ties from country *i* to country *j* indicates country *i* is the acquirer country (containing investors) and country *j* is the target country. Joyez (2017) makes use of a similar approach to construct a country level network of French multinationals and their foreign affiliates.

Recent methodological developments in the field of network analysis combined with increasingly rich databases allow inferences to be made regarding how organisations have changed over time, along with whether their performance is associated with their business group structure, thus adding value to traditional approaches in the field. Furthermore, a network perspective could also allow researchers to identify strategic decisions of multinational groups, more specifically, how a group enters a region or sector. In the context of business groups, network analysis particularly provides a potentially useful contribution as an alternative approach to analyse the behaviour and investment decisions of EMNEs.

2.7 Summary

This chapter has discussed network analysis' contribution to key areas linked to international trade and investment, along with highlighting where network analysis can potentially contribute. The areas examined by this chapter are international trade, foreign direct investments, fragmentation of production, the regionalisation versus globalisation debate and, finally, the role of MNEs.

The extant literature applying NA to international trade highlights how this methodological approach enables to better capture the interdependent nature of trade in the global economy. In addition, the extant network studies of the ITN show how NA can be utilised to identify key players in international trade and track the rise of emerging economies in the world system and consequent changes in the overall trade structure. In addition to the use of descriptive statistics, network analysis can contribute to the understanding of contemporary international trade (and production) through the application of advanced network models, where interdependence is often at the heart of these models.

Studying patterns of FDI represents an area where network analysis can further contribute in order to better map the interdependent nature of investment decisions of firms, along with the aggregated FDI patterns of nations. Increased availability of data at different levels of aggregation and more sophisticated analytical techniques have enabled the application of NA to investment networks of countries, cities and, ultimately firms, with a number of recent publications in this area. The challenge for the future would be to further the construction and development of relevant datasets mapping FDI, to build on the limited studies tackling international investment research questions from a network perspective.

The review of the fragmentation of production literature highlights that this is a key area where network analysis can make a significant contribution. The descriptive studies examining production patterns based on disaggregated trade data demonstrate how network analysis can be used to identify the rise of key suppliers and regional production patterns in the global economy. This is an area where network analysis can further contribute through advanced network models, going beyond identifying key players, rather identifying patterns that characterise production at the sector level.

The review has identified that substantial work has been undertaken to examine regional trade patterns utilising network methods. One area where network analysis can further contribute is a more detailed examination of the effect of trade at the regional level on overall global trade patterns. The present book provides some very good examples of research in this area, addressing questions related to the "distance puzzle."

When examining the literature on MNE activity, the literature review demonstrated that a network analysis of business groups as ownership networks presents significant potential in addressing research questions regarding the strategic decisions of multinationals, along with operationalising theoretical approaches, such as the LLL framework.

2.8 References

Abeysinghe, T. and K. Forbes (2005), "Trade linkages and output-multiplier effects: a structural VAR approach with a focus on Asia", Review of International Economics, 13: 356{375.

Ali-Yrkkö, J., Rouvinen, P., Seppälä, T. and Ylä-Anttila, P. (2011) Who Captures Value in Global Supply Chains? Case Nokia N95 Smartphone, *Journal of Industry, Competition and Trade*, 11(3), pp. 263–278.

Altomonte, C. and Rungi, A. (2013) *Business Groups as Hierarchies of Firms: Determinants of Vertical Integration and Performance*, Fondazione Eni Enrico Mattei, Available at:
http://econpapers.repec.org/RePEc:fem:femwpa:2013.33.

Amador, J. and Cabral, S. (2016a) Global Value Chains: A Survey of Drivers and Measures, *Journal of Economic Surveys*, 30(2), pp. 278–301.

Amador, J. and Cabral, S. (2016b) Networks of Value-added Trade, *The World Economy*, Available at:
http://onlinelibrary.wiley.com/doi/10.1111/twec.12469/full.

Amighini, A., Cozza, C., Rabellotti, R. and Sanfilippo, M. (2014) Investigating Chinese Outward Foreign Direct Investments: How Can Firm-level Data Help?, *China & World Economy*, 22(6), pp. 44–63.

Amighini, A. and Gorgoni, S. (2014) The International Reorganisation of Auto Production, *The World Economy*, 37(7), pp. 923–952.

Amighini, A., Sanfilippo, M. and Rabellotti, R. (2009) The rise of multinationals from emerging countries: A review of the literature, Available at: http://cadmus.eui.eu/handle/1814/21617.

Anderson, J. E. (2010) *The Gravity Model*, Working Paper, National Bureau of Economic Research, Available at: http://www.nber.org/papers/w16576.

Anderson, J. E. and van Wincoop, E. (2004) Trade costs, *Journal of Economic Literature*, 42(3), pp. 691–751.

Anderson, K., Francois, J., Nelson, D. and Wittwer, G. (2016) Intra-industry Trade in a Rapidly Globalizing Industry: The Case of Wine, *Review of International Economics*, 24(4), pp. 820–836.

Artis, M., A.-B. Galv~ao and M. Marcellino (2003), "The transmission mechanism in a changing world", Economics Working Papers ECO2003/18, European University Institute.

Athukorala, P. and Yamashita, N. (2006) Production fragmentation and trade integration: East Asia in a global context, *The North American Journal of Economics and Finance*, 17(3), pp. 233–256.

Backer, K. D. and Yamano, N. (2012) *International Comparative Evidence on Global Value Chains*, OECD Science, Technology and Industry Working Paper, OECD Publishing, Available at: http://ideas.repec.org/p/oec/stiaaa/2012-3-en.html.

Baldwin, R. (2012) *Global Supply Chains: Why They Emerged, Why They Matter, and Where They are Going*, SSRN Scholarly Paper, Rochester, NY, Social Science Research Network. Available at: http://papers.ssrn.com/abstract=2153484.

Baldwin, R. (2006) Globalisation: the great unbundling (s), *Economic Council of Finland*, 20(2006), pp. 5–47.

Baldwin, R. and Lopez-Gonzalez, J. (2015) Supply-chain Trade: A Portrait of Global Patterns and Several Testable Hypotheses, *The World Economy*, 38(11), pp. 1682–1721.

Baldwin, R. and Venables, A. J. (2013) Spiders and snakes: Offshoring and agglomeration in the global economy, *Journal of International Economics*, 90(2), pp. 245–254.

Baltagi, B. H., Egger, P. and Pfaffermayr, M. (2008) Estimating regional trade agreement effects on FDI in an interdependent world, *Journal of Econometrics, The use of econometrics in informing public policy makers*, 145(1–2), pp. 194–208.

Bardhan, A. D. and Jaffee, D. (2004) On intra-firm trade and multinationals: Foreign outsourcing and offshoring in manufacturing, *Revised: April*, 7, Available at: http://faculty.haas.berkeley.edu/jaffee/Papers/ForeignDirectJaffeefBardhan.pdf.

Basile, R., Commendatore, P., De Benedictis, L. and Kubin, I. (2017) The impact of trade costs on the European Regional Trade Network: An empirical and theoretical analysis, *Review of International Economics.*

Bernard, A. B., Jensen, J. B. and Schott, P. (2006) *Intra-Firm Trade*, mimeo, Available at: http://www.ifn.se/Wfiles/Vaxholm-06/mnt_10.pdf.

Blázquez, L. and González-Díaz, B. (2015) International automotive production networks: How the web comes together, *Journal of Economic Interaction and Coordination*, pp. 1–32.

Blöchl, F., Theis, F. J., Vega-Redondo, F. and Fisher, E. O. (2011) Vertex centralities in input-output networks reveal the structure of modern economies, *Physical Review E*, 83(4), p. 046127.

Blonigen, B. A. (2005) A Review of the Empirical Literature on FDI Determinants, *Atlantic Economic Journal*, 33(4), pp. 383–403.

Blonigen, B. A. and Piger, J. (2011) *Determinants of Foreign Direct Investment*, Working Paper, National Bureau of Economic Research, Available at: http://www.nber.org/papers/w16704.

Breiger, R. (1981), \Structure of economic interdependence among nations", in P. M. Blau and R. K. Merton, (eds.), Continuities in structural inquiry, Newbury Park, CA: Sage, 353{80.

Carney, M., Gedajlovic, E. R., Heugens, P. P. M. A. R., Essen, M. V. and Oosterhout, J. (Hans) V. (2011) Business Group Affiliation, Performance, Context, and Strategy: A meta-analysis, *Academy of Management Journal*, 54(3), pp. 437–460.

Cassi, L., Morrison, A. and Ter Wal, A. L. J. (2012) The Evolution of Trade and Scientific Collaboration Networks in the Global Wine Sector: A Longitudinal Study Using Network Analysis, *Economic Geography*, 88(3), pp. 311–334.

Cerina, F., Zhu, Z., Chessa, A. and Riccaboni, M. (2015) World Input-Output Network, *PLoS ONE*, 10(7), p. e0134025.

Chen, H. and Chen, T.-J. (1998) Network Linkages and Location Choice in Foreign Direct Investment, *Journal of International Business Studies*, 29(3), pp. 445–467.

Cingolani, I., Iapadre, L. and Tajoli, L. (2017) International production networks and the world trade structure, *International Economics*.

Coe, N. M., Dicken, P. and Hess, M. (2008) Introduction: global production networks—debates and challenges, *Journal of Economic Geography*, 8(3), pp. 267–269.

Crescenzi, R., Datu, K. and Iammarino, S. (2017) European Cities and Foreign Investment Networks, *Scienze Regionali*, 16(2), pp. 229–260.

Cuervo-Cazurra, A. (2006) Business groups and their types, *Asia Pacific Journal of Management*, 23(4), pp. 419–437.

Cuervo-Cazurra, A. (2012) Extending theory by analyzing developing country multinational companies: Solving the Goldilocks debate, *Global Strategy Journal*, 2(3), pp. 153–167.

De Benedictis, L., Nenci, S., Santoni, G., Tajoli, L. and Vicarelli, C. (2014) Network Analysis of World Trade using the BACI-CEPII dataset, *Global Economy Journal*, 14(3–4), pp. 287–343.

De Benedictis, L. and Tajoli, L. (2011) The World Trade Network, *The World Economy*, 34(8), pp. 1417–1454.

De Masi, G., Giovannetti, G. and Ricchiuti, G. (2013) Network analysis to detect common strategies in Italian foreign direct investment, *Physica A: Statistical Mechanics and its Applications*, 392(5), pp. 1202–1214.

Dedrick, J., Kraemer, K. L. and Linden, G. (2010) Who profits from innovation in global value chains?: a study of the iPod and notebook PCs, *Industrial and Corporate Change*, 19(1), pp. 81–116.

Dietzenbacher, E., Los, B., Stehrer, R., Timmer, M. and de Vries, G. (2013) The Construction of World Input–Output Tables in the Wiod Project, *Economic Systems Research*, 25(1), pp. 71–98.

Dueñas, M. and Fagiolo, G. (2014) Global trade imbalances: A network approach, *Advances in Complex Systems*, 17(03n04), p. 1450014.

Dueñas, M., Mastrandrea, R., Barigozzi, M. and Fagiolo, G. (2017) Spatio-temporal patterns of the international merger and acquisition network, *Scientific reports*, 7(1), p. 10789.

Duernecker, G., Meyer, M. and Vega-Redondo, F. (2012) Being close to grow faster: A network-based empirical analysis of economic globalisation, Available at: http://cadmus.eui.eu/handle/1814/20814.

Dunning, J. H. (2006) Comment on Dragon multinationals: New players in 21 st century globalisation, *Asia Pacific Journal of Management*, 23(2), pp. 139–141.

Dunning, J. H. (2013) *International Production and the Multinational Enterprise (RLE International Business)*, Routledge.

Egger, P. H., M. von Ehrlich and D. R. Nelson (2012), "Migration and Trade", The World Economy, 35: 216{241.

Fagiolo, G. (2017), "The International Trade Network: Empirics and Modeling", in Jennifer Nicoll Victor, Alexander H. Montgomery, and Mark Lubell (Eds.), The Oxford Handbook of Political Networks, Oxford University Press, Oxford.

Fagiolo, G. (2010) The international-trade network: gravity equations and topological properties, *Journal of Economic Interaction and Coordination*, 5(1), pp. 1–25.

Fine, B. (2013) Consumption Matters, *Ephemera*, 13(2), pp. 217–248.

Gereffi, G. (2001) Beyond the Producer-driven/Buyer-driven Dichotomy The Evolution of Global Value Chains in the Internet Era, *IDS Bulletin*, 32(3), pp. 30–40.

Gereffi, G. and Frederick, S. (2010) The global apparel value chain, trade and the crisis: challenges and opportunities for developing countries, *World Bank Policy Research Working Paper Series, Vol*, Available at: http://papers.ssrn.com/sol3/papers.cfm?abstract_id=1596491.

Ghoshal, S. and Bartlett, C. A. (1990) The Multinational Corporation as an Interorganizational Network, *The Academy of Management Review*, 15(4), p. 603.

Gomez, D. M., Torgler, B. and Ortega, G. J. (2013) Measuring Global Economic Interdependence: A Hierarchical Network Approach, *The World Economy*, 36(12), pp. 1632–1648.

Guillén, M. F. and García-Canal, E. (2009) The American model of the multinational firm and the 'new' multinationals from emerging economies, *The Academy of Management Perspectives*, 23(2), pp. 23–35.

Helliwell, J. F. and T. Padmore (1985), "Empirical Studies of Macroeconomic Interdependence", in R. Jones and P. Kenen, (eds.), Handbook of International Economies, Elsevier Science Publishers B.V.

Helpman, E. (1984) A Simple Theory of International Trade with Multinational Corporations, Available at: http://dash.harvard.edu/handle/1/3445092.

Helpman, E. (2006) Trade, FDI, and the organization of firms, *Journal of Economic Literature*, 44(3), pp. 589–630.

Hennart, J.-F. (2012) Emerging market multinationals and the theory of the multinational enterprise, *Global Strategy Journal*, 2(3), pp. 168–187.

Hoskisson, R. E., Wright, M., Filatotchev, I. and Peng, M. W. (2013) Emerging multinationals from Mid-Range economies: The influence of institutions and factor markets, *Journal of Management Studies*, 50(7), pp. 1295–1321.

Iapadre, L. and Plummer, M. (2011) Statistical measures of regional trade integration, In *The regional integration manual: quantitative and qualitative methods*, Routledge London, pp. 98–123.

Iapadre, P. L. and Tajoli, L. (2014) Emerging countries and trade regionalization. A network analysis, *Journal of Policy Modeling, Measuring and Modeling Regional Power and Leadership*, 36, Supplement 1, pp. S89–S110.

Joyez, C. (2017) On the topological structure of multinationals network, *Physica A: Statistical Mechanics and its Applications*, 473, pp. 578–588.

Kali, R., Méndez, F. and Reyes, J. (2007) Trade structure and economic growth, *The Journal of International Trade & Economic Development*, 16(2), pp. 245–269.

Kali, R. and Reyes, J. (2010) Financial Contagion on the International Trade Network, *Economic Inquiry*, 48(4), pp. 1072–1101.

Kareem, O., Fatima and Kareem, I. O. (2014) *Specification and Estimation of Gravity Models: A Review of the Issues in the Literature*, SSRN Scholarly Paper, Rochester, NY, Social Science Research Network, Available at: http://papers.ssrn.com/abstract=2459484.

Kastelle, T., Steen, J. T. and Liesch, P. W. (2006) Measuring globalisation: An evolutionary economic approach to tracking the evolution of international trade, In *DRUID Summer Conference 2006*, Danish Research Unit for Industrial Dynamics, pp. 1–41, Available at: http://espace.library.uq.edu.au/view/UQ:104415.

Keller, W. (2004), "International Technology Diffusion", Journal of Economic Literature, 42:752{782.

Khanna, T. and Yafeh, Y. (2007) Business Groups in Emerging Markets: Paragons or Parasites?, *The Journal of Economic Literature*, 45(2), pp. 331–372.

Kim, S. and Shin, E.-H. (2002) A Longitudinal Analysis of Globalisation and Regionalization in International Trade: A Social Network Approach, *Social Forces*, 81(2), pp. 445–468.

Koch, W. and LeSage, J. P. (2015) Latent Multilateral Trade Resistance Indices: Theory and Evidence, *Scottish Journal of Political Economy*, 62(3), pp. 264–290.

Kogut, B. (2012) *The Small Worlds of Corporate Governance*, Cambridge, Mass, MIT Press.

Koskinen, J. and Lomi, A. (2013) The Local Structure of Globalisation, *Journal of Statistical Physics*, 151(3–4), pp. 523–548.

Krackhardt, D. and Stern, R. N. (1988) Informal Networks and Organizational Crises: An Experimental Simulation, *Social Psychology Quarterly*, 51(2), p. 123.

Krugman, P. (1995), "Growing World Trade: Causes and Consequences", Brookings Papers on Economic Activity, 26: 327{377.

Lejour, A., Rojas-Romagosa, H. and Veenendaal, P. (2014) Identifying hubs and spokes in global supply chains using redirected trade in value added, Available at: http://papers.ssrn.com/sol3/papers.cfm?abstract_id=2426088.

Linden, G., Kraemer, K. L. and Dedrick, J. (2009) Who captures value in a global innovation network?: the case of Apple's iPod, *Commun. ACM*, 52(3), pp. 140–144.

Los, B., Timmer, M. P. and de Vries, G. J. (2015) How Global Are Global Value Chains? A New Approach to Measure International Fragmentation, *Journal of Regional Science*, 55(1), pp. 66–92.

Magerman, G., De Bruyne, K. and Van Hove, J. (2013) Revealed Multilateral Trade Resistance in Gravity Models–A Network Approach, *The World Economy*, Available at: https://lirias.kuleuven.be/handle/123456789/455927.

Mahutga, M. C. (2006), "The Persistence of Structural Inequality?: A Network Analysis of International Trade, 1965-2000", Social Forces, 84: 1863-89.

Maluck, J. and Donner, R. V. (2015) A Network of Networks Perspective on Global Trade, *PLOS ONE*, 10(7), p. e0133310.

Mathews, J. A. (2006a) Dragon multinationals: New players in 21st century globalisation, *Asia Pacific Journal of Management*, 23(1), pp. 5–27.

Mathews, J. A. (2006b) Response to Professors Dunning and Narula, *Asia Pacific Journal of Management*, 23(2), pp. 153–155.

McNerney, J., Fath, B. D. and Silverberg, G. (2013) Network structure of inter-industry flows, *Physica A: Statistical Mechanics and its Applications*, 392(24), pp. 6427–6441.

Metulini, R., Riccaboni, M., Sgrignoli, P. and Zhu, Z. (2017) The indirect effects of foreign direct investment on trade: A network perspective, *The World Economy*, Available at: http://onlinelibrary.wiley.com/doi/10.1111/twec.12504/abstract.

Narula, R. (2012) Do we need different frameworks to explain infant MNEs from developing countries?, *Global Strategy Journal*, 2(3), pp. 188–204.

Narula, R. (2006) Globalisation, new ecologies, new zoologies, and the purported death of the eclectic paradigm, *Asia Pacific Journal of Management*, 23(2), pp. 143–151.

Nemeth, R. and D. Smith (1985), "International Trade and World-System Structure: A Multiple Network Analysis", Review: A Journal of the Fernand Braudel Center, 8: 517{60.

Ng, F. and Yeats, A. (1999) Production Sharing in Asia: Who Does What for Whom, and Why, *Washington: World Bank Policy Research Working Paper*, (2197).

OECD (2013) *Interconnected Economies*, Paris, Organisation for Economic Co-operation and Development, Available at: http://www.oecd-ilibrary.org/content/book/9789264189560-en.

Peng, M. W. (2012) The global strategy of emerging multinationals from China, *Global Strategy Journal*, 2(2), pp. 97–107.

Piccardi, C., Calatroni, L. and Bertoni, F. (2010) Communities in Italian corporate networks, *Physica A: Statistical Mechanics and its Applications*, 389(22), pp. 5247–5258.

Piccardi, C. and Tajoli, L. (2012) Existence and significance of communities in the world trade web, *Physical Review E*, 85(6), p. 066119.

Reyes, J., Schiavo, S. and Fagiolo, G. (2008) Assessing the evolution of international economic integration using random walk betweenness centrality: the cases of east asia and latin america, *Advances in Complex Systems*, 11(05), pp. 685–702.

Reyes, J., Schiavo, S. and Fagiolo, G. (2010) Using complex networks analysis to assess the evolution of international economic integration: The cases of East Asia and Latin America, *The Journal of International Trade & Economic Development*, 19(2), pp. 215–239.

Reyes, J., Wooster, R. and Shirrell, S. (2014) Regional Trade Agreements and the Pattern of Trade: A Networks Approach, *The World Economy*, 37(8), pp. 1128–1151.

Robins, G. (2013) A tutorial on methods for the modeling and analysis of social network data, *Journal of Mathematical Psychology, Social Networks*, 57(6), pp. 261–274.

Sacks, M., M. Ventresca and B. Uzzi (2001), \Global Institutions and Networks: Contingent Change in the Structure of World Trade Advantage, 1965-1980", American Behavioral Scientist, 44: 1579{601.

Smith, D. A. and White, D. R. (1992) Structure and Dynamics of the Global Economy: Network Analysis of International Trade 1965–1980, *Social Forces*, 70(4), pp. 857–893.

Snyder, D. and Kick, E. L. (1979) Structural position in the world system and economic growth, 1955-1970: A multiple-network analysis of transnational interactions, *American Journal of Sociology*, pp. 1096–1126.

Srholec, M. (2006) Fragmentation and trade: A network perspective, In pp. 7–9, Available at: http://etsg.org/ETSG2006/papers/Srholec.pdf.

Sturgeon, T. J. (2008) From commodity chains to value chains: interdisciplinary theory building in an age of globalisation, Available at: http://isapapers.pitt.edu/84/.

Sturgeon, T. J. (2000) How Do We Define Value Chains and Production Networks?, *IDS bulletin*, 32(3), pp. 9–18.

Sturgeon, T. J., Memedovic, O., Van Biesebroeck, J. and Gereffi, G. (2009) Globalisation of the automotive industry: main features and trends, *International Journal of Technological Learning, Innovation and Development*, 2(1), pp. 7–24.

Sturgeon, T. J. and Van Biesebroeck, J. (2011) Global value chains in the automotive industry: an enhanced role for developing countries?, *International Journal of Technological Learning, Innovation and Development*, 4(1), pp. 181–205.

Sturgeon, T. and Kawakami, M. (2010) Global value chains in the electronics industry: was the crisis a window of opportunity for developing countries?, *World Bank Policy Research Working Paper Series, Vol*, Available at: http://papers.ssrn.com/sol3/papers.cfm?abstract_id=1676652.

Tsekeris, T. (2017) Global value chains: Building blocks and network dynamics, *Physica A: Statistical Mechanics and its Applications*, 488, pp. 187–204.

UNCTAD (2013) *Global Value Chains and Development: Investment and Value Added Trade in the Global Economy: A Preliminary Analysis*, United Nations: New York and Geneva, Available at: http://unctad.org/en/PublicationsLibrary/diae2013d1_en.pdf.

Vitali, S., Glattfelder, J. B. and Battiston, S. (2011) The Network of Global Corporate Control, *PLoS ONE*, 6(10), p. e25995.

Wallerstein, I. (1987) World-systems analysis, *Social theory today*, pp. 309–324.

Ward, M. D., Ahlquist, J. S. and Rozenas, A. (2013) Gravity's Rainbow: A dynamic latent space model for the world trade network, *Network Science*, 1(01), pp. 95–118.

Wasserman, S. and Faust, K. (1994) *Social network analysis: methods and applications*, Cambridge; New York, Cambridge University Press.

Xiao, H., Sun, T., Meng, B. and Cheng, L. (2017) Complex Network Analysis for Characterizing Global Value Chains in Equipment Manufacturing, *PLOS ONE*, 12(1), p. e0169549.

Xiao, W., Wang, L., Zhang, Z. and Wang, C. (2017) Identify and analyse key industries and basic economic structures using interregional industry network, *Cluster Computing*, pp. 1–11.

Yang, Z., Algesheimer, R. and Tessone, C. J. (2016) A Comparative Analysis of Community Detection Algorithms on Artificial Networks, *Scientific Reports*, 6, p. 30750.

Yeats, A. (2001) *Just How Big is Global Production Sharing?*, SSRN Scholarly Paper, Rochester, NY, Social Science Research Network, Available at: http://papers.ssrn.com/abstract=597193.

Zhu, Z., Cerina, F., Chessa, A., Caldarelli, G. and Riccaboni, M. (2014) The Rise of China in the International Trade Network: A Community Core Detection Approach, *PLOS ONE*, 9(8), p. e105496.

Zhu, Z., Puliga, M., Cerina, F., Chessa, A. and Riccaboni, M. (2015) Global Value Trees, *PLoS ONE*, 10(5), p. e0126699.

3.

Structure and evolution of the world's historical trade patterns

Benjamin Vandermarliere, Samuel Standaert and Stijn Ronsse

Data: Historical trade integration (hti) index from Standaert, et al. (2016) (https://www.researchgate.net/project/Historical-Trade-Index)
Software: Python (graph-tool)

3.1 Introduction

Social scientists have long tried to discern the structure of the worldwide trade pattern and track its evolution over time. Most of their theoretical and empirical efforts have been focussed on describing and identifying of one of three specific network structures: globalisation, regionalisation, and core-periphery. Globalisation is an amorphous term that is interpreted differently depending on the field. Sometimes it is used simply to refer to an increasingly connected world, but a popular definition links it to the concept of geographic neutrality. A geographically neutral world is one where all countries trade with each other, irrespective of their distance or other geographical concerns. For this reason, this view is also known as the "death of distance" (Jameson, 1984; Caimcross 1997). Regionalisation, on the other hand, is a situation where the trade network is organized into a few regions containing countries that trade intensively with each other, but where inter-regional links are sparse. The core-periphery structure, as defined by Wallerstein's world-system analysis (2004), speaks of a world where there is a small group of very densely connected countries (the core), surrounded by a large peripheral group of countries that trades mostly with the core and not among themselves.

As a mathematical framework to study interactions, network theory is a natural candidate to explore international trade and uncover the patterns underlying worldwide trade. It should come as no surprise that its tools to uncover large-scale structures have been used extensively to address questions on globalisation (Kim and Shin, 2002), regionalisation (Barigozzi et al.,

2011; Reyes et al., 2014) and the core-periphery structure of international trade (Snyder and Kick, 1979; Kali and Reyes, 2007).

The way in which trade networks have been modelled has evolved strongly over time, even within the family of networks where countries are represented by nodes and the edges depict the flow of trade.[1] Initial studies started with the simplest definition of the edges, using binary variables to indicate the presence or absence of trade (import or exports) between two countries (e.g., Smith and White, 1992; Reyes et al., 2014). There are many ways in which the edge definition can be more informative on the actual trade flows between the countries. Edges can be directed to distinguish a situation where trade flows in only one direction (Serrano and Boguñá, 2003; Li et al., 2003; Garlaschelli and Loffredo, 2004, 2005; Kali and Reyes, 2007). The edges can also be weighted with the volume of exports (Fagiolo et al., 2008, 2009; De Benedictis and Tajoli, 2011), allowing us to distinguish countries that trade a lot. These weights can be further refined by making the edges proportional to either the total trade of the country (Tzekina et al., 2008) or to the GDP of the country (Krings et al., 2014), since a million USD in trade will be more important to a small economy that trades little, than to a large country that trades a lot. Finally, these networks can also be linked over time, allowing us to study the changing role of certain countries in the trade network, or examine how the overall structure changes over time.

In parallel with the increasing level of detail at which trade flows are represented, the techniques used to discern the large-scale structures have evolved too. While initially simple network statistics were used like the network density, later papers relied on increasingly complex methods like modularity maximization (Fortunato, 2010). This chapter presents the next step in this methodological evolution by outlining how Peixoto's (2015) temporal stochastic block model (SBM) technique can be used to elicit the structure of worldwide trade patterns and track its evolution over time.

The temporal SBM technique elegantly addresses three limitations that are currently present in the field. To start, it uses all the information contained in the weighted directed network, unlike some of the more coarse-grained alternatives that are limited to unweighted or undirected networks. Secondly, the

[1] Other ways in which trade networks have been modelled focus on transportation infrastructure or the social network among traders or entrepreneurs. Examples of the former include the ORBIS project (Scheidel, 2015), which reconstructed the Roman Empire's transportation network and linked to the overland trade expansion, and Buys et al. (2010) who looked at road networks and overland trade expansion in Sub-Saharan Africa. Van Doosselaere (2009) and Saxe (1979) analysed the social network of traders in medieval Genoa and the eighteenth century Indies, respectively, while Erikson and Bearman (2006) for example combined both the social and transportation networks.

SBM technique uses the temporal dimension of the data and is able to find the best fitting structure describing the network consistently throughout the entire period studied. Other methods either (arbitrarily) aggregate over several years or only discuss a limited set of years. Finally, while most tests look for a particular structure in the data (e.g., communities or a core-periphery structure), SBM is an agnostic procedure that does not make any a priori assumptions about the structure. The flexibility of this more generic approach allows us to better detect the transitions of the network structure as well as uncover patterns that run counter to expectations. In section 2 we dig deeper into the issues of current methodologies and how they are addressed with temporal SBM.

After discussing how globalisation, regionalisation, and the core-periphery structure are analysed in network theory, section 5 sets out to reveal the structure and evolution of the world's trade patterns from the 1880s to the late 1980s. To model the worldwide trade network, we use the historical trade integration (hti) index of Standaert et al. (2016). This index captures the level of trade integration between two countries, i.e., the relative importance of the bilateral import and export flows for each country. By combining various historical data sets and using statistical techniques to address availability problems, the hti index can give us one of the most replete images of trade relations over this hundred-year period. For example, it also includes pre-World War I colonial trade flows. Using the hti index, we construct a temporal weighted directed network that captures trade integration during three consecutive periods: the first wave of globalisation (1880-1913), the interbellum (1919-1939), and the second wave of globalisation up till the disintegration of the former USSR (1946-1989). While the second globalisation wave did not stop after the fall of the Berlin wall, the large geopolitical changes it brought has caused some authors to refer to the post-1990 period as the third globalisation wave. It has been left out of the analysis to increase the homogeneity of the periods under study.

The remainder of this chapter is organised as follows: the next section discusses how international trade concepts like globalisation and regionalisation can be translated to network theory. We then introduce stochastic block models and explain the construction of the historical trade network. Sections 5 and 6 discuss our findings and conclusions.

3.2 Networks and trade patterns

In this section, we discuss four key concepts from the international trade literature and show the link with corresponding concepts in network theory: globalisation, regionalisation, core-periphery idea and the hub-and-spoke pattern.

3.2.1 Globalisation

Since the 1980s, the term globalisation has been used in a myriad of scientific disciplines, each using its own definition(s). Nevertheless, a common denominator to most definitions is the shift of economic transactions from the local toward the global market. In other words, countries increasingly trade with partners all over the world and distance plays an increasingly smaller role in determining those trade flows. This idea, first proposed by Jameson (1984), was summarized by Caimcross (1997) as the "death of distance."

The economic history literature identifies two important waves of globalisation before and after the World Wars and a period of de-globalisation in between. There has been much discussion on the timing of the first phase of globalisation. Some authors believe it started at the end of the nineteenth century (e.g., Estevadeordal et al., 2002; Das, 2004), while others believe that it started from as early as the 1840s (e.g., O'Rourke and Williamson, 2004; Jacks et al., 2010). Regardless of when it started, all agree that the end of the nineteenth century was a part of this first globalisation wave. During this time, mercantilist policies were replaced by free trade regimes, with Great Britain leading the way. The European colonizers also imposed this new trading regime on their colonies and even forced independent countries to open up their trade. At the same time, technological progress, such as the use of steam engines and the construction of an extensive railway network, significantly reduced trading costs. This was helped along by the gold standard, which offered a stable international trading climate (Crafts, 2004).

The rapid liberalization of trade of the first globalisation wave was brought to a halt by the start of the First World War. The subsequent conference of Versailles did little to stabilize international relations and the Great Depression and the protectionist policies it induced further exacerbated the situation. At the time, the USA took over the leading role in the world economy, but it failed to further the free trade agenda and could not pull the world economy out of the recession. The trade policy during the interbellum was marked by beggar-thy-neighbour policies, with countries trying to protect their domestic markets by increasing the quotas and tariffs on international trade.

World War II strengthened the anti-imperialist nationalist and communist states, the disintegrating effect of which lasted till the 1990s. On top of that, globalisation was countered by the use of higher tariffs in support of import-substitution policies, mostly by newly decolonized countries (Findlay and O'Rourke, 2007). Although the decades following the Second World War are entitled as a second wave of globalisation, it was mostly a regional evolution limited to Western Europe and Northern America. This was not only a result of disintegrating communist and anti-imperialist states but also by the protectionist trade politics of newly decolonized countries (Findlay and O'Rourke, 2007). Intensification of trade relations took place but was geographically determined and did not extend to the rest of the world. While the main determinant of the first globalisation wave was the decrease in trade costs, the second wave was mainly driven by geopolitical factors. Globalisation continued to strengthen after the fall of the Berlin wall, a trend that has lasted to this day. Because of the major changes to the geopolitical order, the period after 1989 is sometimes called the third globalisation wave.

In a network context where countries are represented by nodes and their trade by (directed) edges, globalisation and geographic neutrality would be denoted by an increase in the number of edges and an equalization in their distribution over the different nodes. The theoretical extreme would be a completely connected network where each country trades with all other countries. A number of studies have looked for globalisation by studying the network density, but because of data availability issues this research has mostly been focussed on the second half of the 20th century, i.e., the second and third globalisation waves. For example, Kim and Shin (2002), Kali and Reyes (2007) and De Benedictis and Tajoli (2011) all found an increase in the number of edges. Their trade networks were constructed respectively using import data for 1959 and 1975, using import and export data for 1992 and 1998 and using import data for the period 1950 till 2000. All three studies also concluded that the global trade network was far from completely connected: when edges are defined as imports being positive, the density increases from 31% in the 50s to 72% in 2011 in the Direction of Trade Statistics database. However, this strongly overestimates network density as it includes many very small, but still positive trade flows. Using the historical trade integration index, Standaert et al. (2016) were able to compare both globalisation waves. They found that the importance of distance has significantly dropped since the early 1880s and that once you control for the increase in the number of countries over time the network density increased during both waves.

3.2.2 Regionalisation

While globalisation is an indiscriminate increase in the number of trade links between countries, regionalisation implies the emergence of groups of countries that trade strongly amongst themselves but have few linkages to countries outside of their group. These regions might be actual geographical regions, i.e., determined by distance, but can also be seen more broadly as cultural regions, or those determined by (former) colonial powers and their colonies. Multilateral trade agreements like the European Union or the North American Free Trade Agreements are examples of political institutions aimed at increasing the integration among countries in their region above those in the rest of the world. Whether or not regionalisation is the first step to a globalised trade pattern is a hotly debated topic in economics (see, e.g. the building block vs. stumbling block debate surveyed in Panagariya, 1999).

The concept of trade groups and regionalisation has a natural counterpart in network theory: communities and the community-structure. The panels of figure 3.1 show three diagrams representing a network with a typical community structure (Fortunato, 2010). The coloured circles represent nodes and edges are drawn as lines between them. To avoid cluttering the figures, bi-directional connections are indicated with a single line, while edges that only run in one direction get an arrow to indicate the orientation.

First, the left diagram shows the actual network which has three distinct groups of nodes. One can observe that there are many connections among the members of a given group but that there are few connections to members of other groups. This is the signature of a network with a community structure. The centre diagram coarse grains the network and shows a block for each of the corresponding communities. Finally, the right diagram expresses the average number of edges between nodes of a combination of any two groups. The columns show the incoming edge distribution and the rows the outgoing edge distribution. For example, the nodes from block 1 are highly connected with other nodes from block 1 (black) but have a lower outgoing edge density (grey) with nodes from block 2 and no outgoing edges to block 3 (white). In terms of the incoming edges, nodes from block 1 are likely to be connected to the two other blocks but less so than among themselves.[2] In contrast, the same drawing for a perfectly globalised world would look like a single black block of completely connected countries.

Figure 3.1: The community structure-regionalisation

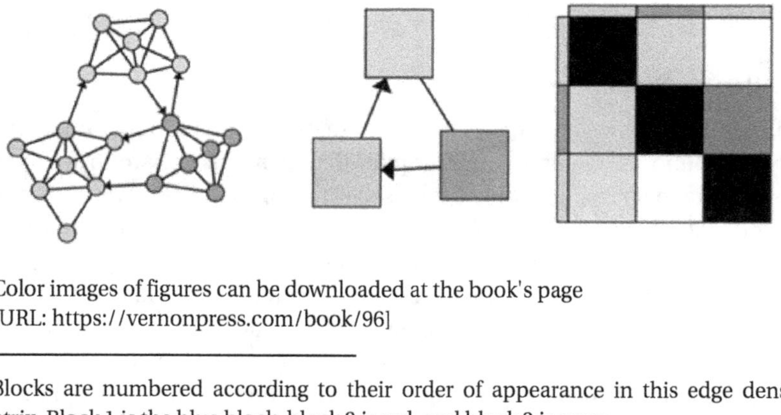

Color images of figures can be downloaded at the book's page
[URL: https://vernonpress.com/book/96]

[2] Blocks are numbered according to their order of appearance in this edge density matrix. Block 1 is the blue block, block 2 is red, and block 3 is green.

Notes: The network is displayed on the left, the middle panel shows the coarse-grained view of the network where nodes with a similar position are in the same block, and the right panel is a matrix showing the average edge density between the nodes in each block (darker colour signals a higher density).

Several studies already investigated the community structure of the international trade network. There are variations in the techniques used as well as the time periods covered. For example, Tzekina et al. (2008) study the structure and evolution of the trade network using a visual inspection of so-called "islands" starting in 1948.[3] Barigozzi et al. (2011) and Reyes et al. (2014) use a more quantitative technique called modularity maximization (Fortunato, 2010) to study the trade network respectively starting in 1992 and 1970.[4] While these studies find some evidence of the existence of a community structure, this turns out to be not highly significant. In other words, they cannot unambiguously conclude that the worldwide trade network consists of clear-cut, close-knitted communities.

3.2.3 Core-periphery

A third structure often claimed to be present in international trade is the core-periphery structure. In his theory, which was first developed by Wallerstein (2004), the world is comprised of a core of industrially developed countries and a periphery of developing countries. The pattern of dependence between the core and periphery is lopsided. The peripheral countries depend predominantly on one or more core countries, while core countries are only connected to other core countries. While Wallerstein's theory also concerns production systems and dependency relations, we will restrict ourselves to the trade pattern associated with the core-periphery model.

The panels of figure 3.2 show the prototypical example of a core-periphery structure using the same three diagrams as above (Borgatti and Everett, 2000). The blue nodes represent the tightly connected core countries, while the sparsely connected periphery is formed by the red nodes. The edge density fingerprint (right panel) illustrates the lop-sided distribution of edges, with the periphery having many outgoing connections to the core but none with to other peripheral countries, while the core only has connections to other core countries.

---

[3] An island is a connected component in which the weights of the arcs within the community are significantly larger than those outside the community. It is a measure implemented in the Pajek library.

[4] A network has a high modularity when the nodes can be partitioned into groups of nodes that have a higher than average intragroup connectivity and lower than average intergroup connectivity. Given a certain network, the modularity maximization algorithm searches the node partitioning that has the highest possible modularity.

Figure 3.2: The core-periphery structure

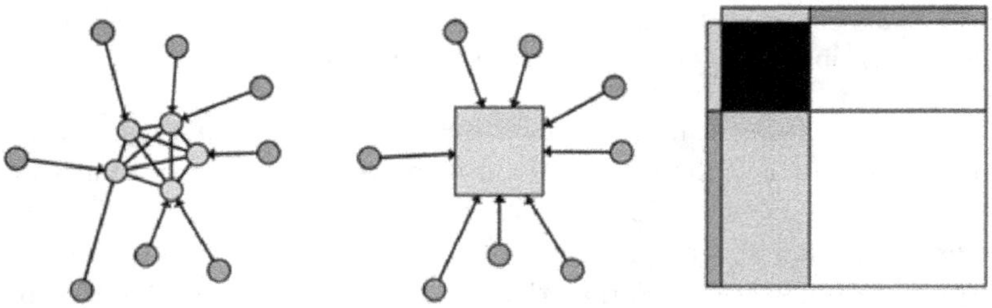

Color images of figures can be downloaded at the book's page
[URL: https://vernonpress.com/book/96]

Notes: The actual network is displayed on the left, the middle panel shows the coarse-grained view of the network where nodes with a similar position are in the same block, and the right panel is a matrix showing the average edge density between the nodes in each block (darker colour signals a higher density).

Kali and Reyes (2007) looked for this echo in the binary (i.e., unweighted) trade network of the 1990s. Using the Lorenz curves of the degree of the countries in the network, they concluded that the world indeed has a core-periphery structure.[5] Snyder and Kick (1979) used a more complex stochastic block model technique to allocate 118 countries into either the core or the periphery between 1955 and 1970. While both studies confirmed the existence of the core-periphery model, they did so using a binary (i.e., unweighted) trade network that covered a relatively limited number of countries and years.

3.2.4 Hub-and-spoke

The fourth network structure, hub-and-spoke, is a combination of the preceding two. Like regionalisation, it features regional groupings that have strong connections between themselves. However, unlike regionalisation, these groups are connected to a central hub. In this aspect, the hub-and-spoke structure resembles the core-periphery model, which also features a highly connected network core. Unlike the core-periphery model though, there is no real periphery as the countries that are not part of the hub are organized into regional groupings that have strong ties among themselves.

As the hub-and-spoke structure lies in between these two other structures, there is a significant risk that it is misidentified when using tests that look specifically for either regionalisation or a core-periphery structure.

[5] The degree of a node in a network is the number of other nodes the node is connected to.

3.3 A general descriptor: stochastic block models

In the previous section, we saw that the research that looks for specific network structures has found evidence of globalisation as well as core-periphery structures and (to a lesser extent) of regionalisation. This is partly because the tests used do not discern well enough between the different possible network structures, either because the test itself is rather crude (e.g., looking at the network density) or because it requires a less informative network (e.g., a binary network). To resolve this problem, we use a temporal stochastic block model (SBM) that uses all information available to see which pattern, if any, the worldwide trade network conforms to and how this evolves over time. An SBM is a flexible way to provide a high level description of the structure of a network (Holland et al., 1983). It uses both incoming and outgoing (weighted) edges, to identify groups of nodes that behave similarly in the graph. To that end, it summarizes the behaviour of the nodes by describing the average relation between nodes from those different partitions.

To illustrate, figure 3.3 shows an example of a general network structure that does not conform to basic structures outlined above. Typically, we start from a graph like the one shown in the left panel where there are clear differences between certain nodes, but it is hard to see an overall structure. The SBM technique separates the nodes into different groups (middle panel) and describes the average interaction of these groups (right panel). It shows us that there are three types of node positions in the network. The nodes from the blue and red blocks are strongly connected with themselves, but there are no links between both blocks. The blue block has reciprocal connections with the green block, while the red block only has edges going to the green block. The nodes from the green block, on the other hand, are only connected to the other two blocks and have no connections among themselves.

Figure 3.3: A block-model structure

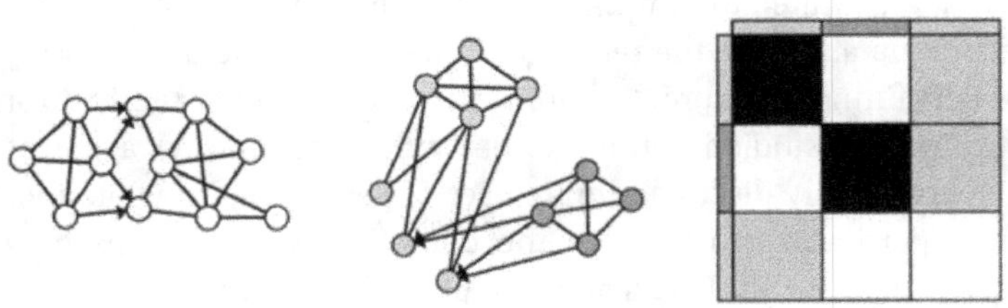

Color images of figures can be downloaded at the book's page
[URL: https://vernonpress.com/book/96]

Notes: The unstructured network is displayed on the left, the middle panel shows the partitioning of this network by the SBM technique, and the right panel is a matrix showing the average edge density between the nodes in each block (darker colour signals a higher density).

Stochastic block models are explicitly designed in order to elicit and describe any type of network structure. It can capture a core-periphery structure, as was done in Snyder and Kick (1979), but it can also distil associative patterns, such as community structures, and nonassociative patterns in the network.

Because of their flexibility, picking the right stochastic block model to describe a network is not an easy task and the number of possible partitions increases exponentially with the number of nodes. To pick the optimal partition, we use the methodology developed by Peixoto (2013, 2014).[6] The algorithm looks for the partition that best describes the network with minimum description length, or in other words that uses the least amount of information. As a result, the number of partitions is only increased when it significantly improves the description of the network. Unlike the other methods described above, Peixoto's (2015) method also takes the time-dimension into account, allowing us to link different blocks over time and ensuring that the partitioning of the dataset remains consistent and optimal through time.

The word stochastic in SBM refers to the fact that these models are estimated using a Monte Carlo Markov Chain technique. As a result, the precise partitioning of the nodes can sometimes be prone to statistical noise. Running the algorithm twice can result in a slightly different partitioning, especially when there are a lot of nodes whose behaviour is difficult to place with one group. The term stochastic also refers to the fact that SBMs are not only used to distil the structure of a given network, they can also be used in the opposite direction. That is, starting from an SBM that describes a certain network structure, one can stochastically generate new networks with the same structure.

In summary, Peixoto's methodology has three particular advantages compared to other techniques. To start, it uses all the information contained in the weighted directed network, unlike some of the more coarse-grained alternatives that are limited to unweighted or undirected networks. Moreover, the SBM technique also uses the temporal dimension of the data and is able to find the best fitting structure describing the network consistently throughout the entire period studied. Other studies either (arbitrarily) aggregate over several years or only discuss a limited set of years. Finally, while most tests look for a particular structure in the data (e.g., communities or a core-periphery structure), SBM is an agnostic procedure that does not make any a priori assumptions about the structure. The flexibility of this more generic approach allows us to better detect the transitions of the network structure as well as uncover patterns that run counter to expectations.

---

[6] An implementation of the algorithms used can be found in the python library graph-tool: https://graph-tool.skewed.de/

3.4 Constructing the historical trade integration network

In order to uncover the patterns underlying worldwide trade flows, we construct a worldwide network of trade integration using the historical trade integration (*hti*) index from Standaert et al. (2016). Trade integration, while based on the bilateral trade flows also takes into account the size of the countries. As a result, it captures the degree of bilateral dependence, i.e., the extent to which the bilateral import and export flows matter for each country. After all, the importance of a million dollars in trade will be vastly different for Estonia than it will be for the United States, both because of the size of their economy and the total size of their imports/exports. In addition, the dependence on a specific trading partner can be either because you import a lot from or export a lot to that country.

The historical trade integration index has a number of advantages over other indicators of trade integration. The most important of which is that it covers a significantly larger fraction of trade flows, especially in the period before the 1950s. Not only does the index go back to the 1880s (excluding the world wars), it also covers trade between colonies and their colonial power as well as trade flows between colonies. While this dataset is far from complete (e.g., it covers only covers the official trade flows), its increased data availability reduces the risk that for example changes in the number of countries are mistaken for actual changes in the structure of worldwide trade flows.

Unlike most other indicators of trade integration, the hti is a composite index, combining various indicators of trade integration into one overall index. This allows the index to present a more discriminating picture of trade integration. Export and import flows are considered separately, allowing us to identify those countries that strongly depend on one particular market for their imports but not their exports, or vice versa. These trade flows are also normalised in different ways, filtering out important trade flows either because they are large relative to the GDP of the country, or because they constitute a significant fraction of total trade. Because these indicators are combined using a state-space model, differences in their availability can be used in an offsetting manner. Instead of reducing the dataset to those observations where all data is available, the state-space model can compute the index even when only partial data is available. It also uses the temporal information in the dataset to further compute the most likely index value for each observation.[7] More technical information on the construction of the index can be found in the appendix. For the complete discussion of its construction and a

---

[7] The index can be downloaded at: http://www.sherppa.ugent.be/hti/hti.html. Technical details on the construction of the *hti* and a comparison with other indicators of trade integration can be found in Standaert et al. (2016).

comparison with other indicators of integration, we refer to Standaert et al. (2016).

The estimation of the *hti* index returns not just the most likely value of the level of integration for each country-pair (or dyad) in each year. Instead, it gives the entire distribution of this value. For example, if the index was computed with only partial data, or if the indicators disagreed on the level of integration, the *hti* index will have a much higher standard deviation. The fact that the entire probability distribution of the index is available can be used in the construction of the trade integration network. Typically, trade flows data is marked by an overabundance of very small, but non-zero trade flows. As a result, either an arbitrary cut-off point has to be chosen, or a much more dense network has to be constructed in which the majority of the edges has a trivial weight.[8] However, as we have the entire distribution of the *hti* index at our disposal, we can distinguish which values of the index are significantly greater than zero –the index value when there is no trade between the country-pair. By only using the significant level of integration, we can construct a much sparser network. Specifically, we construct a weighted directed network by drawing an edge from country A to country B if the $hti_{BA,t}$ is significantly greater than zero at the 5% level. The edge weights are simply the value of the *hti* index.

Figure 3.4 shows the number of nodes and edges of this network over time. The strong increase in the former is for the most part due to the "birth" of new nations over time, like the Austro-Hungarian Empire disbanding into Austria and Hungary in 1918, or the dissolution of the Soviet Union in the 1990s. The sudden increase in the number of nodes in 1950 is caused by the inclusion of a large number of colonial countries to the dataset, whose information is added a number of years before they gained independence. The increase in the number of countries also explains the simultaneous jumps in the number of edges in the network: trade that was previously internal to one country is suddenly counted as international trade between two or more countries. However, even when the number of countries is kept constant, we still see an increase in the network density during 1880-1918 and 1950-2008, meaning that the number of edges increases independently of the change in the number of nodes.

---

[8] This overabundance of meaningless edges risks significantly slowing down the computation of the more complex network characteristics and analyses.

Figure 3.4: Nodes and Edges *hti* network over time

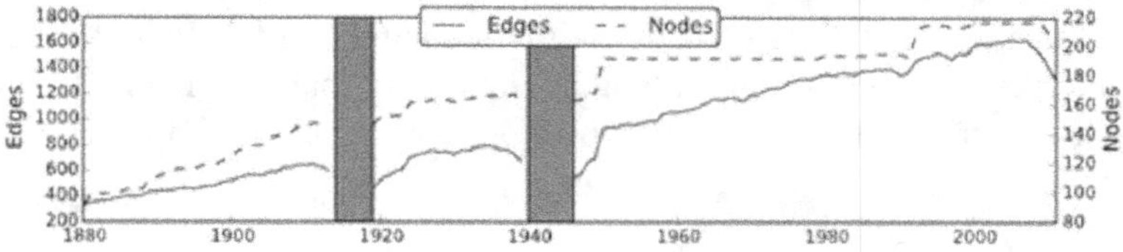

Color images of figures can be downloaded at the book's page
[URL: https://vernonpress.com/book/96]

Notes: number of edges (blue line, right axis) and nodes (dashed line, left axis) in the *hti* network from 1880 to 2015 (source: Standaert, et al., 2016, p. 246).

The network density almost doubles from 1880 to 2010 when the number of countries is kept fixed, rising from 5 to 9%. However, the increase in the number of nodes completely undoes this growth, resulting in density in 2010 that is slightly below that of 1880. That the density is low relative to other trade networks is due to the fact that edges are only drawn for countries whose level of trade integration is statistically significantly different from zero trade. For example, in 1990 close to a seventeen thousand country-couples had positive trade flows, but only 1345 had levels of integration that were significantly greater than zero at the 5% significance level (Standaert et al., 2016).

3.5 Revealing the structure of the world's trade patterns

Having constructed the *hti* network, we are now set to elicit the structure of worldwide trade from the 1880s to 1990s. While the SBM technique can be used to analyse how this structure changes from year to year, we will restrict the analysis in this chapter to a more high-level analysis. To that end, we split up the sample into three periods, separated by the world wars: i.e., the first wave of globalisation (1880-1913), the interbellum (1919-1939), and the second wave of globalisation up till the disintegration of the former USSR (1946-1989).

3.5.1 The first wave of globalisation: 1880-1913

We start our discussion with the first wave of globalisation, in particular, the years 1880-1913. Figure 3.5 shows the results of applying the temporal SBM technique to the *hti* network. The left panel shows the edge density fingerprint, with the grey scale showing the average extent to which the countries in each stochastic block (the rows) is integrated into every other block (the columns). This graph only contains those countries that existed and were significantly integrated with another country at any time during the first globalisation wave. This gives us a total of 146 countries that the SBM algorithm separated into three main blocks. As was explained earlier, this number of blocks is determined by the SBM estimator, which only adds a block when the benefit of the additional descriptive power of the model is greater than the cost of the increase in the description length. The second panel of figure 3.5 shows which countries belong to each of the blocks using coloured dots on a world map.[9]

Figure 3.5: First globalisation wave

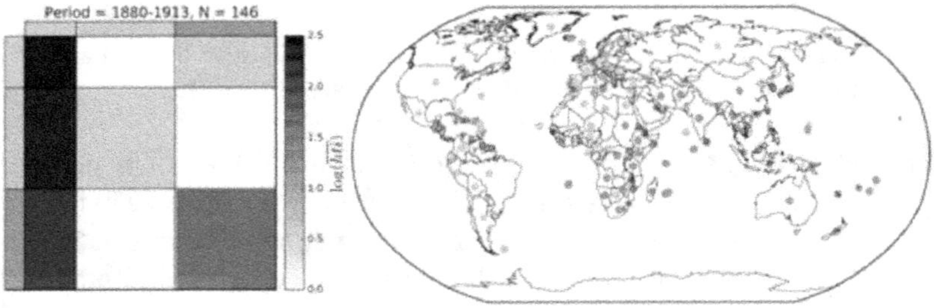

Color images of figures can be downloaded at the book's page
[URL: https://vernonpress.com/book/96]

Notes: The left panel shows a matrix with the (log of the) average index values of links between the nodes in one block with the nodes of any other block and the right panel a world map where countries are coloured according to their block assignment.

What becomes immediately clear is that the graph is far from symmetric. The first column of the degree fingerprint shows that almost all countries are strongly integrated into the blue block (including the blue block itself). The other links are far less strong and the blocks green and red are poorly integrated with themselves. Looking at the countries that make up the different blocks in the second panel, we see that the blue block is centred around Western Europe and North America although it also includes, for example Brazil. The green block roughly consists of former Spanish and French colonies in South-America and the Western part of the African continent, while the red block covers Asia, Oceania and the Eastern part of Africa, lining up more closely with the British colonies at that time.[10] Table 3.1 shows the top

[9] Because borders were subject to change during the years under consideration, we do not use a choropleth map but use a dot to represent a country. The borders are only there for indicative purposes.

[10] The block assignment of some small countries might sometimes seem debatable. Mostly there really is a connection with the block, e.g. France and its overseas territories, but sometimes this is a result of the stochastic nature of the SBM technique. For example we see that for the interbellum Cameroon is assigned to the Scandinavian

five countries according to the indegree or how much the other countries are integrated into them.[11] It shows Great Britain as the top country in the first block –the block which itself has the highest indegree– making it the pivot country during the first globalisation wave.

In terms of the particular network structure, it is clear that the trade pattern formed during the first globalisation wave fits a core-periphery model, where the core consists of the first block (blue) and the periphery is formed by the French, Spanish and English colonies (the green and red block). All three groups of countries are highly integrated into the core, and the periphery's internal links are much weaker than its link to the core. This is particularly strong in the case of the French/Spanish colonies, where the link to the core countries is many times stronger than the links to their own peripheral block. However, there is a difference between the two peripheral blocks in that the former British colonies (red) have much stronger intra-block links than the French/Spanish colonies (green). Moreover, unlike the latter, nodes from the red block also have incoming links from the core countries. Returning to the terminology of Wallerstein's world-system analysis, we see that the green block corresponds to the periphery and the red block to the semi-periphery. Of course, we realize that these findings are not new to the field of economic history. The power of the SBM technique is that it reaches these conclusions using only the raw trade data, without preconceptions on the world functioned during this period.

Table 3.1: Top 5 highest indegree: 1880-1913

Blue	Green	Red
Great Britain	Chile	India
USA	Peru	China
France	Bolivia	Japan
Germany	Ecuador	Australia
Belgium	Columbia	Mauritius

Notes: The top 5 countries per block for the period 1880-1913 according to their indegree.

block. Overall, the bulk of the blocks stays constant when we repeat the partitioning. But sometimes a smaller countries gets reassigned to another block. This reassignment can happen because a country might show behavior which equally likely places it in two different blocks.

[11] While indegree is a relatively simplistic measure, the ordering of the top-5 countries remains the same when more complicated measures like the Katz-centrality are used.

3.5.2 The interbellum: 1919-1939

The second time period we study is that of the inter-war period. The interbellum is particularly interesting not only because it is a period of de-globalisation, but also to study the effects of the First World War on the worldwide trade network. To that end, figure 3.6 shows the SBM decomposition of the trade network during the interbellum. The number of countries (148) is more or less the same as that during the first globalisation wave, with a few minor changes like the end of the Austria-Hungarian Empire.

Comparing the pre-WWI to the post-WWI graphs, we see first of all that the number of blocks has increased from three to five. The former group of core countries has split up into three new blocks. This has resulted in a new group of core countries (blue) that now also includes the newly independent South-American countries, a second block (orange) consisting mostly of Scandinavian countries and a third group (yellow) of countries from Central and South-Eastern Europe. The fourth group (green) now consists of Canada, Mexico and the Caribbean countries, while the final block (red) remains dominated by the (former) British colonies (table 3.2), mainly consisting of countries in South and East Africa and Asia.

Figure 3.6: Interbellum

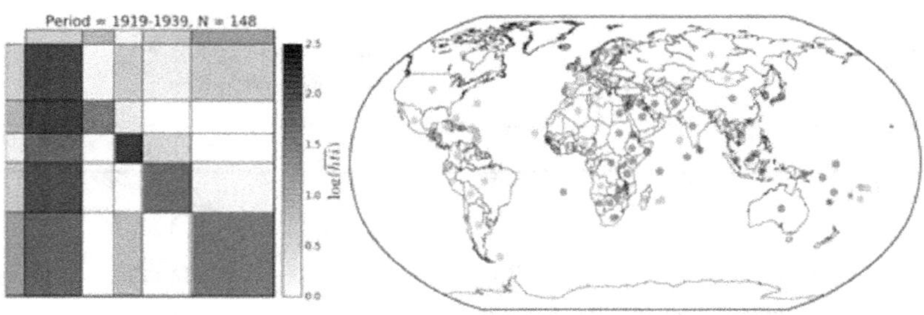

Color images of figures can be downloaded at the book's page
[URL: https://vernonpress.com/book/96]

Notes: The left panel shows a matrix with the (log of the) average index values of links between the nodes in one block with the nodes of any other block and the right panel a world map where countries are coloured according to their block assignment.

While the pre-WWI trade pattern was an almost perfect example of the core-periphery system, we see that this system has started to shift during the interbellum. While the core group of countries (blue) still remains the most linked-to block and keeps its pivotal role in the world trade system, most blocks have started forming much stronger intra-block links. The Eastern-European block (yellow), for example, is more strongly connected to itself than to any other block. In addition, the core countries are also forming stronger ties to countries outside of their block. Similarly, the other blocks have started to form links to blocks outside of the core, although these ties remain weak. At the same time, we notice that distance is becoming a stronger component in the determination of the blocks as the colours now follow a tighter geographical pattern. For example, with the exception of the US, all countries in North and Central America now belong to the same (green) block. Given that the bilateral distance is not explicitly incorporated in the SBM algorithm, it follows that countries increasingly trade with their neighbours over this time period.

Table 3.2: Top 5 highest indegree: 1919-1939

Blue	Orange	Yellow	Green	Red
Great Britain	Sweden	Italy	Canada	Japan
USA	Denmark	Romania	Br. Virgin Is.	India
Germany	Finland	Czechoslovakia	Guyana	Australia
France	Santa Lucia	Austria	Venezuela	China
Belgium	Norway	Greece	Jamaica	Indonesia

Notes: The top 5 countries per block for the period 1919-1939 according to how strongly other countries are integrated into them.

3.5.3 The second wave of globalisation: 1946-1989

Finally, we discuss the second globalisation wave from the late 1940s to the fall of the Berlin wall in 1989. In comparison to the previous two periods, the number of countries increases by almost a third to a total of 193. This is mostly the result of the independence of many North and West-African countries. However, even after their independence most have remained strongly linked to their former colonial power, which is why the majority of these "new" countries are grouped with the former core.

The number of blocks needed to describe the network has further increased to six. The biggest change is the split up of the block that was dominated by British colonies (the red block in figures 3.5 and 3.6). In general, the blocks now follow mostly regional lines (e.g., the Scandinavian block (orange) or the Southern Africa block (purple)), although there are exceptions. For example, as we would expect during the cold-war period, the USSR and the USSR-dominated countries have formed a block separated from the core-group (yellow). Added to this group is a large contingent of South-American countries that were grouped together with the USSR countries because of their similar links to a number of Eastern-European countries rather than their link to the USSR. Finally, table 3.3 also shows the United States taking over the leading role in the trade network.

Figure 3.7: Second globalisation wave

Color images of figures can be downloaded at the book's page
[URL: https://vernonpress.com/book/96]

Notes: The left panel shows a matrix with the (log of the) average index values of links between the nodes in one block with the nodes of any other block and the right panel a world map where countries are coloured according to their block assignment.

In line with the changes made during the Interbellum, the post-WWII period shows a further dismantlement of the core-periphery structure. While the first block still remains the most important block and is still linked to the other blocks, they now also link more strongly to themselves. In other words, both the grouping of countries and the trade links between the groups now suggest a stronger regionalized trade pattern. That being said, Western Europe and North America remain important central players on the world stage, forming links to all other blocks. For example, in spite of their short distance to each other, the two African blocks are linked much more strongly to the core group than to each other. On the whole, we see that with a couple of exceptions, the area of the matrix that is white keeps shrinking over time, meaning that most blocks do form trade ties with the other blocks. While this could be interpreted as a sign of an increasingly globalised world, the main trading partners remain either countries from the same block or those from the first block in Western Europe or North America. In other words, rather than the core-periphery pattern of the previous periods, the second trade globalisation wave follows a hub-and-spoke pattern where strong regional groupings feed into a central hub. The fact that this pattern contains elements from globalisation, core-periphery, and communities explains why earlier papers found evidence of all three structures.

Table 3.3: Top 5 highest indegree: 1946-1989

Blue	Green	Orange	Yellow	Red	Purple
USA	Canada	Sweden	Russia	Japan	Portugal
Great Britain	Venezuela	Denmark	Romania	Australia	South Africa
Germany	Antilles	Norway	Czech Rep.	India	Zimbabwe
France	Trinidad	Finland	Austria	Saudi Arabia	Kenya
Italy	Guyana	Iceland	Argentina	China	Angola

Notes: The top 5 countries per block for the period 1946-1989 according to how strongly other countries are integrated into them.

3.6 Conclusion

This chapter studied the structure of the worldwide trade network from the 1880s to the late 1980s, looking specifically for a pattern corresponding to globalisation, regionalisation or a core-periphery. To that end, we constructed a weighted, directed network that captures the extent to which countries are integrated into each other. We did this using the historical trade integration index that measures the relative importance of trade flows for countries around the world from as early as the 1880s.

The total time-period was split up into three sections: the first globalisation wave (1880-1913), the Interbellum, a period of de-globalisation (1919-1939) and the second globalisation wave until the fall of the Berlin wall (1946-1989). The structure of the network during these periods was analysed using the temporal stochastic block model methodology of Peixoto (2013, 2014, 2015). This method uses all the information in the network (weighted, directed and temporal) to elicit the structure in an agnostic way allowing us to see which particular network structure, if any, underlies in the data.

During the first globalisation wave, we find a very strong core-periphery structure, where the core is made up of countries like the USA and Great Britain, the semi-periphery by India and China, and the periphery by Chile and Peru. However, this structure is slowly dismantled over the next two periods. First of all, an increasing number of countries started forming their own blocks where the strength of the intra-block links often surpasses that of the link to the original core group. The core itself is no longer the same homogenous group it was during the first interbellum, as many former colonies are grouped together with their colonial power. In other words, we see signs of increasing regionalisation, but unlike the strict community structure, the link with the core group remains strong. While most blocks also start forming links with blocks other than the core (a sign of globalisation) these links remain relatively weak. Overall, we find that the start of the second globalisation wave is not marked by globalisation, regionalisation or core-periphery, but rather a hub-and-spoke pattern where strong regional clusters are linked to a central hub.

While the current analyses are high-level studies that summarize the overall network structure over 20 to 43 years, the SBM technique can also be used to draw the network structure in each year and link the different blocks through time. This would allow a much more intricate look at how the network structure has evolved from core-periphery to this hub-and-spoke pattern. For example, it can be used to see whether this change is gradual and happens throughout the period studied, or whether the destabilizing effect of the World Wars is the main contributor to these high-level structural changes. A more detailed look would also allow us to flag countries that do not conform to expectations, which could lead to new insights into the behaviour of countries on this long-time span. We hope to address these and other questions in future research.

3.7 Appendix: The construction of the historical trade index

This appendix aims to provide some technical insight into the construction of the *hti*. For more information, see Standaert et al. (2016).

As we noted in section 4, the *hti* is a composite index, combining four indicators that track bilateral imports and exports relative to total flows as well as the economic size of the sender country. If $X_{ij,t}$ represent the imports of country i from country j in year t and $GDP_{i,t}$ is the gross domestic product of country i in year t, these four indicators can be written as:

$$y_{ij,t} \equiv \left[\frac{X_{ij,t}}{\sum_k X_{ik,t}}, \frac{X_{ji,t}}{\sum_k X_{ki,t}}, \frac{X_{ij,t}}{GDP_{i,t}}, \frac{X_{ji,t}}{GDP_{i,t}}\right]'.$$

If all four indicators were available in each year, they could be easily combined using standard aggregation techniques like the geometric of arrhythmic average. The problem is that bilateral trade is notoriously prone to gaps: often imports are available while exports are not, or vice versa. Equally hard to come by is GDP data that covers all countries continuously from 1880 to the late twentieth century. While gaps abound in the data, particularly in the early 1900s, the number of years where no data is available at all remains relatively limited. In order to combine this data in a way that accounts for the gaps, without having to impute them ex ante, employ a state-space model.

A state-space model is set of equations that describe the behaviour over time of an unknown variable (the state-variable), as well as its relation with a set of observed variables, called the measurement variables. In our example, the measurement variables are the four indicators in $\boldsymbol{y}_{ij,t}$ while the state variable is the unknown level of trade integration $hti_{ij,t}$. The key to state-space model is that there exist simple, iterative algorithms –called the Kalman filter and smoother– that can determine the most likely value of the state-space model (see Kim and Nelson, 1999).

The state-space model used to estimate $hti_{ij,t}$ consists of two linear equations. The first equation (the measurement equation) describes how the four indicators are related $hti_{ij,t}$. As the scaling of the four variables is not uniform, each has unique scaling parameters that are summarized in (4×1) intercept and slope vectors $\boldsymbol{c}$ and $\boldsymbol{z}$. Furthermore, in order to allow for measurement and other errors, we also included a normally distributed error term $\epsilon_{ij,t}$, whose variance is the (4×4) diagonal matrix Σ_ϵ. This results in the following linear *measurement* equation (with variables in bold font indicating matrices or vectors):

$$\boldsymbol{y}_{ij,t} = \boldsymbol{c} + \boldsymbol{z}\, hti_{ij,t} + \epsilon_{ij,t}$$

$$\epsilon_{ij,t} \sim N(0, \Sigma_\epsilon)$$

To complete the state space model, we assume that the unknown level of trade integration follows an autoregressive process with one lag. The extent to which $hti_{ij,t}$ depends on its previous values, T, is determined inside the model, but a distinction is made between the period before World War I, the Interbellum and the period following World War II. The change in the level of integration that does not follow this pattern is captured by $\mu_{ij,t}$, which is also assumed to follow a normal distribution.

$$hti_{ij,t} = T\, hti_{ij,t-1} + \mu_{ij,t}$$

$$\mu_{ij,t} \sim N(0, \sigma_\mu)$$

There are many ways in which this model can be estimated. In this case, we used the Kalman filter and smoother in a Bayesian Gibbs sampling algorithm to compute the model's parameters ($\boldsymbol{c}, \boldsymbol{z}, T, \Sigma_\epsilon$ and σ_μ) and determine the most likely value of $hti_{ij,t}$.

3.8 References

Barigozzi, M., Fagiolo, G. and Mangioni, G. (2011) Identifying the community structure of the international-trade multi-network, *Physica A: statistical mechanics and its applications*, 390(11):2051–2066.

Borgatti, S. P. and Everett, M. G (2000) Models of core/periphery structures, *Social networks*, 21 (4):375–395.

Buys, P., Deichmann, U. and Wheeler, D. (2010) Road network upgrading and overland trade expansion in Sub-Saharan Africa, *Journal of African Economies*, page ejq006.

Caimcross, F. (1997) *The death of distance*, Harvard Business School Press, Cambridge.

Crafts, N. (2004) Globalisation and economic growth: a historical perspective, *The World Economy*, 27(1):45–58.

Das, D. K. (2004) *The Economic Dimensions of Globalisation*, Springer.

De Benedictis, L. and Tajoli, L. (2011) The world trade network, *The World Economy*, 34(8): 1417–1454.

Erikson, E. and Bearman, P. (2006) Malfeasance and the foundations for global trade: The structure of English trade in the east indies, 1601–18331, *American Journal of Sociology*, 112(1): 195–230.

Estevadeordal, A., Frantz, B. and Taylor, A. M. (2002) *The rise and fall of world trade, 1870-1939*, Technical report, National Bureau of Economic Research.

Fagiolo, G., Reyes, J. and Schiavo, S. (2008) On the topological properties of the world trade web: A weighted network analysis, *Physica A: Statistical Mechanics and its Applications*, 387 (15):3868–3873.

Fagiolo, G., Reyes, J. and Schiavo, S. (2009). World-trade web: Topological properties, dynamics, and evolution, *Physical Review E*, 79(3):036115.

Findlay, R. and O'Rourke, K. H. (2007) *Power and plenty: trade, war, and the world economy in the second millennium, volume 51*, Cambridge University Press.

Fortunato, S. (2010) Community detection in graphs, *Physics reports*, 486(3):75–174.

Garlaschelli, D. and Loffredo, M. I. (2004) Fitness-dependent topological properties of the world trade web, *Physical review letters*, 93(18):188701.

Garlaschelli, D. and Loffredo, M. I. (2005) Structure and evolution of the world trade network, *Physica A: Statistical Mechanics and its Applications*, 355(1):138–144.

Holland, P. W., Laskey, K. B. and Leinhardt S. (1983) Stochastic blockmodels: First steps, *Social networks*, 5(2):109–137.

Jacks, S., Meissner, C. M. and Novy, D. (2010) Trade costs in the first wave of globalisation, *Explorations in Economic History*, 47(2):127–141.

Jameson, F. (1984) Postmodernism, or the cultural logic of late capitalism, *New Left Review I*, 146.

Kali, R. and Reyes, J. (2007) The architecture of globalisation: a network approach to international economic integration, *Journal of International Business Studies*, pages 595–620.

Kim, S. and Shin, E.-H. (2002) A longitudinal analysis of globalisation and regionalization in international trade: A social network approach, *Social Forces*, 81(2):445–468, 2002.

Kim, C.-J. and Nelson, C. R. (1999) *State-Space Models with Regime Switching*, MIT Press, Cambridge.

Krings, G. M., Carpantier, J.-F. and Delvenne, J.-C. (2014). Trade integration and trade imbalances in the European Union: a network perspective, *PloS one*, 9(1): e83448.

Li, X., Jin, Y. Y. and Chen, G. (2003) Complexity and synchronization of the world trade web, *Physica A: Statistical Mechanics and its Applications*, 328(1):287–296.

O'Rourke, K. H. and Williamson, J. G. (2004) Once more: When did globalisation begin? *European Review of Economic History*, 8(01):109–117.

Panagariya, A. (1999) The regionalism debate: an overview, *The World Economy*, 22(4):455–476.

Peixoto, T. P. (2013) Parsimonious module inference in large networks, *Physical review letters*, 110 (14):148701.

Peixoto, T. P. (2014) Hierarchical block structures and high-resolution model selection in large networks, *Physical Review X*, 4(1):011047.

Peixoto, T. P. (2015) Inferring the mesoscale structure of layered, edge-valued, and time-varying networks, *Physical Review E*, 92(4):042807.

Reyes, J., Wooster, R. and Shirrell S. (2014) Regional trade agreements and the pattern of trade: A networks approach, *The World Economy*, 37(8):1128–1151.

Saxe, E. L. (1979) *Fortune's tangled web: trading networks of English entrepreneurs in Eastern India*, 1657-1717. PhD thesis.

Scheidel, W. (2015) Orbis: the Stanford geospatial network model of the roman world.

Serrano, M. A. and Boguñá, M. (2003) Topology of the world trade web, *Physical Review E*, 68(1): 015101.

Smith, D. A. and White, D. R. (1992) Structure and dynamics of the global economy: network analysis of international trade 1965–1980, *Social forces*, 70(4):857–893.

Snyder, D. and Kick, E. L. (1979) Structural position in the world system and economic growth, 1955-1970: A multiple-network analysis of transnational interactions, *American journal of Sociology*, pages 1096–1126.

Standaert, S., Ronsse, S. and Vandermarliere, B. (2016) Historical trade integration: globalisation and the distance puzzle in the long twentieth century, *Cliometrica*, pages 1–26.

Tzekina, I., Danthi, K. and Rockmore, D. N. (2008) Evolution of community structure in the world trade web, *The European Physical Journal B*, 63(4):541–545.

Van Doosselaere, Q. (2009). *Commercial agreements and social dynamics in medieval Genoa*, Cam- bridge University Press.

Wallerstein, I. M. (2004) *World-systems analysis: An introduction*, Duke University Press.

4.

A new approach to international trade from Network Geometry. The World Trade Atlas 1870-2013

Guillermo García-Pérez, Marián Boguñá, Antoine Allard, and M. Ángeles Serrano

Data: International trade data from the Correlates of War Project (COW) (COW, 2012).
Software: Python, (SciPy and NumPy for analysis and Matplotlib for visualisation), Mathematica (visualisation), Fortran 77 (analysis) and C++1y.

4.1 Aims and scope

International trade annually moves trillions of dollars and represents one of the main evolving networks of interactions between countries in the world. Beyond the exchange of goods and services, it interplays with other economic, political and social systems and sustains the propagation of different processes, both beneficial and harming, such as innovations or crises. All these interactions shape the complex architecture of the World Trade Web (WTW), which presents typical features of complex networks in very different domains, such as the small-world property, heterogeneous distributions of the number of trade partners, high levels of triadic closure relationships, community structure and nontrivial global distribution of flows (Serrano and Boguñá, 2003; Garlaschelli and Loffredo, 2004; Serrano et al., 2007a; Serrano, 2007; Serrano et al., 2010).

However, many studies still focus on bilateral relationships to understand the International Trade System. Bilateral flows have traditionally been modelled using the gravity model of trade which, in analogy to Newton's law of gravitation, accurately predicts that the volume of trade exchanged between two countries increases with their economic sizes and decreases with their geographical separation (Tinbergen, 1962; Bergstrand, 1985; Squartini and Garlaschelli, 2014). The precision of the gravity model improves when it is supplemented with other factors, such as colony-coloniser relationships, a shared common language, or the effects of political borders and a common currency (Frankel and Rose, 2002; Anderson and van Wincoop, 2004; Bergstrand and Egger, 2011). Despite the success of the gravity model at replicating trade volumes, it performs very poorly at predicting the existence of trade channels between pairs of countries (Dueñas and Fagiolo, 2013a); an obvious limitation that prevents it from explaining the striking regularities observed in the complex architecture of the WTW. One of the reasons for this flaw is that the gravity model focuses on detached bilateral relationships and so overlooks multilateral trade resistance and other network effects. Another drawback is that geography is not the only factor that defines distance in international trade. Distance matters but along many other dimensions.

This chapter reviews in detail our network gravity model (García-Pérez et al., 2016b), a new approach to predict both the existence and the volume of significant trade interactions between pairs of countries in the world based on methodologies and reverse engineering techniques from Network Science (Newman, 2010; Cohen and Havlin, 2010). The network gravity model relies on economic sizes and on effective distances that incorporate the different dimensions affecting international trade—including but not limited to geography—implicitly encoded on the complex patterns of trade interactions. We describe a pure geometric counterpart using hyperbolic space, which has been conjectured to be the natural geometry underlying complex networks (Boguñá et al., 2009; Krioukov et al., 2010; Papadopoulos et al., 2012; Borassi et al., 2015). In the hyperbolic trade space, economic sizes and geographical distances are combined into a sole distance metric as a proxy of aggregate trade barriers, such that the closer countries are in hyperbolic trade space, the greater their chance of being connected. We estimate trade distances from empirical data to represent the WTW through World Trade Maps. The maps are annual and cover a time span of fourteen decades. The collection as a whole is referred to as the World Trade Atlas 1870-2013. We also extended the network gravity model to deal with trade flows such that the same underlying metric space can explain simultaneously the existence and the volume of trade interactions (Allard et al., 2017).

Beyond the obvious advantages of visualisation, the World Trade Atlas increases significantly our understanding of the long-run evolution of the international trade system and helps us to address a number of important and challenging questions. In particular, which is the role of distance in trade, not merely in geographical terms, and how far or close have countries been through recent history? Which role plays each country in the maps and how has this role evolved in time? Are Preferential Trade Agreements (PTAs) consistent with natural communities as measured by trade distance? Has the formation of PTAs led to lower or higher barriers to trade inside blocs? Are historical, economic, and geographical divisions becoming increasingly irrelevant? The answers lead to a clear picture in which the evolution of the international trade system has been shaped by three simultaneous forces: globalisation, hierarchisation, and localisation. We find that the international trade system is becoming more heterogeneous and hierarchical than ever before and, at the same time, more interconnected and clustered into natural trade communities not fully consistent with Preferential Trade Agreements.

4.2 The world trade web as a complex network

Trade, transport, and communication have evolved boosted by waves of globalisation, as periods when a complex series of closely intertwined changes have dramatically increased the interactions and interdependencies between a growing number of people and human organisations in disparate geographic regions. As a result, the world economies exhibit nowadays a high level of global interdependency. Therefore, the analysis of international trade requires a global perspective, taking into account every country and its trade relationships regardless of its population or wealth, which can be based on the representation of the international trade system as a complex network of interactions. Complex networks are formed by a large number of elements linked by nonlinear interactions that self-organise and give place to emerging phenomena. Network Science (Newman, 2010; Barrat et al., 2008; Dorogovtsev et al., 2008) offers a paradigmatic methodological framework for their study, providing tools and techniques that have been successfully applied to a wealth of systems, both natural and manmade, with examples as far apart as the Internet and metabolic networks in the cell. Beyond rich and informative visual representations, the complex network approach is producing a breakthrough in our understanding of the large-scale structure, behaviour and evolution of the international trade system (Serrano and Boguñá, 2003; Garlaschelli and Loffredo, 2004; Serrano et al., 2007b; Serrano, 2007; Serrano et al., 2010; Almog et al., 2015; García-Pérez et al., 2016b).

The World Trade Web (WTW) is the representation of the international trade system as a complex network (Serrano and Boguñá, 2003) in which countries are represented as nodes and commercial relations between them as links. This level of description goes beyond the country-specific and bilateral analyses often used in traditional economic studies of trade. Yearly snapshots of the WTW, reconstructed from empirical data, feature robust non-trivial signatures typical of complex networks across domains, which help in explaining emergent properties and systemic effects like, for instance, unexpected economic influences of one country on another even if their trade exchange is absent or not significant (Serrano et al., 2007b). Next, we revise the most basic topological properties of the WTW as a complex network and discuss how the complex network perspective can be reconciled with the role of distance in international trade.

4.2.1 Structural features of undirected representations

The vast majority of complex networks share common features. Their architecture is not that of a regular lattice neither is it completely random but lies in between. They display the small-world property, which states that the average shortest path length or average topological distance between any pair of vertices, counted as the number of intermediate neighbours, grows at most logarithmically with the system size (in finite systems, the length of the diameter or the average shortest path length between nodes is used as a proxy). The distribution of the number of nearest neighbours of nodes, or degree k, takes the form $P(k)\sim k^{-\gamma}$, with $\gamma \in [2,3]$, which implies an extremely high level of degree heterogeneity where most nodes have a low number of connections while just a few interact with nearly all the system. These distributions are said to be scale-free, meaning that the magnitude of the fluctuations renders the average value uninformative. Degree correlations are also important. Typically, a high clustering coefficient, measuring the probability that the neighbours of a given node are interconnected, is observed. In addition, many economic, technological and biological networks show degree-degree correlations, that account for the probability that a node of a certain degree is connected to a node of a different degree, with a dissassortative pattern meaning that highly connected nodes preferentially attach to poorly connected ones, in contrast to many social systems in which these two-point correlations denote homophily. Apart from this, other properties, such as modular and hierarchical organisation, characterise also the topological structure of complex networks.

The reconstruction of the WTW from empirical data displays all those non-trivial features (Serrano and Boguñá, 2003). The WTW is customarily constructed from public databases reporting import and export exchanges of merchandises between pairs of countries in the world. Exports render an inflow of money into a country and an outflow of goods, while imports generate an outflow of money and an inflow of goods. By selecting and combining import and export information between every pair of countries, different kind of complex network representations with different levels of detail and information content can be constructed, being the most basic one that in which a link between a pair of countries stands for the existence of a trade channel, independently of its directionality or intensity. More sophisticated accounts can be constructed if the directionality of the bilateral flows or the amounts exchanged are considered (Serrano et al., 2007b; Serrano, 2007; Serrano et al., 2010)

However, signatures of the complex organisation of the WTW are obscured by the dramatical increase in the density of connections, in the total amount traded in the world, and in the relative average geographic length of trade channels in the last decades, which has augmented the entanglement of the network despite the growth in the number of countries N in the international trade arena, see figure 4.1. The progressive crumbling of the Imperial Colonies during the sixties and seventies and the former Soviet Union contributed to this fact. The average number of trade partners per country $\langle k \rangle$ increases at a faster rate than that of the number of countries N, Figure 4.1A. As a consequence, the density of connections $\langle k \rangle$ / $(N - 1)$ has boosted from 0.2 to 0.7 in the period under study. The temporal evolution of the total international trade—measured as a percentage of the sum of all national gross domestic products (GDPs)—presents a similar trend, with a major reversal in the inter-war periods, Figure 4.1B. At the same time, the average geographic length of trade channels has been growing as compared to the average distance among all pairs of countries in the system, Figure 4.1C, proving that trade channels have been progressively established with more geographically distant partners.

Figure 4.1: Time evolution of scalar variables in the World Trade Web

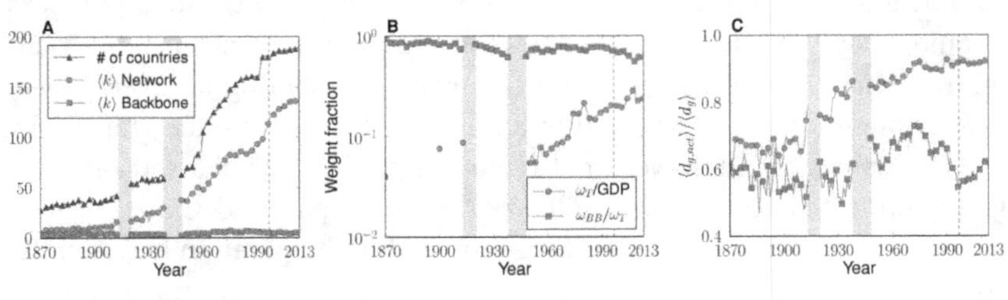

Color images of figures can be downloaded at the book's page
[URL: https://vernonpress.com/book/96]

A: Number of countries, and average number of trade partners per country, $\langle k \rangle$ in the WTW and the corresponding backbone. B: Ratio between total trade ω_T and world's GDP. The sparsity of points before the WWII is due to lack of GDP data. The plot also shows the fraction of total weight that is retained in the backbone (70% ~ 80%). C: Ratio between the average geographic distance of trade channels $\langle d_{g,net} \rangle$ and the average distance among pairs of countries in the world $\langle d_g \rangle$ in the WTW and the corresponding backbone.

In parallel, world trade networks display, especially after World War I (WWI), strong global and local heterogeneity which can be exploited to filter out a sparse subnetwork representing the relevant structure that remains after eliminating the contingent interactions which overshadow the information contained in the system (Serrano et al., 2009). These backbones, see details in next section, retain most of the countries but the number of trade channels is drastically reduced to the statistically significant ones. At the same time, pivotal features denoting the complexity of the international trade system are clearly exposed. The topology of WTW backbones is small-world, so that each pair of countries is very close to each other in topological distance, with an average value very similar to the one expected for a random network of the same size and average degree; it shows a quite neat scale-free distribution of the number of trading partners of countries; it presents disassortative degree-degree correlations, meaning that highly interconnected economies tend to connect to poorly connected ones; and it displays a high level of clustering—much greater than the value corresponding to a random network of the same size—that decreases as a function of degree indicating that countries trading with a well-connected one are poorly interconnected among them. This result, together with the scaling law for two-point correlations, reveals a hierarchical architecture of highly interconnected countries that belong to influential areas that, in turn, connect to other influential areas through hubs. The hierarchical structure of a complex network can also be detected through another important degree correlation measure, the rich club coefficient, which measures the tendency of progressively higher connected nodes to club forming elites (Colizza et al., 2006) or to polarize in competing blocks (Serrano, 2008). The WTW shows a very clear and sharp rich-multipolarisation phenomenon with hub countries sharing on average less trade among them than expected in an unbiased situation—they form fully connected subsets in the weighted representation—and polarised into two tightly connected blocks: the United States and Japan and China, against France, Germany, and the United Kingdom, with the separation between the two blocks exposed by a reduced exchange of merchandise as compared to an unbiased situation (Serrano, 2008). All these properties make the world trade web a complex network, which is far from being well described through a classical portrait based on detached bilateral relationships. We show measurements of some of these features for the WTW in the year 2013 in Figure 4.2.

As a consequence, backbones give a very convenient representation of the most significant trade channels and allow, as we explain in the next sections, to mine and map the international trade system.

Figure 4.2: Backbone of the World Trade Web in 2013

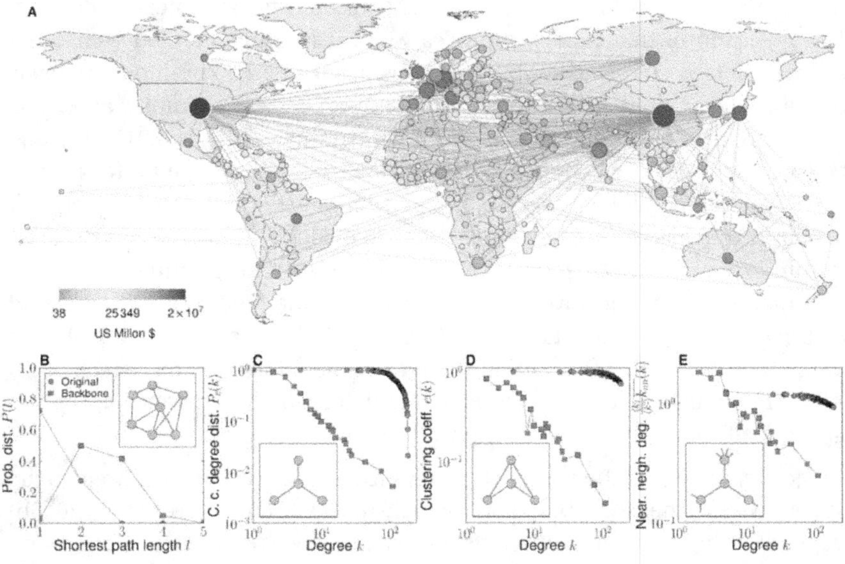

Color images of figures can be downloaded at the book's page
[URL: https://vernonpress.com/book/96]

A: Nodes represent countries and their sizes are proportional to the logarithm of the number of trade partners in the backbone. Nodes are coloured according to the logarithm of GDP values. Topological properties: B: Distribution of shortest path lengths. C: Complementary cumulative degree distribution. D: Average degree-dependent clustering coefficient. E: Normalised average degree of nearest neighbours. Insets: Sketches illustrating the corresponding metrics.

4.2.2 The role of distance

Complex networks are usually represented as topological objects, where nodes are detached from geometrical positions and so links do not have any discriminating length or travel time magnitude. The only source of metric distances in network topologies is the collection of shortest paths, which is not well behaved in the sense that its distribution for pairs of nodes is very homogeneous due to the small-world property, and so different parts of the system cannot be distinguished on the basis of this metric.

However, the evidence suggests that we are far from a distance-free world. In international trade, distance still matters (Engel and Rogers, 1996) and in many dimensions: cultural, administrative or political, economic, and geographic. This is widely supported by different proofs concerning the magnitude of bilateral trade flows. The gravity model of trade (Tinbergen, 1962; Bergstrand, 1985), in analogy to Newton's law of gravitation, accurately predicts that the volume of trade exchanged between two countries increases with their economic sizes and decreases with their geographical separation. The precision of that model improves when it is supplemented with other factors, such as colony–colonizer relationships, a shared common language, or the effects of political borders and a common currency (Frankel and Rose, 2002; Anderson and van Wincoop, 2004; Bergstrand and Egger, 2011). Despite the success of the gravity model at replicating trade volumes, it performs very poorly at predicting the existence of a trade connection between a given pair of countries (Dueñas and Fagiolo, 2013a); an obvious limitation that prevents it from explaining the striking regularities observed in the complex architecture of the world trade web (Serrano and Boguñá, 2003; Garlaschelli and Loffredo, 2004; Serrano et al., 2007a; Serrano, 2007; Serrano et al., 2010). One of the reasons for this flaw is that the gravity model focuses on detached bilateral relationships and so overlooks multilateral trade resistance and other network effects (Schweitzer et al., 2009).

A gravity model for the existence of significant trade channels between pairs of countries in the world based on trade distances (García-Pérez et al., 2016b) is possible in the context of Network Science (Newman, 2010; Cohen and Havlin, 2010). It is based on economic sizes and on an effective distance which incorporates different dimensions affecting international trade, not only geography, implicitly encoded in the complex patterns of trade interactions. These variables are combined into a connectivity law proposed for complex networks with underlying metric spaces (Serrano et al., 2008, 2011) and it can be represented in a pure geometric approach using a hyperbolic space, which has been conjectured as the natural geometry underlying complex networks (Boguñá et al., 2009; Krioukov et al., 2010; Papadopoulos et al., 2012; Borassi et al., 2015). The key topological feature suggesting a geometric origin of complex networks is clustering—the tendency of the neighbours of a node to connect among them—which arises in the topology as a consequence of the triangle inequality in the underlying geometry; namely, if nodes B and C are both near node A in a hidden metric space, then B and C must also be close, since they cannot be further away from one another than the sum of their distances to A. This transitivity of closeness induces a high level of clustering on networks generated on metric spaces, as common neighbours of nodes tend to connect, thus forming triangles. This also works at the level of the intensities of the interactions: if the weights of connections depend on the distance between the connected nodes in the underlying metric space, we expect them to be quantitatively different depending on the clustering properties of the connections so that the same underlying metric space rules the WTW topology and also its weighted organization.

In the hyperbolic trade space, distance combines economic size and effective distance into a sole trade distance metric, such that the closer countries are in hyperbolic trade space, the greater their chance of becoming connected and the greater their expected trade volume. The trade distance can be estimated from empirical data using adapted statistical inference techniques (Boguñá et al., 2010; Serrano et al., 2012) which allow us to represent international trade through World Trade Maps (WTMs). These define a coordinate system in which countries are located in relative positions according to the aggregate trade barriers between them. The collection of annual maps, which cover a time span of fourteen decades, is referred to as a whole as the World Trade Atlas 1870-2013 (García-Pérez et al., 2016b), and is presented via spatial projections and trade distance matrices (García-Pérez et al., 2016a). Beyond the obvious advantages of visualization, the World Trade Atlas 1870-2013 significantly increases our understanding of the long-term evolution of the international trade system and helps us to address a number of important and challenging questions by asserting that, in terms of trade, the world is not flat; it is hyperbolic.

4.3 Network reconstruction

In order to produce World Trade Maps of the international trade system, the first step is to construct a WTW for every year in which the links between the countries carry a weight ω_{ij} equal to the sum of the trade flows from *i* to *j* and from *j* to *i*, i. e. $\omega_{ij} = \omega_{i \to j} + \omega_{j \to i}$, where the arrow represents the direction of the flow of goods. Hence, the resulting networks are weighted and undirected. Bilateral trade data reported by countries can be used. Due to a reliability problem, we avoid working with export data whenever possible. Instead, more accurate reported import values of bilateral trade data can be used, since an export from one country to another is simultaneously an import from the partner; see details in next subsection.

4.3.1 Empirical data

Bilateral trade data to reconstruct weighted versions of the WTW can be found in the websites of the International Monetary Fund (IMF) (IMF, 2015) and the United Nations Commodity Trade Statistics Database (UN, 2015), among others. More conveniently, datasets with curated versions are also available (Gleditsch, 2002; Barbieri et al., 2009). We used the dataset provided in The Correlates of War Project (COW) (COW, 2012), with curated bilateral trade flows from 1870 to 2009 (Barbieri and Keshk, 2012) based on values reported by each country to the IMF. Due to some detected flaws in the data for the last years—like the absence of trade data for Germany after 2006—, we restricted the use of this dataset, referred to as DBI, to the period from 1870 to

1996 (with the only modification of the removal of the flows between Haiti and United Kingdom in 1877, which seem to be outliers). We complemented it with more recent data from the IMF and followed the same curation steps to produce a version with world bilateral trade data from 1997 to 2013, referred to as DBII (García-Pérez et al., 2016b).

Different issues have to be taken into account in the curation process (Barbieri et al., 2009). The first step is to build up a correspondence between IMF and COW codes for countries and to extend the COW's state list from 2011 to 2013. In most cases, the matching is very clear, but there are some special cases. A given country may appear under different names at the IMF. For instance, in the last years, some countries still report trade with the U.S.S.R. A different problem is the case of China, whose trade data does not include the one for the two special administrative regions Hong Kong and Macao, which have been added to China. Also, many entries in the COW state list can correspond to the same country, like "Yugoslavia," "Yugoslavia not specified," "Serbia and Montenegro," "Serbia and Montenegro not specified," "Serbia, Republic of," "Montenegro" and "Kosovo" before its independence. Also, several countries report trade with pairs of countries, like "Belgium-Luxembourg not specified." Following the same steps as the COW Project, we have split every such flow into two, proportionally to the GDP of Belgium and Luxembourg the corresponding year (the GDP data of both countries for this operation was retrieved from the World Bank (WB, 2015)). Finally, there are no trade reports from Taiwan in the IMF database. We have obtained its data from the ROC's Bureau of Foreign Trade (ROC, 2015), matching their country list with the one from the COW Project.

Once the correspondence between codes is established, trade flows can be assigned to links between countries from IMF data. Four numbers are reported for every pair of countries *i* and *j*: $\omega^{i}_{i\to j}$, $\omega^{j}_{i\to j}$, $\omega^{i}_{j\to i}$ and $\omega^{j}_{j\to i}$, where the upper index represents the reporting country. The importer's value is generally more reliable than the exporter's due to the taxes to which imports are subject, so we used the values $\omega_{ij} = \omega^{j}_{i\to j}+\omega^{i}_{j\to i}$ whenever available, substituting importers' by exporters' values $\omega^{i}_{i\to j}$ or $\omega^{j}_{j\to i}$ otherwise. To check the consistency between DBI and DBII, trade volumes for 1997 in the two databases were compared, see Figure 4.3. Indeed, the difference is smaller than 10^{-2} US Million \$ in the 96.1% of cases, which indicates a very good agreement. The minimal observed discrepancies are due to rounding criteria in some cases—we round to the second decimal place if the flow is larger than 1 US Million \$—, and to the absence of some importers' reports when DBI was constructed—the differences between the importers' and the exporters' reported values could be very large (for instance $\omega^{SLV}_{SLV\to ZIM} \approx 160000$ US\$ while $\omega^{ZIM}_{SLV\to ZIM} \approx 15$ US\$). Nonetheless, as stated above, these cases are very rare.

Figure 4.3: Consistency between DBI and DBII in 1997

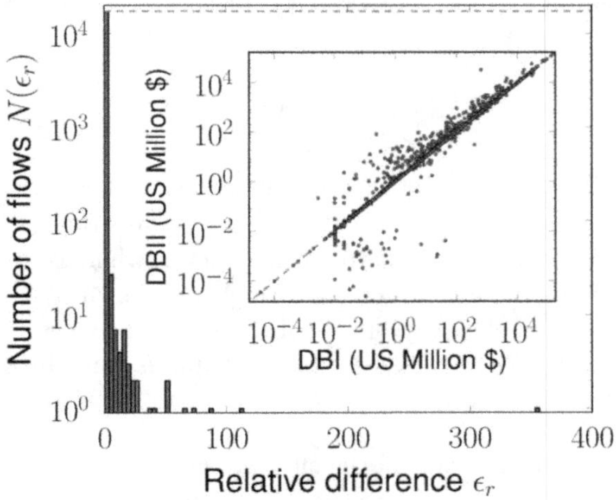

Color images of figures can be downloaded at the book's page
[URL: https://vernonpress.com/book/96]

Histogram of relative differences between trade volumes in the two databases. The red horizontal line indicates the total number of flows. Inset: Each point corresponds to the value of a given trade volume in both databases. Most points lay in the diagonal.

We also collected GDP data obtained from three different sources: The Maddison Project (Bolt and van Zanden, 2014) from 1870 to 1949, Gleditsch's GDP data (Gleditsch, 2015) from 1950 to 2011, and data from the World Bank (WB, 2015) and the CIA World Factbook (CIA, 2015) for the years 2012 and 2013. As in the case of trade data, country codes need to be matched with those in the COW's state list. Moreover, since trade is reported in current US Million $, we have converted the real GDP values into current GDP values using the deflator calculated by comparing Maddison's data with data from (Johnston and Williamson, 2015).

Finally, data for formal Preferential Trade Agreements between countries was obtained from the World Trade Organization (WTO) (WTO, 2015).

4.3.2 Extracting backbones of significant trade channels

The high density of connections observed in the WTW reconstructions, which increases with the passage of time, obscures patterns and regularities within the networks and so prevents the inference of trade distances. At the same time, the networks display, especially after World War I (WWI), a strong heterogeneity in the global distributions of the number of trading partners, the total trade per country and bilateral flows. An increasing heterogeneity is also present at the local level in the distribution of flows between the neighbours of every single country, which we quantify using the disparity measure $k_i Y_i(k_i)$ (Serrano et al., 2007a; Herfindahl, 1959; Hirschman, 1964) for each country i,

$$k_i Y_i(k_i) = k_i \sum_j \left(\frac{\omega_{ij}}{s_i}\right)^2 \quad (4.1)$$

where ω_{ij} is the total flow between countries i and j and $s_i = \sum_j \omega_{ij}$ is the strength (aggregated trade) of country i. If country i distributes its trade homogeneously between its trade partners $k_i Y_i(k_i) = 1$, whereas in the opposite case—if all its trade is concentrated on a single link—$k_i Y_i(k_i) = k_i$. As shown in figure 4.4 for a few selected years, the disparity of all countries in the WTW has been increasing. This indicates that, as countries gained trade partners, they only intensified a few of their trade connections.

Figure 4.4: Disparity in trade volumes for all countries of the WTW in different years

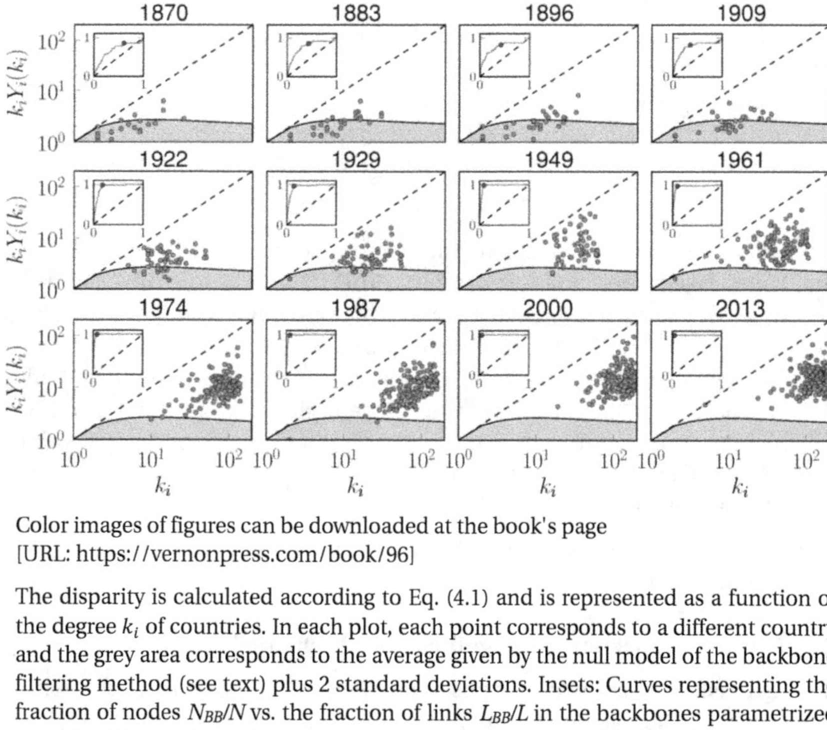

Color images of figures can be downloaded at the book's page
[URL: https://vernonpress.com/book/96]

The disparity is calculated according to Eq. (4.1) and is represented as a function of the degree k_i of countries. In each plot, each point corresponds to a different country and the grey area corresponds to the average given by the null model of the backbone filtering method (see text) plus 2 standard deviations. Insets: Curves representing the fraction of nodes N_{BB}/N vs. the fraction of links L_{BB}/L in the backbones parametrized by α. The blue circles indicate the values that correspond to the backbone with $\alpha = \alpha_c$ which maximizes the vertical distance to the diagonal (constrained by $N_{BB}/N \geq 0.8$ ($N_{BB}/N \geq 0.7$ in 1894) so that most countries remain in the system). Moreover, in order to avoid fluctuations in the topology between years, the 1975 backbone was selected with a higher link fraction than the given by the geometric rule.

These heterogeneities can be exploited to filter out, for each year, a sparse subnetwork representing the relevant structure that remains after eliminating the contingent interactions which overshadow the information contained in the system (Serrano et al., 2009). The disparity filter proceeds as follows. For each trade channel of a given country *i*, we compute the probability α_{ij} that the link takes the observed normalised weight ω_{ij}/s_i according to a null model in which countries assign their aggregated trade among their partners randomly from a uniform distribution. By imposing a significance level α, we can determine the statistical significance of a given trade channel by comparing the obtained p-value α_{ij} to α. Therefore, if $\alpha_{ij} > \alpha$, the flow through that trade channel can be considered compatible with a random distribution (with the chosen significance level α) and is thus discarded. The statistically relevant channels are then those that satisfy

$$\alpha_{ij} = 1 - (k-1)\int_0^{\frac{\omega_{ij}}{s_i}} (1-x)^{k-2}\, dx < \alpha, \quad (4.2)$$

for at least one of the two countries *i* and *j* (Serrano et al., 2009).

By applying this selection rule to all the links in the network, we filter a subgraph containing, in general, fewer links and nodes depending on the value of the significance level α. In order to find an optimal value of α, it is convenient to plot the fraction of remaining nodes in the backbone N_{BB}/N versus the fraction of remaining links L_{BB}/L for different values of α (insets in Figure 4.4). As the filter becomes more restrictive, the number of links decreases dramatically while keeping almost all nodes until a certain critical point α_c after which the number of nodes starts a steep decay. This behaviour is due to the fact that the disparity filter for $\alpha = \alpha_c$ is able to select the minimal set of significant links that preserve the global connectivity, referred to as the backbone. Geometrically, the value α_c defining the backbone can be identified with the value of the significance level whose corresponding point in the $N_{BB}/N - L_{BB}/L$ plane maximizes the vertical distance to the diagonal. Notice that on the diagonal $N_{BB}/N = L_{BB}/L$, so the average degree remains constant ($\langle k \rangle_{BB} = 2L_{BB}/N_{BB} = 2L/N = \langle k \rangle$). Consequently, setting $\alpha = \alpha_c$, where α_c is chosen according to the geometric rule stated above, minimizes the average degree of the backbone $\langle k \rangle_{BB}$. This offers a consistent and systematic criterion to extract the backbones of the WTW at different years. The values of α_c for each year can be found in Table S4 in García-Pérez et al., (2016a).

Apart from preserving almost all countries, backbones show an average degree almost constant in time, figure 4.1A and capture most of the total trade, figure 4.1B. Backbones expose pivotal features of the international trade system as a complex network: the small-world property, heterogeneous degree distributions, degree-degree correlations, and clustering, figure 4.2B-E. Interestingly, the correlation between the degrees of countries within the backbones and their GDPs is always extremely high, figure 4.5A, meaning that these backbones of world trade networks reveal economic size—in terms of GDP—as an underlying variable. The value is well above than the correlation observed in the original networks so that the backbones stand as a more meaningful network representation of the international trade system from an economic point of view.

Backbones differ from the unfiltered networks in the relation between geographic distance and trade connections. Overall, the geographic length of connections relative to the geographic distance between all the countries (located at the coordinates of their capitals) shows a sustained increase in the unfiltered network, see figure 4.1C. This means that trade connections become less dependent on distance over time. However, the significant trade channels within the backbone are comparatively shorter over the whole period, which means that, despite globalisation, countries are more likely to choose their more significant trade partners from among their closest neighbours. The connection probability is almost independent of distance in the unfiltered networks, but it shows a clear power-law decay with a stable exponent in the case of the backbones, figure 4.5B, and showing that geographic distance plays an increasingly important role for the most significant trade channels. Strikingly, the filter that produces the backbones is blind to geography.

Figure 4.5: Comparison of different statistics in the WTW and the corresponding backbone

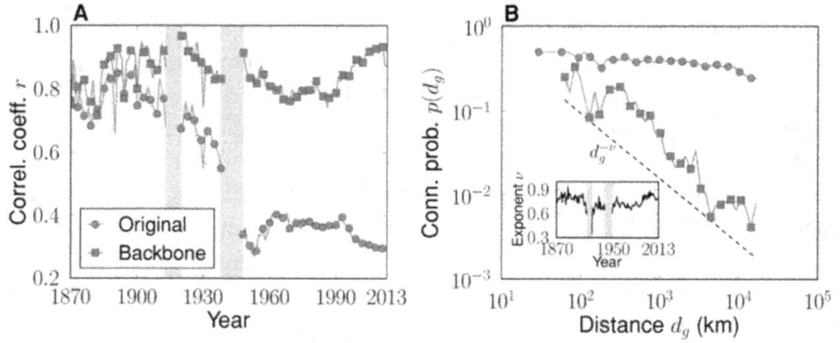

Color images of figures can be downloaded at the book's page
[URL: https://vernonpress.com/book/96]

A: Time evolution of the Pearson correlation coefficient between the number of trade channels of a country and its GDP. B: Probability distribution function of the geographical distance of trade channels in 2013. Inset: Time evolution of the characteristic power-law exponent of that distribution in the WTW backbone.

4.4 Mapping the world trade web

4.4.1 A gravity model for trade channels

WTW backbones are suitable to be mapped onto an underlying trade space in which closer countries have a greater chance of becoming connected by a trade channel. The likelihood of becoming connected is based on a gravity model consisting of economic size factors and effective trade distances. The simplest metric space that can be considered to represent effective distance is a circle on which countries are separated by an angular distance $d_{a,ij} = \min(|\Delta\theta_{a,ij}|, 2\pi - |\Delta\theta_{a,ij}|)$, and where any pair of countries i and j are connected in terms of this distance with probability

$$p_{ij} = \frac{1}{1+\chi_{ij}^{\beta}} = \frac{1}{1+\left(\frac{d_{a,ij}}{\mu\kappa_i\kappa_j}\right)^{\beta}}, (4.3)$$

such that p_{ij} decreases as a function of $d_{a,ij}$ and increases with the expected economic sizes κ (Serrano et al., 2008). This is known as the S^1 model. These economic sizes are strongly correlated with degrees in the backbone and, therefore, with the corresponding GDPs, figure 4.5A. Distances $d_{a,ij}$ incorporate the different factors that shape the complex architecture of the international trade system—not only geography—implicitly encoded in its connectivity pattern. The parameters μ and β govern the average degree and the clustering, respectively, of the network. Note that β is an elasticity measure with respect to trade distances; it calibrates the coupling between the topology and the underlying metric space. Hence, the proposed connection probability resembles Newton's law of gravitation and, therefore, the classical gravity model predicting the volume of bilateral trade flows. Notice, however, that p_{ij} is not used to predict the volume of trade but the existence of a significant trade channel; information which has to be provided a priori in classical gravity models of trade, since they reproduce the existence of a link very badly (Dueñas and Fagiolo, 2013a).

The S^1 gravity model defined by Eq. (4.3) is isomorphic to a purely geometric network model in the hyperbolic plane, see figure 4.6, known as the H^2 model (Krioukov et al., 2010). Hyperbolic geometry has been conjectured as the natural geometry underlying the complex features—e.g., scale-free degree distributions, strong clustering levels, the small-world property, etc.—of real-world networks (Papadopoulos et al., 2012; Krioukov et al., 2009). This geometric interpretation of complex networks can be demonstrated with the gravity law type of connection probability introduced in Eq. (4.3). Indeed, by mapping the variable κ to a radial coordinate r as follows

$$r = R - 2\ln\left[\frac{\kappa}{\kappa_0}\right] \text{ with } R = 2\ln\left[\frac{2}{\mu\kappa_0^2}\right], \quad (4.4)$$

where κ_0 is the economic size of the smallest economy; and by keeping the same angular coordinates. The connection probability, Eq. (4.3) can then be rewritten as

$$p_{ij} = \frac{1}{1+e^{\frac{\beta}{2}(x_{ij}-R)}}, \quad (4.5)$$

where $x_{ij} = r_i + r_j + 2ln\frac{d_{a,ij}}{2} \approx d_{h,ij}$ is a very good approximation of the hyperbolic distance $d_{h,ij}$ between two points at radial coordinates r_i and r_j and angular separation $d_{a,ij}$. The exact hyperbolic distance can be computed with the hyperbolic law of cosines

$$\cosh d_{h,ij} = \cosh r_i \cosh r_j \; - \; \sinh r_i \sinh r_j \cos d_{a,ij} \quad (4.6)$$

The hyperbolic representation condensates in a pure geometric framework the properties of the entire system—economic size and effective distance in the gravity model Eq. (4.3)—; that is, it allows to draw genuine maps of the trade system where different parts can be compared on an equal footing. More specifically, due to the inverse relation between economic size κ and hyperbolic radius *r*, large economies with high degrees are located close to the centre of the disk, whereas small economies are placed near its boundary; the distance between nodes with the same angular separation increases exponentially with their hyperbolic radial coordinates.

Figure 4.6: Gravity model and hyperbolic representation

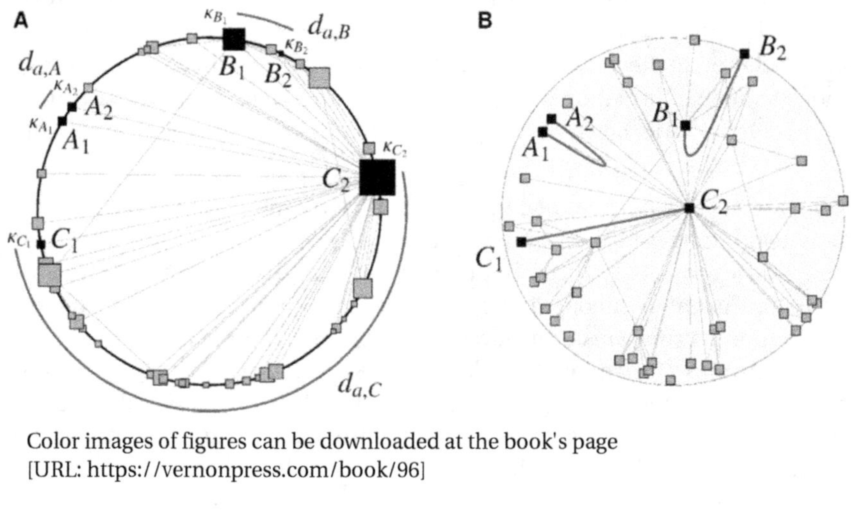

Color images of figures can be downloaded at the book's page [URL: https://vernonpress.com/book/96]

Three different pairs of nodes $A_1 - A_2$, $B_1 - B_2$ and $C_1 - C_2$ have been highlighted. A: S^1 gravity model in which the effective distance d_a is given by the angular separation along the circle. The size of a node is proportional to its economic size κ. B: Hyperbolic space representation of the model in A. The three different pairs of nodes are separated by the same hyperbolic distance. In this representation, nodes are equally sized, but nodes with a higher degree (larger size in A) are positioned closer to the centre in the hyperbolic plane. As an example, nodes $A_1 - A_2$ with small degree and very low angular separation can be very far apart in hyperbolic space.

4.4.2 Embedding method

World Trade Maps are constructed by embedding WTW backbones in hyperbolic space. The embedding assigns coordinates in the underlying space to each country in a backbone such that trade and effective distances can be defined for every pair. The method uses statistical inference techniques to identify the coordinates which maximize the likelihood that the backbone is reproduced by the model. Inferred angular distances represent a measure of trade likelihood, except for the (economic) sizes of the countries. This means that two small countries need to be close in terms of angular distance to increase their chance of becoming connected. The inferred hyperbolic distance, however, incorporates size effects; that is, two countries can be close in hyperbolic space just because of their size. In particular, large economies are in general closer to the rest of the world than smaller economies.

The likelihood function that needs to be maximized is given by

$$L = \prod_{i<j} p_{ij}^{a_{ij}} \left(1 - p_{ij}\right)^{1-a_{ij}}, \quad (4.7)$$

where $\{a_{ij}\}$ is the adjacency matrix, with entries $a_{ij} = 1$ if countries i and j are connected and $a_{ij} = 0$ otherwise. Note that a_{ij} depends on real trade data, whereas p_{ij} depends on the $\{(r, \theta)\}$ coordinates to be inferred. Moreover, the connection probability Eq. (4.5) depends also on the global parameters of the model: number of nodes in the backbone N, average degree in the backbone $\langle k \rangle$, exponent of the power-law degree distribution γ and the clustering controlling parameter β, which must be inferred in order to maximize Eq. (4.7). The likelihood maximization procedure requires thus the following two steps:

- **Estimation of the global parameters**: The value of the exponent γ can be estimated directly from the degree distribution measured in the reconstructed WTW backbone. We use a linear fit to the curve $log P_c(k)$ versus $log\ k$, where $P_c(k) = \int_k^\infty P(k')dk'$ is the complemen-

tary cumulative degree distribution giving the probability for a randomly chosen node in the network to have degree greater or equal to k, less noisy than $P(k)$. A power-law degree distribution with exponent γ, $P_c(k) \sim k^{1-\gamma}$ becomes the straight line $logP_c(k) = (1-\gamma)logk + c$, which allows to obtain γ from its slope. Due to the small number of nodes in the system, we constrain the values of $\gamma \geq 2.15$.
The values of the parameters N and $\langle k \rangle$ need to be estimated carefully. When a synthetic network is generated with the model, some of its nodes may have no connections (which is more likely to occur for very sparse graphs) and we do not consider them as belonging to the system. Hence, the target N and $\langle k \rangle$ in the model can be different from the observed ones. For very large systems, these differences can be estimated analytically, but in this case, we are considering networks with less than 200 nodes.
The value of β is also difficult to estimate. It affects the resulting average clustering coefficient $\bar{C}$ (indeed, $\bar{C}$ increases with increasing β) but the exact value cannot be obtained by analytic means.
We estimate the three parameters N, $\langle k \rangle$ and β by comparing the real WTW backbones to synthetic networks generated with the model using different values for the three target parameters. We detail the procedure next:

1. Measure γ, N_{obs}, $\langle k \rangle_{obs}$ and $\bar{C}_{obs}$, i.e., the exponent of the degree distribution, the number of nodes, average degree and average clustering of the WTW backbone.

2. Initialize the target variables N_{targ}, $\langle k \rangle_{targ}$ and β_{targ} using some values as the initial guess. In our case, we use $N_{targ} = N_{obs} + 10$, $\langle k \rangle_{targ} = 4\langle k \rangle_{obs}$ and $\beta_{targ} = 5.5$.

3. Generate a synthetic network using the target variables and the observed value of γ.

4. Measure N_{synth}, $\langle k \rangle_{synth}$ and $\bar{C}_{synth}$ of the synthetic network.

5. If $|N_{synth} - N_{obs}| < \epsilon_N \wedge |\langle k \rangle_{synth} - \langle k \rangle_{obs}| < \epsilon_{\langle k \rangle} \wedge |\bar{C}_{synth} - \bar{C}_{obs}| < \epsilon_{\bar{C}}$, the synthetic network can be considered similar to the observed one, so the values N_{targ}, $\langle k \rangle_{targ}$ and β_{targ} used to generate it are good estimations to be used in Eq. (4.7). Keep them and stop. If the condition is not fulfilled, go to step 6.

6. If $N_{synth} < N_{obs} \Rightarrow N_{targ} + \delta_N \rightarrow N_{targ}$. Else $N_{targ} - \delta_N \rightarrow N_{targ}$.
If $\langle k \rangle_{synth} < \langle k \rangle_{obs} \Rightarrow \langle k \rangle_{targ} + \delta_{\langle k \rangle} \rightarrow \langle k \rangle_{targ}$. Else $\langle k \rangle_{targ} - \delta_{\langle k \rangle} \rightarrow \langle k \rangle_{targ}$.
If $\bar{C}_{synth} < \bar{C}_{obs} \Rightarrow \beta_{targ} + \delta_\beta \rightarrow \beta_{targ}$. Else $\beta_{targ} - \delta_\beta \rightarrow \beta_{targ}$.
Go to step 3.

The implementation of this algorithm gives good estimations for the global parameters so that the resulting synthetic networks mimic the real backbones. The final values are averages over 20 estimations. Moreover, we set $\epsilon_N = 1$, $\epsilon_{\langle k \rangle} = 0.1\langle k \rangle_{obs}$ and $\epsilon_{\bar{C}} = 0.05$. δ_N is set to 1, while $\delta_{\langle k \rangle}$ and δ_β are withdrawn from the uniform distribution $U(0, 0.2)$ in every iteration of step 6. To ensure the convergence of the method, the value of β is constrained between 2.1 and 6.5.

Once N, $\langle k \rangle$, β and γ are known, the radius R of the hyperbolic disk can be computed as

$$R = 2log\left[\frac{2N}{\langle k \rangle \beta \sin\frac{\pi}{\beta}}\left(\frac{\gamma-1}{\gamma-2}\right)^2\right] \quad (4.8)$$

- **Maximization of the likelihood function**: Once the global parameters are known, Eq. (4.7) can be maximized. We use an adapted version of the Metropolis-Hastings algorithm. Since we are not embedding a single network but a temporal sequence, we take as initial coordinates of a given country the ones obtained in the previous embedding. We first embed the network for the year 2013—the largest—and the rest of them sequentially in decreasing time order. Notice also that it is convenient to maximize the logarithm of L, which we will denote as log-likelihood ln L, instead of L to avoid numerical issues. The steps to embed the network corresponding to year Y are:

    1. **Initial positions:** for every country i in the current network:

        i. If i belongs to the WTW of year $Y+1$, set (r_i, θ_i) to the values of the $Y+1$ embedding (constrain r_i so that it is not larger than R). Else, choose r_i randomly from $U(0, R)$ and θ_i from $U(0, 2\pi)$.

        ii. Set $(\tilde{r}_i, \tilde{\theta}_i) = (r_i, \theta_i)$. These variables will record the maximum-likelihood configuration.

2. **Compute the initial value of the log-likelihood** $\ln L$ using Eq. (4.7). Set $\ln \tilde{L} = \ln L$. This variable will record the highest value of the log-likelihood.

3. **Maximize likelihood:** Repeat $S \times N^2$ times (in all cases, $S =$ 30 is enough to achieve convergence):

   i. Choose a node i at random from the list [2, N]; notice that we never select node 1 (which corresponds to the USA, the most persistent hub in time) in order to keep its angular coordinate unchanged. The reason to do so is that the likelihood L is invariant with respect to global rotations of the system. Hence, not varying the angular coordinate of one of the nodes anchors the embedding by breaking this symmetry.
   Propose a new value for θ_i from $U(0, 2\pi)$.
   Compute the log-likelihood increment. Notice that only $N - 1$ steps are required, as opposed to calculating the new log-likelihood as in step 2.
   If $\Delta \ln L \geq 0$ accept the change of θ_i. Otherwise, accept the change with probability $e^{\Delta lnL} = \frac{L_{new}}{L_{old}} < 1$.
   If the change is accepted, give $\ln L$ the new value $\ln L + \Delta\ln L \rightarrow \ln L$. If $\ln L > \ln \tilde{L}$ set $(\tilde{r}_i, \tilde{\theta}_i) = (r_i, \theta_i)$ for all i and $\ln \tilde{L} = \ln L$.

   ii. Choose a node i at random from the list [1, N].
   Propose a new value for r_i from $U(0, R)$.
   Compute the log-likelihood increment.
   If $\Delta \ln L \geq 0$ accept the change of r_i. Otherwise, accept the change with probability $e^{\Delta lnL} = \frac{L_{new}}{L_{old}} < 1$.
   If the change is accepted, give $\ln L$ the new value $\ln L + \Delta\ln L \rightarrow \ln L$. If $\ln L > \ln \tilde{L}$ set $(\tilde{r}_i, \tilde{\theta}_i) = (r_i, \theta_i)$ for all i and $\ln \tilde{L} = \ln L$.

For every year Y, we repeat the whole algorithm 10 times and keep the configuration with the maximum-likelihood. We then run step 3 starting with such initial configuration but accepting changes if and only if $\Delta \ln L > 0$. It is also important to point out that L has a very complex landscape with many degeneracies, that is, configurations with similar likelihood. Usually, the difference between these configurations is the inversion of a whole community. Such a change mildly affects a small fraction of the pairs of distances $d_{h,ij}$ only and, therefore, L takes a similar value. In order to obtain statistically reliable distances between countries, we average distances (both hyperbolic and angular) and connection probabilities, as well as their fluctuations over 100 embeddings starting with completely random positions, see figure 4.7.

Figure 4.7: Distance matrices between countries in the WTW backbone in 2013

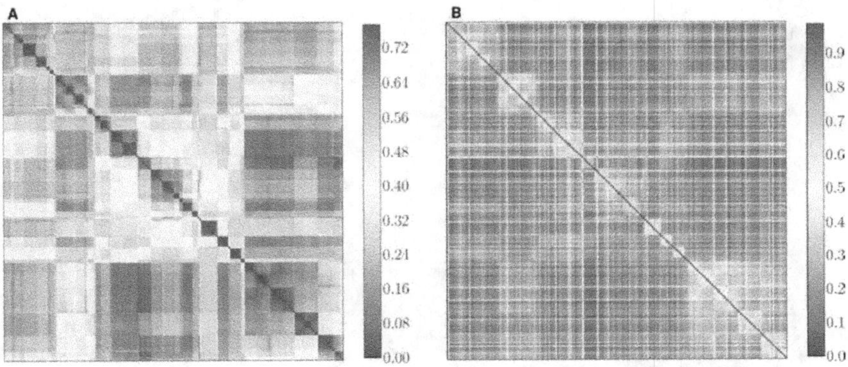

Color images of figures can be downloaded at the book's page
[URL: https://vernonpress.com/book/96]

A: Average normalised angular distances $\langle \tilde{d}_{a,ij} \rangle$. Nodes are ordered such that nearest neighbours are consecutive. The dark squares in the matrix reveal the community structure of the backbone. B: Average normalised hyperbolic distances $\langle \tilde{d}_{h,ij} \rangle$. The ordering of the countries is the same in both matrices.

4.4.3 Hyperbolic maps of WTW backbones

The application of the embedding method to the backbones of annual WTWs from 1870 to 2013 produces 129 World Trade Maps that conform to the World Trade Atlas 1870-2013 (García-Pérez et al., 2016b, a) (WTA 1870-2013). Single embeddings for each year are useful for visualization purposes, figure 4.8, while averaged distances, figure 4.7, are more suitable for computations.

Figure 4.8: World Trade Maps for different years

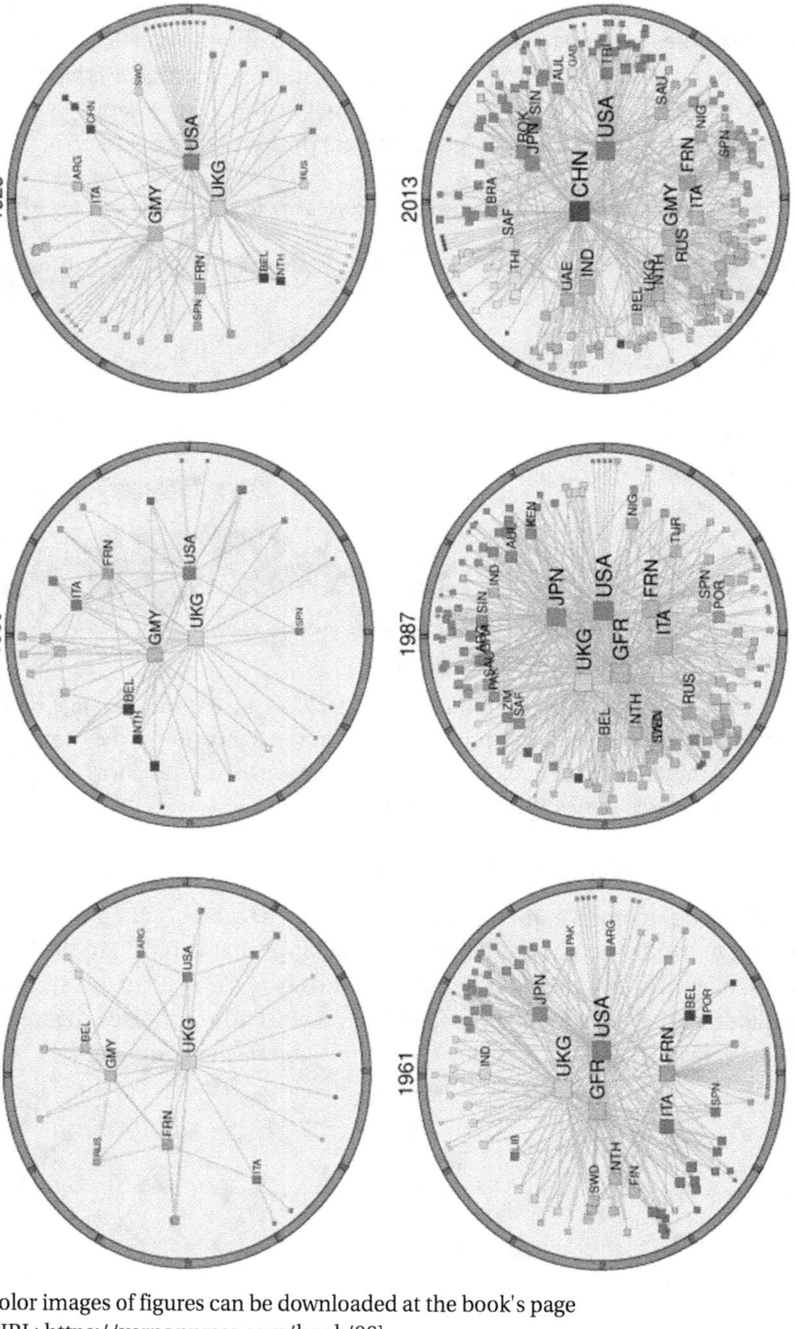

Color images of figures can be downloaded at the book's page
[URL: https://vernonpress.com/book/96]

Representation on the hyperbolic plane. The radial and angular coordinates of countries determine the trade distances between them through Eq. (4.6). Symbol sizes are proportional to the logarithm of the degrees of the countries and colours represent communities revealed by the CGM presented in Sec. "Detecting communities in WTMs: the CGM method." See the online video tool (García-Pérez et al., 2016a) for the country associated with each acronym.

Pairwise quality tests: Figure 4.9A-D demonstrates the power of the gravity model of trade channels to reproduce the topological properties of WTW backbones. This is due, in particular, to the excellent agreement between the empirical and the theoretical probability of connection Eq. (4.5) as a function of the effective distance between countries rescaled by economic size, figure 4.9E- H. To measure the empirical connection probability $\frac{d_{a,ij}}{\mu\kappa_i\kappa_j}$ are binned into M subintervals and, for every bin, the fraction of connected pairs out of all pairs whose effective distances fall into the bin is counted. The expected degrees $\langle k_i \rangle$ of countries, defined as $\langle k_i \rangle = \sum_{j \neq i} p_{ij}$ with p_{ij} given by Eq. (4.5) and the distance calculated using the coordinates of the embedding and Eq. (4.6), match almost perfectly the observed values k_i measured in the backbones, see figure 4.9I-L, in accordance with MLE for expected degrees (Boguñá et al., 2010).

A further demonstration of the quality of the embeddings is given by the temporal evolution of the area under the receiver operating characteristic (ROC) curve or AUC statistics measuring the ability of the model to predict real trade channels. Once a network is embedded, Eq. (4.5) assigns a connection probability p_{ij} to each pair of nodes, independently of whether they are connected or not in the backbone. The ROC curve is produced by computing the *true positive rate* (TPR)—the fraction of existing links predicted by the model—as a function of the *false positive rate* (FPR)—the fraction of links that do not exist in the network but have been predicted to exist by the model—parametrized by the thresholds defined by all possible links. Notice that a perfect prediction would correspond to TPR=1 and FPR=0. The area under the ROC curve (AUC) provides a scalar summarizing the result. The best possible result corresponds to AUC=1; its value is well above 0.975 in all embeddings of the WTA 1870-2013. Figure 4.9M displays the time evolution of the AUC statistic, always almost 1 and, in the inset, the ROC curve for the year 2013.

Finally, a key observation is that the correlation between embedding distances and geographic distances, as shown in figure 4.9N, is significant over the whole period, but far from one; meaning that trade distances encode more than purely geographical information.

Global quality tests: The tests presented so far to assess the quality of the embeddings only take into account pairwise information. We complement the validation by measuring the efficiency of navigation in the embeddings. It has been previously shown that the geometrical information provided by the embedding into hyperbolic space can be used to navigate the network efficiently by following the very simple rule of greedy forwarding: to go from a source node i to a target node j, hop to the source's neighbour that is closest (according to Eq. (4.6)) to destination j, and iterate (Boguñá et al., 2010). Following this procedure, networks which are well described by the embedding model sustain a high number of successful routes in a number of hops not much larger than the topological shortest path length, i.e., the minimum number of hops actually required to go from i to j. This is due to the fact that shortest paths follow closely the geodesics in the underlying space.

We measure the success rate—the fraction of successful paths via greedy forwarding—and the average stretch—the average overall successful routings of the quotient between the number of hops required by greedy forwarding and the topological shortest path length. Notice that, for every pair of countries, both directions must be checked, since the process is not necessarily symmetric. We also compare the results with the ones measured on the same networks with the same radial coordinates but with randomized angular coordinates. The results are displayed in figure 4.9O-P. As the number of countries grows, the success rate for the randomized embeddings decreases, reaching values as low as 0.5, whereas it takes an almost constant value of 1 along the whole period for the embeddings of the backbones. The stretch increases slightly over the last years in both cases but remains very close to one. However, notice that it is always closer to 1 for the real embedding even though it is computed over a much larger set of pairs; indeed, the stretch is defined for successful greedy paths only (about 50% in the randomized case in the last years).

Figure 4.9: Quality of the embeddings

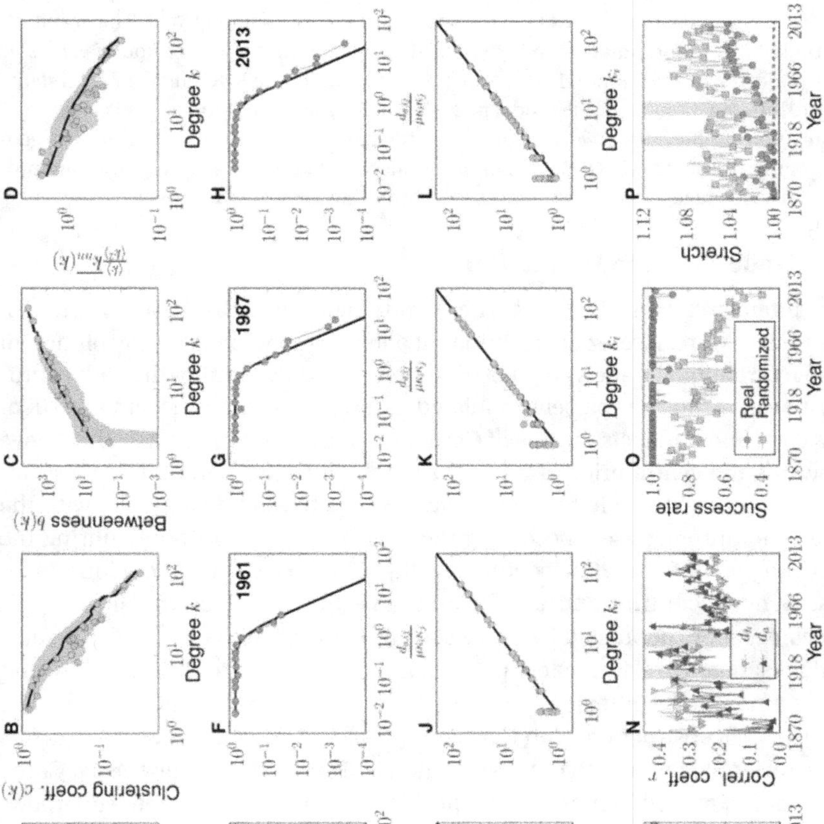

Color images of figures can be downloaded at the book's page [URL: https://vernonpress.com/book/96]

A-D: Comparison of the topology of the WTW backbone in 2013 with 1000 synthetic networks generated by the gravity model of trade channels using the coordinates of the corresponding embedding. A: Complementary cumulative degree distribution. B: Degree-dependent clustering coefficient. C: Country betweenness centrality. D: Average normalised nearest-neighbour degree. The thick black line gives the average over realizations and the green areas indicate the 99% confidence interval. E-H: Empirical connection probability as a function of effective distance rescaled by economic size and measured using the average distances in the corresponding year. The empirical probability is computed from Eq. (4.3). I-L: Expected degree $\langle k_i \rangle$ of node i versus its real degree ki. M: Temporal evolution of the area under the ROC curve, or AUC statistic. Inset: ROC curve of the model in 2013. H: Historical evolution of the Pearson correlation coefficient between hyperbolic and angular distances, d_h and d_a, and geographical distance d_g. O: Evolution of the success rate of the greedy forwarding process. P: Average stretch of successful greedy routing paths for every year.

4.5 Trade since the 19th century

An interactive tool displaying The World Trade Atlas 1870-2013 can be accessed at (García-Pérez et al., 2016a). It allows us to visualize the evolution of the international trade system over fourteen decades. During the 19th century, the atlas shows a sparsely populated trade space with the hegemonic UK at its core; and it reflects the rise of Germany, France, and the USA as they move towards the centre prior to WWI. During the interwar period, the atlas presents a central triangle formed by the UK, the USA, and Germany; with the USA then progressively becoming the new hegemonic economy during the second part of the 20th century. In the 1960s, decolonization introduces many new countries and at the same time the upper intermediate region becomes more populated by actors such as France, Italy, Japan, and the Netherlands; together with, in less prominent positions, India, Russia, Spain, and Belgium, among others. In the 1990s, the European Community starts its process of construction, with Germany, Italy and France coming closer; while the Soviet Bloc remains very close to Russia. During the last few years, China has moved towards a more central position, as a new pretender to superpower status; while the USA, the European Community, and Japan have moved to less central positions following the decline of their relative dominance.

4.5.1 Hierarchies

The evolution of the international trade system at the large scale has been shaped by three simultaneous forces: globalisation—mentioned above—, localisation—discussed in the next subsection—, and hierarchisation. The impact of the first two has already been discussed from many perspectives (Krugman, 1991a, 1995; Baldwin and Martin, 1999; Fujita et al., 1999; Chase-Dunn et al., 2000; Friedman, 2005; Stiglitz, 2006; Ghemawat, 2007). Conversely, the role and implications of hierarchisation at the system level have not been recognised before. However, its effects in the WTMs are keenly discernible. The first sign is the radial stratification of economies according to their size, with that small economies—low-degree countries—always located at the periphery of the disk, while large economies—with high degrees—settling at its centre. A rough measure of the hierarchical position of a country is then given by its radial coordinate, and so by its degree, as compared to the radius, *R*, of the trade space, which measures the hyperbolicity of the whole system or, equivalently, its departure from flatness, figure 4.10A. *R* grows until reaching a stationary value at the end of the interwar period, around which it fluctuates thereafter. Interestingly, the opposite behaviour is observed for the elasticity parameter, β, shown in figure 4.10C, informing about the coupling between the topology of the network and the underlying metric space. Larger values of *R* imply that differences in trade distances are more important for peripheral nodes; that is, they connect to each other less frequently.

Figure 4.10: Hierarchy in World Trade Maps

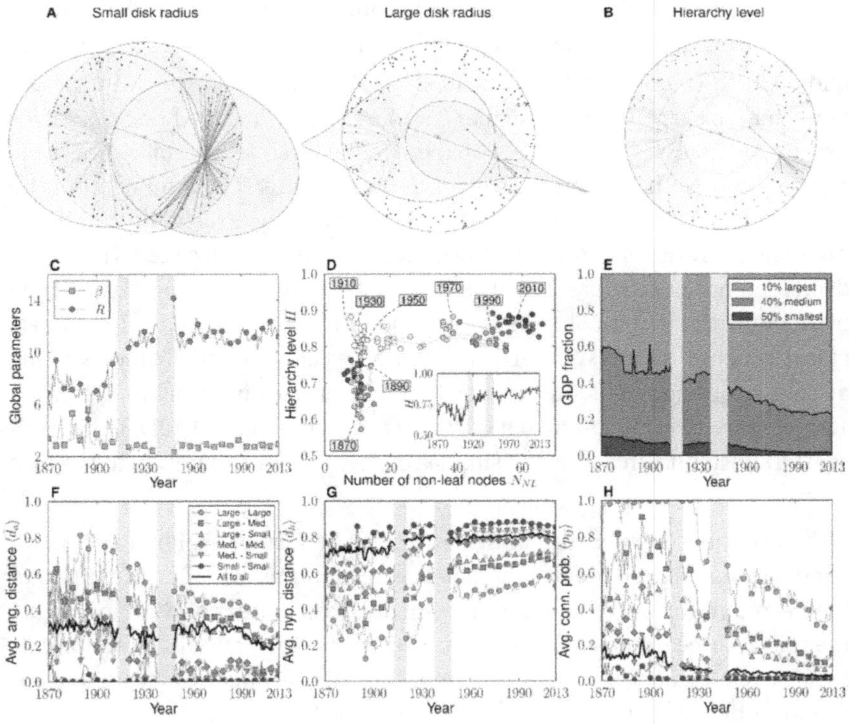

Color images of figures can be downloaded at the book's page [URL: https://vernonpress.com/book/96]

A: Two hyperbolic disks with different radii (rescaled). Within each disk, we drew two circles of the same radius but centred at different locations. For small radius, the two inner circles appear to be similar to Euclidean disks; whereas, for large radius, the inner circles are strongly distorted. B: Sketch illustrating the definition of the hierarchy level, *H*, of two different nodes. Leaf nodes appear in grey. C: Evolution of the radius, R, of the hyperbolic disk and of the elasticity parameter, β. D: Evolution of the hierarchy level, H, as a function of the number of non-leaf countries and of time. Inset: Time evolution of H. Note that the number of non-leaf countries has grown (with some fluctuations) over time, so that the increase of N_{NL} along the x-axis is roughly chronological. E: Evolution of the fraction of total GDP accumulated by the top 10%, 40%, and 50% of countries by economic size. F–G–H: Evolution of: the average normalised angular distance (only connected countries); the average normalised hyperbolic distance; and the average connection probability between countries within the same group and in the different groups defined in E.

A more refined measure is given by the level of hierarchy of the network as a scalar, H, based on angular distances. We define a non-leaf country i as that having at least one trading partner j whose economy is smaller, i.e, with a radial coordinate $r_j > r_i$. For each non-leaf country i with radius r_i, we measure the average angular separation $\overline{d_{a,\iota}}$ with its trading partners for which $r > r_i$ and define its hierarchical level as $h_i = 1 - 2\,\overline{d_{a,\iota}}\,/\pi$, figure 4.10B. If the neighbours have exactly the same angular coordinates as i, $h_i = 1$; whereas $h_i = 0$ for random angular positions. The global hierarchy level, H, is obtained by averaging hi over all non-leaf countries. The evolution of H as a function of the number of non-leaf countries, figure 4.10D, is revealing. Even if the number of non-leaf countries has increased noticeably in the last decades, H has not decreased but has increased. This indicates an expansion of the depth of the hierarchy, from a quasi starlike organization before WWI to a deeper hierarchical structure after WWII, with more countries at intermediate layers acting as local economic hubs. In the long run, H increases from below 0.7 in the 19th century to very close to 0.9 in 2013, see inset of figure 4.10D. This represents a substantial increase and situates the system at extremely high levels of hierarchy.

The economic significance of this effect can be further explored by analysing the evolution of trade distances between countries classified according to their economic size. We rank countries in decreasing order of GDP and divide them into three groups: the top 10%, the middle 40%, and the bottom 50%, figure 4.10E. Figures 4.10F, G and H show the evolution of: the average angular distance (between connected pairs); the average hyperbolic distance; and the average connection probability, for all pairs of countries within the same group and in the different groups. Hyperbolic and angular distances are normalised by the diameter of the space, $2R$ and π, respectively, so that different years are comparable. There is a sharp and persistent stratification according to economic group, denoting a positive correlation between trade distance, or connection probability, and economic status. The average angular distance strongly correlates with economic size. Interestingly, we observe the opposite behaviour for the average hyperbolic distance: it is anti-correlated with economic size. This reversal reflects the different interpretations of the two trade distance measures: the latter governs the formation of trade channels, and the former is an indicator of clusterisation. The hyperbolic distance between economic groups has been steadily increasing since the 1960's, and this increase has been more pronounced for the large economies. In contrast, the angular distance between groups, fluctuating until the end of WWII, has remained very low or decreased over time. This denotes a trend towards concentration of countries in specific regions of the trade space.

Placed in historical perspective, these results indicate that small countries at the bottom of the hierarchy are far from the rest of the world in terms of trade distance. They, therefore, encounter greater difficulties establishing trade channels with other countries, except for the largest economies at the top of the hierarchy, which have more chances of becoming connected worldwide. At the same time, the increase in hyperbolic distance may be a consequence of the increase in hierarchy and of market competition effects; while the decrease in angular distance indicates the formation of better-defined trading blocs that form communities in the trade space.

4.5.2 Detecting communities in WTMs: the CGM method

Hub countries near the centre of the hyperbolic disk are close to many other countries in the system and therefore have a large number of connections, whereas countries at the periphery are close to other small countries only if separated by a small angular distance. Therefore, to partition the network into communities with similar countries, we must take into account their angular coordinates. Indeed, the S^1 model assumes a uniform angular density of nodes in the underlying circle, so the clusterisation of countries around certain angular coordinates reveals regions in which they tend to connect with each other profusely. The Critical Gap Method (CGM) (Serrano et al., 2012) relies on this idea to detect communities by finding angular regions that are densely populated. To that end, it maximizes modularity Q (Newman, 2006), the standard measure for the quality of the partition in community detection algorithms applied to complex networks. This quantity, which is bounded $Q \in [-1, 1]$, compares the fraction of links inside communities with the expected fraction for a random distribution of them and is equal to 0 if nodes are randomly assigned into communities. To define a partition, a critical angular gap separating countries in different communities need to be specified. Once a partition of countries in the international trade system is defined on the basis of their localisation in a WTM and the critical gap, its modularity is evaluated according to the topology of the corresponding backbone and the partition with the highest modularity is chosen. The CGM method for the detection of spatially-based communities in WTMs then reads:

1. Set the value of $\tilde{Q} = -1$. This variable will encode the highest value of Q.
2. Increase the value of the critical gap g_c sequentially from 0 to 1. For every value:
    i. Connect all pairs of nodes (i, j) whose normalised angular distance $\tilde{d}_{a,ij} \leq g_c$.
    ii. Find all the connected components in the resulting graph.
    iii. Assign all nodes in the same connected component to the same community.
    iv. Compute the modularity Q of the partition. If $Q > \tilde{Q}$ set $Q \rightarrow \tilde{Q}$ and keep the partition.

At the end of the process, the partition with the highest modularity is kept. Notice that this method is equivalent to considering all gaps, between consecutive nodes in the circle, larger than g_c as community boundaries; however, this algorithm works also using distances instead of coordinates. This is useful because averaged distances are more reliable than single embeddings. Figures 4.11A-B illustrate the process of community detection using the CGM method. The evolution of the number of CGM communities is shown in figure 4.11C, as compared to those obtained by applying the Louvain algorithm (Blondel et al., 2008) on the topology of the backbones. In terms of modularity, figure 4.11D, the two methods coincide to an extremely high degree. However, the number of communities discovered by CGM is typically twice that of the Louvain method, since Louvain modules may integrate smaller CGM communities. Both modularity and the number of communities increase over time, reaching a maximum at the beginning of the last economic crisis around 2007, with a minor downturn afterwards.

Figure 4.11: CGM space-based communities versus Preferential Trade Agreements

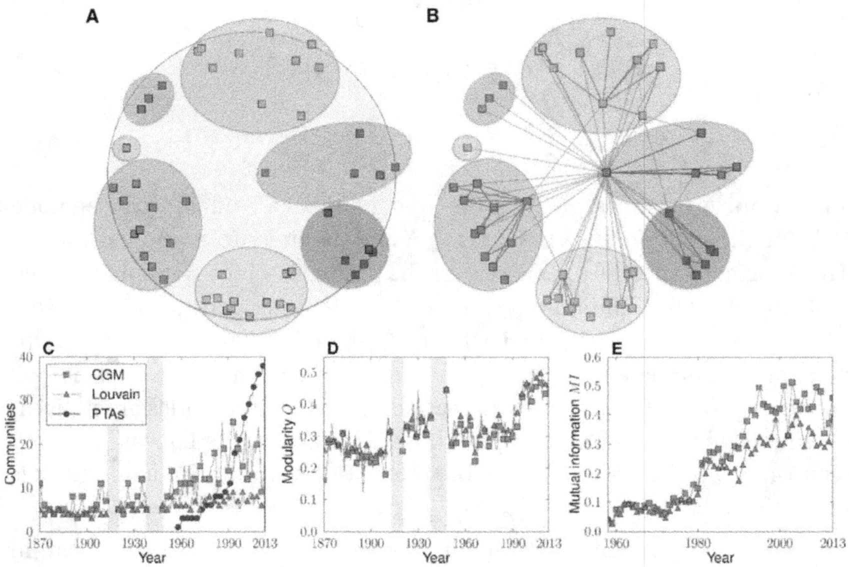

Color images of figures can be downloaded at the book's page
[URL: https://vernonpress.com/book/96]

A: Sketch illustrating the CGM method. Nodes in the hyperbolic plane are partitioned into different communities separated by large enough angular gaps, hence depending on the geometric information only. B: Once the partition is defined, the modularity *Q* is computed by comparing the number of links within the communities (purple links) to the number of links between nodes in different communities (green links). C: Evolution of the number of communities detected by the Louvain method and the CGM, along with the evolution of the number of PTAs. D: Evolution of the modularity, *Q*, for the two community detection methods. E: Mutual information between the CGM or Louvain communities and PTAs.

4.5.3 WTM communities versus PTAs

This tendency towards localism in trade space seems consistent with the proliferation, since the late 1980's, of PTAs as formal trading blocs (Krugman, 1993; Frankel, 1997), figure 4.11C. We use the WTO's Regional Trade Agreements Information System (RTA-IS) (WTO, 2015) to list all plurilateral PTAs in force in 2013 and compare them with natural CGM trade communities. To measure their similarity, we use the normalised mutual information (Cover and Thomas, 2006) (MI). The normalised mutual information of two partitions X and Y is defined as

$$MI = \frac{\sum_{y\in Y}\sum_{x\in X} p(x,y)\log\left(\frac{p(x,y)}{p(x)p(y)}\right)}{\max\{H(X),H(Y)\}} \ (4.9),$$

where $H(X) = -\sum_{x\in X} p(x)\log p(x)$ (4.10)

and $H(Y) = -\sum_{y\in Y} p(y)\log p(y)$ (4.11).

In the above formulas, $p(x,y)$ is the probability for a randomly chosen node to belong to community x in partition X and to community y in partition Y. The marginal probability $p(x)$ ($p(y)$) is the probability for a randomly chosen node to belong to community x (y) in X (Y). Thus, if two partitions X and Y are equal, $p(x,y) = p(x) = p(y)$ and MI = 1. On the other hand, if the two partitions are uncorrelated, $p(x,y) = p(x)p(y)$, the logarithm in Eq. (4.9) is null and, hence, MI = 0. Over the entire period, natural communities are noticeably more congruent with PTAs than those identified by the Louvain method, figure 4.11E. However, the overlap between PTAs and natural communities is not perfect.

This poses a question regarding the progression of barriers to trade within each PTA, which can be assessed from the evolution of the average normalised angular and hyperbolic distances— $\langle \tilde{d}_a \rangle$ and$\langle \tilde{d}_h \rangle$, respectively—between its members. We focus in PTAs with at least ten years of history—31 trading blocs in 2013—for which we find different patterns of evolution, see figure 4.12.

Both average normalised angular and hyperbolic distances remain stable over time in about half (17) of the PTAs, with $\langle \tilde{d}_a \rangle$ typically close but above the geographic value—North American Free Trade Agreement NAFTA, Central American Common Market CACM, Caribbean Community and Common Market CARICOM, Pacific Island Countries Trade Agreement PICTA, Economic Cooperation Organization ECO, and PTAs in Africa, like SADC, WAEMU, CEMAC, ECOWAS, and in Latin America LAIA. In some blocs, $\langle \tilde{d}_a \rangle$ and $\langle \tilde{d}_g \rangle$ are extremely congruent, specifically in PTAs with a worldwide composition—Protocol on Trade Negotiations PTN and Global System of Trade Preferences among Developing Countries GSTP—; or, at the other extreme, with a strong geographical orientation—Southern Common Market MERCOSUR and Commonwealth of Independent States CIS. Strikingly, the value of $\langle \tilde{d}_a \rangle$ is found to be below the geographical average in PTAs interconnecting Russia and the republics of the former Soviet Union—Russian Federation - Belarus - Kazakhstan, Eurasian Economic Community EAEC, Common Economic Zone CEZ—, which denotes communities with reduced trade barriers, even below levels expected given their geographical dispersion.

Figure 4.12: Evolution of effective and trade distances between countries in every PTA

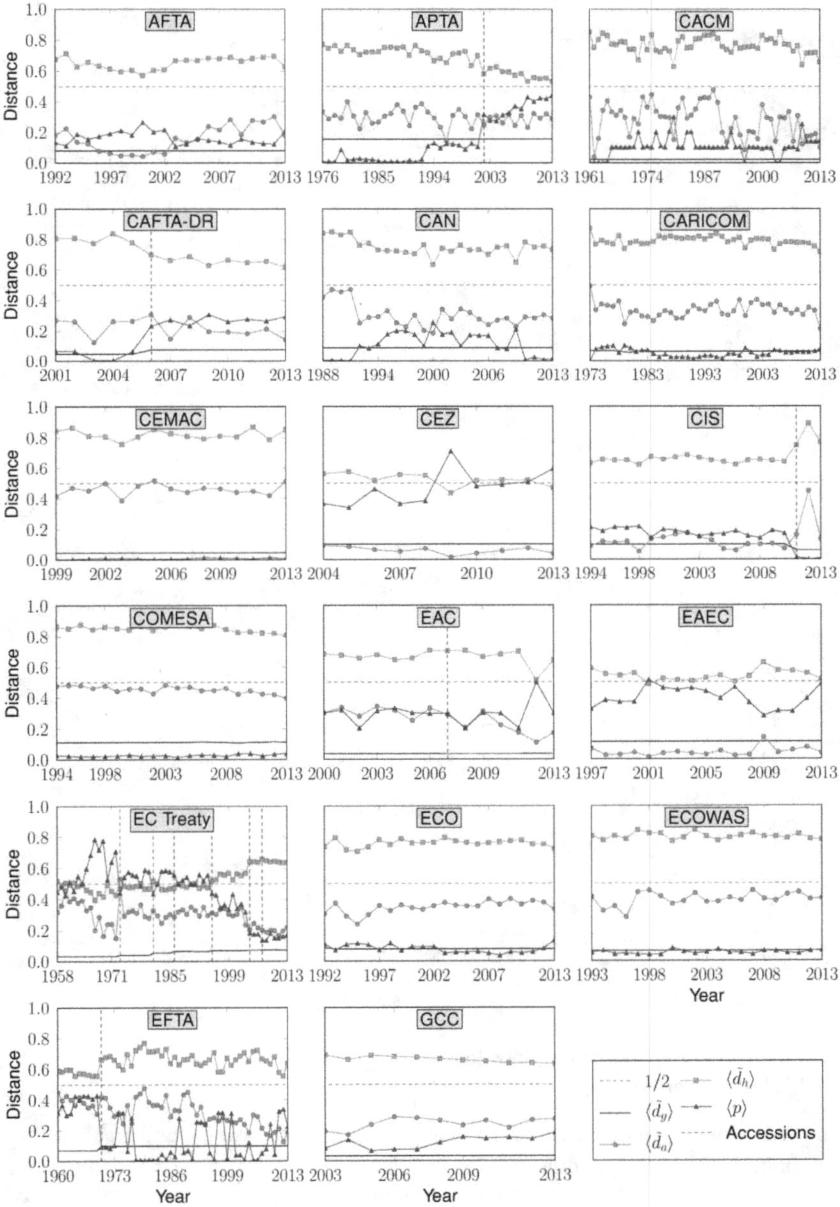

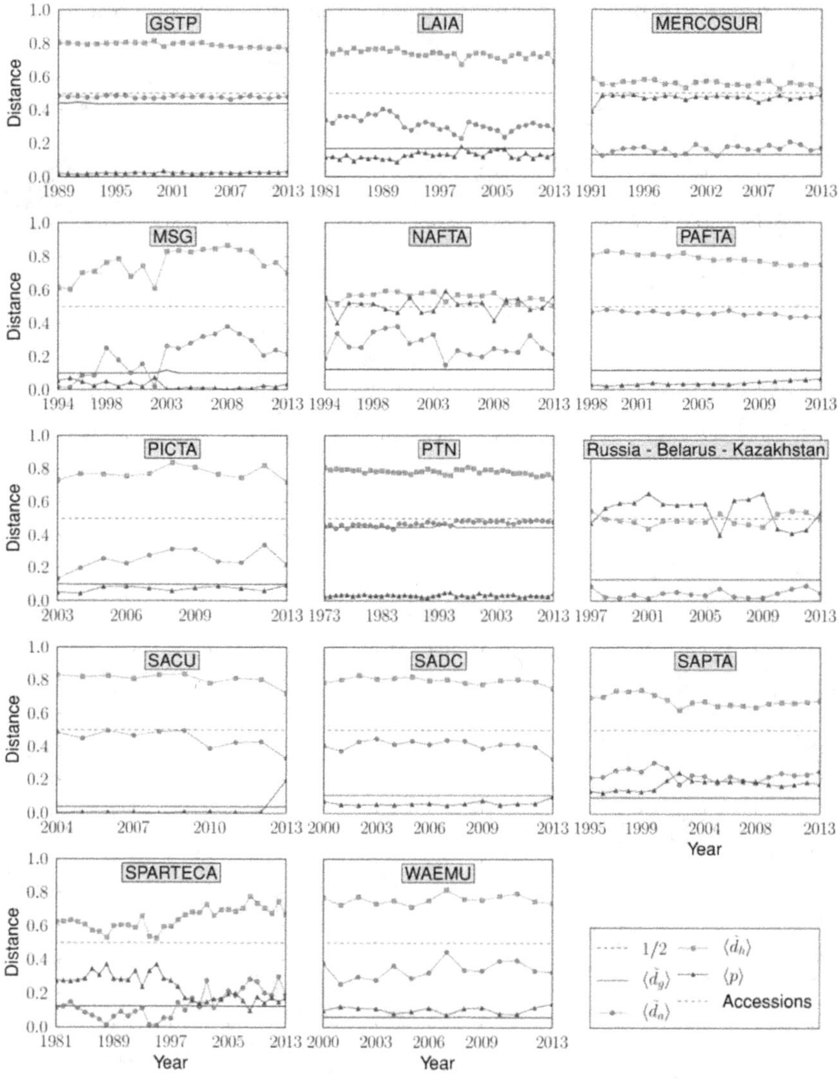

Color images of figures can be downloaded at the book's page
[URL: https://vernonpress.com/book/96]

Evolution of the average normalised distances (geographical $\tilde{d}_g$, angular $\tilde{d}_a$ and hyperbolic $\tilde{d}_h$) and average connection probabilities. The vertical dashed lines represent new accessions into the PTA. The red dashed lines correspond to the 1/2 value. Since distances are normalised with respect to the maximum possible distance in each case, it represents the average separation for both $\tilde{d}_g$ and $\tilde{d}_a$ for a uniform random distribution of points and the radius R in the hyperbolic case.

Distances in the rest of the PTAs show mixed progressions. An interesting case is the Asia-Pacific Trade Agreement (APTA), with $\tilde{d}_h$ steadily decreasing since its inception, even after the accession of China in 2002; whereas $\tilde{d}_a$ has remained fairly stable. This implies a significant increase in the internal connectivity of the PTA, which may be related to the increasing economic size of their members. In other PTAs both the average normalised angular and hyperbolic distances show a very mild decrease—Pan-Arab Free Trade Area PAFTA, Dominican Republic - Central America - United States Free Trade Agreement CAFTA-DR, Andean Community CAN, Southern African Customs Union SACU, Common Market for Eastern and Southern Africa COMESA, East African Community EAC. Finally, both distances present a slight but clear increase in some PTAs, denoting a trend towards trade diversion among their members, as in the South Pacific Regional Trade and Economic Cooperation Agreement (SPARTECA), mainly formed of small islands in the Pacific Ocean.

The European Community (EC) Treaty is the largest and most complex of all the PTAs, accounting for 23.6% of world GDP in 2013. Its evolution has moved through three different stages. The first lasted from its inception until 1972, just before the accession of Denmark, Ireland, and the UK. During this period, both angular and hyperbolic distances reduced significantly and the internal connectivity increased, which indeed indicates an important reduction of barriers to trade. The aforementioned accessions in 1973 reversed the trend, which indicates that the new members were not natural partners of the treaty before they entered the agreement. During the second stage, 1973–2003, many medium/large economies joined, but internal distances remained stable since these new countries were, de facto, natural trade partners of the treaty. Between 2003 and 2004, another transition took place with the accession of a large number of small economies, mainly in Eastern Europe. During the transition, $\langle \tilde{d}_a \rangle$ decreased significantly at the same time as $\langle \tilde{d}_h \rangle$ increased, and so the internal connectivity decreased. Before joining the EC these newly adjoined countries already had members of the EC as their main trading partners. After joining the EC, these new countries kept the same main trading partners but, due to their small size, did not increase trade with them. So, the effect has been augmented internal barriers to trade in the last decade, as the increased localisation due to the addition of small economies could not be compensated for due to the heterogeneity in economic sizes of the members.

In summary, the clear movement towards localism as a tendency to concentrate within natural trade communities only finds a moderate overlap with formal PTAs. Indeed, PTAs have not necessarily reduced barriers to trade between their members, as measured by hyperbolic and angular distances.

4.6 Extension to trade volumes

The representation of the WTW as an unweighted network, taking the interactions between pairs of elements as purely binary, turns out to be a first approximation which captures well the most basic organizing principles. Beyond this, a weighted network approach that incorporates the information about the intensity of trade relationships can greatly improve our knowledge about the international trade system. In such a weighted description, trade relationships have an associated intensity or weight ω, and so countries have associated strengths s—the sum of the weights on the links attached to them—giving the actual magnitude of aggregated imports and exports.

It has been recently discovered that the nature of weights in real complex networks is geometric as well (Allard et al., 2017). The evidence is based on the relationship between clustering, triangle inequality in the underlying space, and weights. If the weights of connections depend on the distance between the connected nodes in the underlying metric space, we expect them to be related also with the clustering properties of the connections since clustering is also a property induced by the transitivity of closeness. However, weights and clustering are known to be strongly influenced by the degrees of endpoint nodes (Barrat et al., 2004; Popovié et al., 2012; Pajevic and Plenz, 2012), which prevents from a direct detection of the metric properties of weights due to the typical heterogeneity in the degrees of nodes in real networks. Thus, to compare links on an equal footing, the weights need to be normalised as $\omega_{ij}^{norm} = \frac{\omega_{ij}}{\overline{\omega}(k_i k_j)}$, where $\overline{\omega}(k_i k_j)$ is the average weight of links as a function of the product of degrees of their endpoint nodes. By doing so, the weights are decoupled from the topology; indeed, if the links are randomly sampled in the network, $\langle \omega_{ij}^{norm} \rangle = 1$ by construction. However, if triangles are randomly sampled instead, the mean normalised weight of their connections in the WTW backbone of 2013 is $\langle \omega_{ij}^{norm} \rangle \approx 1.2$, meaning that trade channels involved in triangles tend to have larger normalised trade volumes than the average link. This result finds a very simple explanation in geometry: the closer two countries are, the higher the number of triangles their connection closes; hence, when sampling from triangles, we are biasing the sampling of trade channels towards closer pairs which, in turn, have higher trade volumes, see figure 4.13A.

Since there is a dependence of trade volumes on the hidden metric distances, the geometric network models S^1 and H^2 can be extended to a two-step gravity model capable of predicting the existence of significant trade channels along with their intensities. In the extension of the S^1 model, weights are assigned in a distance-dependent manner on top of the topology generated by the original gravity model. Apart from the expected economic sizes κ, a second hidden variable σ is associated to each country, such that $\frac{\sigma}{\kappa^{1-\alpha}}$ plays the role of economic size of countries and ensures that, once the network has been assembled, they have expected degree and strength κ and σ, respectively. This new hidden variable can be correlated with κ so that the pair (κ, σ) associated with a given country is drawn from the joint probability distribution function $\rho(\kappa, \sigma)$. The weight of an existing trade channel between two countries with hidden variables κ_i, σ_i, κ_j and σ_j, respectively, and at a metric distance $d_{a,ij}$ in the underlying S^1 circle is then given by

$$\omega_{ij} = \epsilon_{ij} \frac{\nu \cdot \left(\frac{\sigma_i}{\kappa_i^{1-\alpha}}\right) \cdot \left(\frac{\sigma_j}{\kappa_j^{1-\alpha}}\right)}{d_{a,ij}^{\alpha}}. \quad (4.12)$$

In the latter expression, $\nu > 0$ is a free parameter that controls the average strength or aggregated trade volume of countries and can always be chosen such that $\bar{s}(\sigma) = \sigma$; the new hidden variable σ can therefore be interpreted as the expected strength of a country. The parameter $\alpha \in$ dictates a trade-off between the contribution of degrees and geometry to weights. If $\alpha = 0$ weights are independent of the underlying metric space and maximally dependent on degrees, while $\alpha = 1$ implies that weights are maximally coupled to the underlying metric space with no direct contribution of the degrees. Finally, ϵ_{ij} is a noise term, a positive random variable distributed according to a gamma distribution of average $\langle \epsilon_{ij} \rangle = 1$ and with a given second moment $\langle \epsilon_{ij}^2 \rangle$.

The joint probability distribution function $\rho(\kappa, \sigma) = \rho(\kappa)\rho(\sigma|\kappa)$ controls the correlation between degrees and strengths. A deterministic relation between hidden variables σ and κ of the form $\sigma = a\kappa^{\eta}$ is observed in real complex networks (Barrat et al., 2004); (Popović et al., 2012); (Barthelemy, 2011), yielding $\bar{s}(k) \sim ak^{\eta}$. Hence, the weighted extension of the gravity model introduces new global parameters: a, η, ν, α and $\langle \epsilon_{ij}^2 \rangle$. The first two, a and η, can be directly inferred from the observed relation between strength and degree. This yields $a = 3772$ and $\eta = 1.63$ for the backbone of the WTW in 2013. The third one, ν, can be set by imposing $\bar{s}(\sigma) = \sigma$. Inferring the coupling between the weights and the metric space α and the noise parameter $\langle \epsilon_{ij}^2 \rangle$ is subtler and needs to exploit the triangle inequality in the underlying metric space. To that end, the purely geometric version of the weighted model is more convenient and obtained by using the mapping given by Eq. (4.4), such that Eq. (4.12) becomes

$$\omega_{ij} = \epsilon_{ij} \frac{\nu}{\mu^{\alpha}} \frac{\sigma_i \sigma_j}{\kappa_i \kappa_j} e^{-\frac{\alpha}{2}(x_{ij} - R)}, \quad (4.13)$$

from which we can isolate the approximate hyperbolic distance $x_{ij} \approx d_{h,ij}$ between nodes i and j. The triangle inequality, $x_{ij} + x_{jk} \geq x_{ik}$ can then be written as

$$\ln\left[\frac{\omega_{ij}\omega_{jk}}{\omega_{ik}}\left(\frac{\kappa_j}{\sigma_j}\right)^2\right] + \ln\left[\frac{\mu^\alpha}{\nu}\right] - \frac{1}{2}\alpha R \leq \ln\left[\frac{\epsilon_{ij}\epsilon_{jk}}{\epsilon_{ik}}\right]. \quad (4.14)$$

The first term on the left-hand side of this inequality is a function of the actual weights and network topology and, thus, can be empirically estimated from the data using the observed degrees and strengths as proxies for the corresponding hidden variables. The next two terms on the left-hand side have an explicit dependence on α (note that ν also depends on α). The term on the right-hand side is a noise term whose mean value is close to zero.

In synthetic weighted networks generated by the extended model, the inequality should hold approximately for any value of α in Eq. (4.14) equal to or larger than the value of α_{real} used to assign weights in the network, if the noise term is zero. Note that it may not hold exactly even when α is greater than its real value due to the inherent noise in the estimation of the hidden variables κ and σ in Eq. (4.14), as well as the global parameters μ and ν. In Eq. (4.14), α can be considered as a free parameter such that the triangle inequality violation spectrum, $TIV(\alpha)$, defined as the fraction of violations of the triangle inequality (i.e., triangles for which the left-hand side of Eq. (4.14) is positive), can be measured. Fig. 13**B** shows this curve for the WTW in 2013. In the absence of noise, $TIV(\alpha)$ should take a very small value when $\alpha \geq \alpha_{real}$ if the weighted structure of the network is congruent with the existence of an underlying metric space. In real situations, however, noise is typically present and has an impact on $TIV(\alpha)$, so we need an independent measure of the noise to infer the value of α_{real} from the spectrum $TIV(\alpha)$, provided by the square of the coefficient of variation of the strength, $CV_s^2 = \langle s^2 \rangle / \langle s \rangle^2 - 1$. It can be shown (Allard et al., 2017) that this quantity depends on both α and $\langle \epsilon_{ij}^2 \rangle$ as

$$CV_s^2\left(\alpha, \langle \epsilon_{ij}^2 \rangle\right) = \frac{\pi \langle \sigma^2/\kappa \rangle^2 I_2}{N\mu \langle \sigma \rangle^4 I_1^2} \left\langle \epsilon_{ij}^2 \right\rangle, \quad (4.15)$$

where the dependence on α is encoded in the integrals $I_1 = \int \chi^{-\alpha} p(\chi) d\chi$ and $I_2 = \int \chi^{-2\alpha} p(\chi) d\chi$. The actual value of $CV_{s,observed}^2$ can be measured from the network, so the equation $CV_s^2\left(\alpha, \langle \epsilon_{ij}^2 \rangle\right) = CV_{s,observed}^2$ defines a relation between α and $\langle \epsilon_{ij}^2 \rangle$, denoted by $\alpha^*\left(\langle \epsilon_{ij}^2 \rangle\right)$. Using the coupling between both parameters, α_{real} can be found as follows. For a given value of $\langle \epsilon_{ij}^2 \rangle \geq 1$, a synthetic network is generated with the inferred values of μ, β, ν, $\kappa_i = k_i$, $\sigma_i = a\kappa_i^\eta$ and $\alpha = \alpha^*\left(\langle \epsilon_{ij}^2 \rangle\right)$. Then, the triangle inequality violation curve of the synthetic network $TIV_{synthetic}(\alpha)$ is computed and compared to the $TIV_{real}(\alpha)$ curve of the real WTW backbone in 2013 using the χ^2 statistics. The inferred values of $\langle\epsilon_{ij}^2\rangle_{real}$ and α_{real} can thus be found by minimizing the χ^2 statistics as a function of $\langle\epsilon_{ij}^2\rangle$. This method yields $\langle\epsilon_{ij}^2\rangle_{real} = 1.3$ and $\alpha_{real} = 0.41$ in the WTW backbone of 2013, strongly suggesting a geometric origin of trade volumes. As a validation, Fig. 13**B** shows the $TIV(\alpha)$ curve given by a synthetic network, which matches the real one almost perfectly. Figures 13**C-F** also show a very good agreement between the real weighted structure of the WTW and the one generated by the model.

Figure 4.13: Weighted model versus WTW backbone in 2013

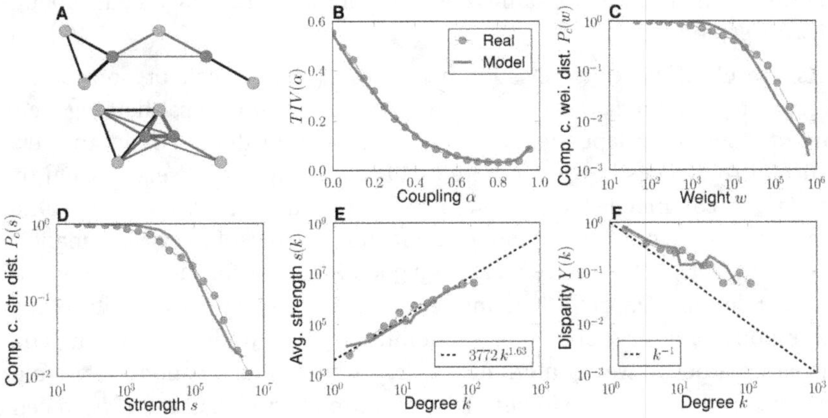

Color images of figures can be downloaded at the book's page [URL: https://vernonpress.com/book/96]

The real network is compared with a synthetic network generated with the parameters inferred from the data. A: An illustrative sketch showing the geometric origin of the relation between weight and multiplicity. In the top picture, the two blue nodes are far, so their connection has a small weight (proportional to the line thickness). In the bottom picture, the two nodes are closer, so their connection has a larger weight. Moreover, notice that nodes that are close to one of the two blue nodes are close to the other one as well, hence closing many triangles. All triangles sharing the link between the blue nodes are shown in red. B: Triangle inequality violation curve. C: Complementary cumulative distribution of trade volumes (weight). D: Complementary cumulative distribution of aggregated trade in countries (strength). E: Average aggregated trade of countries of degree k. F: Disparity of countries as a function of their degree.

4.7 Conclusions and outlook

In terms of trade, two waves of globalisation are identified in recent history corresponding to processes of decolonization and breaking of technical barriers inducing downturns in costs and time expenditures. The first wave is roughly identified from 1870 until the beginning of World War I and was related to lowered costs for transportation of materials and goods triggered by the Industrial Revolution, with steam power encouraging the expansion of railroad networks and oceanic routes and the telegraph connecting the two sides of the Atlantic. The second wave, from 1960 to the present is intimately related to the ease of the exchange of information and ideas facilitated by the Information Technology Revolution, which is causing communications costs to drop dramatically at the same time that information management capabilities are exploding.

As a result of these globalisation processes, the large-scale organization of the world economies exhibits nowadays a high level of local heterogeneity and of global interdependency at the same time. In this scenario, the relevance of trade goes beyond a mere exchange of goods and services. On the one hand, commercial trade flows are indeed highly correlated with other types of cross-country economic interactions—flow of services, financial assets, workers, etc.—and so stand as a good indicator for more general economic relations. On the other, and leaving aside technological, cultural and other noneconomic social aspects that interplay with trade, feedback mechanisms operate between international trade and other economic variables such as production, investment, debt, or currency prices. Trade plays a central role as one of the most important interaction channels between states. It can act, for instance, as a substrate for the transmission of economic policies, cycles, and shocks like the 1997 Asiatic crisis, which shows how economic perturbations originated in a single country can somehow propagate globally in the world. In a broad sense, this implies that the collapse of the barriers in human interactions allows for incidences in one part of the system to affect all the rest.

Therefore, it seems natural to analyse the international trade system from a global perspective taking into account every country and its trade relationships regardless of its size or wealth. This is in contrast to traditional analyses of international commerce that have been based on bilateral interactions. However, the entangled connectivity characterizing international trade points out to a complex system, whose properties depend on its global organization. The complex features of the international trade system are well reproduced, both at the level of trade channels and trade volumes, by a network gravity model based on a hidden metric space of trade distances as aggregated measures that bring together and integrate the different dimensions—

economic, administrative and political, geographical, and cultural—that shape world trade networks. Trade distances determine the likelihood of connections such that two countries close in the natural geometrical embedding space of WTW networks, hyperbolic space, have more chance to interact. The gravity model plus the embedding method conform the framework used to construct the World Trade Atlas 1870-2013 (García-Pérez et al., 2016b, a) that summarizes international trade history between these dates. Most importantly, as stated before by others in an interesting discussion of globalisation (Friedman, 2005; Stiglitz, 2006; Ghemawat, 2007): the world is not flat. We claim, on scientific grounds, that it is hyperbolic.

In contrast to the widespread perception that globalisation has led to a decrease in the importance of distance, we observe that countries preferentially select their significant trade partners from geographically close neighbours, in line with general statistics (Ghemawat and Altman, 2013). According to the World Trade Atlas 1870-2013, the role of trade distance has not decreased but increased over time over the last 14 decades driven by two main forces. First, we report an increased hierarchical organization related to a persistent stratification by economic size, so that not all global trade market competitors have equal opportunities. It was reported previously that elasticity with respect to distance of bilateral trade between high-income countries fell in the period 1962-1996 (Brun et al., 2005), with no trend for the group of low-income countries. The portrait that emerges from our maps is direr. Differences in trade distances are becoming more important, particularly for small economies at the bottom of the hierarchy, which are moving away from the rest of the world. The small economies are encountering more difficulties in establishing trade channels, except for those with the largest economies at the top of the hierarchy, which have more chance of becoming connected worldwide.

Second, we observe a movement towards localism—already encountered before in the context of economic geography (Krugman, 1991b; Fujita et al., 1999)—as a tendency to concentrate within natural trade communities. Interestingly, this trend seems to have been reverted since 2009, maybe as a consequence of the fast rising of China as a new commercial power and due to the effects of the economic crisis. Despite the proliferation of PTAs as formal trading blocs, we only found a moderate overlap with natural communities. Indeed, PTAs have not necessarily reduced barriers to trade between their members, as measured by hyperbolic and angular distances. These results reveal PTAs as tools that may serve purposes other than trade in economics or politics since their ambiguous consequences on the creation or steering of trade depend upon several other conditions (Krugman, 1993; Rosson III et al., 1994). In our framework, we observe that the localisation effect is entangled with that of hierarchisation; that is, with the formation of intermediate hubs that dominate well-delimited angular regions as the number of layers in the hierarchy grows. Both effects, as two sides of the same coin, may have been exacerbated by trade liberalization policies with uneven effects among non-equals (Cage and Gadenne, 2016).

Our framework can be understood as a new generation of gravity models. Classical gravity models predict the volume of flows between elements but cannot explain the observed topology of the interactions among them, as shown in works for the world trade web (Dueñas and Fagiolo, 2013b). Our contribution overcomes this limitation and offers a gravity model that can reproduce both the existence and the intensity of interactions, proving that the same underlying metric space ruling the WTW topology also shapes its weighted organisation.

In perspective, the hidden metric space weighted model and the maps of real complex systems that it enables will lead to a deeper understanding of the interplay between the structure and function of real networks and will offer insights on the impact they have on the dynamical processes they support and on their own evolutionary dynamics. Our discussion has focused on revealing, through a single historical picture, globalisation, hierarchisation, and localisation as the main forces shaping the trade space, which far from being flat is hyperbolic. The World Trade Atlas 1870-2013 can help to shed light on a number of other questions based on trade distances, for instance, those regarding the specific composition of natural communities in trade space, or it can facilitate a new approach to the analysis of the relation between trade and other economic factors.

4.8 References

Allard, A., Serrano, M. Á., García-Pérez, G. and Boguñá, M. (2017), 'The geometric nature of weights in real complex networks', Nature Communications 8, 14103.

Almog, A., Squartini, T. and Garlaschelli, D. (2015), 'A gdp-driven model for the binary and weighted structure of the international trade network', New Journal of Physics 17(1), 013009.

Anderson, J. E. and van Wincoop, E. (2004), 'Trade costs', J. Econ. Lit. 42(3), 691–751.

Baldwin, R. E. and Martin, P. (1999), Two Waves of Globalisation: Superficial Similarities, Fundamental Differences, NBER Working Paper 6904, National Bureau of Economic Research, Inc.

Barbieri, K. and Keshk, O. (2012). Correlates of War Project Trade Data Set Codebook, Version 3.0. [online] Available at http://correlatesofwar.org.

Barbieri, K., Keshk, O. M. and Pollins, B. M. (2009), 'Trading data: Evaluating our assumptions and coding rules', Conflict Management and Peace Science 26(5), 471–491.

Barrat, A., Barthélemy, M., Pastor-Satorras, R. and Vespignani, A. (2004), 'The architecture of complex weighted networks.', Proc. Natl. Acad. Sci. U. S. A. 101(11), 3747–52.

Barrat, A., Barthélemy, M. and Vespignani, A. (2008), Dynamical Processes on Complex Networks, Cambridge University Press, Cambridge.

Barthélemy, M. (2011), 'Spatial networks', Phys. Rep. 499(1-3), 1–101.

Bergstrand, J. H. (1985), 'The gravity equation in international trade: some microeconomic foundations and empirical evidence', Rev. Econ. Stat. 67(3), 474–481.

Bergstrand, J. H. and Egger, P. (2011), Gravity equations and economic frictions in the world economy, in D. Bernhofen, R. Falvey, D. Greenaway and U. Krieckemeier, eds, 'Palgrave Handbook of International Trade', Palgrave Macmillan Press.

Blondel, V. D., Guillaume, J.-L., Lambiotte, R. and ´Etienne Lefebvre (2008), 'Fast unfolding of communities in large networks', J. Stat. Mech. 2008(10), P10008.

Boguñá, M., Papadopoulos, F. and Krioukov, D. (2010), 'Sustaining the Internet with Hyperbolic Mapping', Nature Comms 1, 62.

Boguñá, M., Krioukov, D. and Claffy, K. C. (2009), 'Navigability of complex networks', Nat. Phys. 5, 74–80.

Bolt, J. and van Zanden, J. L. (2014).The Maddison Project: collaborative research on historical national accounts. [online] Available at http://www.ggdc.net/maddison/maddison-project/home.htm.

Borassi, M., Chessa, A. and Caldarelli, G. (2015), 'Hyperbolicity measures democracy in real-world networks', Phys. Rev. E 92, 032812.

Brun, J.-F., Carrère, C., Guillaumont, P. and de Melo, J. (2005), 'Has distance died? Evidence from a panel gravity model', World Bank Econ. Rev. 19, 99–120.

Cagé, J. and Gadenne, L. (2016), 'Tax revenues, development, and the fiscal cost of trade liberalization, 17922006', Working paper, The Warwick Economics Research Paper Series (TWERPS) 1132, University of Warwick.

Chase-Dunn, C., Kawano, Y. and Brewer, B. D. (2000), 'Trade globalisation since 1795: Waves of integration in the world-system', American Sociological Review 65, 77–95.

CIA (2015). The World Factbook. [online] Available at https://www.cia.gov/library/publications/the-world-factbook/.

Cohen, R. and Havlin, S. (2010), Complex Networks: Structure, Robustness And Function, Cambridge University Press.

Colizza, V., Flammini, A., Serrano, M. Á. and Vespignani, A. (2006), 'Detecting rich-club ordering in complex networks', Nat Phys 2, 110–115.

Cover, T. M. and Thomas, J. A. (2006), Elements of Information Theory, second edn, Wiley-Interscience, Hoboken, New Jersey.

COW (2012). The Correlates of War Project. [online] Available at http://www.correlatesofwar.org/.

Dorogovtsev, S. N., Goltsev, A. V. and Mendes, J. F. F. (2008), 'Critical phenomena in complex networks', Rev. Mod. Phys. 80(4), 1275–1335.

Dueñas, M. and Fagiolo, G. (2013), 'Modeling the international-trade network: a gravity approach', J. Econ. Interact Coor. 8, 155–178.

Engel, C. and Rogers, J. (1996), 'How wide is the border?', Amer. Econ. Rev. 86(5), 1112–1125.

Frankel, J. (1997), Regional Trading Blocs in the World Economic System, Institute for International Economics, Washington DC.

Frankel, J. and Rose, A. (2002), 'An estimate of the effect of common currencies on trade and income', Q. J. Econ. 117(2), 437–466.

Friedman, T. L. (2005), The world is flat: A brief history of the twenty-first century, Farrar, Straus and Giroux.

Fujita, M., Krugman, P. and Venables, A. (1999), The Spatial Economy: Cities, Regions and International Trade, MIT Press, Cambridge, MA.

García-Pérez, G., Boguñá, M., Allard, A. and Serrano, M. Á. (2016a). The World Trade Atlas 1870-2013 interactive tool. [online] Available at http://morfeo.ffn.ub.edu/wta1870-2013.

García-Pérez, G., Boguñá, M., Allard, A. and Serrano, M. Á. (2016b), 'The hidden hyperbolic geometry of international trade: World trade atlas 18702013', Scientific Reports 6, 33441.

Garlaschelli, D. and Loffredo, M. I. (2004), 'Fitness-dependent topological properties of the world trade web', Phys. Rev. Lett. 93(18), 188701.

Ghemawat, P. (2007), 'Why the world isn't flat', Foreing Policy 159, 54–60.

Ghemawat, P. and Altman, S. (2013), Depth index of globalisation 2013: And the big shift to emerging economies, Technical report, IESE, ST-310-E, 11/2013.

Gleditsch, K. S. (2002), 'Expanded trade and gdp data', J. Conflict Resolut. 46, 712–724.

Gleditsch, K. S. (2015). Kristian Skrede Gleditsch's data. [online] Available at
http://privatewww.essex.ac.uk/k˜sg/exptradegdp.html.

Herfindahl, O. C. (1959), Copper Costs and Prices: 1870-1957, John Hopkins University Press, Baltimore, MD, USA.

Hirschman, A. O. (1964), 'The paternity of an index', American Economic Review 54, 761– 762.

IMF (2015). International Monetary Fund, Direction of Trade Statistics (DOTS). [online] Available at http://www.imf.org/en/Data.

Johnston, L. and Williamson, S. H. (2015). 'What Was the U.S. GDP Then?', Measuring Worth. [online] Available at http://www.measuringworth.org/usgdp/.

Krioukov, D., Papadopoulos, F., Kitsak, M., Vahdat, A. and Boguñá, M. (2010), 'Hyperbolic geometry of complex networks', Phys. Rev. E 82, 036106.

Krioukov, D., Papadopoulos, F., Vahdat, A. and Boguñá, M. (2009), 'Curvature and temperature of complex networks', Phys. Rev. E 80, 035101.

Krugman, P. (1991a), Geography and Trade, MIT Press, Cambridge, MA.

Krugman, P. (1993), Regionalism versus multilateralism: analytical notes, in J. J. de Melo and A. Panagariya, eds, 'New Dimensions in Regional Integration', Cambridge University Press, Cambridge, pp. 58–89.

Krugman, P. R. (1991b), Geography and Trade, MIT Press, Cambridge, USA.

Krugman, P. R. (1995), 'Growing world trade: Causes and consequences', Brookings Papers on Economic Activity 1995(1), 327–377.

Newman, M. (2010), Networks: An Introduction, Oxford University Press, Inc., New York, NY, USA.

Newman, M. E. J. (2006), 'Modularity and community structure in networks', Proc. Natl. Acad. Sci. USA 103, 8577–8582.

Pajevic, S. and Plenz, D. (2012), 'The organization of strong links in complex networks', Nat. Phys. 8, 429–436.

Papadopoulos, F., Kitsak, M., Serrano, M. Á., Boguñá, M. and Krioukov, D. (2012), 'Popularity versus similarity in growing networks', Nature 489(7417), 537–540.

Popović, M., Štefančić, H. and Zlatić, V. (2012), 'Geometric Origin of Scaling in Large Traffic Networks', Phys. Rev. Lett. 109, 208701.

ROC (2015). ROC's Bureau of Foreign Trade. [online] Available at http://www.trade.gov.tw/English/.

Rosson III, C. P., Runge, C. F. and Hathaway, D. E. (1994), International trade agreements, in M. Hallberg, R. Sptize and D. Ray, eds, 'Food, Agriculture, and Rural Policy into the Twenty-First Century', Westview Press.

Schweitzer, F., Fagiolo, G., Sornette, D., Vega-Redondo, F., Vespignani, A. and White, D. R. (2009), 'Economic networks: The new challenges', Science 325(5939), 422–425.

Serrano, M. Á. (2007), 'Phase transition in the globalisation of trade', J. Stat. Mech. L01002.

Serrano, M. Á. (2008), 'Rich-club vs rich-multipolarization phenomena in weighted networks', Phys. Rev. E 78, 026101.

Serrano, M. Á. and Boguñá, M. (2003), 'Topology of the world trade web', Phys. Rev. E 68, 015101.

Serrano, M. Á., Boguñá, M. and Sagués, F. (2012), 'Uncovering the hidden geometry behind metabolic networks', Mol. BioSyst. 8, 843–850.

Serrano, M. Á., Boguñá, M. and Vespignani, A. (2007a), 'Patterns of dominant flows in the world trade web', J. Econ. Interact. Coord. 2(2), 111–124.

Serrano, M. Á., Boguñá, M. and Vespignani, A. (2007b), 'Patterns of dominant flows in the world trade web', Journal of Economic Interaction and Coordination 2(2), 111–124.

Serrano, M. Á., Boguñá, M. and Vespignani, A. (2009), 'Extracting the mutiscale backbone of complex weighted networks', Proc. Natl. Acad. Sci. USA 106, 6483–6488.

Serrano, M. Á., Garlaschelli, D., Boguñá, M. and Loffredo, M. (2010), The world trade web: Structure, evolution and modeling, in G. Caldarelli, ed., 'Complex Networks', Encyclopedia of Life Support Systems (EOLSS), Eolss Publishers, Oxford, UK.

Serrano, M. Á., Krioukov, D. and Boguñá, M. (2011), 'Percolation in self-similar networks', Phys. Rev. Lett. 106, 048701.

Serrano, M. Á., Krioukov, D. and Boguñá, M. (2008), 'Self-similarity of complex networks and hidden metric spaces', Phys. Rev. Lett. 100, 078701.

Squartini, T. and Garlaschelli, D. (2014), Jan tinbergen's legacy for economic networks: From the gravity model to quantum statistics, in F. Abergel, H. Aoyama, K. B. Chakrabarti, A. Chakraborti and A. Ghosh, eds, 'Econophysics of Agent-Based Models', Springer International Publishing, Cham, pp. 161–186.

Stiglitz, J. E. (2006), Making globalisation work, W. W. Norton & Company, New York, London.

Tinbergen, J. (1962), Shaping the World Economy: Suggestions for An International Economic Policy, The Twentieth Century Fund, New York.

UN (2015). United Nations Commodity Trade Statistics Database (UN COMTRADE). [online] Available at https://comtrade.un.org/db/.

WB (2015). The World Bank open data. [online] Available at http://data.worldbank.org/.

WTO (2015). World Trade Organization, Regional Trade Agreements Information System (RTA-IS), [online] Available at http://rtais.wto.org/UI/PublicMaintainRTAHome.aspx.

5.

Global and local centrality of emerging countries in the world trade network

Luca De Benedictis and Lucia Tajoli

Data: International trade data from UN Comtrade and BACI-CEPII database
Software: R (igraph, intergraph, sna, rms, standardize, mfx, MASS, erer)

5.1 Introduction: Hubs and Satellites

Many changes characterized the world trading system in the past decades. A very relevant and much discussed one concerns the role of the so-called "emerging countries." In general terms, emerging countries are a group of developing countries that attracted much attention by economists and investors because of their rapidly expanding economies. There is no consensus on the exact definition of the term, and the countries which are supposed to be in the process of emergence are often referred to as middle-low income countries under rapid transformation by the IMF World Economic Outlook, or rapidly growing countries (in terms of GDP) by the World Economic Forum, or countries with increasing market shares in world exports by the European Central Bank, or reference is made to some other economic characteristic. One of the reasons for the difficulty in pinning down an exact definition is that emerging countries display quite different characteristics and their economies followed separate paths (Jain, 2006, Aggarwal and Goodell, 2008). In this work, we want to look at emerging countries considering, in particular, their position in the world trading system and comparing their role within such a system.

To obtain a broad and heterogeneous group of emerging countries, among the many possible and evolving classifications (see Section 5.2), in this work we have chosen to follow the list by Kearney (2012), including 27 countries obtained combining various criteria, also used by some other classifications. The countries are Argentina, Brazil, Czech Republic, Chile, China, Colombia, Egypt, Hungary, India, Indonesia, Israel, Jordan, Malaysia, Morocco, Mexico, Pakistan, Peru, Philippines, Poland, Russia, South Africa, South Korea, Taiwan, Thailand, Turkey, United Arab Emirates and Venezuela.[1] This is indeed a miscellaneous group under many perspectives: these countries are scattered in all continents, they are quite different in economic size and population, they present different levels of development, different models of specialization and they followed uneven growth paths. Certainly, they are playing an increasingly important role in changing the patterns of international trade (see Hanson, 2012, Iapadre and Tajoli, 2014). Among them, we will particularly focus our analysis on two cases, the one of China and the one of Mexico. They followed a different trajectory that, according to us, is quite paradigmatic in interpreting the role of emerging countries in world trade. China rises to a hub position, certainly at the regional level and for some specific manufacturing sectors, but also globally to a certain extent. Mexico became the satellite of the US economy. Hubs and Satellites seem the potential strategies for all other emerging countries, exploiting the advantages captured by the notions of degree centrality (a high number of trade partners) and eigenvector centrality (links to the most connected countries of the world, i.e., trade with the most "important" countries).[2]

5.1.1 The evolution of the world trade network

In the past decades, the world trading system in itself has undergone a number of transformations that also involved emerging countries. The number of countries with a relevant role in world trade increased (De Benedictis and Tajoli, 2011), and we can also observe an increased heterogeneity of the important traders, that appear to be at very different stages of development. Finally, trade in commodities, while still important, is by far outpaced by trade in more complex goods. This phenomenon is associated with an increasing share of trade due to intermediate inputs and semi-finished goods, as international fragmentation of production and global value chains have become widespread (Grossman and Rossi-Hansberg, 2008, Johnson and Noguera, 2012, Baldwin and Lopez-Gonzalez, 2015).

These transformations give rise to a changing World Trade Network (WTN). As observed, the density of the WTN (measured by the number of links in the network over the maximum possible number of links) has been growing over time (De Benedictis and Tajoli, 2011, De Benedictis et al., 2014), even if also in

[1] With respect to other classifications the one by Kearney (2012) includes, in addition to the usual suspects, some oil producing countries such as the United Arab Emirates and Venezuela, some African countries such Egypt, Morocco and South Africa, a few OECD countries, and Taiwan.

[2] See section 5.3.2 for the exact definition of different centralities.

this context it is visible the trade shock that followed the international financial crisis.

In a directed network, like the one considered here, density is formally defined as $\gamma = \frac{m}{m_{max}} \equiv \frac{m}{n(n-1)}$, where m is the number of observed arcs in the network, while n is the number of nodes. Among the many properties of the density, two are particularly handy, in the present context: the first one is that being a measure bounded between 0 and 1 it can be interpreted in a probabilistic way; the second one is that it can be decomposed among the different contributions of countries or of group of countries to the overall density.

This decomposition is presented in figure 5.1, where γ - the density of the WTN - is shown split in three time series, one for each group of countries analysed. The overall density γ is rising, with a decreasing slope: the WTN is becoming more connected, as reported by many studies in recent years (Fagiolo et al., 2008, Bhattacharya et al., 2008, Krapohl and Fink, 2013). More specifically, in 1995 the density of the overall trade network was 0.53[3], meaning that two countries picked at random had 53 percent of probability of sharing a common link. In 2010 that probability rose to 0.69, after a peak of 0.70 in 2008 and a sudden drop in the aftermath of the financial crisis.

Splitting the total number of countries into three groups - OECD countries, Emerging countries and a residual category that, lacking a better alternative, we call Others, including Less Developed Countries, Oil producing countries and the rest – we can trace the dynamics of the corresponding sub-densities. During the years between 1995 and 2010, trade links involving Emerging countries were contributing already in a substantial manner to overall density. In 1995, the overall density of 0.53 was due to links involving Emerging countries up to 0.11, as $\gamma^E = \frac{m^E_{1995}}{n(n-1)} = 0.11$, while links involving OECD countries contributed in a similar way for an additional 0.12 and the much larger group of Others made up the remaining 0.30.

The dynamics of the two time series associated with OECD and Emerging countries slowly diverges, pointing to the m_{max} of each group.[4] As for OECD countries, many Emerging countries were already trading with the majority of

[3] The formula of the density in this case $\gamma_{1995} = \frac{m_{1995}}{n(n-1)} = \frac{7553+18666+7301}{178\times177} \equiv 0.53 \equiv 0.11 + 0.30 + 0.12 \equiv \gamma^E_{1995} + \gamma^O_{1995} + \gamma^D_{1995}$; where E stands for Emerging, O stands for Others and D stands for OECD countries.

[4] In the case of Emerging countries $m^E_{max} = \frac{27\times177}{178\times177} = 0.15$, while for OECD countries is $m^D_{max} = 0.14$ and for Others is $m^O_{max} = 0.7$.

possible trading partners in 1995. In facts, the large bulk of the increase in the density of the trade network, between 1995 and 2010, can be attributed to the growing connectivity of the residual category of Others (see figure 5.1). The same group is the one the most affected by the trade effect of the financial crisis, with the Emerging countries showing only a modest negative blip, and OECD countries remaining basically unaffected.

The level of the contribution of each one of the three groups of countries depends, of course, by the numerosity of each group. While the residual category is composed of 125 countries, the OECD countries in our sample set are 26, while the Emerging countries are 27. With a sample of 178 countries, it is not a surprise that the group that contributes the most to the overall density is the one of Others. To make evident why that group is also shaping the dynamics of γ it is convenient to calculate the average degree of each group. In 1995 the average indegree of OECD countries was 160.39: on average an OECD country was importing from a little bit more than 160 country trade partners, over a maximum of 177. The standard deviation was 16.03 and the minimum value was corresponding to Iceland, importing only from 106 trade partners. The statistics on the outdegree are similar for the OECD countries in 1995, showing average intensive trade surplus. On average they were exporting to 168 countries, with a standard deviation of 17.86 and with Iceland exporting to 96 country trade partners. In fifteen years both averages increased, to 168.43 and 173.35 with several OECD countries trading with 177 trade partners, and variances decreasing to 11.26 and 8.1, showing both a mean convergence towards the highest levels of connectivity and a reduction in variance (Barro, 1991, Rodrik, 2012, Acemoglu, 2008)

Figure 5.1: Density of the World Trade Network

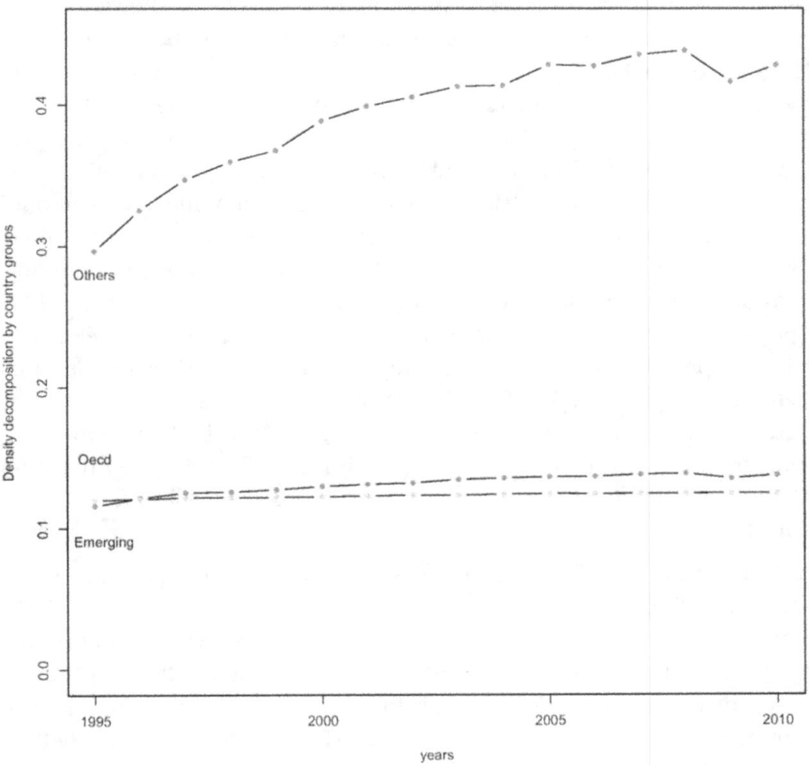

Color images of figures can be downloaded at the book's page
[URL: https://vernonpress.com/book/96]

Source: Authors' elaboration on Comtrade database.

In 1995, the group of Others had an average indegree of 74.94, with a standard deviation of 30.52 (Micronesia was importing from 18 countries, while Hong Kong was from 152 countries), an average outdegree of 70.89, with a standard deviation of 31.55 (with the same two countries exporting to 9 and 198 trade partners), and an average intensive trade deficit. In 2010, the countries in the Others group moved to an average indegree of 106.68 and an average outdegree of 104.09, with the standard deviations slightly increasing to 31.35 and 36.22, respectively, with no σ convergence whatsoever.

The average indegree of Emerging countries in 1995 was 128.85, lower than the one of OECD countries but higher than the one of Others. The in-degree standard deviation was 28.09, comparable to one of the groups of Others. The average outdegree was 141.56, with a very similar outdegree standard deviation of 28.82, showing an average intensive trade surplus. In fifteen years, the group of Emerging countries, also in terms of connectivity showed a high speed of both β and σ convergence. Average indegree and outdegree moved to 156.93 and 165.04, respectively; indegree and outdegree standard deviations decreased to 16.98 and 15.88. Many Emerging countries reached the maximum possible level of connectivity: Brazil, the Czech Republic, Indonesia, India, South Korea, Malaysia, Pakistan, Poland, the Russian Federation, Thailand, Turkey and South Africa, all have both a level of indegree and outdegree higher than the mean value for Emerging countries, but quite similar to the one of the average OECD country. Mexico and China are also among this group. China was fairly connected in 1995, already; with a level of indegree of 160 and a level of outdegree of 176, that reached the level of 176 and 177, respectively, in 2010. Mexico was a follower in 1995, with a level of indegree of 152 and a level of outdegree of 155. It moved fast in terms of indegree, reaching a level of 176 in 2010, but lagged a little bit behind in terms of outdegree, with a level of 170. In spite of this little difference, their trajectories look quite similar, at least in terms of the indicators used so far, degrees and density.

The transformations of the WTN involve much more than a changing density or the distribution of average degree. The overall structure of the WTN changed in the past decades in terms of centralization, clusterisation and hierarchy, and the strength of connections, shifting the relative position of many countries. In this work, the aim is to assess the position of countries at an intermediate level of development in the WTN in order to assess whether they are truly "emerging" within the system and they occupy central positions so to affect the overall connectivity of the WTN. Furthermore, we assess how the position in the WTN of countries is related to their economic changes, using Mexico and China as examples of satellites and hubs among emerging economies.

5.2 Which countries are emerging?

The term emerging countries or emerging economies is normally used to identify a group of countries with an intermediate level of development whose role in the international markets became much more relevant and visible in the recent past. As mentioned, it is not easy to single out the members of this group, as there is no clear-cut consensus on the definition of "emerging." The term initially become widespread especially in the financial literature, usually referring to "emerging markets." In this field of analysis, the links between the financial markets of the advanced and emerging countries have been highlighted to understand to what extent the economic performance of this latter group of countries is exposed to foreign shocks and to the business cycle of the rest of world (Devereux and Mendoza, 2006, Kose et al., 2006, Aggarwal and Goodell, 2008).

But emerging countries have been analysed also from different perspectives and the existing literature provides similar but not overlapping criteria to identify emerging countries: middle-low income countries under rapid transformation, rapidly growing countries in terms of GDP, countries with increasing market shares in world export. Vercueil (2012) proposes a definition of emerging economies that requires applying simultaneously these three criteria, saying that emerging economies display an intermediate level of per capita income, and they are undergoing a process of economic and institutional transformation that generates a high rate of economic growth and increased participation to the world trading system. Applying this definition, there are about fifty or sixty countries that can be defined as emerging. Still, there is no general consensus on the list of countries belonging to this group. The International Monetary Fund in its official publications often refers to "emerging countries," but its definition of this group is not clear-cut.[5] The World Bank explicitly states that it does not use this type of groupings, but it only groups countries by per capita income levels.

Here we want to highlight the role of emerging countries in participating to the transformation of the structure of the trading system, as shown for example by Hanson (2012) and Iapadre and Tajoli (2014). Therefore, we have chosen here to identify as emerging countries the ones listed by Kearney (2012), because this group includes the middle economies mentioned by Hanson (2012) as well as some other important trader with different characteristics. We will focus on dyadic relations among countries, especially on their trade outcomes, starting by considering their market shares, even if we are aware that this is not the only criterion that applies.

5.2.1 The changing role of emerging countries in world trade

According to the calculations by Hanson (2012), using data similar to the one we will shortly report about, since the early 1990s, low- and middle-income economies more than doubled their total share of world exports: the 15 largest middle-income countries had an average annual export growth of 8 per-

[5] On the IMF website it is stated that "the main criteria used by the IMF World Economic Outlook to classify the world into advanced economies and emerging market and developing economies are (1) per capita income level averaged over a number of years, (2) export diversification, and (3) degree of integration into the global financial system [...] Note, however, that these are not the only factors considered in deciding the classification of countries [...] This classification is not based on strict criteria, economic or otherwise, and it has evolved over time."

cent. In particular, between 1992 and 2008, average annual growth in exports was 18 percent in China and 14 percent in India. In the analysis by Iapadre and Tajoli (2014), using a network framework, already in 1995, the so-called BRICs (Brazil, Russia, India, and China, the largest among the emerging economies) appeared well connected and central in the system in terms of degree centrality (with the exception of Russia). All the BRICs catch-up considerably in terms of the number of their connections in the past decade. But that work highlights that with respect to more complex centrality measures, such as eigenvector centrality, the position of the BRICs was much weaker. Even if China has an export market share higher than the USA since 2007, in 2011 its total eigenvector centrality was half of USA's, in spite of an impressive growth over time of this indicator.[6] Here we want to discuss this evidence taking a long run perspective, focusing on two specific years 1995 and 2010, later on.

Figure 5.2: International trade market shares

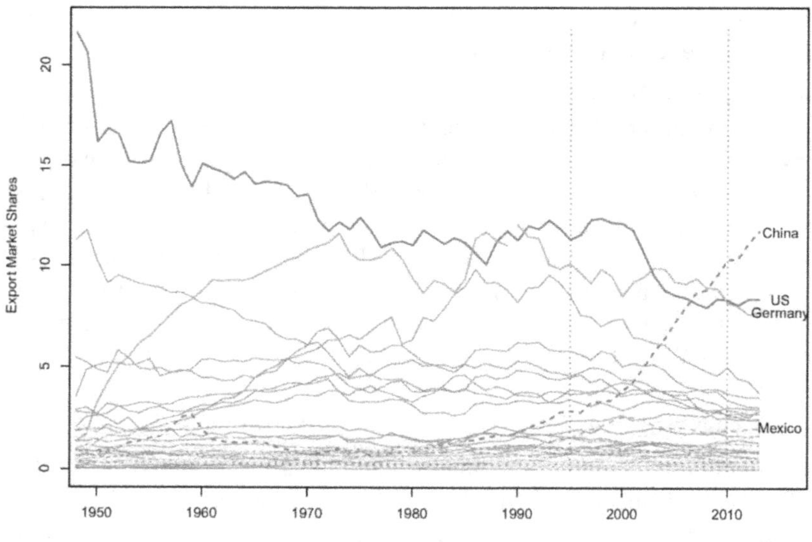

Color images of figures can be downloaded at the book's page [URL: https://vernonpress.com/book/96]

Source: Authors' elaboration on UNCTAD database

[6] A significant improvement is recorded also for India and Brazil, but both countries are still far from the Chinese position in the global scenario. See Iapadre and Tajoli (2014) on that.

In figure 5.2, using historical data on aggregate exports collected by UNCTAD, we are able to plot the long-term dynamics of international trade market shares of each one of the 178 countries in our dataset. Highlighting the evolution of market shares of the US, Germany, Mexico, and China helps us tracing the general trend of OECD countries (shown by continuous lines in figure 5.2), on the one side, and Emerging countries (dotted lines), on the other, since the 1950s.

The US was the leading country, in terms of world trade market share, during the years immediately after the Second World War. With a market share above 20%, they dominated international markets. The negative US trend that marks the period between the 1950s and the second half of the 1980s is almost specular to the one of Germany. From an export market share of less than 2%, Germany rapidly rose at a level around 10% in the 1960s and reached a peak around 12% at the beginning of the 1960s. This is a period of catching-up among OECD countries. The dominant actors of the post-War period, such as the US and the UK, reduce their relative position in favour of rising countries such as Germany, France, Italy and, especially, Japan. All these catching-up OECD countries share an inverted-U long-run trend, reaching its maximum at the end of the 1980s and beginning of the 1990s.

The rebalancing of world trade takes a different direction after the 1980s. The group of Emerging countries, characterized by a level of export market share around 1% in the 1950s, recovered a little in the first place but then as a group, with only a few exceptions, they reduced their market shares in the 1960's, as they cut their colonial ties and many of them turned toward a more autarchic development policy. After a couple of decades of full dominance of advanced countries in world trade, toward the end of the 1980s, market shares of emerging countries begin to grow, and by the beginning of the new millennium a dramatic change in the distribution of market shares has occurred, and it keeps going. In our period of observation, the striking feature is the growth of China's market share, whose trend started rising in the 1980s and has become steeper in the new millennium. A number of other emerging countries display a significant change in their market shares, even if not comparable to China. Mexico is one of those cases.

5.2.2 Two cases: China and Mexico

As mentioned, we want to consider the cases of China and Mexico as paradigmatic of different paths followed in developing the countries' export position.

A key feature of emerging economies in the high growth rate of their GDP and their exports. Table 5.1 presents a comparison of GDP growth rates over the period 1995-2010.

Table 5.1: GDP growth rates in 5-year periods

	1995 – 1999	2000 – 2005	2006 – 2010
World	5.34%	41.27%	28.46%
Emerging countries	6.72%	61.85%	69.72%
China	48.93%	88.71%	121.67%
Mexico	68.55%	26.72%	8.89%

Source: Authors' elaboration on World Bank database.

As expected, emerging countries grew at a rate significantly higher than the one recorded for the world average over the entire period. The GDP growth rate accelerated dramatically in the new millennium, and it further increased between 2006 and 2010, when the world economy slowed down because of the international financial crisis. But as the data suggest, the path was quite different from country to country. Mexico displayed a very high GDP growth rate in the late 1990s, earlier than many other Emerging countries, right after joining the North America Free Trade Agreement that fostered its trade with the US. In that period, Mexico consolidates its position as a crucial production and assembly platform for many US manufacturing firms, and its export growth was spurred also by the country participation to the North American production chains, increasing its export market share to 2.57% in 2000, more than double with respect to ten years earlier. In the early 2000s, the growth of the Mexican economy was still strong, but lower than the world average and much lower than the growth recorded by the Emerging countries, while at the same time its export share was flattening out. From 2006 to 2010, Mexico, with strong links to the U.S. economy and hardly hit by the crisis, slowed down well below its previous records, even if maintaining or even slightly increasing its export share.

China's growth was remarkable already in the late 1990s, but it continued to accelerate even in the last time span observed here, like other Asian countries, more than doubling its GDP in a few years. At the same time, it kept increasing its export share on world markets. Even if starting with an export market share very similar to Mexico in the late 1980s, China expanded rapidly from the 1990s, with an acceleration after 2001, following its entrance in the WTO, and reaching by 2010 a world market share over 10%. Given that China already had a high outdegree in the late 1990s, the impact of joining the WTO was mainly on its out strength (i.e., its export volumes) and on its incoming trade links. Also for China, like for Mexico, it seems that joining a trade agreement had a sharp impact on its trade, even if for China this was a global multilateral agreement rather than a regional one.[7] China's export as well was helped by the participation of its industries to international production chains, but China's production linkages were also quite global rather than regional, being deeply involved in the production and assembly of consumers' goods commercialized by American and European multinational enterprises.

We will see that these differences are apparent also in the network position of these countries.

5.3 Emerging countries' position in the World Trade Network

The traditional descriptive empirical analysis put forward so far lacks two elements, which are crucial in understanding the changes that occurred in the 1980s and the 1990s in world trade, and characterize the recent evolution of the trade system: (a) how much are the changes occurring in one country related to other countries? (b) Have those changes had a systemic effect on the structure of international trade nowadays?

To answer these questions, we expand the use of Network Analysis tools to describe the level of connectivity among countries or different group of countries. We focus just on two sample years 1995 and 2010, the ones depicted in figure 5.2 by the two grey vertical dotted lines on the right. A time in which Emerging countries were taking off and were accelerating their participation in World markets, like China, or were falling back and then stabilizing their position, like Mexico.

5.3.1 Visualization

In order to examine the structure and evolution of the WTN, we move from aggregate trade date to bilateral trade data. We use the UN Comtrade / BACI-CEPII database (Gaulier and Zignago, 2010), reporting bilateral trade flows measured in U.S. dollars among 178 countries, allowing to obtain a weighted directed network for the two years 1995 and 2010. As in De Benedictis et al. (2014) and Zhou et al. (2016), to visualize the WTN we need to sparsify the Trade Matrix to reduce the trade density that impedes any meaningful visualization. We operate a two-steps procedure to select the information contained in the 178×178 Weighted Trade Matrix: (a) for every country we rank export flows in a descending order; (b) for every obtained number, we substi-

---

[7] On the impact of trade agreements on the structure of connections of countries see Iapadre and Tajoli (2014) and Piccardi and Tajoli (2015).

tute the higher export flows with a 1 and all the remaining value (also the missing values and the zeros) with a 0. The resulting Trade Matrix is binary and includes trade relations only with the two major exporting international markets for every country. Isolates are ruled out by construction.

For the case of the WTN in 1995, this procedure transforms the weighted network $\mathcal{G}_{1995} = (\mathcal{V}_{1995}, \mathcal{L}_{1995}) = (178{,}16760)$ into the binary network $\mathcal{G}^*_{1995} = (\mathcal{V}^*_{1995}, \mathcal{L}^*_{1995}) = (178{,}356)$ where $\mathcal{V}$ and $\mathcal{L}$ represent the number of nodes and the number of links respectively). The reduction in the number of arcs is substantial, but the selection procedure allows the major arcs from each country to determine the resulting visualization. Since those arcs account for more than 60% of total world trade in 1995, the cost of losing some information is compensated by the possibility of visualizing the bulk of the structure of trade flows. The case of the WTN in 2010 is analogous: the procedure transforms the weighted network $\mathcal{G}_{2010} = (178, 21766)$ into the binary network $\mathcal{G}^*_{2010} = (178, 356)$.

The resulting visualization is plotted in figure 5.3, with the 1995 WTN plotted in the left pane and the 2010 WTN plotted in the right one. Country-node labels are the ISO3 country codes. Whether the outdegree of each node is fixed to two, the size of the circle associated with each country is proportional to the indegrees, which are highly heterogeneous. Different colours correspond to different country groups: OECD (yellow), Emerging (red) and Others (grey). Finally, the position of a country in the resulting topological space depends on the influence exerted by all other countries, both the ones directly connected to the country under scrutiny and the ones which are not directly connected to it. The location of a node is, therefore, *relative* to the position of all other nodes.

The algorithm that generates the networks in figure 5.3 tends to bring together connected nodes, putting them in the same area of the topological space, while disconnected nodes are put far apart. Nodes that are highly connected (due to the high number of receiving links) tend to be at the centre of the network, the ones that are not, tend to be placed at the periphery.

Figure 5.3: The World Trade Network in 1995 and 2010

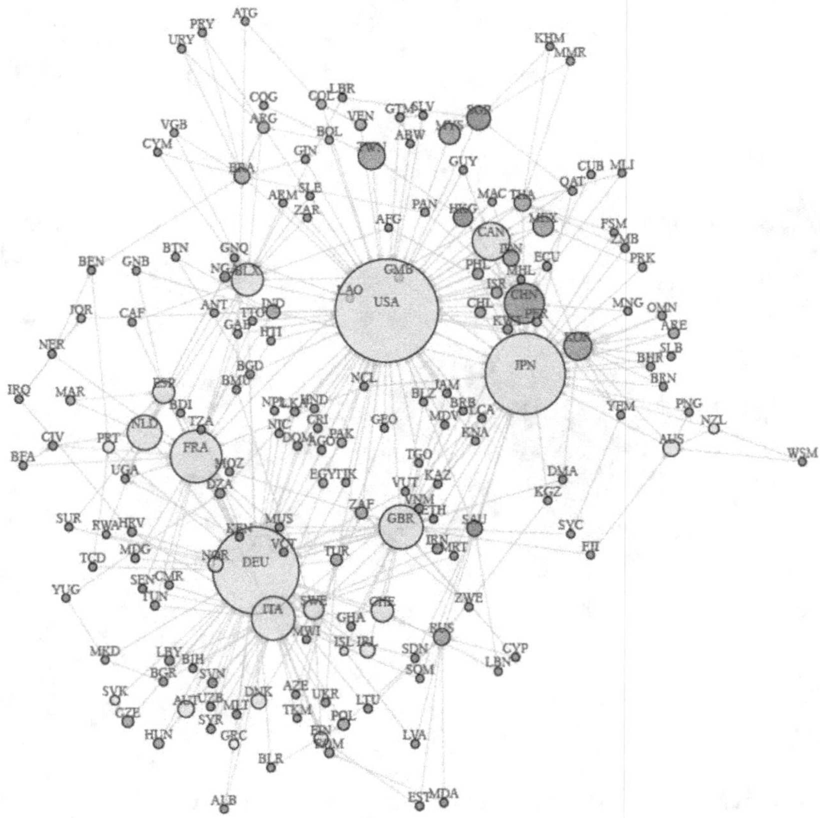

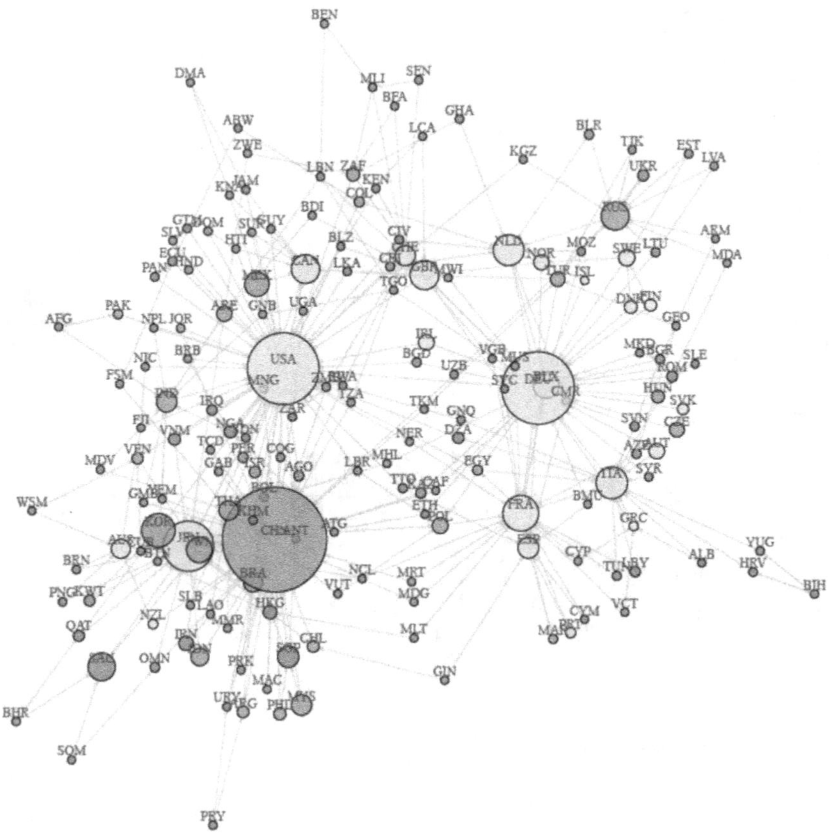

Color images of figures can be downloaded at the book's page
[URL: https://vernonpress.com/book/96]

Source: Authors' elaboration on Comtrade database. The 1995 WTN is plotted on the left, while the 2010 WTN is plotted on the right. Country labels are the Iso3 country codes. For each country, only the export flows toward the first and second main trade partner are considered. Weights of trade flows are disregarded in determining the position of nodes. The size of the circle associated with each country is proportional to indegrees. Different colours correspond to different country groups: OECD (yellow), Emerging (red) and Others (grey). The algorithm used for the visualization is the traditional Fruchterman and Reingold (1991) algorithm.

In 1995, the OECD are well placed at the core of the network[8]; they show the higher dimension in terms of indegree, and a bi-polar structure with one cluster of countries gravitating around the main European economies, and a second cluster gravitating around North America and Japan. The position of Emerging countries replicates the same structure, with Asian and Latin American countries close to Japan and the US and Canada, and transition economies close to European countries. African countries are linked to their former colonial rulers, and India and Pakistan placed in intermediate positions. Countries pertaining to the group of Other are not neatly separated from the Emerging countries, and a clear hierarchical structure is not really evident.

In 2010, the structure of the WTN changed, as the bipolarity gave rise to a three-polar structure, with China, the US, and Germany playing a pivotal role. China is now a major world trade partner and a regional hub, but the star structure is still more evident for Germany and the US. Mexico, on the other side, has increased its proximity to the US and it is now in its close orbit. Overall, rather than a core-periphery conformation, there seems to be a multi-hub-and-satellites structure, with the Emerging countries assuming an intermediate position, and other developing countries at the periphery, which has become thinner.[9]

The visualization of the WTN shows some elements of the structure of the network and of the relative position of countries but needs to be integrated by less subjective statistical analysis.[10]

5.3.2 Network statistics: Centrality

The position of countries can be asserted through the use of local and global centrality measures, as in De Benedictis et al. (2014).

The network visualization of figure 5.3 is based on the information included in $\mathcal{G}_t^* = (\mathcal{V}_t^*, \mathcal{L}_t^*)$, for $t = 1995; 2010$, where $\mathcal{L}_t^*$ is binary- reporting the existence ($\mathcal{L}_{ijt}^* = 1$) or non-existence ($\mathcal{L}_{ijt}^* = 0$) of a trade link – and $\mathcal{L}_t^* \ll \mathcal{L}_t$. In the calculus of the relative position of nodes we need to exploit all the information included in the network:$\mathcal{N}_t = (\mathcal{G}_t(\mathcal{V}_t, \mathcal{L}_t), \mathcal{W}_t, \mathcal{P}_t)$, where the elements included in the *line value function* $\mathcal{W}$ indicate the strength of the link between country i and country j (e.g. the export volume).

---

[8] With the notable exceptions of small countries, such as Austria or Finland; transition economies, such as the Slovak Republic; and remote countries, such as New Zealand and Australia.

[9] For a discussion on the difference of these network structures, see Newman (2010) and Csermely et al.(2013).

[10] Any network visualization is prone the projection-bias associated the bi-dimensional projection of an n-dimensional object. See De Benedictis et al. (2014) on that.

The degree centrality, C_D, is the simplest measure of the position of a node in a network: it just counts the number of direct connections of a node, as we did already in the Introduction. Here we make use a normalised version of the degree centrality, using - for t = 1995; 2010 – the total number of possible neighbours excluding self, $n - 1$, as a normalised factor:

$$C^n_{D_{out}} = \frac{\sum^n_{j\neq i} \mathcal{L}_{ij}}{(n-1)} \qquad C^n_{D_{in}} = \frac{\sum^n_{j\neq i} \mathcal{L}_{ji}}{(n-1)} \quad (5.1)$$

This indicator ranges from 0 to 1: the more is the degree centrality close to 1, the more a country is directly connected to the rest of the network. In a directed network there will be two measures of degree centrality: *in-degree* centrality, measuring the number of arcs pointing to ego, and *out-degree* centrality , measuring the number of arcs exiting from ego.[11]

Moving to the weighted version of the network, we calculate the strength centrality, considering trade volumes instead of trade partnerships. Given the very strong heterogeneity among trade flows, strength centrality measures will differ from degree centralities. Unweighted and weighted networks conceive different information (Newman, 2004).

In equation 5.2, the centrality measure is computed aggregating over of the weights of the arcs (export or imports flows) connected to the node and normalizing by (n – 1). The index we obtain is a measure of the out-strength and in-strength.

$$C^n_{S_{out}} = \frac{\sum^n_{j\neq i} w_{ij}}{(n-1)} \qquad C^n_{S_{in}} = \frac{\sum^n_{j\neq i} w_{ji}}{(n-1)} \quad (5.2)$$

If we normalize the in-strength and out-strength by total world trade ($\sum_i \sum_j w_{ij} = \sum_i \sum_j w_{ji}$) we obtain:

$$C^P_{S_{out}} = \frac{\sum^n_{j\neq i} w_{ij}}{\sum_i \sum_j w_{ij}} \qquad C^P_{S_{in}} = \frac{\sum^n_{j\neq i} w_{ji}}{\sum_i \sum_j w_{ij}} \quad (5.3)$$

which measure the strength centralities in percentage terms. Obviously, the measures defined in equation 5.3 are fully equivalent to the trade shares we examined in the Introduction: export market shares are a measure of (out)strength centrality.

The measure of global centrality that we use for comparative purposes with respect to out-strength centralities is the eigenvector centrality measured over outgoing links. As we showed in figure 5.3, it is not irrelevant for the relative position of a node if the same node is connected to central players or to

---

[11] In the case of out-degree, $\sum^n_{j\neq i} \mathcal{L}_{ij}$ is the total number of countries toward which country i is exporting; in the case of in-degree, $\sum^n_{j\neq i} \mathcal{L}_{ji}$is the total number of countries from which country i is importing.

peripheral ones. The basic idea, as stated in De Benedictis et al. (2014) is that "... a node's *eigenvector centrality* is determined by the eigenvector centrality of its neighbours. It is not the country's centrality itself that matters, what really matters is the centrality of the countries linked to him."[12] The circularity of the argument is evident but can be tackled using some matrix algebra.

Starting from a binary trade-matrix, it is possible to use the Bonacich (1987) eigenvector centrality to define the centrality of country i as the sum of the eigenvector centralities of its neighbours. That is:

$$C_E(i) = \mathcal{L}_{i1}C_E(1) + \mathcal{L}_{i2}C_E(2) + \cdots + \mathcal{L}_{i(n-1)}C_E(n-1) + \mathcal{L}_{in}C_E(n) \quad (5.4)$$

The system of equations can be rewritten in matrix form as:

$$(I - \mathcal{L})\overrightarrow{C_E} = 0 \quad (5.5)$$

where I is a $n \times n$ identity matrix, $\mathcal{L}$ is the adjacency matrix of the trade network and $\overrightarrow{C_E}$ is the $n \times 1$ vector of countries' eigenvector centralities.[13]

Figure 5.4: Comparing local and global centralities: 1995 and 2010

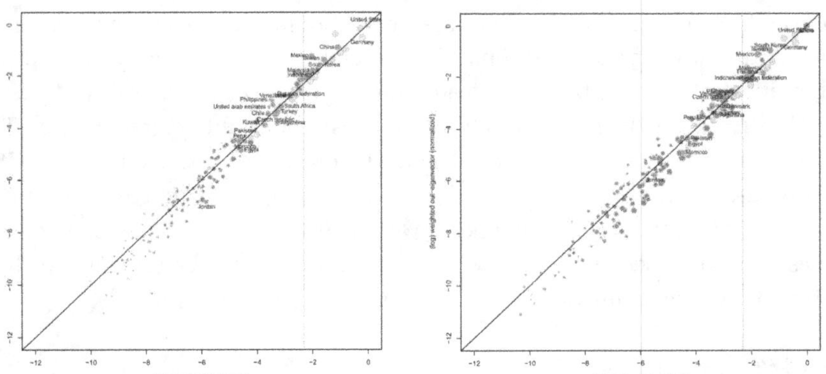

Color images of figures can be downloaded at the book's page
[URL: https://vernonpress.com/book/96]

Source: Authors' elaboration on Comtrade database. The local (horizontal axis) and global centralities (vertical axis) in 1995 are plotted on the left, while the equivalent for 2010 is plotted on the right. The size of the circle associated with each country is proportional to indegrees. Different colours correspond to different country groups: OECD (yellow), Emerging (red) and Others (grey).

---

[12] In general, countries with a high value of eigenvector centrality are the ones which are connected to many other countries which are, in turn, connected to many others.

[13] Equation 5.5 is the trade-matrix characteristic equation for an eigenvalue $\lambda=1$. See De Benedictis et al. (2014) on that.

The weighted version of the out-eigenvector centrality measure, $C_{E_{out}}^{NW}$, is calculated using the trade data for 1995 and 2010 and is plotted on a log-log scale against the strength centrality in figure 5.4.

The comparison of the local centrality, captured by the out-strength centrality (i.e., the export market shares), and the global centrality, measured by the weighted out-eigenvector centrality, shows how the two measures are correlated in such a dense network as the WTN, both in 1995 and in 2010. The dots representing the various countries grouped within OECD, Emerging and Others nicely align along the 45-degree line in the left and in the right panes of figure 5.4. At the same time, there is quite a bit of variability around that very line. Local and global centralities correlate, less so for some countries. Whether OECD countries tend to align, Emerging countries distinguish themselves from Others because they tend to group above the 45-degree line, while the latter tend to place themselves below the line in greater number.

The simple interpretation of being below or above the line is based on the value that neighbours have in increasing the centrality of a country. Countries above the line receive a plus from their neighbours, the ones below receive a penalization. China appears unaffected, being in itself much more central than most of its neighbours. Instead, Mexico's eigenvector centrality is positively affected by the high centrality of its most important neighbour, the US, suggesting that it is getting an advantage from being a satellite of the US economy. And Mexico is maintaining its rank among the Emerging countries in spite of a degree centrality much lower in 1995 that other Emerging countries. The same seems to be true for South Korea, Chile, Venezuela and the Philippines (see figure 5.4). Less so for Argentina, Egypt or Jordan.[14]

5.3.3 Regressions

How relevant is the position of the Emerging countries in the WTN in affecting their economic performance? To address this question, we test the conditional correlation between the centrality indices discussed above with other economic variables. As a first step, we verify that the position of countries in the WTN (and not only their export market share) is a good indicator of a

[14] Most European countries are below the 45 degree line, indicating that they hold relatively large market shares, but they are not as well connected worldwide. This might be the result of the high level of regionalization of European trade. Instead, among OECD countries, Canada is above that line, thanks to their strong ties to the USA. Most smaller and less developed countries are below the line and have a small number of trade links: they still have relatively small market shares, but more than that, they are not well connected and often not to the main traders.

country being or becoming Emerging. In fact, from the results of the proportional odds of logistic regressions reported in Table 5.2, we observe a positive and significant correlation between the probability of being an Emerging country and out eigenvector centrality, both weighted and not.

Taking into account the general tendency to increase connectivity along time - that is controlled for by the use of year fixed effects – the increase of outdegree by one standard deviation makes 4.039 times more likely to be in a higher category, as shown in column 1 of table 5.2.[15] The corresponding predicted probability when outdegree is at mean value is for an OECD country 0.13, while the one of being and emerging country is 0.15, and the one of being an "Others" is 0.71. In other terms, the former two categories tend to be more connected than a random country in the latter category. The marginal effects indicate, in fact, that the change in probability when outdegree increases by one standard deviation is 0.170 for "Others," 0.022 for "OECD" and 0.148 for "Emerging',' much higher for this latter category. Qualitatively similar results are obtained with the other centrality measures (columns 2, 3, and 4 in table 5.2). Interestingly enough, unweighted centrality measures (columns 1 and 3 of table 5.2) result in similar probabilities and similar fitting of the model, the same being true for the weighted centrality measures (columns 2 and 4 of table 5.2), resulting in lower probabilities and lower fitting.

When the model includes both local and global centralities, the general picture is confirmed. In column 5, we report the outcome of the proportional odds logistic regression when outdegree and outeigenvector centralities are included as regressors. In the absence of time fixed effects, the coefficients of the two unweighted centrality measures add up to a probability very close to one of column 1 or column 3. When a time fixed effect is included, as in column 6, and the general tendency of increasing trade connectivity is controlled for, the two coefficients show opposite signs. Il is possible to further qualify this issue looking at the marginal effects for the three categories: the change in probability when outdegree increases by one standard deviation is negative for "Others" (-0.441) and positive for the other two categories (0.385 for "Emerging" and 0.056 for "OECD"); on the other hand, change in probability when outeigenvector increases by one standard deviation is positive for "Others" (0.214) and negative for the other two categories (-0.187 for "Emerging" and -0.027 for "OECD"). Countries in the "Others" category seems to be

[15] Being the dependent variable an ordered variable taking value 1 if the country is in the "Others" category, 2 if the country is "Emerging", and 3 if the country is "OECD," the odds of moving to an higher category is 304% (e.g. (4.039 - 1)×100) when the variable oudegree increases by one standard deviation.

characterized by different structural position with respect to the other two categories. The "Emerging" seems to be the most sensitive category to change in centrality, both local (with a positive marginal effect) and global (with a negative marginal effect). The results in terms of weighted centralities show the relevance of the intensive margin of trade.

Table 5.2: Emerging countries: Proportional odds logistic regressions

	Dependent variable:							
	Group categorical variable: Others, Emerging, and OECD							
	1	2	3	4	5	6	7	8
outdegree	4.039*** (1.17)				2.003*** (0.312)	6.823*** (0.813)		
out strength		2.182*** (0.344)					1.711*** (0.727)	3.231*** (-0.246)
out eigen vector			4.798*** (0.217)		2.438*** -0.32	-3.303*** (0.865)		
w-out eigen vector				1.758*** (0.191)			0.404* (0.242)	0.007 (0.169)
year fixed effect	yes	yes	yes	yes	no	yes	yes	yes
pseudo R-squared	0.494	0.209	0.486	0.193	0.490	0.497	0.211	0.220
Residual Deviance	2295.97	3589.70	2334.33	3665.72	2314.21	2286.86	3581.26	3221.38
AIC	2331.97	3625.70	2370.33	3701.72	2322.21	2324.86	3619.26	3259.38
N	2848	2848	2848	2848	2848	2848	2848	2832

Note: *p<0.1; **p<0.05; ***p<0.01. Bootstrapped standard errors in parenthesis for (1), (2), (3); clustered robust s.e. for (4), (5) and (6).

Considering the marginal impact of centrality on each ordered category of countries, we see that the stronger impact for all indicators is always on the Emerging group, confirming that a relevant position in trade, in particular, access to relevant export markets - as a hub or as a satellite - is a relevant feature of an emerging economy. We also verify how the results are driven by the special case of China, removing China from the sample (column 8 in table 5.2). In this last case, the w-outeigenvector centrality becomes statistically insignificant showing the role of China as a hub, also for other Emerging countries.[16]

Having confirmed the relevance of trade, we then test the correlation between a country's centrality in the WTN and the most general indicator of economic performance, that is GDP growth. It is never easy to specify correctly a growth regression, as a country's growth is affected by such a large set of factors that mis-specification and omitted variables are always a problem in this type of regression (Baldwin, 2004, Acemoglu, 2008). For this reason, we try to be as less restrictive as possible and we start from a simple bivariate non-parametric regression. As shown in figure 5.5, the scatter plots and the associated bivariate nonparametric regression don't show a significant correlation between different centrality indices and annual GDP growth after five years, for the whole sample of countries. This result is not surprising, as it is driven by the group of Other countries (in grey in figure 5.5), making up the bulk of our sample, generally non-central and with very different growth performances over our observation period. But if we restrict the analysis to Emerging countries only (in red in figure 5.5), we find that the general absence of a relation between eigenvector centrality and GDP growth is not confirmed for a subset of countries for which the correlation is inverted-U shaped. This result confirms not only the relevance of trade for emerging countries but the importance of choosing the appropriate partners and markets for export.

---

[16] The marginal effects corresponding to the no-China case show that the change in probability when outstength increases by one standard deviation is negative for "Others" (-0.691) and positive for the other two categories (0.438 for "Emerging" and 0.254 for "OECD"); while the change in probability when w-outeigenvector increases by one stan-dard deviation is also negative for "Others" (-0.002), and positive for "Emerging" (0.001) and "OECD" countries (0.001). In all cases the marginal effect of global centrality is really very small.

Figure 5.5: Nonparametric unconditional relation between centrality and growth I

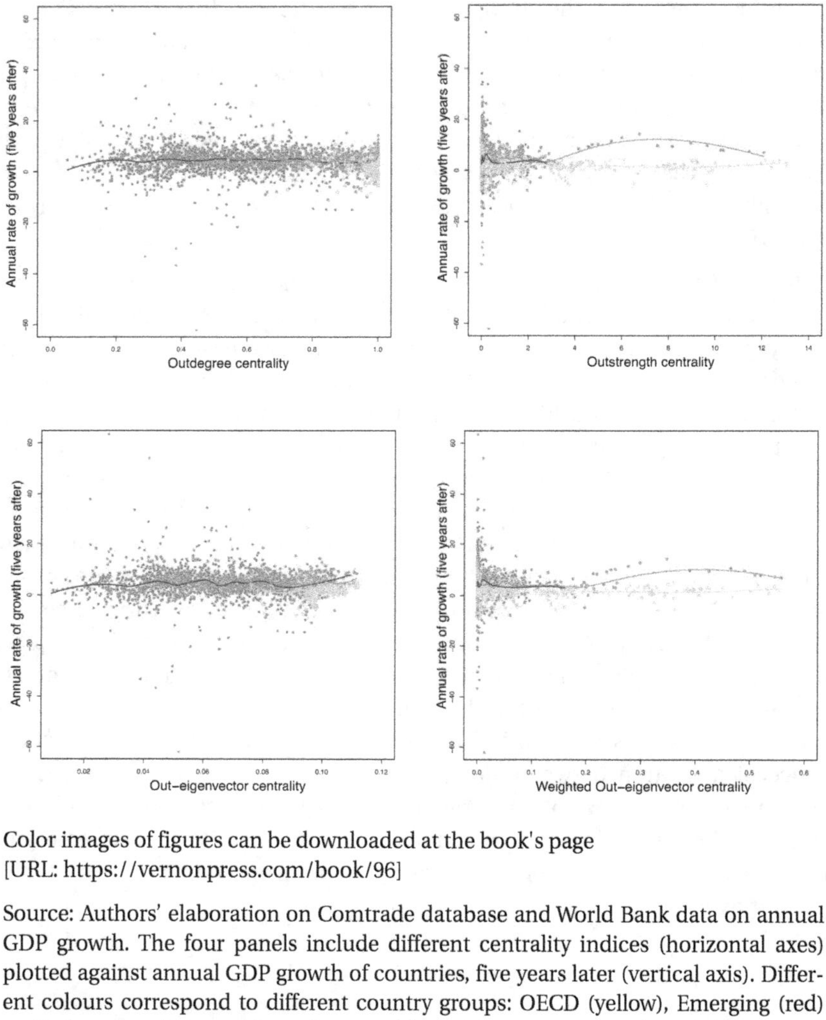

Color images of figures can be downloaded at the book's page [URL: https://vernonpress.com/book/96]

Source: Authors' elaboration on Comtrade database and World Bank data on annual GDP growth. The four panels include different centrality indices (horizontal axes) plotted against annual GDP growth of countries, five years later (vertical axis). Different colours correspond to different country groups: OECD (yellow), Emerging (red) and Others (grey). Smoothing splines are plotted for every group of countries.

In figure 5.6 we plot, just for the subsample of Emerging countries, the marginal effects of centrality measures on annual GDP growth after five years of a semi-parametric regression that includes year and country fixed effects. The bandwidth is set optimally and jointly including the role of fixed effects through aic expected Kullback-Leibler, as in Hurvich, Simonoff, and Tsai (1998). Once controlling for year and country heterogeneity through fixed effects, both outdegree and out-eigenvector centralities show a U-shaped relation: increasing the connectivity after being already connected with more than 50% of the countries in the WTN is negatively correlated with annual GDP growth. This is especially true for eigenvector centrality: connecting with central countries becomes effective only in a second stage. Finally, weighting both centrality measures with trade volumes shows that the effect is always positive on the intensive margin of trade, while it is non-linear in the extensive margin.

Figure 5.6: Nonparametric unconditional relation between centrality and growth II

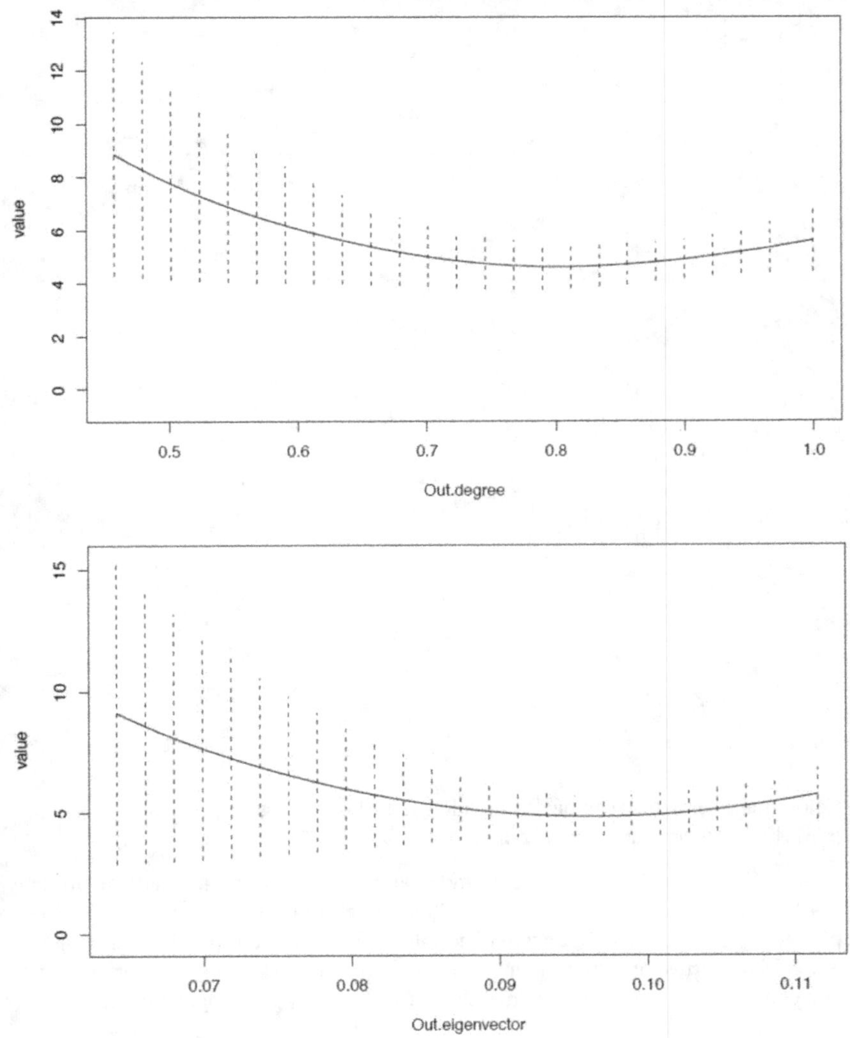

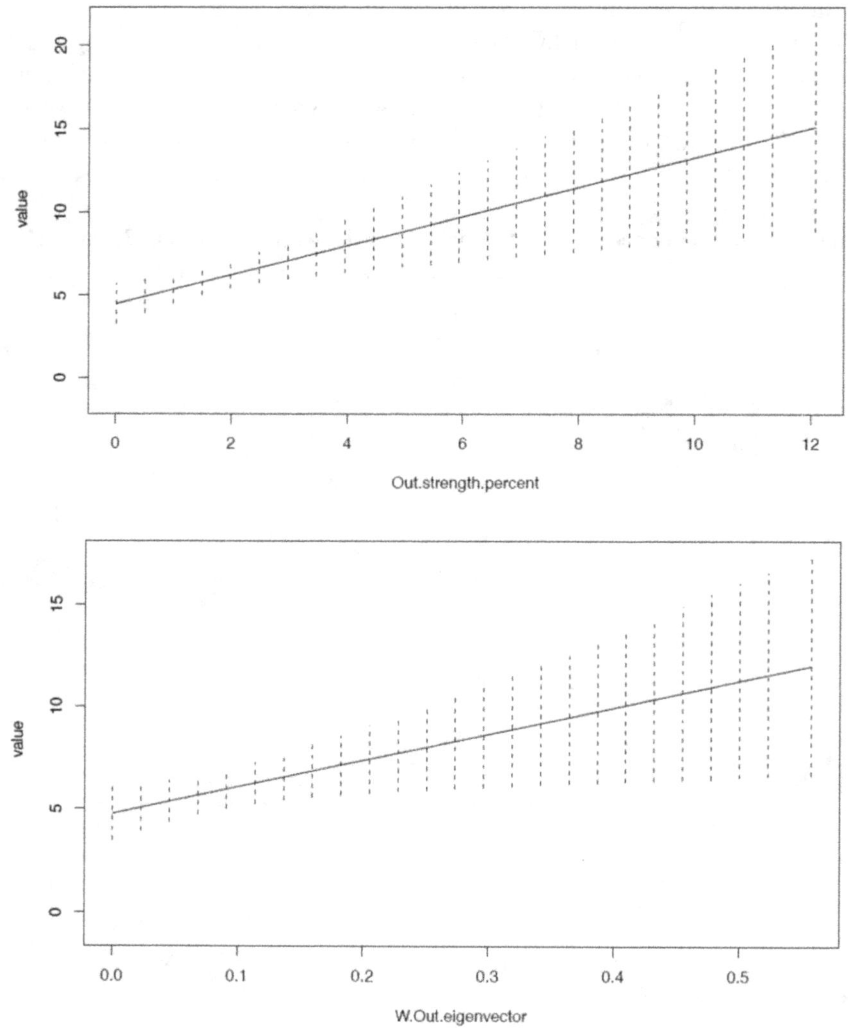

Color images of figures can be downloaded at the book's page
[URL: https://vernonpress.com/book/96]

Source: Authors' elaboration on Comtrade database and World Bank data on annual GDP growth. The four panes include different centrality indices (horizontal axes) plotted against annual GDP growth of countries, five years later (vertical axis). Different colours correspond to different country groups: OECD (yellow), Emerging (red) and Others (grey). Smoothing splines are plotted for every group of countries.

5.4 Concluding remarks

The analysis of the World Trade Network shows that relevant changes occurred in the last two decades and the changing position of emerging countries contributed significantly to the shift observed. Nowadays we observe a network composed by a system of hubs and satellites, with emerging countries occupying different positions in this structure. China has become one of the main hubs, but a few other emerging countries play the role of regional hubs. Instead, other emerging countries appear as satellites, like Mexico, being strongly linked to important central markets. In any case, the analysis confirms the crucial role of trade links for emerging economies. The WTN position can be relevant for a country's growth, but at this stage it is still impossible to establish a robust relationship between the two variables at a global level, as many nodes in the WTN are still in uncertain positions. But a positive relationship between centrality and growth can be found for emerging countries, confirming the existence of a relationship between trade and growth as far as the intensive margin of trade is concerned. Observing the recent evolution of the WTN, we can expect that emerging economies will shape the trade network still for quite some time.

5.8 References

Acemoglu D. (2008) Introduction to Modern Economic Growth, Princeton University Press.

Aggarwal R. and Goodell J.W. (2008) Equity premia in emerging markets: National characteristics as determinants, Journal of Multinational Financial Management, 18, 4, 389 – 404, international Influences on Asset Markets.

Baldwin R. and Lopez-Gonzalez J. (2015) Supply-chain trade: A portrait of global patterns and several testable hypotheses, The World Economy, 38, 11, 1682–1721.

Baldwin R.E. (2004) Openness and growth: What's the empirical relationship?, in: Challenges to Globalisation: Analyzing the Economics, Baldwin R. and Winters L., eds., University of Chicago Press.

Barro R.J. (1991) Economic growth in a cross section of countries, The Quarterly Journal of Economics, 106, 2, 407–443.

Bhattacharya K., Mukherjee G., Sarämaki J., Kaski K. and Manna S. (2008) The international trade network: Weighted network analysis and modeling, Journal of Statistical Mechanics: Theory Exp. A, 2, P02002.

Bonacich P. (1987) Power and centrality: A family of measures, American journal of sociology, 92, 5, 1170–1182.

Csermely P., London A., Wu L.Y. and Uzzi B. (2013) Structure and dynamics of core/periphery networks, Journal of Complex Networks, 1, 2, 93–123.

De Benedictis L., Nenci S., Santoni G., Tajoli L. and Vicarelli C. (2014) Network Analysis of World Trade using the BACI-CEPII Dataset, Global Economy Journal, 14, 287–343.

De Benedictis L. and Tajoli L. (2011) The World Trade Network, The World Economy, 34, 1417–1454.

Devereux M.B. and Mendoza E.G. (2006) Emerging markets and macroeconomic volatility: Lessons from a decade of financial debacles, Journal of International Economics, 69, 1, 1 – 5.

Fagiolo G., Schiavo S. and Reyes J. (2008) On the topological properties of the world trade web: A weighted network analysis, Physica A, 387, 3868–3873.

Fruchterman T.M. and Reingold E.M. (1991) Graph drawing by force-directed placement, Software: Practice and experience, 21, 11, 1129–1164.

Gaulier G. and Zignago S. (2010) BACI: International Trade Database at the Product-Level, CEPII Working Paper, 23, 128.

Grossman G. and Rossi-Hansberg E. (2008) Trading tasks: A simple theory of offshoring, American Economic Review, 98, 5, 1978–1997.

Hanson G.H. (2012) The rise of middle kingdoms: Emerging economies in global trade, Journal of Economic Perspectives, 26, 2, 41–64.

Iapadre P.L. and Tajoli L. (2014) Emerging countries and trade regionalization. A network analysis, Journal of Policy Modeling, 36, 1, 89110.

Jain S.C. (2006) Emerging economies and the transformation of international business: Brazil, Russia, India and China (BRICs), Edward Elgar Publishing.

Johnson R. and Noguera G. (2012) Accounting for intermediates: Production sharing and trade in value added, Journal of International Economics, 86, 2, 224–236.

Kearney C. (2012) Emerging markets research: Trends, issues and future directions, Emerging Markets Review, 13, 2, 159 – 183.

Kose M.A., Prasad E.S. and Terrones M.E. (2006) How do trade and financial integration affect the relationship between growth and volatility? Journal of International Economics, 69, 1, 176 – 202.

Krapohl S. and Fink S. (2013) Different paths of regional integration: Trade networks and regional institution-building in Europe, Southeast Asia and southern africa, Journal of Common Market Studies, 51, 3, 472–488.

Newman M. (2010) Networks. An introduction, Oxford University Press.

Newman M.E.J. (2004) Analysis of weighted networks, 70, 5, Part 2, 056131.

Rodrik D. (2012) Unconditional convergence in manufacturing, The Quarterly Journal of Economics, 128, 1, 165–204.

Vercueil J. (2012) Que nous apprennent les BRIC? Trois conjectures sur les économies émergentes, Mondes en developpement, 2, 158, 25–34.

Zhou M., Wu G. and Xu H. (2016) Structure and formation of top networks in international trade, 2001–2010, Social Networks, 44, 9–21.

6.

World input-output network: applications, implications, and future directions

Massimo Riccaboni and Zhen Zhu

Data: World Input-Output Database (WIOD)
Software: Python

6.1 Introduction

International production has seen a rapid increase of fragmentation across countries in recent decades, especially in the 2000s. A product (with its components) may need to travel across country borders for multiple times before ending up in the hands of a consumer. Therefore, the rise of Global Value Chains (GVCs)[1] has made the conventional trade statistics less informative and even misleading and has greatly complicated the analysis of international trade and macroeconomics as trade in gross terms keeps deviating from trade in value-added between countries (Johnson, 2014). For example, if measured in value-added, the trade deficit of the United States with China will drop by 30-40% immediately (Johnson and Noguera, 2012).

Using the recently available Inter-Country Input-Output (ICIO) tables and more sophisticated accounting techniques, significant efforts have been made to detect the presence and measure the magnitude of the GVCs at the macroeconomic level (Johnson and Noguera, 2012; Timmer et al., 2014; Baldwin and Lopez-Gonzalez, 2015; Los, Timmer and Vries, 2015). They provide quantitative answers to questions such as how global the GVCs are and how much value-added is exchanged between countries. However, they do not explicitly consider the intricate interconnections between sectors or explore the underlying structural changes.

---

[1] A recent survey on the drivers and measures of GVCs is by Amador and Cabral (2016).

This chapter takes a network approach to investigate the GVCs at the macroeconomic level. Network science, a nascent but highly active research field, provides valuable methodologies and tools well suited for studying complex systems such as the GVCs. The approach explicitly takes into account the interconnections between players and quantifies the relationships in a rigorous yet intuitive way and has found fruitful applications in economics and finance (Schweitzer et al., 2009; Elliott, Golub and Jackson, 2014; Acemoglu, Ozdaglar, and Tahbaz-Salehi, 2015).

Belonging to the national accounting framework, the input-output tables are typically only available for individual countries and with more than one year recurrence interval. Yet the study of GVCs requires an integrated set of ICIO tables across countries and at least over the most relevant decade, the 2000s. Fortunately, the ICIO tables in such a form have become available in recent years (Tukker and Dietzenbacher, 2013). The main ICIO data source for this chapter is the World Input-Output Database (WIOD) 2016 release, which covers 43 major countries in the world for the period from 2000 to 2014 (Timmer et al., 2016).

Our applications in this chapter first start with mapping an ICIO table into what we call a World Input-Output Network (WION), where the nodes are the individual sectors in different countries and the links are the input-output relationships between them (Cerina et al., 2015). As a result, the network statistics at both node and network levels can be computed and a number of stylized facts can be established. Second, given that Markov chain is the backbone of input-output analysis, we propose a Markov chain based community detection method to find the clusters on the WION in a natural way (Piccardi et al., 2018). The community detection method enables us to visually detect the presence and significance of GVCs. Third, we transform the WION into a Global Value Network (GVN) by decomposing the final demand of each sector into the value-added contributions from all over the world. We prune the GVN to generate what we call a Global Value Tree (GVT) to show the most important value-added relationships for a selected sector (Zhu, Puliga, et al., 2015). For the selected sector, we can also examine its GVTs over time and detect the structural changes.

We select the WIOD data for the years 2000 and 2014 (the first and the last years respectively of the data set) to exemplify the above process of network analysis. Our results provide valuable insights into understanding the structure and dynamics of GVCs. Moreover, the methods and tools we provide in this chapter are highly customizable. For example, the interested readers may want to generate the GVTs for some specific sectors and countries and track the evolution over time for their particular purposes. In the end, we also provide suggestions for future research directions on this topic.

6.2 Data

A number of ICIO databases have become available in recent years (Tukker and Dietzenbacher, 2013). One such database is the WIOD, whose development was initially funded by European Commission (Timmer et al., 2015). The latest version of the WIOD is its 2016 release, which covers 56 sectors for each of the 43 countries (and the residual country Rest-of-World) for the period from 2000 to 2014 (Timmer et al., 2016). Table A6.1 and Table A6.2 in the appendix provide the lists of countries and sectors respectively.

For each year, there is a harmonized ICIO table recording the input-output relationships between any two sectors in any two countries. The numbers in the WIOD are in current basic (producers') prices and are expressed in millions of US dollars. Table 6.1 shows an example of an ICIO table with two countries and two sectors. The 4 by 4 inter-sector component (highlighted in the dashed box) is called the transactions matrix and is often denoted by Z. Note that the diagonal domestic submatrices (transactions between sectors in the same country) are shaded while the off-diagonal submatrices are the transactions crossing country borders. The rows of Z record the distributions of the sector outputs throughout the two countries while the columns of Z record the composition of inputs required by each sector. Note that in this example all the sectors buy inputs from themselves, which is often observed in real data. Besides intermediate sector use, the remaining outputs are absorbed by the additional columns of final demand, which includes household consumption, government expenditure, and so forth (Here we only show the aggregated final demand for the two countries). Similarly, production necessitates not only inter-sector transactions but also labour, management, depreciation of capital, and taxes, which are summarized as the additional row of value-added.

Table 6.1: A Hypothetical Two-Country-Two-Sector ICIO Table

		Country 1		Country 2		Final Demand		Total Output
		Sector 1	Sector 2	Sector 1	Sector 2	Country 1	Country 2	
Country 1	Sector 1	35	20	10	5	25	5	100
	Sector 2	15	80	5	20	60	20	200
Country 2	Sector 1	5	8	585	255	12	135	1000
	Sector 2	5	10	50	500	135	800	1500
Value-Added		40	82	350	720			
Total Output		100	200	1000	1500			

There are 56 sectors for each of the 44 countries[2] ICIO table in the WIOD. So, in this case, the dimension of the transactions matrix Z is 2464 by 2464.

6.3 World Input-Output Network

6.3.1 Network Approach

The simplest definition of a network is probably a collection of nodes and links between them. To have the corresponding network to each ICIO table, we need first to define clearly the nodes and the links. The ICIO tables, in their original form, can be readily converted to networks. For example, the relationships between sectors are already captured by the transactions matrix Z (see Table 6.1). So here we simply use Z as the weighted adjacency matrix to construct the so-called World Input-Output Network (WION).[3] Back to the example of Table 6.1, the four sectors (of the two countries) will be the nodes and there will be 16 links in the network (the 4 nodes are fully connected with each other by 12 directed links between nodes and 4 self-loop links pointing to themselves). We follow the direction of material flow so that, for instance, the link will point from Sector 1 of Country 2 to Sector 2 of Country 1 with the amount of 8.[4] Note that in this way the WION is weighted (the magnitudes of

[2] Again, one country is actually the residual Rest-of-World.

[3] Of course, there are many alternative ways to specify the network. For example, we may consider the extra nodes to capture the final demand and the value-added information in the ICIO table, the supply-side versus the demand-side perspectives (see Piccardi et al. (2018)), or the value-added decomposition (see Section 4.5 below).

[4] By convention, the material inputs will be supplied from row sectors to column sectors in an input-output table.

the transactions between sectors), directed (transaction relationships are not necessarily symmetric), and with self-loops (a sector sources inputs from itself).

Figure 6.1 and figure 6.2 show the WION in 2000 and in 2014 respectively.[5] For the nodes, each different colour represents a different country. It is easy to see for both years that the nodes belonging to the same country tend to cluster together. In the meanwhile, the WION involves more nodes and gets more complex from 2000 to 2014.[6]

Figure 6.1: WION in 2000

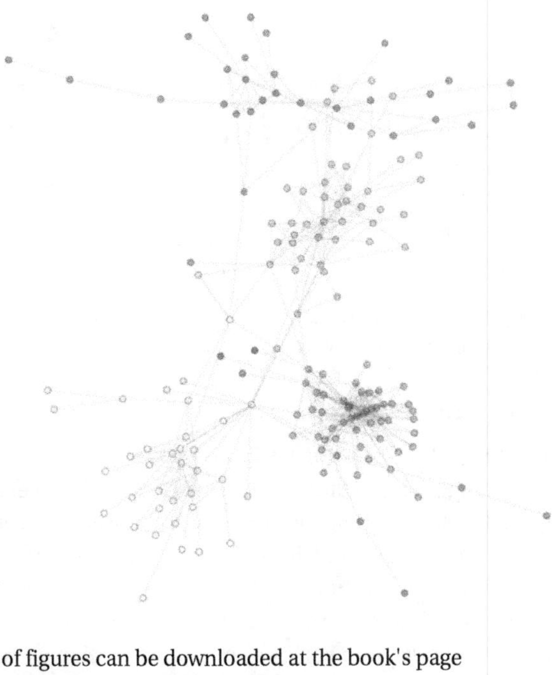

Color images of figures can be downloaded at the book's page [URL: https://vernonpress.com/book/96]

[5] To simplify the visualization, we only show the giant component after converting the original WION to an undirected network and removing the links with weight less than 5000 millions of US dollars. Note that the link width and node size are uniform for the network.

[6] This may be due to the effect of inflation. But in the following analysis we show that the network does become denser over time by the network density measure.

Figure 6.2: WION in 2014

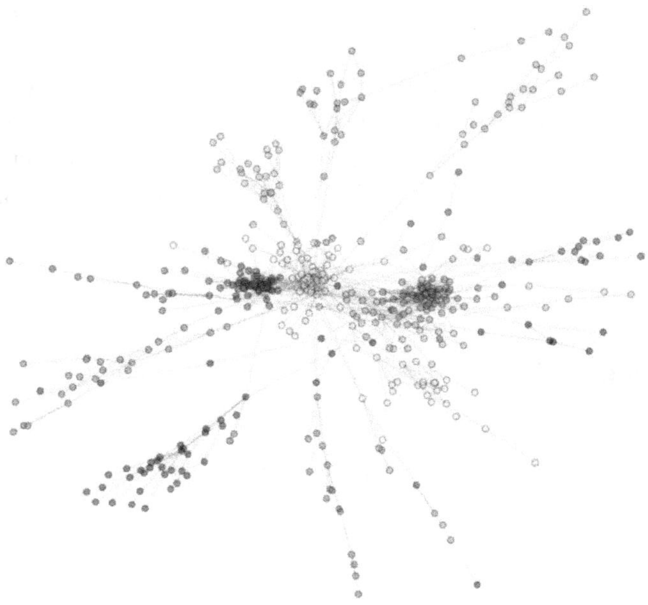

Color images of figures can be downloaded at the book's page
[URL: https://vernonpress.com/book/96]

6.3.2 Aggregate Statistics

To complement the qualitative information observed in the above figures, we also calculate some aggregate statistics to summarize the overall features of the WIONs. Figure 6.3 shows the time series of the domestic weight (which is the sum of all the domestic submatrices of Z[7] over the sum of Z) and the network density (which is the number of links observed in Z over the maximum number of links in principle given the number of nodes[8] in Z). It is straightforward to see that the two time series almost always display reverse behaviour. The negative correlation makes sense because as the network density gets higher, the domestic weight is more likely to shrink due to a higher chance of interactions between countries. It is also important to note that, while the high level of network density indicates the presence of a large number of links between countries, the high level of domestic weight means that most transactions in terms of monetary value happen within the country borders.

---

[7] See the shaded parts in Table 6.1 for an example.

[8] The number of nodes in Z will always be 2464 over time.

Figure 6.3: Time series of the domestic weight and the network density

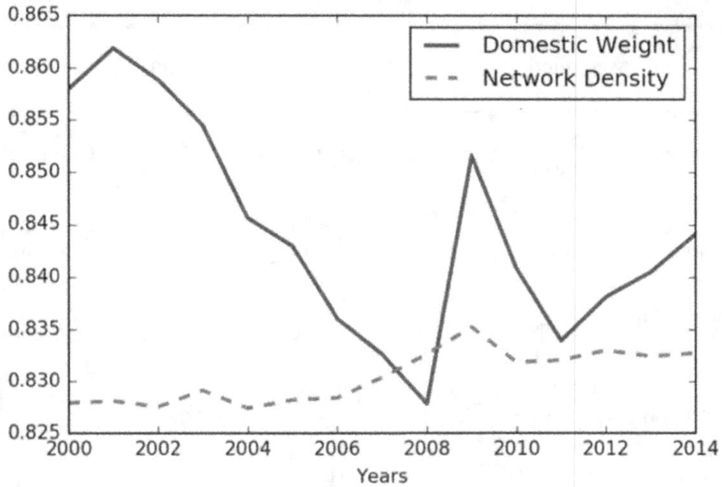

Color images of figures can be downloaded at the book's page
[URL: https://vernonpress.com/book/96]

6.3.3 Centrality Measures

Network science also provides handy tools to measure the positions of the individual nodes. Here we highlight three centrality measures: in-degree (the number of adjacent incoming links for each node), out-degree (the number of adjacent outgoing links for each node), and PageRank (a variant of the eigenvector centrality and a systematic measure accounting for not only the number of links but also the weights of the linked nodes (Page et al., 1999)).

Table 6.2 shows the top five sectors in terms of the three kinds of centralities in the WION for 2000 and 2014.[9] First, even for the top five positions, the different centralities produce different results. For instance, Japan's health sector is much more important if measured by the systematic PageRank centrality than by others in 2000. However, sectors such as USA's public administration appears to be central and robust against different measures and over time. Compared with 2000, 2014 has China emerging as a new player in the top five. Finally, the top sectors are basically service sectors in advanced economies such as Japan and USA while China's central sectors can be manufacturing ones, which implies the different stages of developments and the structural rebalancing of the world economy.

---

[9] The rankings are based on the modified WION after removing the links with weight less than 5000 millions of US dollars. Also, the sectors belong to Rest-of-World are excluded from the rankings.

Table 6.2 : Top Five Sectors of the WION Based on In-Degree, Out-Degree, and PageRank Centralities

	Year 2000			Year 2014		
	In-Degree	**Out-Degree**	**PageRank**	**In-Degree**	**Out-Degree**	**PageRank**
1	USA-Public Admin	USA-Admin	USA-Public Admin	USA-Public Admin	CHN-Wholesale	USA-Public Admin
2	USA-Health	USA-Legal	JPN-Health	CHN-Construction	USA-Admin	CHN-Construction
3	USA-Construction	USA-Wholesale	USA-Health	USA-Health	USA-Wholesale	JPN-Health
4	JPN-Construction	USA-Real Estate	JPN-Wholesale	CHN-Other Machinery	USA-Legal	USA-Health
5	USA-Wholesale	USA-Financial Service	USA-Real Estate	CHN-Chemicals	CHN-Financial Service	GBR-Health

Thus far, we have focused on the salient facts of the WION. Built on the WION framework, the following two sections introduce respectively the applications of community detection and network pruning in the study of GVCs. In particular, the community detection technique in Section 6.4 enables us to detect the presence and significance of GVCs whereas the network pruning technique in Section 6.5 enables us to trace the evolution of GVCs over time.

6.4 Community Detection

Community detection is a subfield in network science concerning the discovery of significant sub-network structures.[10] Since Markov chain is the backbone of the classical input-output analysis, we propose here also a Markov chain based algorithm to detect communities in the WION (Piccardi, 2011; Piccardi et al., 2018). We can think of a random walker walking through the network with the probabilities specified by the network configuration. The intuition is that a significant community is found if the random walker spends a significant amount of time within it as if she is trapped in the community.

[10] A recent survey is by Fortunato (2010).

Below in figure 6.4 and figure 6.5, we show two results of the community detection of the WION in 2000 and 2014 respectively. The 43 countries[11] are arranged by rows and the 56 sectors are arranged by columns so that each cell represent an individual sector. Each different colour represents a community detected while the patched cells represent data-unavailable sectors. The rows are arranged in such a way that from top to bottom the size of the community decreases. Within each community, the top three core sectors are highlighted with integer numbers inside the cells.[12]

[11] We exclude Rest-of-World from the community detection analysis.

[12] See Piccardi et al. (2018) for the method of detecting the cores of each community. The intuition is to find the node with the shortest average distance to other community members to be a core. Other methods and applications of community core detection can be seen in Cerina et al. (2014) and Zhu et al. (2014).

Figure 6.4: Community Detection of the WION in 2000

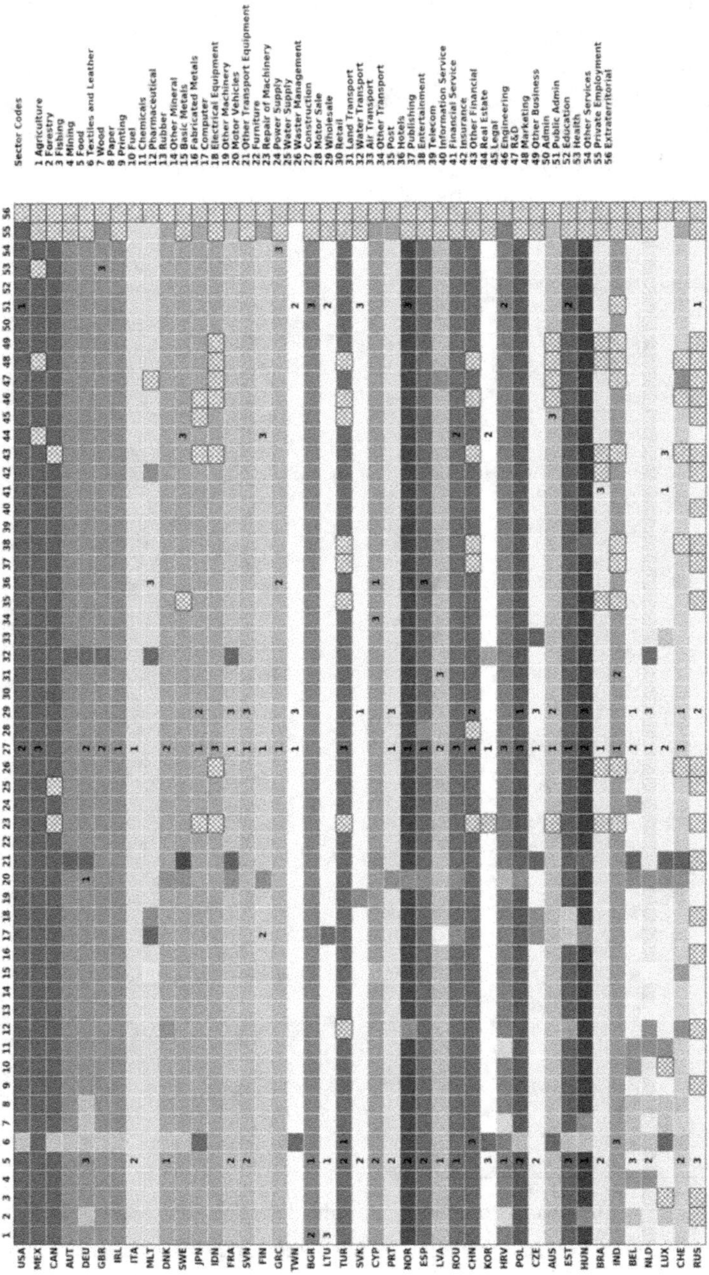

Color images of figures can be downloaded at the book's page
[URL: https://vernonpress.com/book/96]

Figure 6.5: Community Detection of the WION in 2014

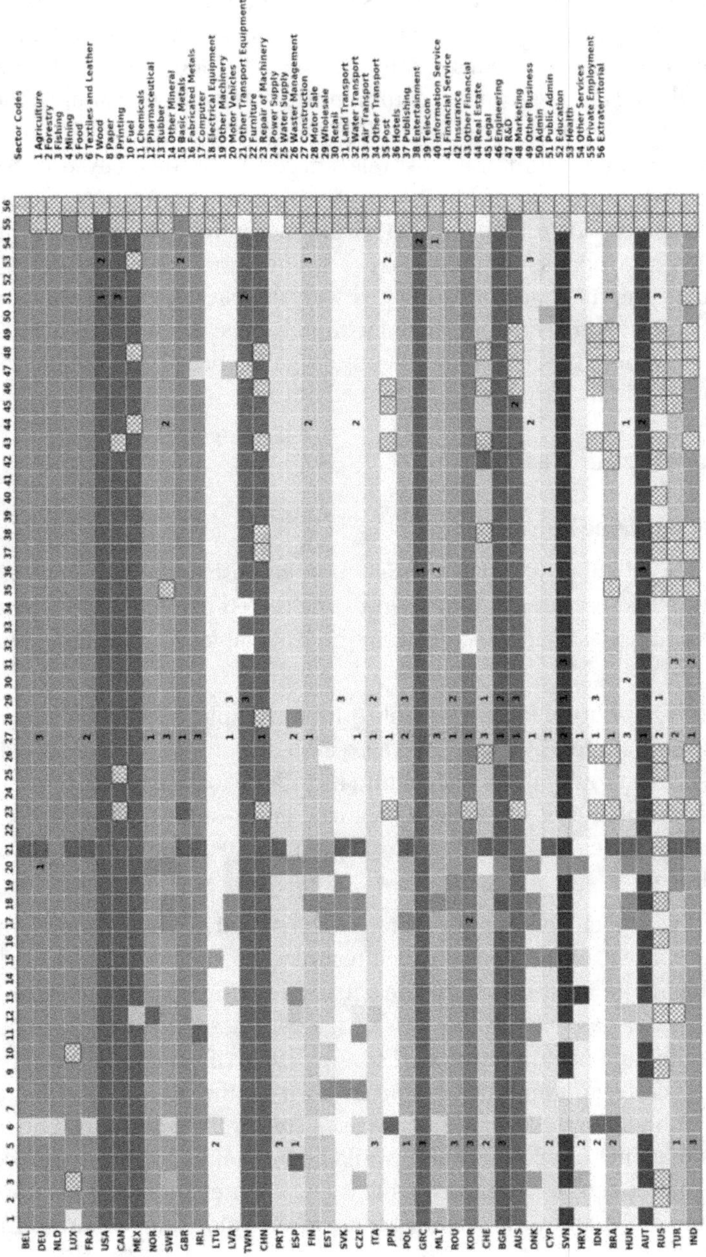

Color images of figures can be downloaded at the book's page
[URL: https://vernonpress.com/book/96]

There are several interesting findings in our results. First, most communities are row-based. That is, the sectors belonging to the same country tend to cluster together, which echoes the visual impression from figure 6.2 above and the fact that most transactions still happen domestically (figure 6.3). Second, there are cross-country communities detected. For example, for both years our algorithm captures the NAFTA (North American Free Trade Agreement) community. Third, the most relevant result for the analysis of GVCs is that we find some column-based communities penetrating across countries within a sector. For example, in 2014, the motor vehicles sector centred in Germany also spans vertically across many other countries. The other transport equipment sector associated with the NAFTA community and the textiles and leather sector associated with Italy have the same pattern. Therefore, our method detects the presence and significance of GVCs at the sectoral level in a vivid way based on solid mathematics.

6.5 Global Value Tree

6.6.1 Global Value Network

As mentioned above, there is a variety of relationships between sectors and the nature and usefulness of networks constructed depend on the definition of links and nodes. Here we transform the ICIO tables into value-added relationships.

For an input-output table (see Table 6.1 for example), the final demand vector is often denoted by f and the value-added vector is often denoted by v. Finally, the last row and the last column record the total sector outputs and its vector is denoted by x. Note that a balanced input-output table has the same total output for each sector by summing up the items either horizontally or vertically.

If we divide each column of the transactions matrix Z by its corresponding total output in x, we get the so-called technical coefficients matrix A. Then it holds that $Ax + f = x$. Rearranging the equation as $(I-A)x = f$, where I is an identity matrix, we can solve x as $x = (I-A)^{-1}f$, where $(I-A)^{-1}$ is often denoted as L and is called the Leontief inverse (Leontief, 1936). If we divide each element of v by its corresponding total output in x, we get the value-added share vector and denote it by u. Moreover, if we use U to denote a diagonal matrix with u on its diagonal (everywhere else would be 0), then the value-added contribution matrix can be computed as $G = UL$. Each element in G is bounded between 0 and 1 and G_{ij} is sector i's share of the value-added contribution to sector j's final demand, f_j.

Finally, we can build the Global Value Network (GVN) using G as its weighted adjacency matrix.

6.6.2 Network Pruning

A network pruning algorithm is used to reveal the most essential value-added relationships for a selected root node.[13] The resulted sub-network is called Global Value Tree (GVT). Since we can generate the GVTs for each sector in the world and for each year available, we can trace the evolution of the GVTs for a given sector or compare the GVTs across countries, sectors, and over time.

Below in figure 6.6 and figure 6.7, we show two examples of the GVTs. They are rooted in South Korea's computer sector and for 2000 and 2014 respectively. The GVTs are generated by a threshold of 0.02 (2% value-added contribution).[14] For the nodes, each different colour represents a country. The red links indicate cross-country relationships while the grey ones indicate domestic relationships. And the links point from value-added providers to receivers. Finally, the link width is proportional to the link weight.

[13] The algorithm is explained in detail in Zhu et al. (2015).

[14] The threshold to generate the most diverse set of GVTs in terms of tree size (measured by the number of nodes) is empirically found to be around 0.02 (Zhu, Puliga, et al., 2015). We choose this value to highlight the topological differences between the GVTs.

Figure 6.6: GVT Rooted at South Korea's Computer Sector (KOR_17) in 2000

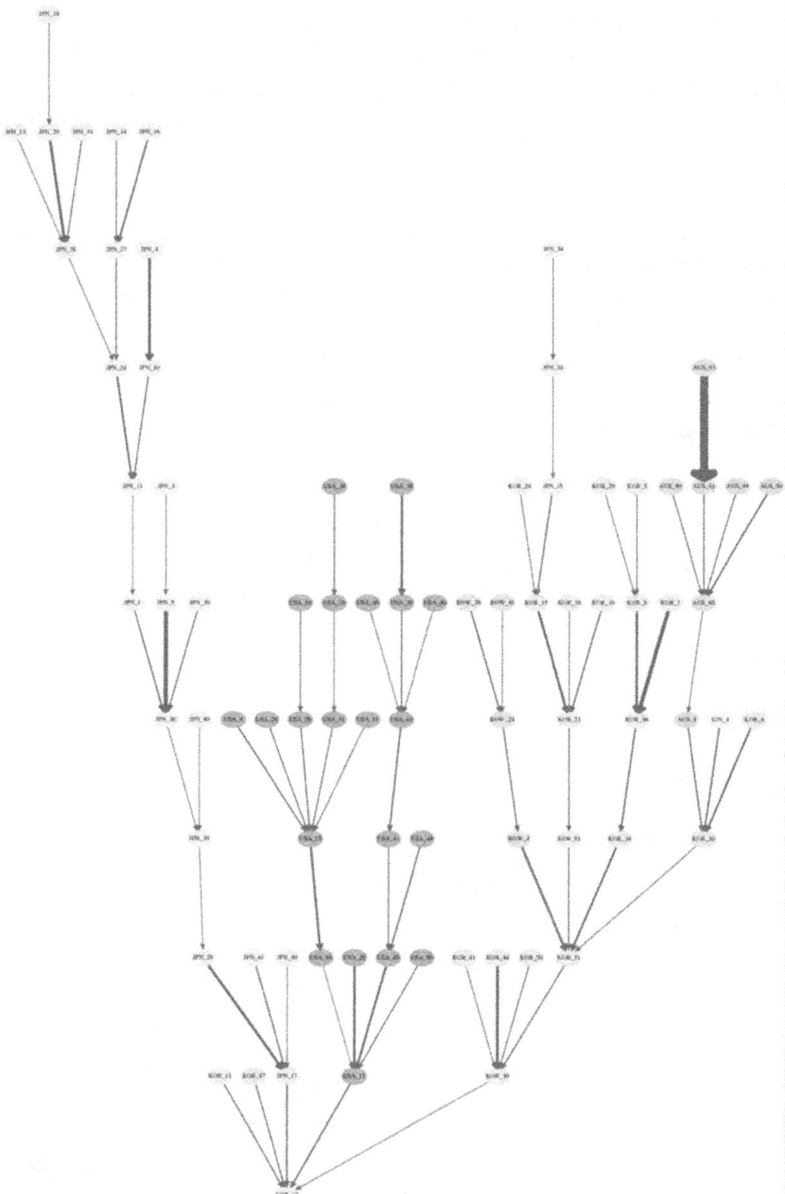

Color images of figures can be downloaded at the book's page
[URL: https://vernonpress.com/book/96]

Figure 6.7: GVT Rooted at South Korea's Computer Sector (KOR_17) in 2014

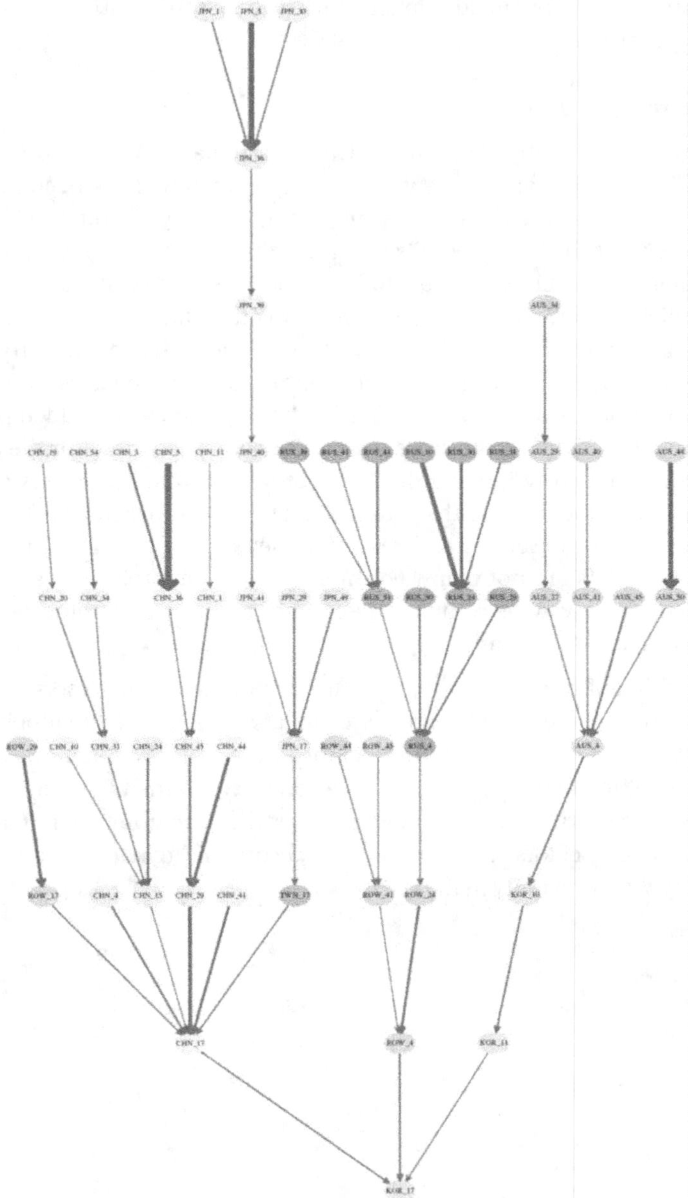

Color images of figures can be downloaded at the book's page [URL: https://vernonpress.com/book/96]

It is very interesting to note that, for South Korea's computer sector, the most important value-added relationships switched from Japan and USA to China over the years.

6.6 Future directions

Using the latest available World Input-Output Database (WIOD) 2016 release, this chapter provides an overview of a line of research we have been doing to bridge the gap between traditional input-output analysis and network science. We expect that the methods and algorithms developed here will open up exciting opportunities to both students and seasoned scholars. The examples highlighted here can be easily extended to other dimensions of the WIOD 2016 release or other similar databases. The interested readers may try other specifications of the networks more relevant to their particular research topics. For example, the GVTs can be built for the upstream value-added providers to the root sector (like what we do in this chapter) and also for the downstream value-added receivers from the root sector. What needed is only to alter the search direction in the algorithm. As stated above, the GVTs can be generated for all the sectors and years. So, they can be visually compared if the relevant GVTs are not many. For more general patterns, we also seek to find a systematic way to compare them across sectors and countries (Zhu, Morrison, et al., forthcoming).

Another line of research highlighting the importance of networks is to understand the microeconomic origins of macroeconomic fluctuations (Acemoglu et al., 2012; Carvalho, 2014). So, for future work, we plan to examine the impact of the network position of a given sector in the WION on its macroeconomic performance and to test whether the synchronization (comovement) between sectors in terms of macroeconomic dynamics can be explained by their proximity in the WION.

6.7 Appendix

Table 6. A1: Countries in the WIOD 2016 Release

Euro-Zone		Non-Euro EU		NAFTA		East Asia		Other	
Country	**Code**	**Country**	**Code**	**Country**	**Code**	**Country**	**Code**	**Country**	**Code**
Austria	AUT	Bulgaria	BGR	Canada	CAN	China	CHN	Australia	AUS
Belgium	BEL	Croatia	HRV	Mexico	MEX	Japan	JPN	Brazil	BRA
Cyprus	CYP	Czech Rep.	CZE	USA	USA	South Korea	KOR	India	IND
Estonia	EST	Denmark	DNK			Taiwan	TWN	Indonesia	IDN
Finland	FIN	Hungary	HUN					Norway	NOR
France	FRA	Latvia	LVA					Russia	RUS
Germany	DEU	Lithuania	LTU					Switzer-land	CHE
Greece	GRC	Poland	POL					Turkey	TUR
Ireland	IRL	Romania	ROU					Rest-of-World	ROW
Italy	ITA	Sweden	SWE						
Luxem-bourg	LUX	UK	GBR						
Malta	MLT								
Nether-lands	NLD								
Portugal	PRT								
Slovakia	SVK								
Slovenia	SVN								
Spain	ESP								

Table 6. A2: Sectors in the WIOD 2016 Release

Nr.	ISIC Rev. 4 Code	Full Name	Short Name
1	A01	Crop and animal production, hunting and related service activities	Agriculture
2	A02	Forestry and logging	Forestry
3	A03	Fishing and aquaculture	Fishing
4	B	Mining and quarrying	Mining
5	C10-C12	Manufacture of food products, beverages and tobacco products	Food
6	C13-C15	Manufacture of textiles, wearing apparel and leather products	Textiles and Leather
7	C16	Manufacture of wood and of products of wood and cork, except furniture; manufacture of articles of straw and plaiting materials	Wood
8	C17	Manufacture of paper and paper products	Paper
9	C18	Printing and reproduction of recorded media	Printing
10	C19	Manufacture of coke and refined petroleum products	Fuel
11	C20	Manufacture of chemicals and chemical products	Chemicals
12	C21	Manufacture of basic pharmaceutical products and pharmaceutical preparations	Pharmaceutical
13	C22	Manufacture of rubber and plastic products	Rubber
14	C23	Manufacture of other non-metallic mineral products	Other Mineral
15	C24	Manufacture of basic metals	Basic Metals
16	C25	Manufacture of fabricated metal products, except machinery and equipment	Fabricated Metals
17	C26	Manufacture of computer, electronic and optical products	Computer
18	C27	Manufacture of electrical equipment	Electrical Equipment
19	C28	Manufacture of machinery and equipment n.e.c.	Other Machinery

20	C29	Manufacture of motor vehicles, trailers and semi-trailers	Motor Vehicles
21	C30	Manufacture of other transport equipment	Other Transport Equipment
22	C31_C32	Manufacture of furniture; other manufacturing	Furniture
23	C33	Repair and installation of machinery and equipment	Repair of Machinery
24	D35	Electricity, gas, steam and air conditioning supply	Power Supply
25	E36	Water collection, treatment and supply	Water Supply
26	E37-E39	Sewerage; waste collection, treatment and disposal activities; materials recovery; remediation activities and other waste management services	Waste Management
27	F	Construction	Construction
28	G45	Wholesale and retail trade and repair of motor vehicles and motorcycles	Motor Sale
29	G46	Wholesale trade, except of motor vehicles and motorcycles	Wholesale
30	G47	Retail trade, except of motor vehicles and motorcycles	Retail
31	H49	Land transport and transport via pipelines	Land Transport
32	H50	Water transport	Water Transport
33	H51	Air transport	Air Transport
34	H52	Warehousing and support activities for transportation	Other Transport
35	H53	Postal and courier activities	Post
36	I	Accommodation and food service activities	Hotels
37	J58	Publishing activities	Publishing
38	J59_J60	Motion picture, video and television programme production, sound recording and music publishing activities; programming and broadcasting activities	Entertainment
39	J61	Telecommunications	Telecom
40	J62_J63	Computer programming, consultancy and related activities; information service activities	Information Service

41	K64	Financial service activities, except insurance and pension funding	Financial Service
42	K65	Insurance, reinsurance and pension funding, except compulsory social security	Insurance
43	K66	Activities auxiliary to financial services and insurance activities	Other Financial
44	L68	Real estate activities	Real Estate
45	M69_M70	Legal and accounting activities; activities of head offices; management consultancy activities	Legal
46	M71	Architectural and engineering activities; technical testing and analysis	Engineering
47	M72	Scientific research and development	R&D
48	M73	Advertising and market research	Marketing
49	M74_M75	Other professional, scientific and technical activities; veterinary activities	Other Business
50	N	Administrative and support service activities	Admin
51	O84	Public administration and defence; compulsory social security	Public Admin
52	P85	Education	Education
53	Q	Human health and social work activities	Health
54	R_S	Other service activities	Other Services
55	T	Activities of households as employers; undifferentiated goods- and services-producing activities of households for own use	Private Employment
56	U	Activities of extraterritorial organizations and bodies	Extraterritorial

6.8 References

Acemoglu, D., Carvalho, V. M., Ozdaglar, A. and Tahbaz-Salehi, A. (2012) The network origins of aggregate fluctuations, *Econometrica*, 80(5), pp. 1977–2016.

Acemoglu, D., Ozdaglar, A. and Tahbaz-Salehi, A. (2015) Systemic risk and stability in financial networks, *The American economic review*, 105(2), pp. 564–608.

Amador, J. and Cabral, S. (2016) Global value chains: a survey of drivers and measures, *Journal of Economic Surveys*, 30(2), pp. 278–301.

Baldwin, R. and Lopez-Gonzalez, J. (2015) Supply-chain Trade: A Portrait of Global Patterns and Several Testable Hypotheses, *The World Economy*, 38(11), pp. 1682–1721.

Carvalho, V. M. (2014) From micro to macro via production networks, *The Journal of Economic Perspectives*, 28(4), pp. 23–47.

Cerina, F., Chessa, A., Pammolli, F. and Riccaboni, M. (2014) Network communities within and across borders, *Scientific reports*, 4, [online] Available at: https://www.ncbi.nlm.nih.gov/pmc/articles/PMC3971449/ (Accessed 29 September 2017).

Cerina, F., Zhu, Z., Chessa, A. and Riccaboni, M. (2015) World input-output network, *PloS one*, 10(7), p. e0134025.

Elliott, M., Golub, B. and Jackson, M. O. (2014) Financial networks and contagion, *The American economic review*, 104(10), pp. 3115–3153.

Fortunato, S. (2010) Community detection in graphs, *Physics reports*, 486(3), pp. 75–174.

Johnson, R. C. (2014) Five facts about value-added exports and implications for macroeconomics and trade research, *The Journal of Economic Perspectives*, 28(2), pp. 119–142.

Johnson, R. C. and Noguera, G. (2012) Accounting for Intermediates: Production sharing and trade in value added, *Journal of International Economics*, 86(2), pp. 224–236.

Leontief, W. W. (1936) Quantitative input and output relations in the economic systems of the United States, *The review of economic statistics*, pp. 105–125.

Los, B., Timmer, M. P. and Vries, G. J. (2015) How global are global value chains? A new approach to measure international fragmentation, *Journal of Regional Science*, 55(1), pp. 66–92.

Page, L., Brin, S., Motwani, R. and Winograd, T. (1999) *The PageRank citation ranking: Bringing order to the web.*, Stanford InfoLab, [online] Available at: http://ilpubs.stanford.edu:8090/422 (Accessed 24 September 2017).

Piccardi, C. (2011) Finding and testing network communities by lumped Markov chains, *PloS one*, 6(11), p. e27028.

Piccardi, C., Riccaboni, M., Tajoli, L. and Zhu, Z. (2018) Random Walks on the World Input-Output Network, *Journal of Complex Networks*, 6(2), pp. 187-205.

Schweitzer, F., Fagiolo, G., Sornette, D., Vega-Redondo, F., Vespignani, A. and White, D. R. (2009) Economic networks: The new challenges, *science*, 325(5939), pp. 422–425.

Timmer, M. P., Dietzenbacher, E., Los, B., Stehrer, R. and Vries, G. J. (2015) An illustrated user guide to the world input–output database: the case of global automotive production, *Review of International Economics*, 23(3), pp. 575–605.

Timmer, M. P., Erumban, A. A., Los, B., Stehrer, R. and de Vries, G. J. (2014) Slicing up global value chains, *The Journal of Economic Perspectives*, 28(2), pp. 99–118.

Timmer, M. P., Los, B., Stehrer, R., de Vries, G. J. and others (2016) *An anatomy of the global trade slowdown based on the WIOD 2016 release*, Groningen Growth and Development Centre, University of Groningen, [online] Available at: https://ideas.repec.org/p/gro/rugggd/gd-162.html (Accessed 22 September 2017).

Tukker, A. and Dietzenbacher, E. (2013) Global multiregional input–output frameworks: an introduction and outlook, *Economic Systems Research*, 25(1), pp. 1–19.

Zhu, Z., Cerina, F., Chessa, A., Caldarelli, G. and Riccaboni, M. (2014) The rise of China in the international trade network: a community core detection approach, *PloS one*, 9(8), p. e105496.

Zhu, Z., Morrison, G., Puliga, M., Chessa, A. and Riccaboni, M. (forthcoming) The Similarity of Global Value Chains: A Network-Based Measure, *Network Science*.

Zhu, Z., Puliga, M., Cerina, F., Chessa, A. and Riccaboni, M. (2015) Global value trees, *PloS one*, 10(5), p. e0126699.

7.

Local and trans-local linkages in the aerospace industry: an emerging small world?

Raja Kali, Ekaterina Turkina, and Ari Van Assche

Data: Firm level data from official company reports, approved lists of suppliers, company websites, and news articles
Software: MATLAB, Netdraw

7.1 Introduction

The increase in international economic integration of the last few decades has affected the nature of international trade in profound ways, nowhere more so than in the rise of global value chains. These vertically organized production processes spread across international borders have been associated with deep changes in the fragmentation, location, and organization of production. While considerable recent research has been geared toward understanding these issues, less attention has been given to how global value chains have evolved over time, and their impact on the nature of industrial clusters previously considered a mainstay of regional economic growth and development.

In a recent paper, we have drawn attention to this question by investigating how the structure of network linkages of cluster firms in the aerospace industry has altered with the rise of global value chains (Turkina et al., 2016). For this purpose, we took advantage of hand-collected data on the network of formal firm linkages within and across 56 aerospace clusters in North America and Greater Europe over the period 2002-2014. Using community detection techniques, we found that cluster firm connections are less and less agglomerated within the geographical boundaries of clusters, and more and more clustered within value chain boundaries that cross multiple locations. We have provided supporting evidence that this transformation is due to the fact that industrial clusters in the aerospace industry are gradually transforming from sectoral to functional specialization, where they are now specializing in finer sliced value chain stages.

In this chapter, we complement our previous paper by investigating whether changes in the structure of the global aerospace cluster network has allowed it to become an increasingly "small world." As we explain in more detail later, a general result in the literature on complex networks is that high-performance networks in many settings have the "small-world" property, which has come to be associated with the efficient functioning of the network. Our key findings can be summarized as follows. First, we find that changes in the configuration of trans-local and local linkages are transforming the topology of the overall network into a "small-world." A small-world is a network whose topology combines high clustering among nodes with short average distance (path length) across nodes.[1] As we explain in Section 5.2, a small-world can be considered an "efficient" configuration of the network. This has come about because a growth in trans-local linkages has reduced average distance in the network while the persistence of many local linkages has maintained a high level of clustering in the network. Second, digging deeper, we find that the reduction in average distance is largely driven by the trans-localisation or offshoring of buyer-supplier and investment linkages. At the same time, what is keeping local industrial clusters intact is a growth in local partnership linkages. Third, we find important regional trends: traditional clusters in developed countries are reorienting their supply chains and investments towards emerging industrial clusters in Eastern Europe and Mexico, while trans-local partnership linkages develop mainly between clusters specialized in similar value chain stages. Taken together, our findings suggest that the organization of the network of global linkages across industrial clusters is becoming more efficient over time. In addition, we find that industrial clusters are transforming from sectorial to functional specialization over time. That is, the benefits of co-locating with firms specializing in the same functional task or value chain stage are starting to over-shadow the forces that benefit the agglomeration of firms due to simple physical proximity.

The rest of the chapter is structured as follows. Section 5.2 presents a brief overview of the recent literature on linkages within and across industrial clusters. Section 5.3 connects this literature to social network analysis and provides theoretical guidance for the empirical analysis. Section 5.4 describes the data and methodology. Section 5.5 contains the empirical analysis. Section 5.6 discusses the results and concludes.

---

[1] The average distance, is the average number of links connecting any two nodes in the network.

7.2 Global cluster network

A recognition that both local and trans-local linkages are important for a cluster's economic prospects has pushed scholars to go beyond the traditional local-global dichotomy which has dominated the cluster literature. Clusters are rarely self-sufficient in terms of the knowledge base they draw upon, and it is, therefore, limiting to consider them as closed or isolated systems (Wolfe and Gertler 2004). Rather, local and global cluster spheres are intrinsically interwoven (Bathelt and Turi 2011). Bathelt and Li (2014), for example, show that local cluster characteristics affect the number and types of trans-local connections that a cluster develops (Bathelt and Li 2014). At the same time, Sturgeon et al. (2008) show that a cluster's trans-local connectedness affects local cluster dynamics since it pushes firms to alter their local production and learning patterns.

As the focus has shifted toward understanding the network of linkages that cluster firms have, there has also been a growing interest in analysing variations across linkage types. Studies on global value chains have focused mainly on trends in vertical buyer-supplier linkages. Sturgeon et al. (2008), for example, document that lead firms in the automotive industry have outsourced a growing share of their production to external suppliers, which are increasingly located in emerging clusters. Li (2014), in contrast, has conducted a systematic analysis of the role of horizontal linkage networks on local and trans-local learning processes in China's Hangji toothbrush industry. Taken together, the results of these studies suggest that clustering dynamics may well vary significantly across linkage types.

A natural tool that is increasingly adopted to investigate the interwoven nature of linkages within and between industrial clusters is social network analysis (Giuliani and Bell 2005; Lorenzen and Mudambi 2013). As a starting point, a cluster is depicted as a network of local linkages between firms, which is embedded in a larger "global cluster network" of exchanges that spans within and across clusters and varies by linkage types (Ter Wal and Boschma 2009). Applying network theory to this setting has generated a number of new insights. First, learning in the global cluster network should not simply amount to being in the right place (i.e., the industrial cluster), but also being in the right position of the network (Ter Wal and Boschma 2009). Indeed, Giuliani and Bell (2005) and Lorenzen and Mudambi (2013) point out that actors located in the same cluster often have very different network positions. Second, the clustering of linkages need not correspond to the geographical boundaries of an industrial cluster. Knowledge diffuses primarily through network linkages which may be particularly dense between local firms, but which also span trans-locally (Ter Wal and Boschma 2009).

7.3 Propositions related to the small-worldness of the global cluster network

In this section, we take the concept of a "global cluster network" as a starting point and use the knowledge-based theory of industrial clusters as a guiding perspective for developing expected properties of the network's small-worldness. This theory-based inductive approach will help us identify the appropriate social network techniques to evaluate the topology and evolution of this global cluster network.

A first property we should expect is that the global cluster network exhibits "small world" properties (Andersen and Lorenzen 2007). One of the general results of the literature on complex networks is that high-performance networks in many settings (biological, technological, social, economic) have the "small-world" property (Watts and Strogatz, 1998; Watts, 2004; Albert and Barabasi, 2002, Goyal et al., 2006). A small-world is a network whose topology combines high clustering among nodes with short average distance (path length) across nodes. A high clustering coefficient means that an actor's linkages are on average also more likely to be connected to each other. A short path length suggests that the average node-to-node distance between actors is low. Inherent in most networks is a trade-off between short distance across nodes and high clustering among nodes, since one comes at the expense of the other if link formation is costly. By balancing this trade-off, the small-world is an "efficient" topology. There are important reasons to believe that the global cluster network exhibits both properties. First, linkages should be tightly knit within the geographic boundaries of industrial clusters due to the existence of location-based knowledge externalities that acts as a driver for firms to collocate in the same location (Maskell and Malmberg 1999). At the same time, the existence of trans-local pipelines that companies build to acquire knowledge pockets from distant locations (Bathelt et al. 2004; Owen-Smith and Powell 2004) infers that the network structure should ensure a short path length between any pair of actors in the global cluster network, in the sense that actors in one industrial cluster are able to access knowledge developed in another industrial cluster through just a few intermediate linkages. This conjecture can be summarized as follows:

Proposition 1: The global cluster network is a small-world.

The network topology should not be the same for horizontal and vertical linkages. First, since a firm's motivation to locate in an industrial cluster varies across the horizontal and vertical dimensions, the clustering dynamics may well differ across linkage types (Li 2014). Horizontally, firms tend to collocate with similar firms since it provides access to pockets of knowledge through the monitoring of rivals. Vertically, in contrast, firms collocate with related firms that are part of the same value chain since it allows them to optimize their input-output interactions (Lundvall 1992). Since firm agglomeration is driven by different factors, we should expect clustering dynamics to differ across linkage types. There is some evidence to back this up. Malmberg and Power (2005) report that vertical linkages are generally more spread out trans-locally than horizontal linkages.

Second, we should not expect the average path length to be the same across linkage types either since a firm's motives to create trans-local linkages also varies across the horizontal and vertical dimension (Bathelt and Li 2014). Horizontally, firms located in developed-country clusters have the incentive to establish horizontal linkages with other firms or subsidiaries located in other developed-country clusters to gain access to complementary knowledge and labour pools. Vertically, in contrast, they often have the incentive to develop trans-local linkages with firms in less advanced clusters to take advantage of comparative advantage forces.

Taken together, this implies that the global cluster network may exhibit different properties when we divide it up into sub-networks by linkage types. This conjecture can be summarized as follows:

Proposition 2: The small-world properties of the global cluster network vary across linkage types.

The structure of the global cluster network should be evolving over time. Digitalization and globalisation are considered to be two forces that have been altering the configuration of firm linkages both within and across industrial clusters (Morgan 2004). Reductions in tariffs and transportation costs have further fuelled this process by reducing the cost of transporting material goods across national and regional borders (Behrens et al. 2015; Hummels 2007).

Digitalization and globalisation should affect the configuration of linkages differently depending on the linkage type. Concerning vertical linkages, it has been widely argued that the improvements in communication technology and reductions in trade costs have led to the trans-localisation of many vertical linkages over time as companies move value chain stages offshore (Blinder 2006; Leamer and Storper 2001; Yi 2003). Since companies are able to codify the knowledge that they need to exchange with their buyers and suppliers, they see the benefit of collocating with their suppliers diminishing. Therefore, firms start replacing their existing local buyer-supplier linkages by new trans-local connections with firms at remote yet cheaper locations. Reductions in tariffs and transportation costs can further strengthen this trend if linkages lead to the transportation of material goods. This process is considered a key driver behind the rise of global value chains (Sturgeon et al. 2008).

One should not expect a similar degree of trans-localisation for horizontal linkages, however. As mentioned above, the key benefit of horizontally collocating with competitors is that it gives a firm the ability to monitor its rivals as well as gain access to a pool of location-based expertise. Since a lot of the sought-for information and knowledge is tacit and therefore locationally sticky, these forces of geographic agglomeration are not necessarily diminished by improvements in communication technology and reductions in trade costs, or at least not at the same extent as for vertical linkages (Morgan 2004; Rodriguez-Pose and Crescenzi 2008). On the contrary, one may even expect that the trans-localisation of buyer-supplier linkages reinforces the geographic clustering of horizontal linkages (Duranton and Puga 2005; Grossman and Rossi-Hansberg 2012). Indeed, as companies gain the ability to separate a specific value chain activity from other parts of the value chain, they have the incentive to locate that activity in an industrial cluster that is specialized in that specific value chain sliver, leading to an increase in horizontal linkages within the industrial cluster.

Taken together, these arguments suggest we should expect that the trans-localisation of vertical linkages reduces average distance in the network over time. At the same time, the persistence and perhaps even increase in localised horizontal linkages should lead to the maintenance of a high level of clustering in the network. We summarize this conjecture as follows:

Proposition 3: The global cluster network is becoming increasingly small-world like over time. Average distance falls, but clustering remains high in the network.

7.4 Data and Methods

Our dataset maps the network of local and trans-local firm linkages in the aerospace industry within and across 52 industrial clusters in North America and (Greater) Europe over the period 2002-2014. We have conducted a number of steps to create the dataset. First, we have used information from the European Cluster Observatory, US Cluster Mapping Project, Canadian Cluster Database and Mexico's INADEM to identify the key aerospace clusters in North America and Europe. Next, we have used individual cluster databases to identify the list of firms located in each industrial cluster. Finally, we have combed through official company reports, approved lists of suppliers, company websites and news articles to carefully map each firm's local and trans-local linkages. In doing so, we have made a distinction between three types of firm ties: (1) intra-firm investment linkages; (2) inter-firm buyer-supplier linkages and (3) inter-firm partnership linkages (e.g., R&D partnership, joint training program, participation in a joint project). In total, our dataset consists of 16,146 local linkages and 34,654 trans-local linkages across 52 clusters during the three time periods 2002-2005, 2006-2009 and 2010-2014.

We distinguish between three types of linkages:

- *Buyer-supplier linkage*: a firm is considered a supplier of another firm if it features on the approved supplier list and is located in one of the clusters in our dataset;
- *Investment linkage:* headquarter-subsidiary or subsidiary-subsidiary relation between two firms owned by the same company. To operationalize this, we assume that all subsidiaries of a company have an investment linkage with all other subsidiaries of the same company.
- *Partnership linkage*: a firm has a formal partnership with another firm. This could, for example, be a joint R&D program, a joint venture or a formal training partnership;

We consider buyer-supplier and partnership linkages as proxies for vertical and horizontal inter-firm linkages, respectively. We treat investment linkages separate and recognize the limitation that we cannot identify if it is horizontal or vertical.

We describe the data collection procedures in detail in Turkina, Van Assche, and Kali (2016). Note that while the span of our dataset does not cover the entire globe, we will continue to refer to the overall network as the "global cluster network" to simplify the exposition of the paper.

We focus on the aerospace industry as it has several key characteristics that are particularly relevant for our study. Companies in the industry rely heavily on formal inter-firm collaboration along both the vertical and horizontal dimension. Horizontally, aerospace companies often form inter-firm partnerships with other similar firms to pool resources and benefit from economies of scale. Vertically, the industry is characterized by a high rate of subcontracting along the supply chain. Also, as is well known, aerospace companies tend to agglomerate in a small number of industrial clusters around the world. In addition, the value chains of aircraft have globalised. For example, in the case of the Boeing 787 Dreamliner, more than 300 companies are involved that build parts at over 5000 factories worldwide. More details on the aerospace industry can be found in Turkina et al. (2016).

To provide an idea how the universe of linkages for a single firm looks like in our dataset, in Figure 7.1 we map the ego network of firm linkages for the Aeromontréal-based company Bombardier Aerospace for 2010-2014. Linkages within the square are Bombardier Aerospace's local linkages, while linkages outside of the square are its trans-local linkages. For example, Bombardier Aerospace has a local buyer-supplier linkage with the Canadian division of French manufacturer THALES Avionics SA which provides the spoiler system for Bombardier's *Learjet* 85 program. It also has a local research partnership linkage with Bell Helicopter aimed at developing advanced flow simulation methods that will shorten time to market and increase aviation safety. And it has a trans-local investment linkage in Queretaro, after investing over $250 million in setting up a greenfield plant to produce fuselages, wings, and electrical harnesses.

Figure 7.1: Bombardier Aerospace (Montreal unit) ego network 2010-2014

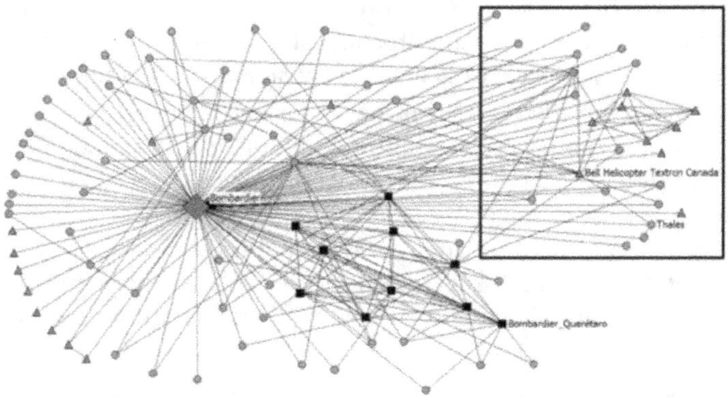

Color images of figures can be downloaded at the book's page
[URL: https://vernonpress.com/book/96]

Note: red triangles are partnership linkages, blue circles are buyer-supplier linkages, and black squares are investment linkages. In the graph, Bombardier does not have any local investment linkages.

Table 7.1 gives some sense of the coverage of our database across time periods and linkage types. Our dataset consists of 16,146 local linkages and 34,554 trans-local linkages across 52 aerospace clusters and three time periods.[2]

Table 7.1: Number of local and trans-local linkages, by type and time period

Linkages	Local			Trans-local		
	2002-2005	2006-2009	2010-2014	2002-2005	2006-2009	2010-2014
Buyer-supplier	4307	3237	2901	906	2681	3383
Partnership	692	1685	2468	1592	1905	2201
Investment	331	281	244	6117	7693	8076
Total	5330	5203	5613	8615	12279	13660

[2] The high number of trans-local investment linkages reflects full cohesion of firm-level investment sub-networks.

7.4.1 Previous analysis

In Turkina et al. (2016), we identified a number of interesting trends over time which are in line with the emergence of global value chains: in the aerospace industry, we witness a significant increase in the share of trans-local linkages between 2002-2005 and 2010-2014. This is largely due to a spatial reconfiguration of intra-firm and buyer-supplier linkages. Trans-local buyer-supplier and intra-firm linkages have increased by 15.3% and 14.2% respectively, while their local counterparts have decreased 12.1% and 13.7%. In contrast, partnership linkages have behaved differently: they have grown trans-locally but have increased even faster at the local level. We have attributed this trend to the fact that industrial clusters over time have started specializing increasingly in fine-grained slices of global value chains rather than in entire industries.

Figure 7.2: Growth in number of linkages (%), 2002-05 to 2011-14

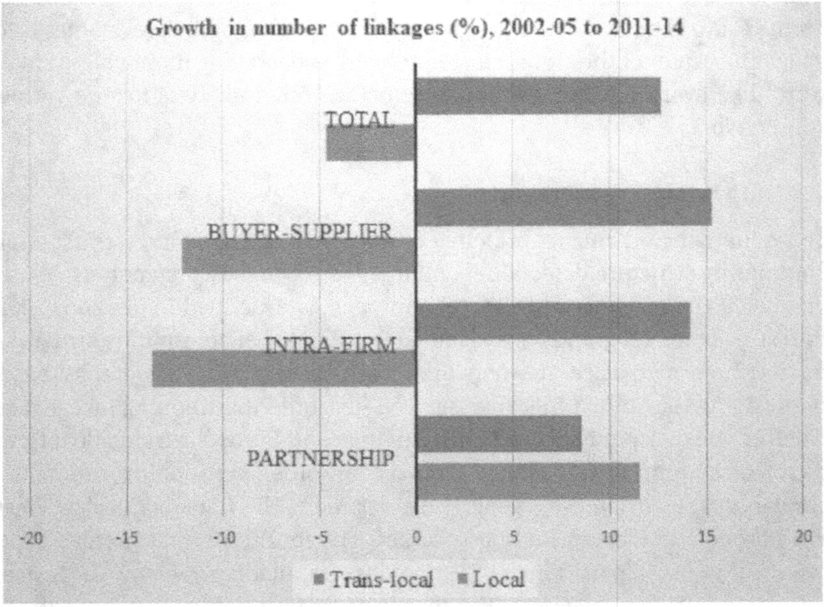

Color images of figures can be downloaded at the book's page [URL: https://vernonpress.com/book/96]

7.4.2 Methods

Our goal here is to examine the propositions developed in section 7.3 by analysing the topology and dynamics of the global cluster network. In this section, we describe the set of techniques that we will use in this paper for uncovering latent communities that underlie the network of linkages within and across clusters.

In a first step, we apply community structure detection techniques to social network analysis to examine the extent to which geography has eroded as an important organizing principle of the global cluster network. Then, we will examine whether the global cluster network, as well as the sub-networks by linkage type, are "small-world" like. As described earlier, a small-world network is one which combines high clustering of linkages (not to be confused with high geographic agglomeration of linkages) with short average distance between nodes. In order to examine this feature empirically, we will calculate the clustering coefficient and average path length of the observed global cluster network and then compare these measures to the properties of a simulated random network upon the same nodes. The idea behind comparing the actual network to a random one is to provide us with a sense of the extent to which the same properties could have arisen by chance, or randomly, as it were. As described below, the properties of the random network, which is used as a benchmark for comparison to the actual network, are obtained by Monte Carlo simulations. Performing this comparison over time enables us to gauge the extent of the global cluster network is becoming more or less small-world like over time. We will also conduct a similar analysis for the various sub-networks.

7.5 Data analysis and results

To evaluate the organizing principle of the aerospace network, we first apply community structure detection techniques to social network analysis. To this end, we use a maximum likelihood approach as described in Jackson (2008) to test whether geography is a significant predictor of community structures in the three aerospace sub-networks. We use four-order geography-based partitioning to conduct this analysis. The first-order partitioning investigates whether the division between North America and Europe is a significant predictor of community structure. The second-order partitioning conducts a similar analysis using the 5 geographic partitions US, Canada, Mexico, Western Europe and Eastern Europe & Turkey. The third-order partitioning separates between 14 partitions (4 US regions, 2 Canadian regions, 3 Mexican regions, 5 European regions). The fourth-order partitioning separates the 52 industrial clusters.

Table 7.2 presents the results of the analysis applied to the overall network and the subnetworks. As far as the whole network is concerned, the results show significant geography-based clustering (i.e., geographical agglomeration of linkages) in the period 2002-2005 with the first-order and second-order partitionings significant at the 10 percent level. At the same time, we find evidence that over time the geographic partitioning reflects less well the "true" underlying community structure. Between 2002-2005 and 2010-2014, the p-values of the fitness tests have declined for all four orders of partitioning for the overall network. In 2006-2009 and 2010-2014, none of the four-order partitionings are significant at the 10% level.

Table 7.2 also presents the same analysis for the three sub-networks separately. It is important to note that we cannot conduct this analysis for the investment sub-network since it is composed of the islands of fully cohesive but disconnected firm-level sub-networks. Instead, we compute the firm-level statistical probability that the focal firm conducts investment in its own local cluster, in its region, in its country, and finally, in its continent.

Table 7.2: Statistical significance of different partitioning schemes (p-value of the fitness test)

Partitioning order	Buyer-supplier			Partnership			Investment			Global aerospace network		
	2002-2005	2006-2009	2010-2014	2002-2005	2006-2009	2010-2014	2002-2005	2006-2009	2010-2014	2002-2005	2006-2009	2010-2014
First order (North America vs. Europe)	0.000	0.003	0.021	0.218	0.264	0.352	0.054	0.127	0.255	0.054	0.102	0.205
Second order (US, Canada, Mexico, Western Europe and Eastern Europe)	0.000	0.148	0.623	0.152	0.239	0.584	0.383	0.421	0.662	0.092	0.413	0.511
Third order – (4 US regions, 2 Canadian regions, 3 Mexican regions, 5 European regions)	0.003	0.072	0.664	0.469	0.383	0.217	0.473	0.564	0.706	0.384	0.567	0.586
Fourth order (the number of industrial clusters in the sample)	0.000	0.046	0.055	0.201	0.098	0.052	0.739	0.805	0.871	0.209	0.218	0.221

Concerning the buyer-supplier sub-network, the results in table 7.2 are similar to the overall network. There is clear geography-based clustering in the period 2002-2005 with all of the four-order partitionings significant at the 1 percent level. At the same time, we find evidence that over time the geographic partitioning reflects less well the "true" underlying community structure. Between 2002-2005 and 2010-2014, the p-values of the fitness tests have declined for all four orders of partitioning for the buyer-supplier sub-network. In 2010-2014, only the first-order partitioning remained significant at the 5% level. Combining this result with the results of our small-world analysis, it seems that the trans-localisation of buyer-supplier linkages is rendering geography a poorer predictor of the buyer-supplier sub-network's community structure.

As far as the partnership sub-network is concerned, we once again see an opposing trend. In 2002-2005, geographic partitioning was a poor predictor of the true community structure in the partnership sub-network. Over time, nonetheless, the p-values of the fitness tests decline for some of the partitionings. In 2010-2014, we find that the fourth-order partitioning becomes significant at the 10% level. These results suggest that the increased localisation of linkages in the partnership sub-network is starting to render geography as a predictor of the partnership sub-network's community structure.

Following the approach pioneered by Watts and Strogatz (1998) and Palla et al. (2005), we then analyse the small world properties of our global cluster network in the aerospace industry over the three time periods to examine the extent to which the global topology of the network is becoming more or less like a small-world network over time.

The small-world property implies that the global aerospace network would be highly clustered, yet have small characteristic path lengths, like random graphs. To analyse these properties, we apply an algorithm that computes the average shortest network path for all possible vertices and the clustering coefficient in the aerospace network. Then we compare these properties with those created by simulation of random linkages in our networks. To construct the clustering coefficient and average path length for the random network, we used Monte Carlo simulation and ran the random network 100 times and took the average. Table 7.3 reports the average shortest path lengths and clustering coefficients for the actual aerospace cluster network and the random networks for the three time periods.

Table 7.3: Small world analysis (whole network)

	Aerospace cluster network		Random network	
	Average Shortest Path Length	**Clustering Coefficient**	**Average Shortest Path Length**	**Clustering Coefficient**
2002-2005	4.654	0.421	10.911	0.154
2006-2009	3.516	0.471	11.302	0.152
2010-2014	3.087	0.496	11.714	0.151

The results in table 7.3 suggest that the global topology of the aerospace cluster network exhibits small-world network properties with an average path length smaller and the clustering coefficient higher than in the randomly simulated network for each of the three time periods. This finding supports our first proposition suggesting that the global cluster network of the aerospace network is a small world.

In line with proposition 3, the results in table 7.3 also show that the aerospace cluster network is becoming even more small-world-like over the sample period. Over time, the average shortest path length of the aerospace cluster network decreases (in 2010-2014, almost four times smaller than the one in the simulated network and statistically significantly smaller than in the 2002-2005 aerospace network (mean test, 0.000 p-value), while the clustering coefficient gradually increases. This implies that the topology of the overall network is changing and becoming ever more efficient over time.

It is important to caution that we should not interpret the increasing clustering coefficient as evidence of a growing concentration of linkages within the geographic boundaries of industrial clusters. Indeed, the clustering coefficient simply measures the cliquishness of nodes in a network. More specifically, the clustering coefficient measures the extent to which the direct connections of a node (both locally and trans-locally) are also connected to each other, averaged over all possible triples of nodes in the network. The clustering coefficient takes into consideration connections occurring both locally and trans-locally. It is thus entirely possible that the clustering coefficient of the aerospace cluster network increases despite of declining importance of local linkages compared to trans-local linkages.

To gain further insights into what is driving the small-world properties of the aerospace cluster network, we break up the network into three sub-networks by linkage type and replicate the analysis conducted in table 7.4. The analysis of the buyer-supplier and partnership sub-networks presented in tables 7.4a and 7.4b show important similarities with that of the overall network. Both sub-networks tend to exhibit small-world properties in the three time periods, even though these properties are clearly stronger for the buyer-supplier sub-network than for the partnership sub-network. For both sub-networks, these small-world properties tend to strengthen over time.

Table 7.4a: Small world analysis (buyer-supplier sub-network)

	Aerospace cluster network		Random network	
	Average Shortest Path Length	**Clustering Coefficient**	**Average Shortest Path Length**	**Clustering Coefficient**
2002-2005	5.283	0.290	8.002	0.158
2006-2009	4.328	0.321	9.508	0.155
2010-2014	3.412	0.348	10.013	0.153

Table 7.4b: Small world analysis (partnership network)

	Aerospace cluster network		Random network	
	Average Shortest Path Length	**Clustering Coefficient**	**Average Shortest Path Length**	**Clustering Coefficient**
2002-2005	6.795	0.169	6.994	0.161
2006-2009	6.121	0.268	7.830	0.160
2010-2014	5.683	0.301	8.201	0.159

Note that we cannot conduct a similar small-world analysis on the investment sub-network due to its intrinsic properties. Since by definition we assume that all subsidiaries of a company have an investment linkage among each other, the investment sub-network simply consists of islands of fully cohesive linkages between subsidiaries of the same firm with an absence of connections between firms. Due to these features, it is not possible to run small-world network algorithms on the investment sub-network.

Combining the results of our small-world analysis with the community structure detection, it seems that geography is becoming a poorer predictor of the overall network's community structure.

7.6 Discussion of findings, limitations and directions for future research

In this paper, we have combined a unique and new dataset of firm linkages within and between aerospace clusters with network methods to examine the small-world properties of the global aerospace network. Our analysis yields the following stylized facts.

First, we observe that high clustering in the network cannot simply be attributed to geographical boundaries. The community structure detection analysis we conducted in section 7.5 suggests that while geographical partitioning is helpful to predict the clustering in the initial network, it becomes a poor predictor in the later years of our data samples.

Second, we find that the global cluster network exhibits small-world properties that have strengthened over time. Linkages in the network are highly clustered, and this clustering of linkages has increased over time. Furthermore, there is short average distance between nodes due to the existence of trans-local pipelines that connect industrial clusters, and this average distance has decreased over time.

Third, we find that it is important to distinguish between different linkage types to explain these stylized facts. The configuration of buyer-supplier, partnership, and investment linkages have transformed very differently over time. Between 2002-2005 and 2010-2014, many buyer-supplier and investment linkages have moved trans-locally (i.e., offshore) and often to emerging clusters in developing countries such as Mexico, Turkey, and Eastern Europe. This pattern is consistent with the findings of numerous studies which document the rise of global value chains and their expansion into developing countries (Feenstra 1998; Johnson and Noguera 2012). Conversely, partnership linkages have become more localised. This trend helps explain why industrial clusters seem to keep intact despite the large expansion of global value chains. At the same time, we found that trans-local partnership linkages grow between clusters specializing in similar functions.

Future work could also advance our findings by modelling linkages through a value based approach instead of the binary scale that we used. In addition, an even more fine-grained distinction between linkage types could further our understanding which type of connectedness matters more for local cluster dynamics. This can be done by breaking investment linkages further up into a horizontal and vertical dimension. Or it can also be done by distinguishing between different types of partnership linkages.

Finally, it would be interesting to explore how the changes in the structure of the global cluster network affect the network position, performance and upgrading pattern of individual clusters. Which factors explain the network position of an industrial cluster? How does this affect an industrial cluster's performance? Are there industrial clusters that have been able to improve their performance by altering their network position? Finally, what can policymakers do to adapt their policies to this new cluster reality?

7.7 References

Albert, R., and A. Barabási. 2002. Statistical mechanics of complex networks. *Reviews of modern physics* 74(1): 47-98.

Alfaro, L. and A. Charlton. 2009. Intra-industry foreign direct investment. The American Economic Review 99(5): 2096-2119.

Andersen, K., and M. Lorenzen. 2007. The stretching of weak ties: clusters, pipelines, and the creation of small worlds. Mimeo.

Bathelt, H. and F. Li. 2014. Global cluster networks – foreign direct investment flows from Canada to China. *Journal of Economic Geography* 14(1): 45-71.

Bathelt, H., A. Malmberg, and P. Maskell. 2004. Clusters and knowledge: local buzz, global pipelines and the process of knowledge creation. *Progress in Human geography* 28(1): 31-56.

Bathelt, H., and P. Turi. 2011. Local, global and virtual buzz: The importance of face-to-face contact in economic interaction and possibilities to go beyond. *Geoforum*, 42(5), 520-529.

Behrens, K., T. Bougna, and M. Brown. 2015. The world is not yet flat: Transport costs matter! CEPR Discussion Paper No. 10356.

Blinder, A. 2006. Offshoring: the next industrial revolution? *Foreign Affairs* 85(2): 113-128.

Boschma, R. and A. Ter Wal. 2007. Knowledge networks and innovative performance in an industrial district: the case of a footwear district in the South of Italy. *Industry and Innovation*, 14(2): 177-199.

Bresnahan, T. and A. Gambardella. 2004. *Building a High-Tech Cluster: Silicon Valley and Beyond.* Cambridge: Cambridge University Press.

Cano-Kollmann, M., T. Hannigan, R. Mudambi, and H. Ra. 2014. Thriving innovation amidst manufacturing decline: the Detroit auto cluster and the stickiness of local knowledge. Mimeo.

Delgado, M., M. Porter, and S. Stern. 2010. Clusters and entrepreneurship. *Journal of Economic Geography* 10(4): 495–518.

Delgado, M., M. Porter, and S. Stern. 2014. Clusters, convergence, and economic performance. *Research Policy* 43(10): 1785–1799.

Duranton, G., and D. Puga. 2005. From sectoral to functional urban specialisation. *Journal of Urban Economics* 57(2): 343-370.

Dyer, J., and H. Singh. 1998. The relational view: cooperative strategy and sources of interorganizational competitive advantage. *Academy of Management Review*, 23(4): 660-679.

Feenstra, R. 1998. Integration of trade and disintegration of production in the global economy. *The Journal of Economic Perspectives*, 12(4): 31-50.

Feldman, M. and D. Audretsch. 1999. Innovation in cities: science-based diversity, specialization, and localised competition. *European Economic Review* 43(2): 409–29.

Fortunato, S. Community detection in graphs. 2010. *Physics Reports* 486(3): 75-174.

Giuliani, E., and Bell, M. 2005. The micro-determinants of meso-level learning and innovation: evidence from a Chilean wine cluster. *Research policy,* 34(1): 47-68.

Glaeser, E. and W. Kerr. 2009. Local industrial conditions and entrepreneurship: how much of the spatial distribution can we explain? *Journal of Economics and Management Strategy* 18(3): 623–63.

Glückler, J. 2007. Economic geography and the evolution of networks. *Journal of Economic Geography* 7(5): 619-634.

Goyal, S., M. Van der Leij, and J. Moraga-Gonzalez. 2006. Economics: An Emerging Small World. *Journal of political economy* 114(2): 403-412.

Hummels, D. 2007. Transportation costs and international trade in the second era of globalisation. *Journal of Economic Perspectives* 21(3): 131-54.

Jackson, M. 2008. *Social and Economic Networks,* Princeton University Press.

Johnson, R., and G. Noguera. 2012. Accounting for intermediates: Production sharing and trade in value added. *Journal of International Economics,* 86(2): 224-236.

Kamada, T., and S. Kawai. 1989. An algorithm for drawing general undirected graphs. *Information processing letters* 31(1): 7-15.

Leamer, E., and M. Storper. 2001. The economic geography of the internet age. *Journal of International Business Studies* 32(4): 641-665.

Li, P.-F. 2014. Horizontal versus vertical learning: divergence and diversification of lead firms in the Hangji toothbrush cluster. *Regional studies* 46.

Lorenzen, M. and R. Mudambi. 2013. Clusters, connectivity and catch-up: Bollywood and Bangalore in the global economy. *Journal of Economic Geography* 13(3): 501-534.

Lundvall, B. (Ed.). 1992. *National Systems of Innovation: Towards a Theory of Innovation and Interactive Learning.* London: Pinter Publishers.

Malmberg, A., and P. Maskell. 2006. Localised learning revisited. *Growth and Change* 37(1), 1-18.

Malmberg A., and D. Power. 2005. (How) do (firms in) clusters create knowledge? *Industry and Innovation* 12: 409–431.

Maskell, P. 2001. Towards a knowledge-based theory of the geographical cluster. *Industrial and corporate change* 10(4): 921-943.

Maskell, P., and A. Malmberg 1999. Localised learning and industrial competitiveness. *Cambridge Journal of Economics,* 23(2): 167-185.

Morgan, K. 2004. The exaggerated death of geography: learning, proximity and territorial innovation systems. *Journal of Economic Geography* 4(1), 3-21.

Newman, M. 2004. Fast algorithm for detecting community structure in networks. *Physical Review E* 69(6): 066133.

Niosi, J., and M. Zhegu. 2010. Aerospace clusters: local or global knowledge spillovers? *Industry & Innovation* 12(1): 5-29.

Owen-Smith, J., and W. Powell. 2004. Knowledge networks as channels and conduits: The effects of spillovers in the Boston biotechnology community. *Organization science,* 15(1), 5-21.

Palla, G., I. Derényi, I. Farkas, and T. Vicsek. 2005. Uncovering the overlapping community structure of complex networks in nature and society. *Nature* 435(7043): 814-818.

Porter, M. 1990. *The Competitive Advantage of Nations.* New York: Free Press.

Porter, M. 2003. The economic performance of regions. *Regional Studies* 37(6): 549–78.

Rodríguez-Pose, A., and R. Crescenzi. 2008. Mountains in a flat world: why proximity still matters for the location of economic activity. *Cambridge Journal of Regions, Economy and Society,* 1(3): 371-388.

Romero, J. 2011. Centripetal forces in aerospace clusters in Mexico. *Innovation and Development* 1(2): 303-318.

Saxenian, A. 1994. *Regional Advantage: Culture and Competition in Silicon Valley and Route 128.* Massachussetts: Harvard University Press.

Storper, M., and A. Venables. 2004. Buzz: face-to-face contact and the urban economy. *Journal of Economic Geography,* 4(4): 351-370.

Sturgeon, T. 2002. Modular production networks: a new American model of industrial organization. *Industrial and Corporate Change,* 11(3): 451-496.

Sturgeon, T. 2003. What really goes on in Silicon Valley? Spatial clustering and dispersal in modular production networks. *Journal of economic geography* 3(2): 199-225.

Sturgeon, T., J. Van Biesebroeck and G. Gereffi. 2008. Value chains, networks and clusters: reframing the global automotive industry. *Journal of economic geography* 8(3): 297-321.

Ter Wal, A. and R. Boschma. 2009. Applying social network analysis in economic geography: framing some key analytic issues. *The Annals of Regional Science,* 43(3), 739-756.

Traud, A., C. Frost, P. Mucha and M. Porter. 2009. Visualization of communities in networks. *Chaos* 19(4).

Turkina, E., Van Assche, A, and R. Kali 2016, Structure and evolution of global cluster networks: evidence from the aerospace industry, *Journal of Economic Geography,* doi: 10.1093/jeg/lbw020

Von Hippel, E. 1989. *Cooperation between rivals: informal know-how trading.* Springer Netherlands: 157-175.

Watts, D. 2004. The "new" science of networks. *Annual review of sociology*: 30: 243-270.

Watts, D., and S. Strogatz. 1998. Collective dynamics of 'small-world' networks. *Nature* 393(6684): 440-442.

Wolfe, D., and M. Gertler. 2004. Clusters from the inside and out: local dynamics and global linkages. *Urban Studies* 41(5-6): 1071-1093.

Yi, K.-M. 2003. Can vertical specialization explain the growth of world trade? *Journal of Political Economy* 111(1): 52-102.

8.

The international fragmentation of production: a multilevel network approach

Matthew Smith, Sara Gorgoni and Bruce Cronin

Data: International trade data (UNComtrade) and Bureau Van Dijk's Orbis
Software: UCINET, R (statnet and tnet), Visone and MPNet

8.1 Introduction

Twenty-first century production is fragmented into a number of stages, geographically spread internationally, which has led to a rise in the level of international trade in intermediate goods and intra-firm trade (Helg and Tajoli, 2005; UNCTAD, 2013). Fragmentation is due to outsourcing (Jones and Kierzkowski, 2005), as well as to the development of what Hanson et al. (2005) call "vertical production networks," which describes the trade between a parent company and affiliates located abroad.

Traditional approaches used to investigate international trade and FDI, such as gravity models, generally fail to recognise the interdependencies which characterise trade and investment patterns. These models assume that firm decisions to export, import and invest in a nation are made in isolation of other trading and investment relationships. This is a strong assumption, and in a world characterised by interdependent production strategies, a different modelling approach is called for. Yet attempts to address this via network analyses of international trade (Cingolani et al., 2017) or corporate ownership (Kogut, 2012; Altomonte and Rungi, 2015) consider these two phenomena in isolation, disregarding the fact that country-level patterns of trade are a result of firm-level activity.

This chapter aims to fill this gap by presenting a strategy for combining firm and country-level data to overcome the abstract separation between the micro and the macro level. We examine the challenges of building a multilevel relational dataset using firm ownership data from Orbis and country-level international trade data from UN Comtrade. We then propose a multilevel network model that could be used with such data to investigate the micro determinants of ties observed at the macro-level. We consider potential challenges and propose solutions to such a modelling approach.

The chapter is structured as follows: section two reviews the extant literature applying network analysis to the reorganisation of production. This section outlines the rationale for a multilevel network perspective, along with the contributions of a multilevel analysis. Section three describes the opportunities and challenges in constructing a multilevel dataset from Orbis and UN Comtrade databases. Section four develops advanced models that that could be employed to analyse such a multilevel network and considers potential modelling challenges. This is followed by concluding comments and suggestions for further applications.

8.2 Literature review

8.2.1 Network analysis and the fragmentation of production

The international fragmentation of production provides a number of challenges to standard methodological approaches, in particular, the independence assumption. These challenges to standard techniques have led to a variety of methodological approaches. One of the most frequently applied methodological frameworks is that of Global Value Chains (GVCs) ; where the production of a good is mapped from its conception to end use and beyond over a wide geographic space (Gereffi et al., 2005). The GVC approach primarily addresses research questions such as where is value added along the chain, and who reaps the value? (Nielsen et al., 2011; Nielsen et al., 2017) Whilst a very useful conceptual tool in examining production patterns, a significant limitation of the GVC approach is that the qualitative case study method it rests on provides limited generalisability.

A strand of literature that considers the fragmentation of production in a more quantitative manner, outside the GVC framework, is that which analyses multinational production.[1] This stream of literature clearly argues the need to consider the firm as the unit of analysis to uncover patterns of trade and the interaction with multinational production; a large amount of firm heterogeneity lies behind aggregated international trade data at the country-level (Ramondo et al., 2012). However, detailed datasets on firm trade are

[1] Antràs and Yeaple (2013) provide a review of the state of the literature on international trade and multinational firms, primarily considering the contributions and empirical implementation of more quantitative models.

widely unavailable, and those distinguishing between intra-firm and arm's length trade do not exist.

A limited number of studies have applied network analysis to international trade within particular industries, allowing the analysis of global value chains in an extensive and quantitative manner (Srholec, 2006; Amighini and Gorgoni, 2014; Blázquez and González-Díaz, 2015). A key contribution is Amighini and Gorgoni (2014), who examine disintegrated production patterns in the automotive sector. However, while the analysis of international trade within an industry is indicative of inter- and intra-industry production patterns, the reliance on country-level trade data alone leaves potentially important firm-level relationships obscured.

8.2.2 The contribution of a multilevel network approach

A crucial issue in investigating the international organisation of production is the fact that the majority of studies lack recognition – in terms of empirical analysis – of the multilevel nature of the phenomenon.

Studies generally examine international trade in isolation of Foreign Direct Investment (FDI) decisions, yet this is clearly not a realistic assumption in a world where production is a globally fragmented process, with many multinational and corporate groups utilising FDI and locational assets in their manufacturing activities to retain competitive advantages (Gray, 1996). Gammeltoft et al. (2010) recognise that studies that make use of FDI stock and flow statistics only illustrate overall country patterns. This approach elides the fact that FDI stock and flow data are an aggregation of the international investment activity of individual firms and that therefore trade and investment flows are dependent on corporate networks (Park and Park, 2015). Altomonte and Rungi (2013) define these corporate networks of firms linked by ownership as "business groups." They argue that business groups play a key role in the fragmentation of production; UNCTAD (2013) noted that these groups accounted for 80 percent of total world trade in 2010.

Sgrignoli (2014) makes an attempt to investigate the interplay between international trade and FDI through a network perspective, examining how the FDI network influences the trade network through a set of gravity models, more specifically to assess whether FDIs complement or substitute trade. However, within this study, inferences are made at the broad macro sector level (manufacturing and services), neglecting the vast differences in trade and investment patterns across industries. In the study the FDI network is a country-level network constructed by aggregating a large firm-level dataset, disregarding additional key information, such as corporate group affiliation. In any case, given the increasing complexity of the production process, there is a need to consider the interplay of FDI and trade beyond the classification of these as complements or substitutes.

The need to combine firm-level and country-level data has been acknowledged by several scholars (amongst them Miroudot et al., 2009). Current datasets, however, lack the required information, especially in relation to the rise of intra-firm trade, suggesting a need to combine bilateral trade data with firm-level information. Feenstra et al. (2010) recognise this in their examination of the state of available data for the study of international trade and FDI. They suggest that in order to better understand the complex nature of production as it is today, there is a need for this complexity to be reflected in the datasets used, capturing the increasing importance of MNEs and intra-firm trade. The rise of GVCs requires the creation of new datasets that can be used in quantitative studies; a factor additionally recognised by international economic organisations. For instance, a WTO-OECD collaborative initiative has resulted in a new dataset, Trade in Value Added, which maps value added patterns utilising aggregate industry level input-output tables (OECD, 2013).

In this chapter, we show how secondary data sources at different levels can be combined and used in a multilevel network analysis to shed light on the location of value and the positions of firms in GVCs.

8.3 Data considerations

There are a number of issues and challenges in combining data sources to create a multilevel international trade and production dataset. First, the data sources need to be sufficiently disaggregated to distinguish production and trade at a level that firms might arguably influence. Second, the macro-level and micro-level datasets must be classified in similar units to allow meaningful comparisons and consideration of interactions between levels. In this case, this means similar classification of product or commodity and of geographic location of activity. Third, to allow network analysis, the combined dataset must contain a sufficiently diverse set of nodes of activity and with sufficient linkages in terms of production and trade to constitute a network, rather than a set of dyadic relationships for example; this involves decisions on thresholds for inclusion of meaningful data.

8.3.1 Dataset construction

The selection of appropriate data is a key component in investigating the phenomenon of the fragmentation of production and, as this chapter utilises a multilevel perspective, matching the data at both micro and macro levels is essential. Drawing inspiration from the insight generated by the GVC approach on a case basis, we take the product as the framing level, considering product trade at the macro and the product production at the micro. The perspective of the product (or function or task, as it has also been referred to) has been argued as more relevant than the aggregated sector level when critically discussing issues in the area of the fragmentation of production (Grossman and Rossi-Hansberg, 2008; Baldwin and Robert-Nicoud, 2014), as a finished product is now generated through trade in intermediate goods (Timmer et al., 2013).

There are two approaches one could use to map the fragmentation of production at the country-level. Firstly, input-output (I-O) tables can be used to measure trade in intermediate inputs; alternatively, the trade patterns of components with a high level of disaggregation can be examined (Srholec, 2006). I-O tables provide useful, relevant data on inter-industry purchases, particularly recent extensions that include estimates of industry-level imports and exports (Timmer et al., 2015). But I-O tables are only constructed at high levels of aggregation, typically at no more than a two-digit level, for example, "C27, manufacture of electrical equipment." By contrast, trade data is available at a highly disaggregated level from the UN Comtrade database, for example, the five-digit Standard International Trade Classification (SITC) "77421, manufacture of x-ray, radiography, or radiotherapy apparatus."

The data from UN Comtrade can be used to build a macro-level, international trade network, where a tie is directed from the exporter to the importer. Because the analytical methods assume dichotomous data, a threshold needs to be applied to the data to ensure that only the most relevant ties are retained yet preserving the network structure. This procedure also helps in omitting countries which do not significantly contribute to trade yet increase levels of reciprocity. The appropriate threshold can be determined by examining the proportion of world trade that is retained by applying the threshold, to ensure the network represents the majority of global trade. A 0.01 percent threshold on SITC 7741, for example, retains 97 percent of world trade but reduces the number of countries included from 166 to 95.

Bureau van Dijk's Orbis database provides suitable data to build a micro-level ownership network and a firm-country affiliation network. This database has been used in the construction of ownership networks in a variety of studies (Glattfelder and Battiston, 2009; Vitali et al., 2011; Vitali and Battiston, 2013). The main challenge in the construction of the micro-level network the selection of firms that produce the product classified in the SITC used in the macro-level network. Firms are classified in Orbis on the basis of producing industry rather than traded commodity, principally the Statistical Classification of Economic Activities, in French Nomenclature Statistique des Activités

Économiques dans la Communauté Européenne (NACE). So, a mapping between the NACE industry and SITC trade codes is needed.

Eurostat maintains a set of correspondence tables among different statistical classification systems (Eurostat, 2017). There are no direct correspondence tables between NACE and SITC classification systems, but an indirect link is available via correspondence tables between NACE and the International Standardised Industry Classification (ISIC), ISIC and the United Nations Harmonised System (HS) and between HS and SITC. Thus, linking the correspondence tables NACE-ISIC-HS-SITC provides a method of systematically mapping NACE classifications to SITC classifications (ISDATA, 2017). By this means it is possible to, for example, map NACE code 266 "Manufacture of irradiation, electromedical and electrotherapeutic equipment" to SITC code 77421 "Manufacture of x-ray, radiography, or radiotherapy apparatus."

So, a firm's network of production of a product in internationally dispersed subsidiaries can be compared to the macro-level inter-country trade of that product. This involves the creation of two further datasets. The first, the micro-level ownership network, has firms as actors and ownership relations as ties, directed from the parent firm to the subsidiary. This positional strategy in defining the ownership network boundary ensures that only firms directly occupying a place in the manufacture of a particular product are included, yet this strategy generally results in a number of disconnected actors, with a set of small, separate connected components lacking ties between them (Knoke and Yang, 2008). The second dataset, the firm-country affiliation network, is constructed from the national location information of each of the firm's branches, where they have production, distribution and sales sites.

The full multilevel network, therefore, contains three types of ties: trade flows between countries, ownership ties between firms and the ties between firms and countries, based on the location of firms. Visualisations of an example full multilevel networks can be found in figure 8.1, where red nodes represent firms and blue nodes countries. In the remainder of the chapter, the firm-level ownership network is referred to as the micro-level, the international trade network as the macro-level and the firm-country affiliation network as the meso-level, in line with the terminology utilised in multilevel network analysis

Figure 8.1: Example full multilevel network

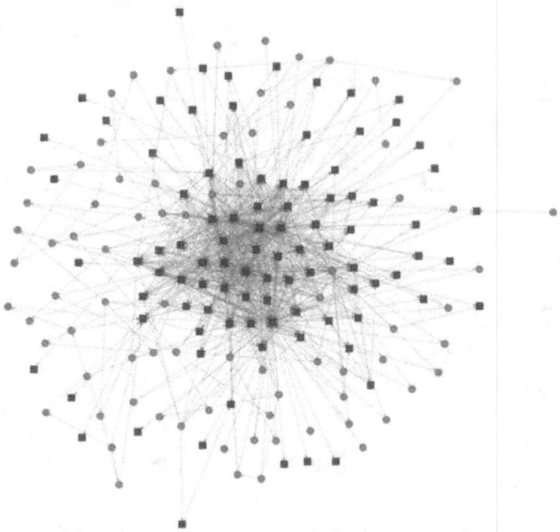

Color images of figures can be downloaded at the book's page [URL: https://vernonpress.com/book/96]

Note: Blue squares are countries and red circles are firms

8.3.2 Descriptive analysis of multilevel networks

This section provides a descriptive analysis of an example international production and trade network, examining the three levels separately, allowing the identification of the most prominent firms and nations.[2] The example used is broadly categorised as the medical and precision instruments industry, which includes items such as ultrasound machines and MRI systems (NACE code 266 "Manufacture of irradiation, electromedical and electrotherapeutic equipment").

Table 8.1 provides a summary of the network level statistics for both the international trade and ownership networks. The trade network is characterised by low reciprocity (two-way ties), suggesting a hierarchical structure. The trade network is also characterised by a high out-degree centralisation score, which suggests that export ties are not evenly distributed, rather there are a small number of countries with exports to many other countries. The in-degree centralisation score indicates that imports are relatively evenly distributed amongst countries in the network (when compared to exports).

[2] The descriptive network statistics are calculated using a combination of UCINET (Borgatti et al., 2002) and the R packages Statnet (Handcock et al., 2014) and tnet (Opsahl, 2009). The network visualisations were created using Visone (Baur et al., 2001).

Table 8.1: Descriptive Statistics for Trade and Ownership Networks

	Trade Network	Ownership Network
Size (No. of Nodes)	95	68
Density	0.0648	0.0105
Reciprocity	0.3247	0
Transitivity	0.4910	0
Average Degree	12.1895	1.4118
Out-Degree Centralization	0.6871	0.2165
In-Degree Centralization	0.1603	0.0046
Clustering Coefficient	0.7319	0

The macro-level network visualisation, presented in figure 8.2 indicates that the trade network is characterised by a core-periphery structure; Table 8.2 presents the members of the core along with the core-periphery density matrix and final fitness for the network. The core-periphery structure indicates that the trade within this sector is characterised by a tightly connected group of countries accounting for most of the trade. Where there is clearly a very dense core, with a core-core density score of 0.814. This contrasts with the low periphery-periphery density, which points towards members of the periphery excluded from a high number of trading relationships, and dependent on trade with the core. These results indicate a hierarchical structure of international trade, and therefore production, of medical and precision instruments.

Figure 8.2: Macro-level international trade network

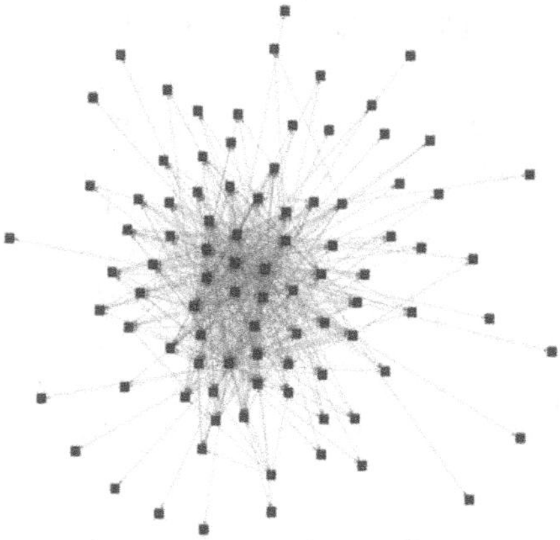

Color images of figures can be downloaded at the book's page
[URL: https://vernonpress.com/book/96]

Table 8.2: Core-periphery analysis of the international trade network

Core	USA, Germany, China, Japan, Netherlands, UK, Finland, France, Italy Republic of Korea, Spain, Switzerland, Malaysia	Density Matrix		C	P	Final Fitness	0.789
			C	0.814	0.343		
			P	0.046	0.006		

The core is prominently dominated by European nations, along with the USA, the key areas in terms of demand in the industry. The Republic of Korea's prominent position in the network may be a result of the Korean firm Samsung Electronics and its investment in the medical devices industry in 2011, along with the country's proximity to the related electronics value chain.

The micro-level ownership network is presented in figure 8.3 where the green triangles represent key lead firms in the network, that is, the firms which dominate the sector, for example, Medtronic Inc. Kogut and Walker (2001) note that ownership networks are characterised by a low density and are sparsely populated, while Todeva (2006) further emphasises that ownership networks involve hierarchical control. These characteristics can be clearly seen in the ownership network under examination. Figure 8.3 is clearly asymmetrical, centred on certain focal firms; these are often referred to as orchestrating or lead firms that often hold strategic positions in firm networks (Kano, 2017). In figure 8.3 these are represented by the green triangles.

Figure 8.3: Micro-level ownership network

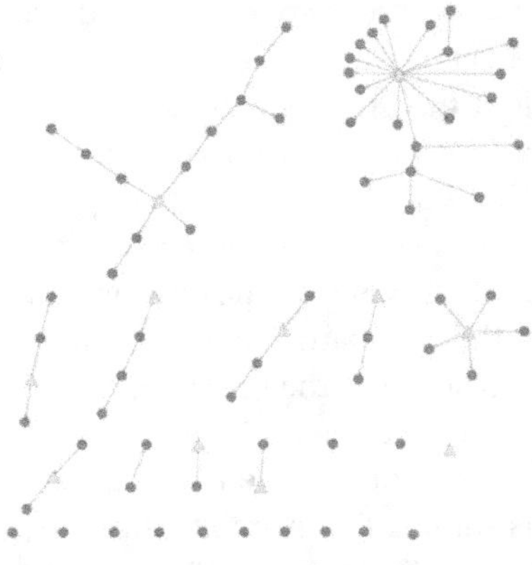

Color images of figures can be downloaded at the book's page [URL: https://vernonpress.com/book/96]

Note: Green triangles represent key lead firms in the network

8.4. Modelling multilevel networks

Models for multilevel network analysis have only really become available relatively recently, thanks to Wang et al. (2013) who introduced an extension of the Exponential Random Graph Model (ERGM) to the multilevel case. Since, there has been an influx of interest in multilevel network models due to the increased availability of rich datasets that can be analysed using these techniques (Lomi et al., 2016; Lazega and Snijders, 2016).

8.4.1 Exponential Random Graph Model (ERGM)

ERGMs are a well-established methodology to examine features of networks, with a number of empirical applications found in political science (Ingold and Leifeld, 2014; Heaney, 2013), sociology (Lubbers and Snijders, 2007) and managerial studies (Arrieta-Paredes and Cronin, 2016). ERGMs are used to test whether there is a tendency for reciprocity, transitivity and the spread of ties in a network, along with how nodal attributes shape how actors connect in the network. However, these applications focus on applying ERGMs to a single network, rather than a multilevel setting,

ERGMs are parameterized in terms of patterns of local network substructures, termed network configurations. The parameter values indicate the weight and direction of the network configurations in explaining the global network structure. The configurations are often used as indicators of network processes, and therefore the parameter values can offer information about the processes that potentially underpin the network (Lusher et al., 2013; Robins, 2013).

The types of parameters that can be specified in an ERGM framework can be split into three groups: structural effects, node covariates, and dyadic covariates. Structural effects are at the heart of the ERGM framework and allowing direct modelling of the interdependencies characterising a network. Second, the nodal covariates account for the formation of network ties as an outcome of the attribute of the actors themselves. Are nodes with a specific attribute more (or less) likely to send (or receive) ties? Node-based effects can also be used to test for homophily in the network; are ties more likely to occur between actors with the same attribute? In terms of international trade, we can test whether countries from the same region are more likely to trade. For continuous node-based covariates, there are also difference terms, which allow testing of whether a tie between two actors is more likely when the value of the actors is similar. For example, this allows the testing of whether countries of a similar size (in terms of GDP) are more likely to trade. Dyadic covariate effects model how another network (or relationship) influences the formation of ties, for example, how does the geographic distance matrix include global trade?

Wang et al. (2013)'s extension of the ERGM to the multilevel case is a probability distribution where the structure of a typical graph is a cumulation of the local process both within and across levels. This extension takes into account the multiple networks involved, the macro-level network (denoted by A), the micro-level network (denoted by B) and the meso-level network (denoted by X).

This extension is expressed in the form:

$$P(A = a, B = b, X = x) =$$

$$\frac{1}{k(\theta)} \exp(\sum \theta_Q z_Q(a) + \theta_Q z_Q(x) + \theta_Q z_Q(b) + \theta_Q z_Q(a, x) + \theta_Q z_Q(b, x) + \theta_Q z_Q(a, x, b))$$

Where:

$z_Q(a)$ and $z_Q(b)$ are the within level network statistics for the micro and macro levels.

$z_Q(x)$ is the network statistic for the structural effects in the bipartite meso-level .

$z_Q(a, x)$ and $z_Q(b, x)$ are the network statistics for the interactions between the macro and meso-level networks and the micro and meso level networks respectively.

$z_Q(a, x, b)$ are the network statistics for the configurations that involve ties from all three networks.

Limitations of the multilevel ERGM are discussed by Zappa and Lomi (2015) and are mainly concerned with the models' inability to deal with weighted ties and longitudinal data. An important drawback of this model is that it requires the trade and ownership linkages to be dichotomized, as multilevel ERGMs can only deal with binary data. Nevertheless, this approach still provides a valuable tool for the analysis of the structure and patterns of international trade and investment.

8.4.2 Multilevel network configurations

Local network configurations are an important part of ERGMs; they consist of a small subset of nodes and ties, which can represent a theoretical process, the model can then test the propensity for this theoretical process in the observed network. These local configurations represent the interdependencies between ties, and in the multilevel case, between levels. As noted by Zappa and Lomi (2015) in their detailed description of an empirical multilevel ERGM, typical statistical approaches often fail to capture these dependencies or treat them as part of the error term. In a multilevel estimation, a level is usually fixed; for example, the structure of the ownership network might be fixed, as the variable used to explain trade and investment patterns in the industry. Consequently, local network configuration is not needed for that level. This practice is observed in the application of multilevel ERGMs, which often consider the micro (or macro) level and the meso-level as exogenous (Zappa and Robins, 2016; Brennecke and Rank, 2016), hence reducing the complexity of the model.

Given the focus of this chapter is on multilevel analysis, we will omit to discuss in detail the macro- and meso-level configurations, referring the reader to Lusher et al. (2013) for a more thorough explanation. We would like to mention, however, that these configurations can be used to test key research hypothesis, such as for example, at the macro-level, whether trade exhibits preferential patterns and is concentrated in a handful of nations; whether exports and imports are evenly distributed; whether there is a tendency for nations that import intermediate inputs to also export; whether nations are more likely to trade with nations that they share multiple trading partners and many more.

The multilevel configurations span across the different levels and involve the trade ties between nations, the firm-country affiliation ties and the ownership ties amongst firms. These configurations are outlined in Table 8.3, along with their economic interpretation. These configurations allow testing of a wide range of informative structures in the data and have the potential to address a variety of research questions considering the organisation of production in the modern global economy.

For example, the *alternating affiliation*-based *closure* tests whether two countries are more likely to trade when they receive investments by the same firms. The *affiliation based trading/popularity/activity* effects allow investigation of how investment shapes international trade patterns, where we can test whether countries with a high level of investment have numerous import or export ties respectively in the international trade network. There is also the possibility to test whether there is a tendency for parents and subsidiaries to be located in the same nation through the *domestic subsidiary* effect.

The *intra-firm trade* parameter represents a form of cross-level exchange; here the assumption is made that the parent and subsidiary trade. The investigation of patterns of intra-firm trade is a valuable aspect of the application of the multilevel ERGM to these data, given that data on intra-firm trade is widely unavailable. Furthermore, identifying when trade is characterised as intra-firm can provide additional insights into the investment motives of multinational groups (Ivarsson and Johnsson, 2000).

Table 8.3: Multilevel ERGM – example multilevel configurations

Configuration	Representation	Economic Interpretation
Alternating affiliation-based closure		Propensity for a set of firms based in two nations to trigger a trade tie between them.
Affiliation based trading	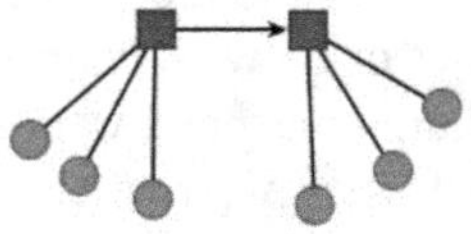	Propensity for nations with high levels of firm investment to trade.
Affiliation based popularity	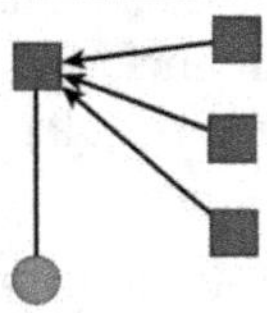	Propensity for countries with high levels of investment to establish several import ties in the international trade network.
Affiliation based activity	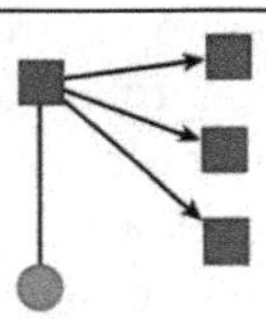	Propensity for countries with high levels of investment to establish several export ties in the international trade network.
Domestic Subsidiary	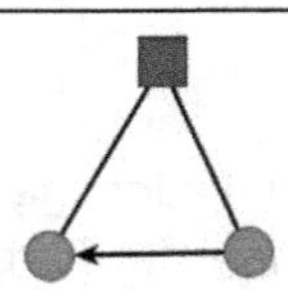	Propensity for two firms linked by ownership to be based in the same nation, i.e. the propensity for domestic subsidiaries.
Intra-firm trade	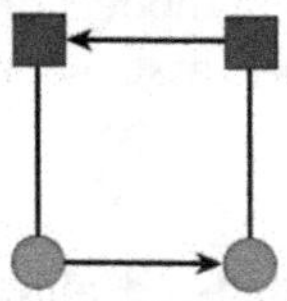	Propensity for intra-firm trade
Lead Firm Affiliation	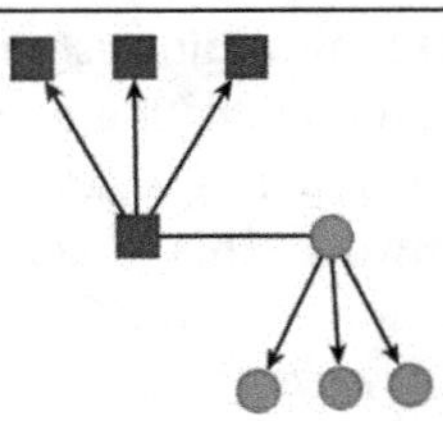	Propensity for countries with investment from firms with a high number of subsidiaries (lead firms) to establish several export ties in the international trade network, that is, the presence of lead or orchestrating firms.

Color images of figures can be downloaded at the book's page [URL: https://vernonpress.com/book/96]

Note: Red circles are firms and blue rectangles are nations.

8.4.3 Additional parameters

Although in this chapter we have focused on hypotheses we can test with the multilevel configurations, these are not the only parameters specified in the multilevel network model. Our key interest here is in the interdependencies between levels, and what these can reveal about the structure of international trade and investment (and therefore production). When modelling these, however, we can also specify effects at the macro (country to country trade network) and meso (firm-country affiliation network) levels as controls. There a number of structural parameters at the macro level which can be used to control for the spread of trade ties or network centralisation (spread parameters), transitivity (closure and shared partner parameters) and reciprocity (for a full discussion of the additional types of parameters that can be specified in single level ERGMs see Snijders et al., 2006; Lusher et al., 2013; Wang et al., 2009). Additional nodal covariates are included in the macro level to control for country size (GDP), market affluence (GDP per capita), regional homophily (region match) and geographic distance.

A range of parameters at the meso-level (firm-country affiliation network) can be included as control variables to control for certain features of the country-firm affiliation network. A country isolates parameter could be used to control for countries that are present in the international trade network, but where no firm from the micro-level ownership network is affiliated with them. Further parameters are also needed to control for the spread of ties in the meso-level.

In addition, it is necessary to include two multilevel level control parameters: subsidiary and parent-firm affiliation parameters. These parameters control for the absence of connections in the ownership and firm-country affiliation network, which would assist model convergence with a good fit and does not suffer from degeneracy issues associated with sparse networks.

8.4.4 Estimation considerations

The multilevel network models discussed above are fully implemented in MPNet software (Wang et al., 2014), providing estimation and goodness of fit procedures. The procedures involve simulating a large number of networks from the estimated ERGM and comparing characteristics of the simulated networks with the observed network. This is computationally challenging with large datasets, where simulations may run for several days. And as alluded to in the last section, when networks are sparse models may not converge to a stable result.

Parameter values resulting from estimation of the particular model provide an indication of the likelihood of each network configuration, given the other network configurations and effects specified in the model. A positive and significant configuration parameter indicates that the configuration is more likely to be observed in the network under examination than by random chance. A goodness of fit measure tests how well the estimated model as a whole is able to reproduce the salient characteristics of the observed network.

In the international trade and production case, since the network configurations are multilevel, estimation allows the identification of links between firm activity and trading patterns, providing sophisticated insights beyond simply noting associations between the two levels. In particular, the multilevel ERGM applied to this novel dataset construction provides a unique opportunity to test for intra-firm trade, the role of FDI, lead firms and locations of firm operations across an industry internationally, going beyond the single country-level approaches seen in the literature (De Backer and Yamano, 2012).

8.5 Concluding Comments

The problem of creating and analysing datasets that combine firm-level and country-level network data in order to better explain the international fragmentation of production is something that many scholars and international organisations are currently trying to address. This chapter has presented a method of constructing such a dataset and discussed how the application of a multilevel network model to this has the ability to explain the organisation of production in that sector and provide greater insight into patterns of intra-firm trade, investment patterns, and motives, than possible with existing approaches.

Although there are limitations to the multilevel ERGM approach presented here, namely the models' inability to deal with weighted ties and longitudinal data, the chapter demonstrates the value of this type of approach. There is a clear research agenda in applying this technique to a variety of internationally distributed industries to uncover distinctive types of organisation, which we would suggest would best begin with comparisons across industries with different technological content.

8.6 References

Altomonte, C. and Rungi, A. (2013) *Business groups as hierarchies of firms: Determinants of vertical integration and performance*, Fondazione Eni Enrico Mattei, Available at: http://econpapers.repec.org/RePEc:fem:femwpa:2013.33.

Altomonte, C. and Rungi, A. (2015) Firm performance and the optimal organization of business groups. Conference Paper, University of Birmingham, available at <https://www.birmingham.ac.uk/Documents/college-social-sciences/business/research/gvc/gvc-seminar-paper-29-10-2015.pdf>

Amighini, A. and Gorgoni, S. (2014) The international reorganisation of auto production, *The World Economy*, 37(7), pp. 923–952.

Antràs, P. and Yeaple, S. R. (2013) *Multinational firms and the structure of international trade*, Working Paper, National Bureau of Economic Research, Available at: http://www.nber.org/papers/w18775.

Arrieta-Paredes, M.-P. and Cronin, B. (2016) Exponential random graph models for management research: A case study of executive recruitment, *European Management Journal*, Available at: http://www.sciencedirect.com/science/article/pii/S0263237316300937.

Baldwin, R. and Robert-Nicoud, F. (2014) Trade-in-goods and trade-in-tasks: An integrating framework, *Journal of International Economics*, 92(1), pp. 51–62.

Baur, M., Benkert, M., Brandes, U., Cornelsen, S., Gaertler, M., Köpf, B., Lerner, J. and Wagner, D. (2001) Visone software for visual social network analysis, In *Graph Drawing, Lecture Notes in Computer Science*, Springer, Berlin, Heidelberg, pp. 463–464.

Blázquez, L. and González-Díaz, B. (2015) International automotive production networks: How the web comes together, *Journal of Economic Interaction and Coordination*, pp. 1–32.

Borgatti, S. P., Everett, M. G. and Freeman, L. C. (2002) *Ucinet for Windows: Software for social network analysis*, Harvard, MA, Analytic Technologies.

Brennecke, J. and Rank, O. N. (2016) The interplay between formal project memberships and informal advice seeking in knowledge-intensive firms: A multilevel network approach, *Social Networks*, 44, pp. 307–318.

Cingolani, I., Iapadre, L. and Tajoli, L. (2017) International production networks and the world trade structure, *International Economics*.

De Backer, K. and Yamano, N. (2012) *International comparative evidence on global value chains*, OECD Science, Technology and Industry Working Paper, OECD Publishing, Available at: http://ideas.repec.org/p/oec/stiaaa/2012-3-en.html.

Eurostat (2017) *RAMON - Reference and management of nomenclatures*, European Commission, Available at: http://ec.europa.eu/eurostat/ramon.

Feenstra, R. C., Lipsey, R. E., Branstetter, L. G., Foley, C. F., Harrigan, J., Jensen, J. B., Kletzer, L., Mann, C., Schott, P. K. and Wright, G. C. (2010) *Report on the state of available data for the study of international trade and foreign direct investment*, Working Paper, National Bureau of Economic Research, Available at: http://www.nber.org/papers/w16254.

Gammeltoft, P., Barnard, H. and Madhok, A. (2010) Emerging multinationals, emerging theory: Macro-and micro-level perspectives, *Journal of International Management*, 16(2), pp. 95–101.

Gereffi, G., Humphrey, J. and Sturgeon, T. (2005) The governance of global value chains, *Review of International Political Economy*, 12(1), pp. 78–104.

Glattfelder, J. B. and Battiston, S. (2009) Backbone of complex networks of corporations: The flow of control, *Physical Review E*, 80(3), p. 036104.

Gray, P. (1996) The eclectic paradigm: The next generation, *Transnational Corporations*, 5(2), pp. 51–65.

Grossman, G. M. and Rossi-Hansberg, E. (2008) Trading tasks: A simple theory of offshoring, *American Economic Review*, 98(5), pp. 1978–1997.

Handcock, M. S., Hunter, D. R., Butts, C. T., Goodreau, S. M., Krivitsky, P. N., Bender-deMoll, S. and Morris, M. (2014) Statnet: Software tools for the statistical analysis of network data, *The Statnet Project (http://www. statnet. org). R package version.*

Hanson, G. H., Mataloni, R. J. and Slaughter, M. J. (2005) Vertical production networks in multinational firms, *Review of Economics and Statistics*, 87(4), pp. 664–678.

Heaney, M. T. (2013) Multiplex networks and interest group influence reputation: An exponential random graph model, *Social Networks*, Available at: http://www.sciencedirect.com/science/article/pii/S0378873312000664.

Helg, R. and Tajoli, L. (2005) Patterns of international fragmentation of production and the relative demand for labor, *North American Journal of Economics and Finance*, 16, pp. 233–254.

Ingold, K. and Leifeld, P. (2014) Structural and institutional determinants of influence reputation: A comparison of collaborative and adversarial policy networks in decision making and implementation, *Journal of Public Administration Research and Theory*, p. muu043.

ISDATA (2017) *The industrial symbiosis data repository*, Available: http://isdata.org.

Ivarsson, I. and Johnsson, T. (2000) TNC strategies and variations in intra-firm trade: The case of foreign manufacturing affiliates in Sweden, *Geografiska Annaler: Series B, Human Geography*, 82(1), pp. 17–34.

Ivarsson, I. and Jonsson, T. (2003) Local technological competence and asset-seeking FDI: an empirical study of manufacturing and wholesale affiliates in Sweden, *International Business Review*, 12(3), pp. 369–386.

Jones, R. W. and Kierzkowski, H. (2005) International trade and agglomeration: An alternative framework, *Journal of Economics*, 86(1), pp. 1–16.

Kano, L. (2017) Global value chain governance: A relational perspective, *Journal of International Business Studies*, pp. 1–22.

Knoke, D. and Yang, S. (2008) *Social network analysis*, Sage.

Kogut, B. (2012) *The Small Worlds of Corporate Governance*, Cambridge, Mass, MIT Press.

Kogut, B. and Walker, G. (2001) The small world of Germany and the durability of national networks, *American Sociological Review*, 66(3), p. 317.

Lanz, R. and Miroudot, S. (2011) *Intra-firm trade*, OECD Trade Policy Papers, Paris, Organisation for Economic Co-operation and Development, Available at: http://www.oecd-ilibrary.org/content/workingpaper/5kg9p39lrwnn-en.

Lazega, E. and Snijders, T. A. B. (eds.) (2016) *Multilevel network analysis for the social sciences*, Cham, Springer International Publishing.

Lomi, A., Robins, G. and Tranmer, M. (2016) Introduction to multilevel social networks, *Social Networks*, 44, pp. 266–268.

Lubbers, M. J. and Snijders, T. A. B. (2007) A comparison of various approaches to the exponential random graph model: A reanalysis of 102 student networks in school classes, *Social Networks*, 29(4), pp. 489–507.

Lusher, D., Koskinen, J. and Robins, G. (2013) *Exponential random graph models for social networks: theory, methods, and applications*,.

Miroudot, S., Lanz, R. and Ragoussis, A. (2009) *Trade in intermediate goods and services*, OECD Publishing, Available at: http://www.abhatoo.net.ma/index.php/fre/content/download/15082/262506/file/Trade_in_Intermediate_Goods_and_Services.pdf.

Nielsen, B. B., Asmussen, C. G. and Weatherall, C. D. (2017) The location choice of foreign direct investments: Empirical evidence and methodological challenges, *Journal of World Business*, 52(1), pp. 62–82.

Nielsen, P. B., Denmark, S., Linden, G., Gereffi, G. and Brown, C. (2011) Direct measurement of global value chains: collecting product-and firm-level statistics on value added and business function outsourcing and offshoring, In Available at: http://www.irle.berkeley.edu/conference/2012/materials/Sturgeon_Direct_Measurement.pdf.

OECD (2013) *Interconnected economies*, Paris, Organisation for Economic Co-operation and Development, Available at: http://www.oecd-ilibrary.org/content/book/9789264189560-en.

Opsahl, T. (2009) Structure and evolution of weighted networks, Queen Mary, University of London, Available at: http://ethos.bl.uk/OrderDetails.do?uin=uk.bl.ethos.507253.

Park, I. and Park, S. (2015) Modes of foreign direct investment and patterns of trade: An alternative empirical approach, *The World Economy*, 38(8), pp. 1225–1245.

Ramondo, N. (2014) A quantitative approach to multinational production, *Journal of International Economics*, 93(1), pp. 108–122.

Ramondo, N., Rappoport, V. and Ruhl, K. J. (2012) Horizontal versus vertical foreign direct investment: Revisiting evidence from US multinationals, Available at: http://exchan.ecares.org/ecaresdocuments/seminars1213/rappoport.pdf.

Ramondo, N., Rappoport, V. and Ruhl, K. J. (2016) Intrafirm trade and vertical fragmentation in U.S. multinational corporations, *Journal of International Economics*, 98, pp. 51–59.

Robins, G., Pattison, P. and Wang, P. (2009) Closure, connectivity and degree distributions: Exponential random graph (p*) models for directed social networks, *Social Networks*, 31(2), pp. 105–117.

Sgrignoli, P. (2014) The world trade web: A multiple-network perspective, *arXiv preprint arXiv:1409.3799*, Available at: http://arxiv.org/abs/1409.3799.

Snijders, T. A., Pattison, P. E., Robins, G. L. and Handcock, M. S. (2006) New specifications for exponential random graph models, *Sociological Methodology*, 36(1), pp. 99–153.

Srholec, M. (2006) Fragmentation and trade: A network perspective, In pp. 7–9, Available at: http://etsg.org/ETSG2006/papers/Srholec.pdf.

Timmer, M. P., Los, B., Stehrer, R. and Vries, G. J. (2013) Fragmentation, incomes and jobs: an analysis of European competitiveness, *Economic Policy*, 28(76), pp. 613–661.

Timmer, M. P., Dietzenbacher, E., Los, B., Stehrer, R. and de Vries, G. J. (2015) An illustrated user guide to the world input–output database: The case of global automotive production", *Review of International Economics*, 23(3), pp. 575–605.

Todeva, E. (2006) *Business networks,* London, Routledge.

UNCTAD (2013) *Global value chains and development: investment and value added trade in the global economy: A preliminary analysis,* United Nations: New York and Geneva, Available at: http://unctad.org/en/PublicationsLibrary/diae2013d1_en.pdf.

Vitali, S. and Battiston, S. (2013) *The community structure of the global corporate network,* SSRN Scholarly Paper, Rochester, NY, Social Science Research Network, Available at: http://papers.ssrn.com/abstract=2198974.

Vitali, S., Glattfelder, J. B. and Battiston, S. (2011) The network of global corporate control, *PLoS ONE,* 6(10), p. e25995.

Wang, P., Robins, G. L., Pattison, P. E. and Koskinen, J. H. (2014) MPNet: Program for the simulation and estimation of (p*) exponential random graph models for multilevel networks, Melbourne School of Psychological Sciences, The University of Melbourne, Melbourne, Australia.

Wang, P., Sharpe, K., Robins, G. L. and Pattison, P. E. (2009) Exponential random graph (p∗) models for affiliation networks, *Social Networks,* 31(1), pp. 12–25.

Zappa, P. and Lomi, A. (2015) The analysis of multilevel networks in organizations models and empirical tests, *Organizational Research Methods,* p. 1094428115579225.

Zappa, P. and Robins, G. (2016) Organizational learning across multi-level networks, *Social Networks,* 44, pp. 295–306.

9.
The network of European outward foreign direct investments

Giulia De Masi and Giorgio Ricchiuti

Data: fDi markets
Software: Pajek

9.1 Introduction

The fragmentation of production is a major feature of modern economies. This process has a strong and visible impact on economic agents and on firms' strategies as they have to deal with a more competitive environment. The firms' ability to survive in the new context created by the fragmentation of production depends upon their capacity to innovate their products and processes as well as on their ability to penetrate new markets. The impressive growth in the number of firms involved in exports, FDI and global outsourcing reveals that firms react to globalisation by developing internationally oriented strategies. Business relations were the prevailing form of internationalization until some years ago, on the contrary, nowadays firms use more complex modes to become international. Major international integration has been associated with strong manufacturing reorganization both domestically and internationally. The uncertainties surrounding the developments of internationalization have made politicians, businessmen and ordinary citizens of every nation aware of the need to constantly monitor the evolution of international markets. This way agents can promptly analyse the changes and limit the possible adverse effects on the economic system, particularly in terms of employment. At the same time, by being aware of the new spatial distribution of firms, due to the fragmentation of production, policymakers could better understand the long-run economic trends. Finally, a deeper comprehension of this phenomenon, clearly pervasive in the economic system, could provide insights on the development of the economy.

In his seminal paper, Melitz (2003) links the role of heterogeneity with the decision to export, highlighting that only the more productive firms are able to bear the cost of exporting and therefore to access international markets. Less productive firms are confined to domestic markets, or they have even to exit the market. In a similar way, but accounting for more complex modes of internationalization, Helpman et al. (2004) generalize these results, incorporating horizontal Foreign Direct Investment (FDI). The underlying idea is that there are relatively few firms able to compete in international markets and these firms are more productive, pay higher wages, employ more skilled workers and invest more in R&D. Theoretical works have therefore highlighted a clear-cut ranking in the productivity of firms such that the most productive firms will invest abroad, the second most productive will serve foreign markets through exports, and the least productive will 'stay domestic'. Empirical studies, based on this approach, have also shown heterogeneity among firm size, wages paid, as well as strategies adopted to penetrate foreign markets. However, the clear-cut ranking is valid only on average. The empirical distribution of productivity, net worth or size among firms adopting different internationalization modes have some area of overlapping. For example, while, on average, exporters are more productive, there are domestic firms with productivity higher or equal to exporters. This overlapping can be easily explained by the coexistence of different sources of heterogeneity which may affect the chosen modes of internationalization. Indeed, the international literature has already moved far beyond, introducing other sources of heterogeneity such as innovation activity (Bustos, 2011), product quality (Hallak and Sivadasan, 2013, Manova and Zhang, 2012, Crino' and Epifani, 2012), demand factors and uncertainty (Albornoz, et al 2012, Di Comite et al. 2014) and financial fragility (Chaney, 2005; Manova 2013; Assenza et al., 2016).

The distributions of the variables of interest are also strongly dispersed, detecting that heterogeneity is pervasive not only between but also within groups. Giovannetti et al. (2015), through econometric analysis on Italian data, shed light on the sources of heterogeneity in productivity among foreign direct investors; in particular, they investigate the links between parent productivity and affiliates characteristics such as their number, location, turnover and sectoral characteristics. They try to explain the heterogeneity (in terms of productivity) within foreign direct investors, looking at the strategies firms adopt: how far they go, what features the countries of destination have, if they prefer greenfield investments to M&A and so on. In the same line, but in a complementary way, De Masi et al. (2013) build and study the network of Italian firms that invest abroad, highlighting the linkages among firms and identifying the key nodes of the system (both in terms of firms and countries of destination). They show that even foreign direct investors that operate within the same sector can adopt different internationalization strategies: some firms invest abroad (horizontal FDI) using middle-large countries as a productive platform to export to neighbouring countries through commercial affiliates; other firms are global players (vertical FDI), and their production is carried out for cost-saving reasons, and/or in search of professional skills; finally, most foreign activities seem to be linked to commercial purposes, in the attempt to promote exports. Thus, by means of network analysis, they introduce an additional aspect in the debate: heterogeneity is also strong within the same sector.

The present analysis is in line with applications of complex network theory to Economic systems (Schweitzer et al., 2009). In the last decade, complex networks have been set up as a cross-cutting research field in various disciplines of natural sciences (physics and biology) and social sciences (Dorogovtsev, Mendez 2003). Complex network theory, which has only recently been applied to Economics, allows identification and evaluation of the structures underlying the relationships between different economic units. By way of example, the foreign trade series for Latin American and South-East Asian countries follow the same pattern; however, the network analysis is able to show how the degree of centralization decreased rapidly in Latin America, whereas it grew in South-East Asia. This implies a change in the structure of international trade in the two regions (see Reyes et al., 2008). In the empirical literature, network analysis is mostly used to study the structure of the interbank market (Iori et al., 2008), bank-firm credit market (De Masi et al., 2011; Battiston et al. 2007), financial market investments (Garlaschelli et al., 2005), the world trade network (De Benedictis and Tajoli, 2011), and the world trade web (Fagiolo et al., 2011). Few studies can be found in the literature on FDI at a global level. Wall et al. (2011) analyse the network of the top 100 global multinational and ownership linkages in more than 2000 cities worldwide, distinguishing between all industrial sectors and producer service sector. More recently, Alfaro and Chen (2014) analyse a worldwide establishment-based database of multinationals using measurements of network density to study agglomeration phenomena. Finally, relative to European countries, network analysis has been applied to Italian foreign investment data (De Masi et al., 2013) and French data (Joyez, 2017).

Within this strand of literature and in line with De Masi et al. (2013), in this paper, we reconstruct the network of the European (EU28) firms investing abroad. Our analysis makes use of the database 'fDi markets': a rich global, detailed database developed by the Financial Times, through which we analyse the relevance of heterogeneity on the network of worldwide foreign direct investments. fDi markets are the main online global database of FDI information; it allows for real-time monitoring of investment projects to track and profile companies investing overseas. Since 2003, the database has recorded globally over 10 trillion of dollars invested from over 80,000 companies. It is worth noting that only greenfield FDI is recorded and in what follows we will refer interchangeably to affiliates and 'projects,' the term used in fDi markets. We study - separately - the years 2003 and 2015, in order to compare the structural change on the longest available period, and we try to identify changes before and after the crises. In future work, we will study the entire period, analysing the evolution of the network year by year. In order to create the network, a bipartite graph has been generated, where the nodes are both investors and host countries, and a link is drawn if a parent company invests in a certain host country. Our main aim is to use the network to reveal the existence of heterogeneity between and within sectors and/or the possible presence of common behaviours between firms. To pursue this aim, we detect the presence of subnets (or subnetworks) and main hubs (countries/firms) also within specific sectors. Finally, we qualitatively analyse the main actors to discover whether the choice to develop new projects is correlated to specific features of these actors.

In section 9.2, we present the methodology applied here; then, after presenting the dataset (section 9.3), first we discuss the main features of the whole sample (section 9.4), and then of three relevant sectors: Textile, Machinery, and Coal (section 9.5).

9.2 Network: the method

Network analysis investigates the topological properties of the complex structure of economic relationships. In order to help the readers, we briefly report the main elements of the network theory used throughout the chapter. Networks are represented as graphs, that is a set of nodes and links. From a mathematical point of view, a network is represented by an adjacency matrix. The element of the adjacency matrix a_{ij} indicates that a link exists between nodes i and j.

9.2.1 Bipartite network

In the empirical application for this paper, a bipartite network is defined (see De Masi, 2008). A network is called bipartite when two kinds of nodes are present, in our case firms and countries. From a mathematical perspective, distinguishing two kinds of nodes C (countries) and I (investors), the graph G_{C+I}, with a total set of nodes $(C+I)$ is defined. A link is drawn if a firm invests in a specific host country, therefore $a_{ij} = 1$ if investor i goes to country j; otherwise $a_{ij} = 0$. A simplified example of a bipartite network of countries and firms is plotted in figure 9.1, top panel.

Figure 9.1: Bipartite and projected graph

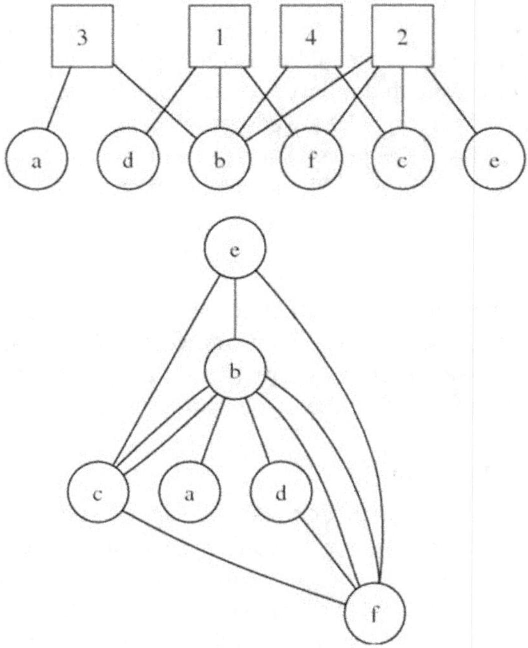

Color images of figures can be downloaded at the book's page
[URL: https://vernonpress.com/book/96]

Top panel: bipartite graph, considering the set of investors (circles) I = a, b, c, d, e, f and countries C = 1, 2, 3, 4 (squares). Bottom panel: corresponding projected graph on firm's space.

9.2.2 Projected network

In the study of a bipartite graph, a widely used approach is to study separately two networks defined from the original one. In particular, we extract from the overall graph two graphs, each one composed of just one kind of nodes (countries or investors in our case). These two networks are called projected networks, as they are obtained as a projection of the initial graph in the subspace composed by nodes of the same kind. The two new projected networks are defined G_C and G_I, and they are made up by only nodes of the C or I kind respectively (Peltomaki and Alava, 2006; Sneppen et al., 2004; Guillaume and Latapy, 2004). For the purpose of this paper, I is the network of investors (parent firms investing in the same countries) and C the network of countries (where the firms invest). In figure 9.1, starting from the bipartite network in the top panel, the network projected into the subspace of the firm is plotted in the bottom panel.

Firms could have a link regardless the number of countries they have in common. However, to retain this kind of information, we define a weighted network[1]: the weight of the link between two firms represent the number of countries they are both connected to in the bipartite network. This leads to the definition of a weighted adjacency matrix W in the firm subspace: the weight associated with the link between two firms is the number of common countries they choose.[2] Therefore, starting from the adjacency matrix of investor-country relationships a_{ic}, the general element of the matrix W is given by

$$w_{ii'} = \sum_{cc'} a_{ic} \cdot a_{i'c'} \cdot \delta_{cc'} \quad (9.1)$$

Where δ is Kronecker-delta function: its value is 1 if $c = c'$, otherwise 0. The meaning of the above equation is that two investors i and i' are linked if they invest at least in one common country. The number of common countries they both invest is the weight $w_{ii'}$ of the link between the two investors.

9.2.3 Network visualization

The visualization of a graph is a crucial point in the study of a network. The study of automatic drawing is a very active field of research. The aim is to obtain a way to represent in the Euclidean space an object (the graph) which is defined only on the topological space. Many algorithms have been proposed. Among them, the Kamada-Kawai algorithm (Kamada and Kawai, 1989) is based on the idea that the suitable geometric distance between two vertices in the drawing represents the topological distance between them in the graph. The network is represented as a set of particles (nodes) connected by springs. The final network visualization is based on the minimization of the energy associated with this set of coupled harmonic oscillators. This approach allows us to represent close to each other nodes pertaining to the same group (connected by many links).

The visualization process is certainly the first hint to identify common strategies (if any) between different investors. The Kamada-Kawai layout algorithm indeed allows us to disclose the presence of highly clustered nodes and lowly clustered or even isolated nodes. High clustering shows common strategies between those nodes (investors), meaning that they tend to invest in the same countries. On the other hand, low clustering and isolation of a particular node is an indicator of a singular strategy of that node, different from those of other nodes.

---

[1] For the sake of graphs' clearness, we do not show the weights in the plots below: there is high level of heterogeneity, very fat and thin links coexist. Therefore, we only discuss weights from a statistical point of view.

[2] We do not use the value of investments as weight because it is really disperse; moreover, for many projects this values is only estimated by fDi markets.

9.2.4 Topological measurements

Topological measurements allow us to understand the roles of different nodes in the network of firms (or countries). The nodes with more connections are called hubs of the network. From an economic perspective, we could assume that the hub is a network leader: highly interconnected, with many links and high level of centrality (see below). In the network of firms, for instance, a highly connected hub is also usually a very central firm which has a diversified strategy and shares different strategies with many firms. These firms are a driver of the network and their behaviour may affect one of small players. In this sense, a hub can be considered an economic leader. At the same time, the less connected nodes can be considered the followers in investing activities.

We now turn to the description of relevant measures considered in this work. The basic measure is the degree of node *i*, which is given by the number of its links and defines its relevance:

$$k_i = \sum_j a_{ij} \quad (9.2)$$

The strength of a node is defined instead as the sum of the weights of its links.

$$s_i = \sum_j w_{ij} \quad (9.3)$$

For our purposes, this measure gives us an insight of projects carried out, but above all of their spatial dispersion. Moreover, to identify the hubs, many definitions of 'centrality' have been proposed in network analysis. We will consider three of them. The normalised degree centrality is achieved dividing the degree by the maximum possible nodes of the network

$$dc_i = k_i/(N-1) \quad (9.4)$$

where N is the total number of nodes. This measure will be used here to detect the hubs of the subnet (i.e., the sector in this paper).

A second definition, the betweenness centrality (Brandes, 2001), is based on dynamical properties of the graph and is given by the number of times that one vertex k is crossed by the minimal path from one vertex i to j. Let's define d_{ij}, the distance between two vertices i, j, as the shortest number of edges to go from i to j, that is:

$$d_{ij} = min\left\{\sum_{k,l \in \mathcal{P}_{ij}} a_{kl}\right\} \quad (9.5)$$

Where $\mathcal{P}_{ij}$ is a path connecting vertex i and vertex j. Therefore, the betweenness centrality b_i is defined:

$$b_i = \sum_{\substack{j,l=1,N \\ i \neq j \neq l}} \frac{d_{jl}(i)}{d_{jl}} \quad (9.6)$$

where d_{jl} is the total number of different shortest paths (distances) going from j to l and $d_{jl}(i)$ is the subset of those distances passing through i. The sum runs over all pairs with $i \neq j \neq l$. Let's assume that, in order to minimize the distance, other firms should necessarily pass through a specific node (a firm). In the network we created, it means that the latter invests in many countries, sharing its own strategy with many other firms. It has a high betweenness and it is a hub. The last measure of centrality employed is the normalised closeness centrality (see Freeman, 1977 and Sabidussi, 1966):

$$cl_i = \frac{N-1}{\sum_j d_{ij}} = \frac{1}{d_i} \quad (9.7)$$

which is the reciprocal of the average distance of one node from the other nodes. In order to be a hub, a firm should not be very far from all the others.

9.3 The Dataset

The dataset is drawn from fDi Markets-Financial Times business, which is a global database of greenfield foreign direct investment (fDi) information. Since 2003, it allows real-time monitoring of FDI projects, classified by business function, across all sectors. It has globally tracked over 10 trillion of investments from over 80,000 companies. It also includes capital investments and job creation, by tracking and profiling companies investing overseas. To enrich the database, the Financial Times uses different sources: media, project data from industry organizations, information from investment agencies, and data captured from official publications of the companies. In order to validate the data recorded, each project is cross-referenced through multiple sources. Different studies have employed data from fDi markets, but with the exception of Crescenzi et al. (2017), they have not used it to construct a network of European FDI. Among others, Crescenzi et al. (2014) studying EU25, seek to identify the determinants of localisation of direct investment separating the role of states from that of regions. Crescenzi et al. (2016) use fDi markets to analyse expansion / localisation strategies of EU25 of multinationals in emerging countries; then they compare these strategies with those adopted by multinationals in advanced countries.

For the purpose of this paper, our database comprises outward FDI from each of EU28 (countries of origin) to the rest of the world. The countries of destination may be also within the EU28 itself: for example, an Italian company with a greenfield investment in Germany. We employ data for 2003 and 2015 in order to compare the possible change of the FDI-network, following the recent financial crisis. Finally, it is worth noting that differently from De Masi et al. (2013), we do not consider the stock of FDI but the flow (the projects).

9.4 The Network of EU FDI

In order to create the network, a bipartite graph has been generated, where the nodes are both investors and host countries; a link is drawn if a parent company invests in a certain host country. We project the links on two subspaces so that two new projected networks are obtained: the network of investors and that of countries. We first analyse the whole set of firms, then we focus on three specific sectors: Textile, Machinery, and Coal.[3] These sectors are relevant both in terms the number of projects and their value. As in De Masi et al. (2013), the choice of these three sectors allows us to show that firms are heterogeneous within the same sector as well; this means that heterogeneity is pervasive. In what follows, focusing on the three sectors identified above, we will try to understand:

1. the geographical patterns;
2. what are the main hubs (countries/firms) within the sectors;
3. the presence of subnets;
4. whether the main actors present specific features and the characteristics of their projects.

In Tables 9.1-9.4, we report descriptive statistics both for the whole database and the selected sectors. Within the whole database there are 1586 and 2984 investors in 2003 and 2015 respectively and corresponding 3141 and 5235 projects respectively. On average, an investor had 2 projects in 2003 and 1.7 in 2015, but we register large heterogeneity across the sectors with a minimum equal 1 and a maximum equal to 32 in 2003 and 75 in 2015. The topological measures of the bipartite graph for the whole sample disclose a large increase of both degree (number of investment flows) and strength (intensity of these flows) (Table 9.3). It has to be noted that in 2003 the node with the highest strength is a company from a traditional sector (Chemistry), whereas, in 2015, the highest level is achieved by a company in the Service sector (Serviced Office Spaces, Virtual Offices, Co-working Spaces). Moreover, as evident from Table 9.4, there has been a reduction in the betweenness centrality indicator between the two years considered (0.001 in 2003 and 0.0003 in 2015) whereas closeness centrality remains constant at 0.05. This is due to a change of investor network structure: in 2003 it consists of a highly compact cluster, while in 2015 several connected clusters emerge, decreasing the average value of betweenness but keeping the closeness centrality constant. We identify the hubs using centrality measures. It is worth noting that looking at the whole net-

---

[3] Differently from De Masi et al. (2013), in this paper we have information of the specific sector of the projects and not of the investors

work, while in 2003 the leader is a global firm in the Coal sector with interests in almost all countries, in 2015 the leader is a firm in the service sector (sub-sector rental and leasing) with a focus on retailing. Adding this element to what we have found looking at strength, we can confirm that there has been a change in the leading sectors from 2003 and 2015: specifically, manufacturing has given way to service.

Table 9.1: Number of nodes and projects: projected investor network

Sector	Year	Nodes	Projects
		(Investors)	
Whole sample	2003	1586	3141
Whole sample	2015	2984	5235
Coal	2003	49	128
Coal	2015	36	73
Text	2003	51	64
Text	2015	42	67
Mach	2003	101	159
Mach	2015	323	455

Table 9.2: Most connected countries (hubs) in all sectors networks and sector by sector networks.

All	All	Coal	Coal	Mach	Mach	Text	Text
2003	2015	2003	2015	2003	2015	2003	2015
CHN	USA	MEX	GBR	CHN	USA	CHN	USA
RUS	CHN	RUS	CHN	BRA	CHN	BGR	CHN
BRA	IND	USA	IND	USA	DEU	BRA	ESP
USA	GBR	IND	MEX	GBR	IND	HKG	FRA
ESP	DEU	DEU	RUS	IND	RUS	HUN	DEU

Network analysis allows the identification of leaders by looking at their centrality value, while through the Kamada–Kawai algorithm ex-post common strategies can be detected, without any ex-ante hypothesis on the existing relationships. Hence, we are not only able to identify the main receiving countries but also those countries that share many projects with their neighbours; by way of example, we can see that companies investing in the US have also projects in China and so on.

Looking at the geographical distribution of affiliates (Table 9.2), two main markets of destination emerge in 2003: US and China. These were closely followed by the UK, Germany, France, Hungary, Czech Republic, Russia, India, and Poland. On the other hand, in 2015, UK is the main market of destination, surrounded (not surprisingly) by US, China, Germany and France that are now flanked by Spain, Australia, and Mexico. Therefore, there is a change in the projects' flow from European newcomers (with the exception of Romania) to countries outside the EU.

Table 9.3: Degree and strength measures: projected investor network

Sector	Year	Nodes	Degree			Strength		
		(Investors)	Mean	St. dev.	Max	Mean	St. dev.	Max
Whole Sample	2003	1586	120.5	121.2	883	205.7	348.7	3979
Whole Sample	2015	2984	300.2	294.3	2057	463.2	748.6	16781
Coal	2003	49	3.9	3.6	22	6.7	9	58
Coal	2015	36	3.6	2.3	9	4.2	3.3	14
Text	2003	51	2.4	1.2	4	2.8	1.6	16
Text	2015	42	4.1	2.9	12	4.6	3.7	16
Mach	2003	101	11	9	38	13.5	12.5	61
Mach	2015	323	31.9	28.5	463.2	36.2	36.8	258

Table 9.4: Centrality measures: projected investor network

Sector	Year	Nodes	Degree Centrality			Betweenness			Closeness		
		(Investors)	Mean	St. dev.	Max	Mean	St. dev.	Max	Mean	St. dev.	Max
Whole Sample	2003	1586	0.08	0.08	0.56	0.001	0.003	0.04	0.5	0.1	0.7
Whole Sample	2015	2984	0.1	0.1	0.69	0.0003	0.002	0.05	0.5	0.1	0.8
Coal	2003	49	0.08	0.07	0.45	0.018	0.051	0.326	0.3	0.1	0.5
Coal	2015	36	0.1	0.06	0.25	0.005	0.015	0.071	0.1	0.1	0.3
Text	2003	51	0.05	0.02	0.08	0.001	0.002	0.008	0.1	0	0.1
Text	2015	42	0.1	0.07	0.29	0.004	0.016	0.072	0.2	0.1	0.3
Mach	2003	101	0.11	0.09	0.38	0.008	0.026	0.204	0.3	0.1	0.4
Mach	2015	323	0.1	0.09	0.45	0.005	0.019	0.212	0.4	0.1	0.5

9.5 A focus on Three Sectors

As stated above, we focus only on three manufacturing sectors (Coal, Machinery, and Textile) that seem to us representative of the greenfield FDI activities in terms of number and magnitude of the projects, and allow us to qualitatively analyse both the structure of the network and the behaviours of leaders.

9.5.1 Coal

As for the coal sector, Table 9.1 shows that both the number of investors and affiliates is reduced between 2003 and 2015. This may be due both to the merging process (of affiliates and investors) and an increase in near-shoring.

Comparing the key destination countries of Coal investors (see Table 9.2), we notice a slight change between the two periods considered. While in 2003, the largest recipient was Mexico (followed by Russia, USA, and India), in 2015, Great Britain was the most important country, followed by China and India, with Mexico and Russia.

In the figures 9.2 and 9.3, the graphs projected on Coal firms are represented. The network has clearly changed between the two periods. Using the Kamada-Kawai layout algorithm, we find the key players in the industry at the heart of the network. In 2003, there is clearly a key player/hub; it is not only investing in many markets but also indirectly connected with all the other investors. Indeed, according to *fDi markets*, the largest number of projects undertaken by the key player (32) were done in 2003. *fDi markets* also report that the main investor's new projects were motivated by the domestic market growth potential, the proximity to markets or customers, and skilled workforce availability. Moreover, in 2003, the most important area of destination for the main hub has been Asia-Pacific, followed by North-America. The 2015 network is very different especially because of the presence of several segmented subnets. The 2003 leader is still present and important, but only for a subnet. We also register an additional subnet, with its own leader, and four other small networks. The change of structure is not surprising because Coal's investors build partnerships to lower international transaction management costs. The subnets represent groups of companies that operate jointly within the same countries, as it is evident also from the strong reduction in the values of strength (Table 9.3), which declined from 6.7 to 4.2 between 2003 and 2015. Moreover, not surprisingly, the key players have reduced (but not eliminated) the projects soon after the crisis.

Figure 9.2: Projected Network for Firms: Coal 2003

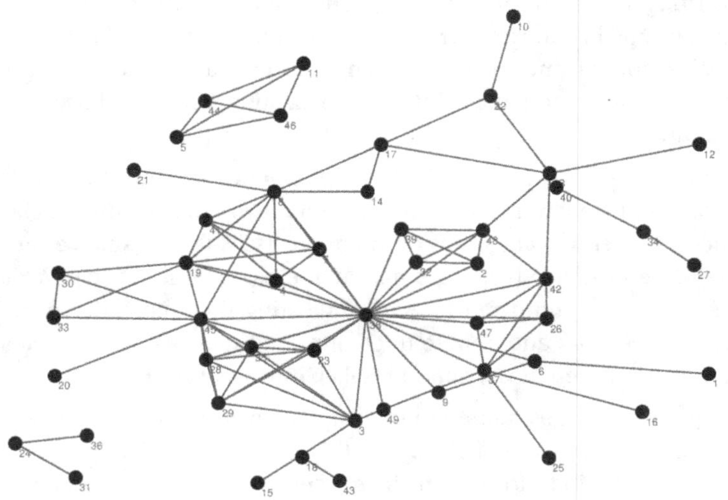

Color images of figures can be downloaded at the book's page
[URL: https://vernonpress.com/book/96]

Figure 9.3: Projected Network for Firms: Coal 2015

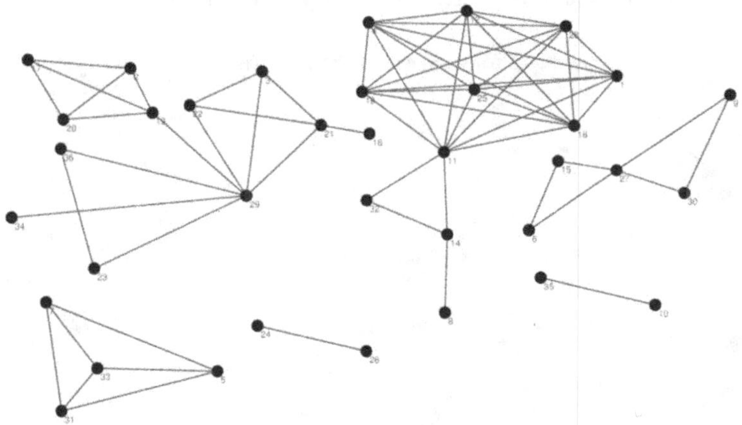

Color images of figures can be downloaded at the book's page
[URL: https://vernonpress.com/book/96]

9.5.2 Textile

Table 9.1 shows that both the number of investors and projects, in the Textile sector, have remained constant in 2003 and 2015. However, the major destination countries have changed. In 2003, priority was given to developing countries such as China, Brazil or eastern European countries such as Bulgaria and Hungary. In 2015 instead, in addition to China, the main destinations are all developed countries, such as USA, Spain, France, and Germany. As for the Coal sector, this may be explained by the fact that, following the financial crisis, the leading companies' internationalization strategies have turned to closer markets.

Looking at betweenness (Table 9.4), it is noteworthy that the textile subnetwork has much lower values than the other two sectors. This means that it is difficult to identify large hubs or, more precisely, that businesses are fairly segmented and divided into groups. At the same time, average closeness increased in 2015 compared to 2003, indicating the emergence of relevant hubs in the network and a more interconnected network. Average closeness has doubled between the two periods taken into account.

The figures 9.4 and 9.5 represent the graphs projected on firms from the textile sector. As in the case of Coal, also this network has clearly changed between the two periods. In 2003 the investments are more related to manufacture, but progressively the increasing number of retailers creates new links between nodes that were previously isolated. It is evident that the 2015 network is more connected, at least in the central part. There are still islands, but a large group of firms moves together and in the same markets. This is also evident from the increased values of both degree and strength from 2003 to 2015 (Table 9.1), with the mean strength moving from 2.8 to 4.6.

Figure 9.4: Projected Network for Firms: Textile 2003

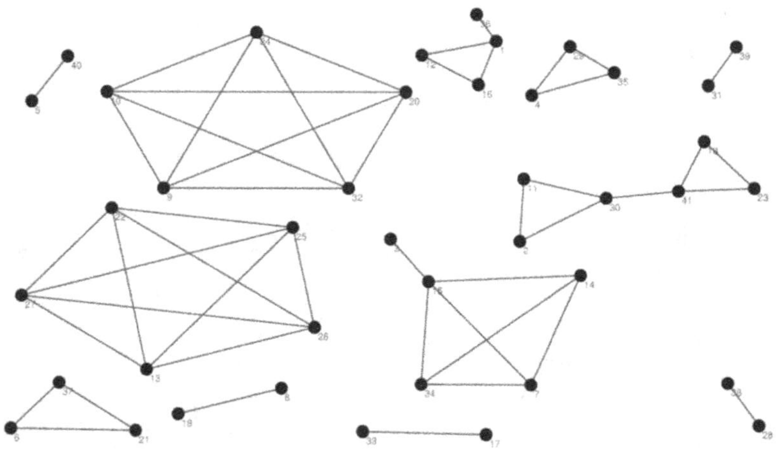

Color images of figures can be downloaded at the book's page [URL: https://vernonpress.com/book/96]

Figure 9.5: Projected Network for Firms: Textile 2015

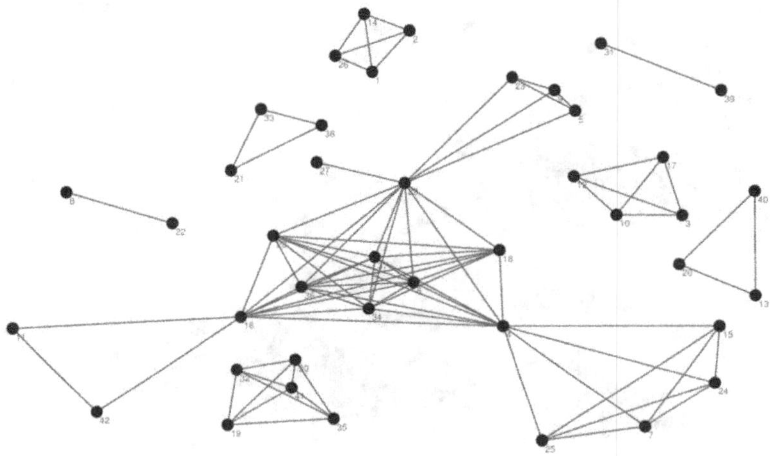

Color images of figures can be downloaded at the book's page
[URL: https://vernonpress.com/book/96]

The most connected nodes (in terms of both degrees and betweenness) of 2003 engage in the design, development, and manufacture of footwear products. And they mainly operate abroad as retailers. In that year, China and USA are the most important countries of destination with respect to job creation and value of investment. On the other hand, in 2015, the two emerging main leaders are focused on manufacturing textile products. Moreover, their projects are related to sales, marketing, and logistics.

9.5.3 Machinery

The last sector we analyse is the machinery sector. This sector presents the largest number of investing and affiliated companies. Moreover, the number of both investors and affiliates tripled over the period under investigation.

In a forthcoming work, analysing the evolution of the network, we try to analyse and understand what this increase is due to. At present, we can imagine that it may be due to several factors such as the greater integration of EU countries, following the enlargement to the East in 2004 and 2009. The increase could as well be a response to the crisis: more fragmentation of production makes it possible to diversify risk and reorganize production. Or it could be just a structural behaviour of the industry as it is a highly connected sector. The betweenness centrality doesn't reach the levels of the Coal sector, but the closeness is higher, indicating greater interconnection in the network. This emerges clearly from figures 9.6 and 9.7, where the networks for the two considered years are reported.

Figure 9.6: Projected Network for Firms: Machinery 2003

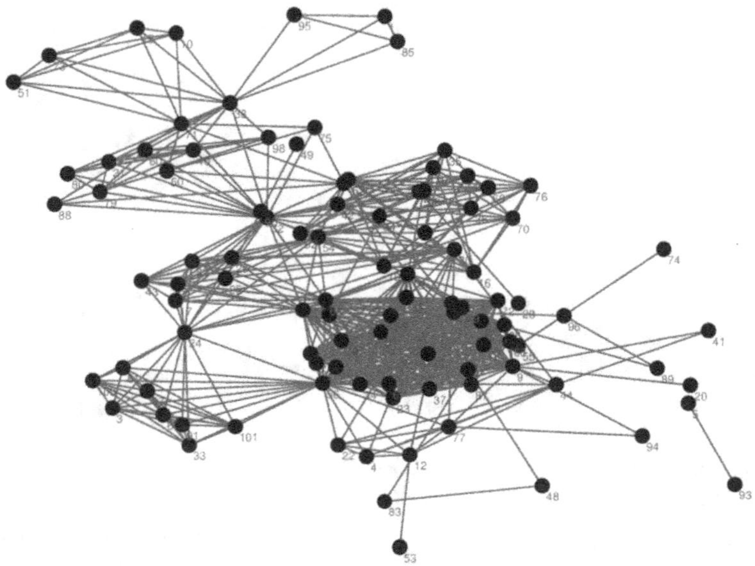

Color images of figures can be downloaded at the book's page
[URL: https://vernonpress.com/book/96]

Figure 9.7: Projected Network for Firms: Machinery 2015

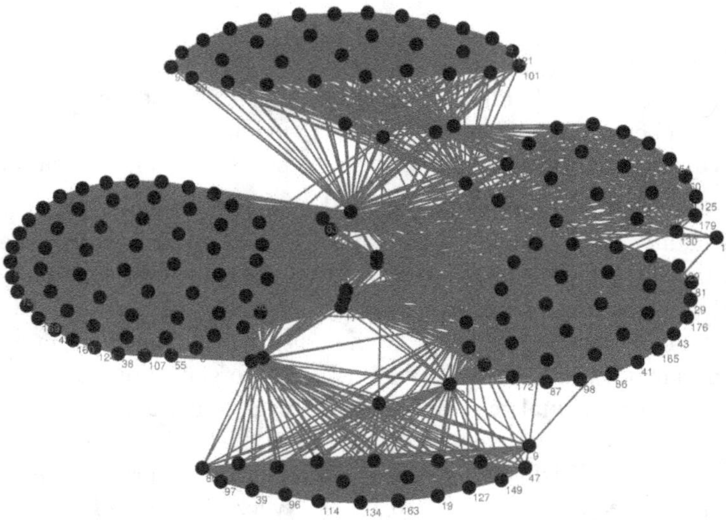

Color images of figures can be downloaded at the book's page
[URL: https://vernonpress.com/book/96]

It is difficult to unambiguously detect the leader of the network and we should rather talk about leaders, a homogeneous group of international firms with similar network indexes. Their maximum degree is high (38 in 2003 and 146 in 2015), as well as their strength and their betweenness, which are much higher than those of the textile sector, indicating the global character of these firms. Moreover, sector leaders produce mechanical and electronic components and their projects are mainly related to manufacturing products.

9.6 Conclusions

In the last decades, foreign investments have changed the geography of production. Starting from the empirical evidence, international economists have stressed the role of heterogeneity among firms to account for the choice of different modes of internationalization. We argue that heterogeneity is pervasive, regarding not only productivity (as in the Melitz's model) but also other firm's characteristics such as innovation strategies or financial robustness. Recently, authors have shown that firm heterogeneity is also present within firms in the same sector (i.e., De Masi et al., 2013). A better understanding of firm heterogeneity could improve our understanding of the evolution of the fragmentation of production.

In line with De Masi et al. (2013), we use network analysis to detect different foreign investment strategies among EU firms. In our view, this tool has been under-utilised in the context of FDI. However, we can detect the links among firms, and single out which of them are hubs (the leaders) of the network. Moreover, analyzing those firms, we are able to identify common or heterogeneous patterns in the process of internationalization. Moreover, it allows to empirically detect and, therefore, analyse the strategy used by the main actors of the network.

We reconstruct and discuss the network of European (EU28) foreign investing firms, relying on measures from complex network analysis. Keeping in due consideration both sector and countries of the destination, and without ex-ante priors, we singled out the linkages among investors. Three sectors have been selected (Coal, Machinery, and Textile) for our analysis.

Moreover, using network indexes and examining the projects, we highlight the evolution of network's structure, in terms of both countries of destination and activities of the main 'leaders'. We use data from the 2003 and 2015, trying to compare the structure before and after the crisis. Considering the three sectors analysed, we observe a structural change from 2003 to 2015 with the formation of sub-networks or clusters. This can be due to the diffused feeling of confidence before the crisis and leading to broad range investments. This has changed after the crisis-producing more prudent investment strategies, which become directed to some specific countries.

This is particularly evident in the Machinery sector, which most probably experienced near-shoring of manufactures and for Coal, where we observe both merging and near-shoring phenomena after the crisis. The opposite behaviour is observed for the Textile sector; this can be easily explained by the increasing tendency to invest not only in manufactures but more and more in retailers.

In a future work, we will study the entire period, analysing the evolution of the network year by year and focusing the analysis on each sector, and on the amount of investment and the jobs created.

Future work should be aimed at identifying how specific crises, in particular, the 2008 recession, impacted on FDI strategies in selected industries and on their network structure.

9.7 References

Albornoz, F., Calvo-Pardo, H., Corcos, G., Ornelas, E., 2012, 'Sequential exporting', Journal of International Economics 88 (1), 17-31.

Alfaro, L., Chen, M., 2014, 'The Global Network of Multidimensional Firms', Journal of International Economics, Volume 94, Issue 2, Pages 263-276

Assenza T, Delli Gatti D., Grazzini J, Ricchiuti G. (2016) 'Heterogenous Firms and International Trade: The role of productivity and financial fragility', CESifo Working Paper Series 5959, CESifo Group Munich

Battiston S., Delli Gatti D., Gallegati M., Greenwald B., Stiglitz J. E., Credit chains and bankruptcy propagation in production networks, J. Economic Dynamic and Control, Volume 31, Issue 6, Tenth Workshop on Economic Heterogeneous Interacting Agents - WEHIA 2005, June 2007, Pages 2061-2084

Brandes U. ,2001, 'A Faster Algorithm for Betweenness Centrality', Journal of Mathematical Sociology. 25(2):163-177.

Bustos P., 2011, 'Trade Liberalization, Exports and Technology Upgrading: Evidence on the Impact of MERCOSUR on Argentinean Firms', American Economic Review, 101 (1), 2011, 304-340.

Chaney T. (2005) 'Liquidity Constrained Exporter', unpublished phd thesis

Crescenzi, R., Datu, K. and Iammarino, S. (2017) European Cities and Foreign Investment Networks, *Scienze Regionali*, 16(2), pp. 229–260.

Crescenzi R., Pietrobelli C., and Rabellotti R., 2014, 'Innovatin drivers, value chains and the geography of multinational corporations in Europe', Journal of Economic Geopgraphy,14, pp. 1053 - 1086

Crescenzi R., Pietrobelli C., and Rabellotti R., 2016, 'Regional Strategic Assets and the Location strategies of emerging countries' multinationals in Europe', European Planning Studies 24:4, 645 - 667

Crinô R. and Epifani P., 2012. 'Productivity, Quality and Export Behaviour', Economic Journal, Royal Economic Society, vol. 122(565), pages 1206-1243, December.

De Benedictis L. and Tajoli L., 2011, 'The World Trade Network', The World Economy, Wiley Blackwell, vol. 34(8), pages 1417-1454, 08.

De Masi G., Giovannetti G., Ricchiuti G., 2013, Network Analysis of Italian Foreign Direct Investments, Physica A 392, 1202-1214

De Masi G., Fujiwara Y., Gallegati M., Greenwald B., Stiglitz J.E., 2011, Japanese Financial Credit Networks, Evolutionary and Institutional Economics Review, 7(2): 209–232

De Masi G., 2008, Empirical analysis of the architecture of the interbank and credit market using network theory, in Networks, Topology and Dynamics, Springer Series Lecture Notes in Economics and Mathematical Systems, Vol. 613, Springer Edition

Di Comite F., Thisse, J.F. and Vandenbussche H., 2014, 'Vertizontal differentiation in export markets', Journal of International Economics, Elsevier, vol. 93(1), pages 50¬66.

Dorogovtsev, S.N. e J.F.F Mendez, Evolution of networks, Oxford University Press, 2003.

Fagiolo G., Squartini T. and Garlaschelli D., 2011, Null Models of Economic Network: The Case of the World Trade Web, LEM Papers Series 2011/26, Laboratory of Economics and Management (LEM), Sant'Anna School of Advanced Studies, Pisa, Italy.

Freeman, L. C., 1977, A set of measures of centrality based on betweenness. Sociometry, 40:35, 41.

Garlaschelli D., Battiston S., Castri M., Servedio V. D.P., Caldarelli G., 2005, The scale-free topology of market investments, Physica A, Volume 350, Issues 2-4, 15, Pages 491-499

Giovannetti G., Marvasi E. and Ricchiuti G., 2015, 'The Heterogeneity of Foreign Direct Investors: Linking Affiliates to Parent Productivity', WP13/2015 DISEI Uni-versitàdi Firenze

Guillaume J.L. and Latapy M., 2004, 'Bipartite structure of all complex networks', Inf. Process. Lett., 90 (5)

Hallak J.C. and Sivadasan J, 2013, Product and Process Productivity: Implications for Quality choice and Conditional Exporter Premia Journal of International Economics, 91(1), pp. 53-67, September 2013.

Iori, G., G. De Masi, O. Precup, G. Gabbi e G. Caldarelli, 2008, 'A network analysis of the Italian overnight money market', J. Economic Dynamic and Control, Volume 32, Issue 1, Pages 259-278

Helpman, E., Melitz, M., Yeaple, S., 2004, 'Exports versus FDI with heterogeneous firms', The American Economic Review 94 (1), 300 316.

Joyez, C., 2017, On the topological Structure of Multinational network, Physica A 473, 578-588 (2017)

Kamada T. and Kawai S., 1989, An algorithm for drawing general undirected graphs. Inf. Process. Lett., 31(1):7-15.

Manova K. B., 2013, 'Credit Constraints, Heterogeneous Firms, and International Trade' Review of Economic Studies 80, p.711-744.

Manova K, Zhang Z., 2012. Multi-product frms and product quality. NBER Work. Pap. 18637

Melitz, M., 2003, 'The Impact of Trade on Intra-Industry Reallocations and Aggregate Industry Productivity' Econometrica, Econometric Society, vol. 71(6), pp. 1695 - 1725

Pajek, Program for, Large Network Analysis, url: http://vlado.fmf.uni-lj.si/pub/networks/pajek/

Peltomaki M. and Alava M. 2006, Correlations in bipartite collaboration networks, J. Stat. Mech., P01010

Reyes, J, Schiavo S, and Fagiolo G., 2008, 'Assessing the evolution of international economic integration using random walk betweenness centrality: the cases of East Asia and Latin America', Advances in Complex Systems, Vol. 11, No. 5 685 - 702

Sabidussi, G., 1966, The centrality index of a graph. Psychometrika,31:581-603.

Schweitzer, F., Fagiolo, G., Sornette, D., Vega-Redondo, F., Vespignani, A., White, D. R., 2009," Economic Networks: The New Challenges", Science, 24 July 2009, Vol. 325, No. 5939, pp. 422-425.

Sneppen K., Rosvall M. and Trusina A., 2004, Europhys. Lett., 67 (3), pp. 349-354

Wall, R.S., van der Knapp G.A., Sectoral Differentiation and Network Structure within Contemporary Worldwide Corporate Networks, 2011, Economic Geography 87 (3), 267-308

10.

Free trade agreements network: structure and evolution

Silvia Sopranzetti

Data: Regional Trade Agreement (RTA) data from the WTO database on RTAs
Software: R (statnet), Pajek

10.1 Introduction

The last twenty years have witnessed a proliferation of the number of trade agreements all over the world. Excluding the successive rounds of enlargement of the European Union (EU), preferential trade agreements have been a sideshow aspect of the international economy for a long time and, until the 1980s, except for minor integration among developing countries, were substantially pioneered by the EU. Recent development such as the Asian countries shift in favour of free trade agreements has changed dramatically this picture involving more countries and changing the characteristics of the agreements (Acharya 2016).

According to the World Trade Organization (WTO) RTA database, there are 279 trade agreements in force in 2017, nearly 75% of which are free trade agreements (FTAs). Almost every country in the world is now part of some sort of preferential agreement and, following the notification of the trade agreement between Mongolia and Japan in June 2016, all WTO members now have an RTA in force; countries such as Mexico and Singapore have more than duplicated their number of FTAs in ten years. As reported by the WTO, more than half of the global commerce is conducted under the rule of some preferential agreement, while the rest is mainly trade between EU, US, Japan, and China, which is not (yet) regulated by any preferential trade agreement.

The literature has focused mainly on why countries sign free trade agreements, or what are the political and economic attributes of countries that increase the probability of being part of an agreement (Baier and Bergstrand 2004; Baier et al. 2014; Martin et al. 2008), while the general structure of the free trade agreements system and the relative position of the individual countries has not been investigated in depth. With respect to the extant literature, this chapter tries going beyond the dyadic setting and investigate the effect of the relative country position in the global FTA network. Since the power of a country in the network arises from its ties, a country's strategy in Free Trade participation may be related not only to the characteristics of the two countries involved, but also to the participating countries' existing FTA relationships with third countries. In this chapter, we argue that every FTA participation could not be considered as independent from the general structure of free trade agreements since FTAs are overlapped and strongly interdependent. Accounting for the network structure of FTAs helps to explain some aspects of FTA formations that would not otherwise be explained by countries' economic characteristics.

The interaction between overlapping free trade agreements, characterizing the FTAs global structure, points to a complex structure whose properties remain largely unexplored. To understand the structure of global trade agreements, a convenient analytical framework is to consider it as a network. Using this approach, countries are represented as nodes and trade agreements between countries as links.

In this chapter, the aim is to understand the global and the local topological properties of FTAs networks and their evolution over time. Therefore, we will analyse the evolving structure of the FTAs network and the relative position of the most important actors over time.

While the World Trade Network has been analysed in depth, in both the unweighted (Serrano and Boguña 2003, Garleschelli and Loffredo 2005, Squartini et al. 2011) and the weighted specification (Fagiolo et al. 2009, Bhattacharya et al. 2008, De Benedictis and Tajoli 2011, De Benedictis et al. 2014), few contributions have focused on the FTAs network formation and its characteristics.

Goyal and Joshi (2006) and Furusawa and Konishi (2007) study the evolution of free trade agreements from a theoretical point of view, following an endogenous network formation approach. Lee (2012) focuses on the free trade agreements' network in East Asia, analysing the evolution of the network and the different strategies followed by the signatory countries. Manger et al. (2012) explore, using network analysis, the patterns of the formation of trade agreements, focusing on hierarchy among countries and triadic closure. Lee and Bai (2013) apply the concepts of transitivity and homophily to FTA network considering in which way the formation of a tie in the network depends on political institutions, regionalism, and economic attributes of the countries.

Compared to these works, in our study, we consider how multiple FTAs interact and evolve over time, considering the evolution of the network characteristics over a large time span from 1960 to 2016. Moreover, we apply novel statistical techniques never employed before in the study of FTA networks, in order to fully characterise the structure of the network. The paper is organised in two main parts. First, we explore the structure of the global network of FTAs and its evolution. We examine the evolution of the network's statistics from 1960 to nowadays, specifically checking if the network has become denser over time. We explore whether countries prefer to link via FTAs with well-connected countries to gain a good position and to have a preferential access to an already very open market. To do this, we test if the degree distribution of the networks fits a power law distribution and we measure the degree assortativity of the network, since we suppose that the network formation follows a preferential attachment process in which connected countries tend to become even more connected via FTAs over time (as new actors try to link to them in order to enjoy indirect position gains). Our second research question is whether geographical proximity is a condition affecting the probability of two countries to sign an FTA. Specifically, we aim to analyse if the FTA network formation follows a path of globalisation or regionalisation and if those have changed over time. To test this, we apply intra- and interregional density to verify whether FTA network configuration is formed on the basis of their partner's geographic attributes as the literature suggests.

Then, in the second part of the paper, we characterise the nodes in the network by analysing the different positions of countries in the FTAs network. Considering how the relative position of countries has changed over time, and the position of the countries every country chooses to connect with, we try to define what are the main strategies followed by selected countries to gain importance in the overall system of trade agreements. To assess this, we consider the core-periphery structure of the networks and the centrality of the actors involved.

The rest of the chapter is organised as follows. Section 10.2 defines and discusses our data. Section 10.3 analyses the structural characteristics of the FTAs Networks from 1960 to 2016. Section 10.4 explores the different positions of countries in the networks and, finally, section 10.5 concludes.

10.2 Network Analysis

Network analysis is concerned with the investigation of the structure of relations between actors. In this chapter the presence of a link g_{ij} represents the presence of an FTA agreement between country i and country j. Given this basic framework, where relations are bilateral and symmetric, we have an unweighted network.

To develop our network analysis, we will use the WTO database on RTAs, which considers all the Regional Trade Agreements Notified to the GATT/WTO and in Force by Date of Entry into Force, which is available on the

WTO website. From the list, we drop the Global System of Trade Preferences among Developing Countries (1988) and the Protocol on Trade Negotiations (1971) because they are very different from the other treaties considered, and cannot be easily compared to other FTAs since they are non-reciprocal trade agreements. We disaggregate the agreements according to the bilateral ties or dyads, for example, the NAFTA agreement will be represented as three bilateral links connecting the US, Canada, and Mexico. Clearly, all FTAs have remarkable differences: they vary in terms of economic weights, the distance between them, and the level of development among partners. No less important, they also vary in size (bilateral or regional agreements). For the sake of comparability between different agreements we choose to consider them as equal, trying during the rest of work to characterized them. In our final dataset, we consider 179 countries. For the sake of tractability, in the representation of the networks, we consider the EU as a single actor. This is because every free trade agreement signed by the EU is binding for all Member states (since 1958, the Commission of the European Communities has negotiated all trade agreements on behalf of the member states). Moreover, to improve the clarity of graphs, we choose not to represent graphically the links describing the agreements between EU and the Overseas Countries and Territories.

10.3 The general structure of the network

The analysis of the structure of the FTAs network gives us some relevant information about how the global support toward free trade agreements has changed over time.

Table 10.1: Statistics for the FTAs network in various year

Year	Number of countries	% of the world total	FTA links	Density	Average Degree
1960	18	12.4	42	0.274	4.61
1970	37	11.7	104	0.156	5.62
1980	41	22.2	195	0.237	10.51
1990	55	27.5	281	0.189	10.21
2000	126	64.2	869	0.115	13.79
2010	160	76.1	1551	0.12	11.17
2016	179	86.8	3085	0.187	34.13

These simple statistics show how the FTA network has changed from 1960 to nowadays. In fact, all over the time span considered the number of countries involved in free trade agreements, the number of FTAs, and the average number of countries every actor is connected with, all increased. We can notice how, after 1990, the number of countries who choose to sign at least one agreement has more than tripled, including not only countries traditionally more open to free trade, but almost every country in the world. In the last six years, with a modest increase in the number of new actors in the network, the average degree almost doubled, meaning that the countries involved are tightening up their relations and opening their markets to an increased number of foreign countries.

To check properly how tight the actors are connected, we need to consider the network density, i.e., what percentage of possible links is covered by a tie. Apparently, it does not appear that the density has increased: it was 27.4% in 1960, while only 18.7% in 2003. One factor to take into account in interpreting density is that the size of the network has grown from 18 countries in 1960 to 179 in 2016.The size of all the possible links within the network grows exponentially as the number of nodes increases linearly, leading to difficulty in determining what changes in measures such as density actually mean. If we focus on the last six years, in which we roughly have the same network size, density increased sharply confirming that the level of interconnection within the network has increased significantly.

We now move to study, more accurately, the structure of the network. If the network has no defined structure, the links will be randomly distributed among the actors, so that the degree distribution of such networks would be normally distributed, and we would find only a small share of countries with a very small or a very large number of FTAs. If we depict graphically the network share of actors against the number of FTAs they have, we expect to find some sort of bell curve. However, this is not what we found in figure 10.1. The distribution of FTAs within the network, in 2016, is much more likely to be a power law curve in which few countries have a huge number of FTAs, while the bulk has few agreements.

Figure 10.1: The distribution of FTAs in the network 2016

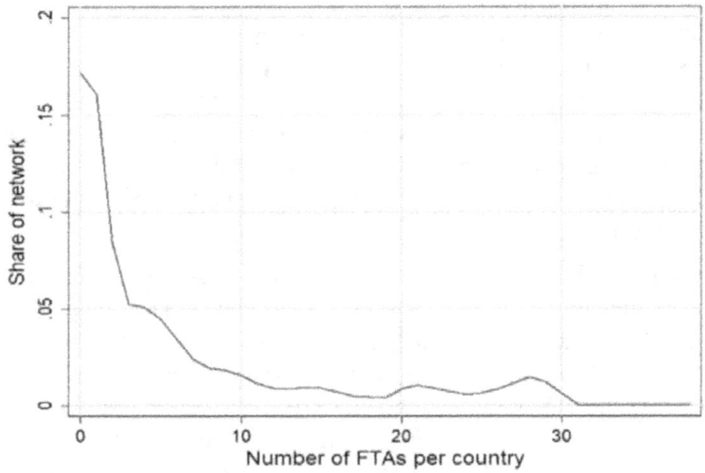

Color images of figures can be downloaded at the book's page
[URL: https://vernonpress.com/book/96]

The long tail of the distribution in figure 1 suggests that the FTA network is not simply random, therefore, to study the structure of the network we will analyse the degree distribution in order to detect some sort of power law behaviour.

To test the goodness-of-fit of our data to a power law, we will use the Kolgomorov-Smirnov statistic. To make sure our data do not fit better with a different distribution, we also consider exponential and log-normal distribution using the same technique (Table 10.2).

Table 10.2: Power law, Exponential and Log-Normal Fits of degree partitions

Year	Power law		Exponential		Log-normal	
	Statistics	P value	Statistics	P value	statistics	P value
1960	0.213	0.382	0.195	0.014	0.166	**0.835**
1970	0.294	0.402	0.923	0.047	0.107	**0.805**
1980	0.276	0.280	0.233	0.000	0.281	**0.576**
1990	0.206	0.258	0.229	0.188	0.086	**0.486**
2000	0.205	0.112	0.085	0.493	0.107	**0.578**
2010	0.175	**0.894**	0.113	0.550	0.127	0.525
2016	0.109	**0.986**	0.109	0.000	0.116	0.271

Albert and Baràbasi (1999) propose a mechanism that explains the origin of the power law distribution: the preferential attachment. When the network size increases, and new nodes are added and linked to existing ones, the new edges are not chosen uniformly, but the new node is linked to an existing one with a probability that is proportional to the degree of the existing node, a sort of "the rich get richer" effect. The main feature of this model is the scale-free distribution since the well-connected nodes tend to become, as the network grows, even better connected (hubs). The preferential attachment nature of the FTAs network has emerged only in the last twenty years. Before 2000, we have not enough statistical support for the power law hypothesis, and the log-normal distribution, given the higher p-value seems more plausible.

We can also explain this preferential attachment process considering the so-called "domino-effect" (Baldwin 2006). After 2000, when the number of new agreements signed and the number of countries part of the network increased sharply, some countries, relatively more open to free trade, rapidly became hubs. The countries outside (or relatively less involved) in the network have been pushed to sign FTAs with already very central actors in the network, because they found it profitable to set FTAs with well-connected countries to have a preferential access to markets in which, given the number of FTAs signed, discrimination could be higher for countries outside the network.

To further check this hypothesis, we consider degree assortativity. This metric considers to what extent nodes in a network associated with other nodes in the network with a similar degree. If our hypothesis is correct, we expect to find that in the last sixteen years the general assortativity of the network has decreased, because countries with a low degree have connected preferentially with hub countries to compete on equal terms in the hub market.

Table 10.3: Degree assortativity in various year

Year	Degree Assortativity
1960	0.813
1970	0.803
1980	0.735
1990	0.815
2000	0.569
2010	0.251
2016	0.019

The degree assortativity index can vary between -1 and 1, with 1 meaning perfect assortative mixing patterns and -1 perfect dissortative mixing patterns. Until 1990, our networks show almost a perfect assortative behaviour meaning that countries were connected only with countries with a similar degree. In 2000 and 2010 the degree assortativity decreased sharply continuing, however, to show mainly an assortative behaviour. In 2016 the assortative index value was 0.019 the lowest value from 1960. These results strengthen our hypothesis showing how in the last years the assortative index has decreased sharply. Of course, since we are considering the whole network we do not expect to find a disassortative behaviour but only a general decrease in the assortative one. This can be explained by the fact that new countries tend to choose to preferentially link with hub countries, but it does not mean that hubs stop to link with other hubs nor that countries already in the network connect only with hubs. Moreover, if we calculate the coefficient excluding European countries (EU members and EFTA countries), which are all hub countries linked all together, we find some signs of disassortative behaviour.

The next characteristic we would like to test is how important are regional connections in the network. If we observe the FTA network in the Sixties, we can observe how it was structured in 3 separate components, each of them representing a regional agreement, while the network nowadays presents a totally different structure in which regional connections may have lost some of their importance.

According to Krugman (1991) and Frankel et al. (1997) a FTA between geographically close countries is more likely to be welfare enhancing since trade diversion is minimized due to the higher transport costs with the other countries outside the agreement: the more two countries trade with each other relative to the rest of the world before signing an FTA, the less the trade diversion implied by that FTA. Other authors such as Nitsch (1996) and Bhagwati and Panagariya (1996) contrast this idea pointing out the importance of the intra-regional transport costs respect to inter-regional ones and the lack of symmetries between "natural" trading partners. If the first hypothesis is correct we expect to find a substantial amount of agreements between countries in the same region, on the other hand, if the critiques are correct FTA formation would not reflect regional composition.

To observe how the regional dimension has changed we compare graphically the FTA networks in 2000 and 2016. Figure 10.2 below depicts the global FTAs network in 2000. We color-coded for the different geographical areas and we weighted the size of each country's circle by degree centrality, simply the number of partner every actor has.

Figure 10.2: The global FTAs network in 200

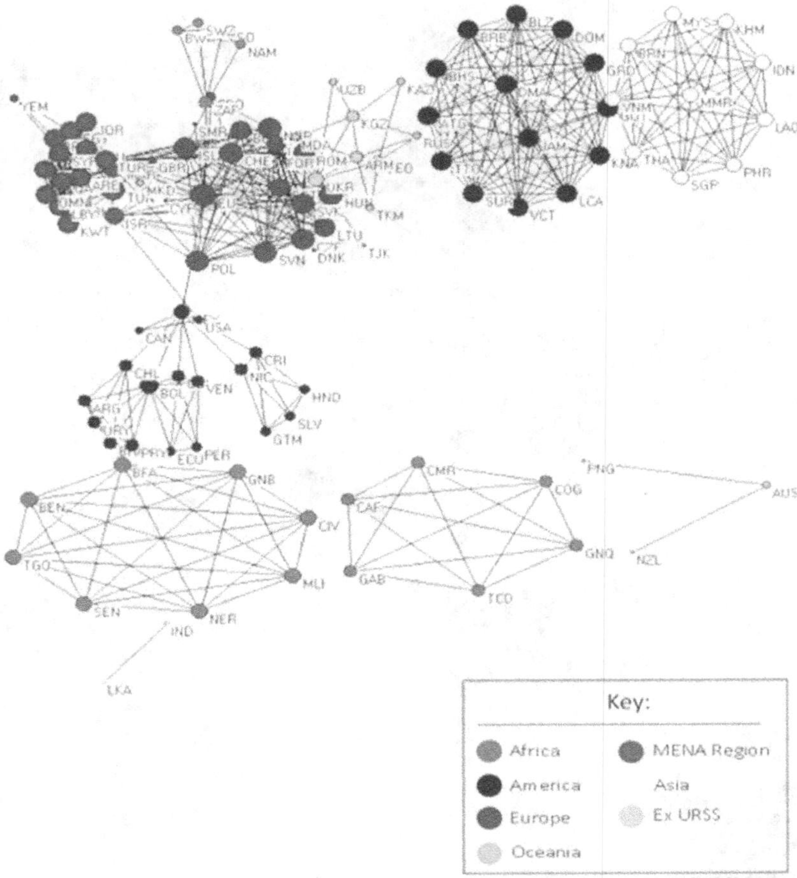

Color images of figures can be downloaded at the book's page
[URL: https://vernonpress.com/book/96]

Figure 10.3: The global FTAs network in 2016

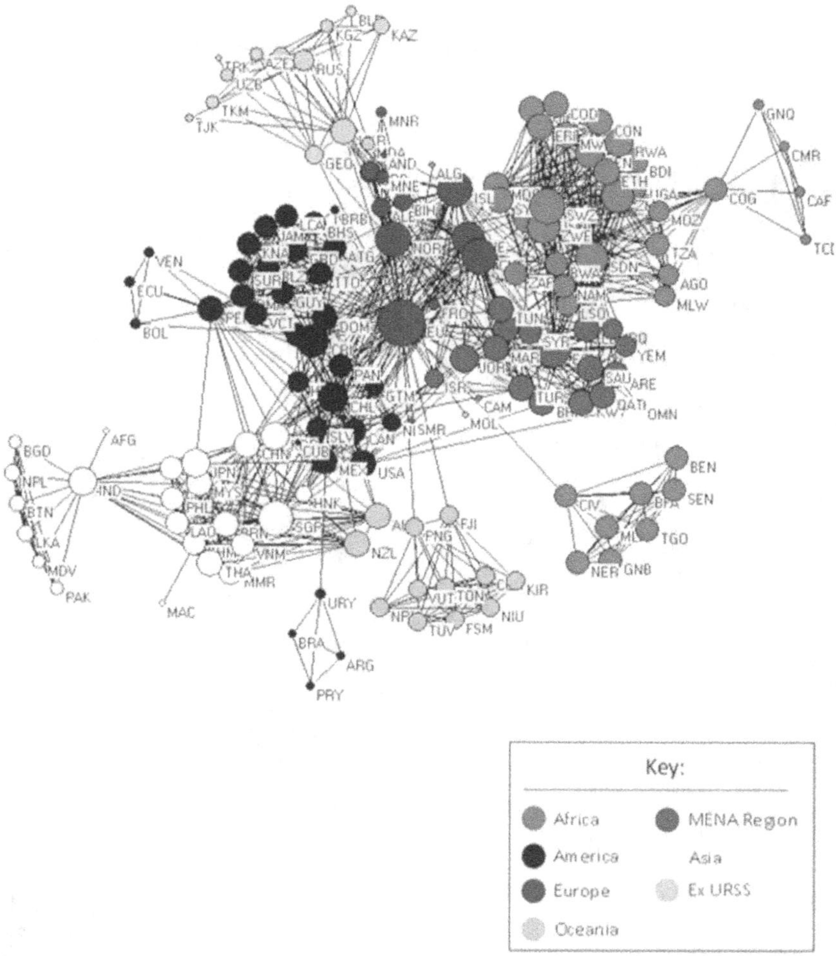

Color images of figures can be downloaded at the book's page [URL: https://vernonpress.com/book/96]

Figure 10.3 shows the network in 2016. As we can see, comparing the two figures, from 2000 to 2016 the FTA network changed significantly. While in 2000 the graph is organized in separate components except for Europe, North Africa, and the Middle East, suggesting that the global system of FTAs was organized mainly around multilateral, regional agreements, in 2016 all the countries are directly or indirectly mutually connected.

In 2016, the FTAs network is still organized in a regional cluster with the European Union, which is the one with the highest number of neighbours, in the middle as pivoting point. As we can see from the graph, most of the clusters correspond to specific regions, which are linked by few countries acting as a bridge, connecting different multilateral, regional agreements. We can see a notable exception to this statement for the countries of Europe and Central and Latin America, which form a larger cluster and are moving to create a mega-region. To properly assess the importance of regional connections, in this section we will analyse the evolution of geographical homophily. Homophily has been defined as the tendency to form social ties with actors showing similar attributes, in our case we will observe, using mixing matrix, if the countries have the tendency to tie with other countries part of the same region. In every cell, we have the actual number of ties between regions for the considered years and, in parenthesis the structural density. Diagonal cells in the matrix refer to homophily in one region while off-diagonal refer to heterophily between regions.

According to the United Nations geographic classification scheme, the world consists of eleven regions: North America, Central America, South America, Western Europe, Eastern Europe, East Asia, South Asia, Southeast Asia, Oceania, Africa, and Southwest Asia-North Africa. Since the sample sizes are small in some regions, for the sake of simplicity, we collapse them into seven regions: Africa, America, Europe, North-Africa and the Middle East, Asia and Oceania and former URSS.

Table 10.4: Mixing matrix by regions 2000

	Europe	America	Africa	NA & ME	Asia & Oceania	Former URSS
Europe	422 (0.8)	15 (0.014)	15 (0.014)	67 (0.019)		2 (0.006)
America		122 (0.246)	13 (0.02)	1 (0.002)	1 (0.002)	
Africa			53 (0.279)			
NA & ME				94 (0.691)		
Asia & Oceania					47 (0.516)	
Former URSS						17 (0.378)
Total	422	137	81	162	48	19

Note: In parenthesis, the structural density. The matrix is symmetric so we omit the lower part

Table 10.5: Mixing matrix by regions 2010

	Europe	America	Africa	NA & ME	Asia & Oceania	Former URSS	Total
Europe	571 (0.812)	63 (0.045)	41 (0.028)	215 (0.314)	8 (0.008)	10 (0.024)	907
America		195 (0312)	26 (0.019)	11 (0.017)	24 (0.026)	5 (0.013)	261
Africa			106 (0.222)	41 (0.06)	17 (0.017)		164
NA & ME				129 (0.843)	2 (0.004)		131
Asia & Oceania					65 (0.2)		65
Former URSS						23 (0.418)	23
Total	571	257	173	396	116	38	1551

Table 10.6: Mixing matrix by regions 2016

	Europe	America	Africa	NA & ME	Asia & Oceania	Former URSS	Total
Europe	778 (0.904)	609 (0.347)	247 (0.143)	284 (0.356)	94 (0.077)	94 (0.172)	2106
America		175 (0.236)	27 (0.012)	11 (0.131)	50 (0.044)	5 (0.008)	268
Africa			290 (0.354)	49 (0.063)	17 (0.011)		356
NA & ME				139 (0.779)	6 (0.011)	1 (0.004)	146
Asia & Oceania					167 (0.411)		167
Former URSS						42 (0.538)	42
Total	778	784	564	483	334	142	3085

Table 10.4, 10.5 and 10.6 represent the mixing matrix for 2000, 2010 and 2016 respectively. We omit the matrix for the previous years because almost all the FTAs were signed by countries part of the same region with an exception for Europe and North Africa, and the Middle East. Until 2000 the FTAs system shows a strong tendency to be homophilous by regions. In fact, the FTAs network was structured mainly on geographically based trade blocks in

which the countries opened to trade within their regional partners moving protectionism from a national to a regional level.

In 2000 the FTAs network shows changes in this regional trade blocks structure with European and American countries which started to sign an increasing number of FTAs outside their region. This trend of decreasing homophily by region is confirmed also in the 2010 matrix in which also countries in the Asia and Oceania region massively embedded in the larger networks of agreements.

The picture in 2016 is the one of a semi-globalised world (Ghemawat 2003). Countries still have agreements more likely within their region since FTA ties are concentrated on the diagonal of the matrix, and the structural density within regions is increasing sharply (with Europe almost close to being a maximal connected subnetwork). However, while FTA agreements are clustered into regional networks, these clusters are not independent of each other. In fact, the number of FTAs between countries from different regions is increasing and, this phenomenon, even not significant for some regions such as Asia and Oceania, is significant for the trade relationship of European and American countries. Therefore, we can say that there have been real and meaningful changes in the FTAs system, even if economic integration is not complete.

Consistently to Krugman and Frankel idea that countries prefer to sign FTAs with partners within the same region, probably because they allow gains from trade creation while at the same time reducing the negative effects of trade diversion, we observe a notable number of links within the same geographic region in all the years considered. Nevertheless, in the last years, we also observe an increase in the number of inter-regional agreements. This result could still be explained by the Krugman hypothesis, according to which the higher inter-regional transport cost could increase the profitability of a regional trade agreement compared to an inter-regional one. In the last years transport costs decreased sharply (Hummels 2007), therefore, the magnitude of inter-continental costs has lost importance as an explanation of the net benefits of a FTA. With lower transport costs, this positive geographic proximity effect decreases, and other factors gain importance in considering FTAs formation, making profitable otherwise not profitable agreements.

10.4 The actors' position

So far, we treated nodes as if they were anonymous, not considering which countries display higher or lower network properties. Now, we analyse the different position of the countries in the FTA network. Considering how the relative position of the countries has changed over time, the position of the countries, and how every country chooses to connect with it, we try to define what are the main strategies followed by selected countries to gain importance in the overall system of agreements.

The first dimension we consider is the position of each node in the network described as a particular pattern of ties. We want to underline the core-periphery structure of the network by identifying the core countries (Borgatti and Everett 2000). In the core-periphery structure, trade agreements occur predominantly within the core and between the core and the periphery, therefore, the core countries are the "central" ones in the network.

We expect to distinctly find a hierarchical structure in the network because the relative economic development of countries strongly influences which countries are likely to sign an FTA with one another (Baier and Bergstrand 2004). High-income countries are the most likely to form an agreement with each other and with middle-income ones, while they have lower incentives to enter into an agreement with a least developed country. Finally, low-income countries have the weakest incentives to conclude FTA with each other. Therefore, we do not expect to find developing countries in the core countries group.

Table 10.7: Core countries selected years

1990	2000	2010	2016
EU,EFTA, Israel	EU, EFTA, Israel, Turkey	EU, EFTA, Israel, Turkey, Egypt, Jordan, Tunisia, Mexico, Chile, Costa Rica	EU, EFTA, Israel, Turkey, Egypt, Jordan, Tunisia, Mexico, Chile, Costa Rica, Korea, Singapore, Morocco, Colombia, Peru, Honduras Nicaragua, US

From Table 10.7 we can identify an evolution of the community structure from a few major core countries in 1990 to a more decentralized topology in 2016. Not only the number of core countries increased but also their geographical origin. In fact, while in 2000 the core countries were fundamentally European with Turkey and Israel closely connected with the European system of free trade agreements, in 2016 we have at least one core country in every region with a remarkable number of core countries in Central and Latin America. Interestingly only in 2010, and mostly in 2016, middle-income countries have entered in the core countries groups, while a high incomes country such as the US become a core country only in 2016. This is because, compared to other high-income countries, US started relatively later to sign FTAs, and in particular FTAs outside its region.

To better address the different ways in which a country could be well connected in the network, we consider centrality. We study centrality because we assume that more central positions within the FTAs network are related to higher degrees of international economic integration of the countries.

There are a huge number of different measures for centrality, each considering different nodes' characteristics, to assess what is the meaning of being a central actor in a network. In this chapter, we consider degree, betweenness and hub centralities. The degree centrality is simply the number of neighbours that a node has in the network. Betweenness centrality (Freeman 1977) is the ratio between the number of shortest path that flows through the given node, divided by the total number of path which flows through that node, is equal to $g(v) = \sum_{s \neq v \neq t} \frac{\sigma_{st(v)}}{\sigma_{st}}$, with σ_{st} representing the total number of shortest paths from node s to node t and $\sigma_{st(v)}$ equal to the total number of shortest paths from node s to node t that pass through v; it measures how much a node links otherwise unconnected parts of the network. It represents the general connectivity and the ability of a country in bridging clusters. Hub centrality is an out-degree variant of eigenvector centrality, and it measures the relative importance of a node in the network. Every node value is proportional to the sum of the scores of his neighbours, and it accounts not only for the number of paths a node has, but also for the rank of the nodes it is connected with (Kleinberg 1999).

Table 10.8: Higher degree centrality countries in various years

1990		2000		2010		2016	
Country	**Value**	**Country**	**Value**	**Country**	**Value**	**Country**	**Value**
EU countries	19	EU countries	35	EFTA countries	54	EU countries	88
Finland	18	EFTA countries	31	Chile	52	Egypt	64
Island	17	Hungary	29	Egypt	51	EFTA countries	61
Norway	17	Czech Republic	29	Jordan	46	Chile	54
Austria	17	Bulgaria	29	EU countries	44	Korea	54
Switzerland	17	Israel	25	Mexico	43	Costa Rica	53

Note: We omitted years before 1990 because the networks were mainly organized in full connected separate components

Table 10.9: Higher hub centrality countries in various years

1990		2000		2010		2016	
Country	**Value**	**Country**	**Value**	**Country**	**Value**	**Country**	**Value**
EU countries	0.2356	EU countries	0.1873	EFTA countries	0.1667	Chile	0.1689
Finland	0.2271	EFTA countries	0.1765	Estonia	0.1608	Costa Rica	0.1446
Island	0.2182	Polonia	0.1654	EU countries	0.1597	EU countries	0.1024
Norway	0.2182	Bulgaria	0.1518	Hungary	0.1567	Egypt	0.0899
Switzerland	0.2182	Romania	0.1506	Turkey	0.1449	Swaziland	0.0876

Note: We omitted years before 1990 because the networks were mainly organized in full connected separate components

Table 10.10: Higher betweenness centrality countries in various years

1990		2000		2010		2016	
Country	**Value**	**Country**	**Value**	**Country**	**Value**	**Country**	**Value**
Israel	0.02655	Tunisia	0.0867	Chile	0.0244	EU countries	0.046
USA	0.01396	South Africa	0.0405	Costa Rica	0.0209	Korea	0.0394
EU countries	0.00165	Bolivia	0.02757	Mexico	0.0104	Chile	0.0367
Australia	0.00069	Romania	0.02562	Australia	0.0093	India	0.0278
Finland	0.00032	Chile	0.01883	USA	0.0093	Singapore	0.0243

Note: We omitted years before 1990 because the networks were mainly organized in full connected separate components

Observing the degree centrality of the actors in the network, we notice immediately how the European countries, except in 2010, represent the most central nodes. Since the formation of the European Economic Community in 1958, free trade was one of the most important value of the European project. With the following enlargements, the countries that choose to become part of this common market automatically became part of all the trade agreements signed by the European countries, increasing sharply the number of partners in the FTA network and setting the European countries at the centre of the global FTA network. The surge of FTA partners for Europe, in 2016, can be explained with the new strategy developed in the last years. The resounding success of European integration pushed EU countries to extend trade preference to many neighbouring countries and former colonies, often for political rather than economic reasons. Moreover, given the fact that EU is the largest trading block in the world with the highest number of free trade agreements, many countries would rather be in an agreement with the EU to avoid being discriminated in the access to a major hub.

If we consider hub centrality, we can notice the comparatively low rank for the EU countries probably because many of the EU's agreements have been concluded with partners that are not very central in the global network. Considering also the rise in the value of betweenness centrality in 2016, we can suppose that EU countries have chosen to exploit the opportunity to become a gatekeeper in the global network (to avoid marginalization in the network due to the new activism of some countries such as the US and Japan) and to connect with otherwise not connected countries, maintaining their status as a "preferential partner" of many countries.

The EU countries are not the only ones who became a hub. The current trend of "crisscrossing" trade agreements between countries has created what Baldwin (2006) and Bhagwati (2003) called "the spaghetti bowl," a very complex interaction between different and often overlapping FTAs. This complex framework may convert some countries into hubs and some others into spokes, according to the number of FTAs each country has. In figure 10.4 we represent for every year the number of new hubs countries. In the last twenty years the number of new hubs has strongly increased, still, some countries become hub multiple times with respect to a distinct set of spokes. The countries with the highest frequency of being a hub are the European ones, the EFTA ones, Turkey, Israel, Mexico and the US (Hur et al. 2010).

Figure 10.4: New hub countries per year

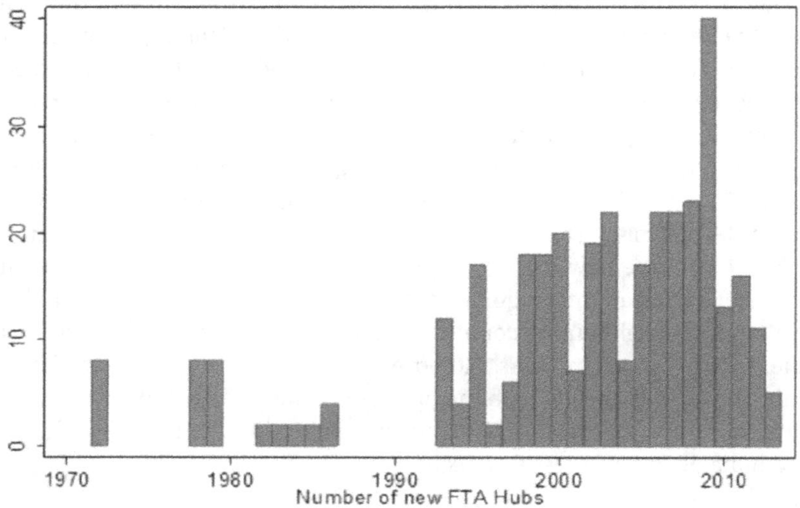

Color images of figures can be downloaded at the book's page
[URL: https://vernonpress.com/book/96]

In the last years, some new countries have entered in the group of most central countries. If in 2000 those countries were mainly the East European ones, involved in FTAs in order to meet the requirements needed to join the EU, in the last sixteen years countries as Chile, Costa Rica, Egypt, South Korea, and Mexico have pursuit a new active policy of FTAs formation. These countries are members of several multi-party FTAs that place them centrally in certain regions and have signed also FTAs with big markets outside their regions, connecting it with the overall network. In those agreements, often are included conditions that help to attract FDI since the PTA acts as a commitment instruments that guarantees investment-friendly policies (Tornell and Esquivel 1995), and locks in an open trade policy in the future (Maggi and Rodrıguez-Clare 2007).

The activism of middle-income countries in FTAs is not completely a new phenomenon. Already in the Sixties, some countries, especially in Latin America and Africa chose to enter into regional trade agreements. Unfortunately, regional integration failed to bring the economic development expected and those regional agreements weakened. In the last ten years, because of the WTO impasse in negotiation, many countries turned back to bilateralism. However, differently, from regionalism in the Sixties, these countries try to sign agreements with large developed market even outside their region (De Melo et al. 2015).

In particular, Mexico, Chile, and Costa Rica have been carrying out a very dynamic policy for the negotiation of free trade agreements. In fact, in addition to an extensive ego-network of trade agreements with almost all the countries in their region, they have also been linked with Asian and industrialized countries not part of their regional network. They started in the middle of the 1990s to negotiate outside Central and Latin America, and now they have FTAs with European Union countries, EFTA countries, US and Canada , all central actors in the network which gave to Mexico, Chile and Costa Rica a high hub centrality values for 2016.

The Chinese case differs. Since 2001, the year in which China entered in the WTO, the country has been increasingly active in its pursuit of regional and bilateral trade agreements. In 2016, China was a member of 14 FTAs with 22 partners. While that is similar to other countries in East Asia (Japan and South Korea, for example), China initially chose to focus on smaller partners (Iceland and Hong Kong) that were easier to negotiate with, before moving to larger and difficult agreements like the one with the ASEAN. Now the Chinese free trade agenda is mainly focused on Asia and the Pacific region.

Figure 10.5: Betweenness centrality versus degree in 2016 selected countries

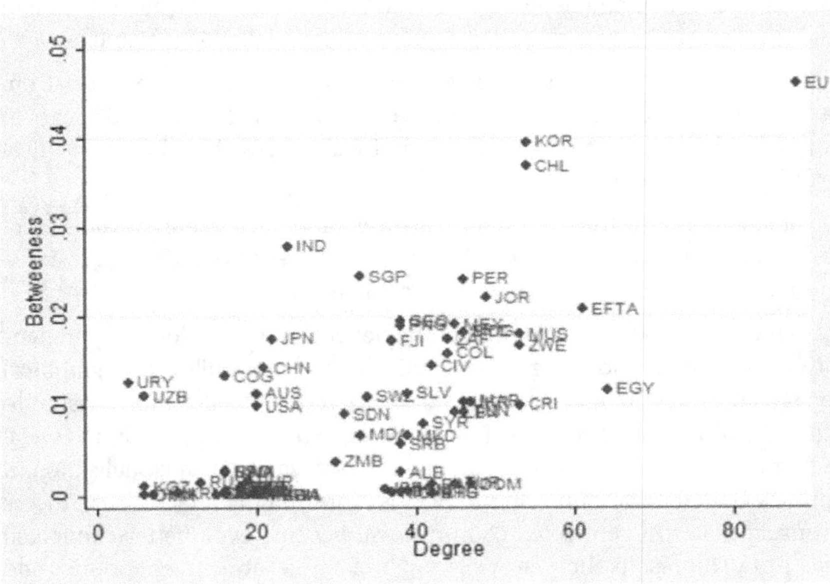

Color images of figures can be downloaded at the book's page [URL: https://vernonpress.com/book/96]

In figure 10.5, we depict betweenness centrality versus degree centrality in 2016 for selected countries. This graph shows how, on average, countries with high betweenness centrality tend to be hubs in the FTAs global network in the sense that they tend to have the largest degrees. However, we have also countries with high degree that do not have high betweenness centrally such as Egypt and Costa Rica or countries with high betweenness centrality that do not have high degree such as Korea, Chile, and India.

In the first group of countries, we have countries that are used to negotiate multilateral rather than bilateral agreements, in this way the country increases its number of partners without increasing its betweenness (as the majority of its partners are already connected between them).

In the second group, we have the so-called "bridge" countries, i.e., countries that connect with otherwise non-connected countries, thereby connecting their region with the rest of the global network. In this way, they can take advantage of being the only connection between two countries.

10.5 Conclusion

In this chapter, we have applied various tools of network analysis to better understand how the general structure of the free trade agreements system and the relative position of the countries in it have changed over time.

More specifically, we analyse the evolution of the global FTA network from 1960 to 2016. We use data comprising 179 countries and covering 56 years to construct the global FTA network to empirically assess its main topological properties.

Our analysis starts from the empirical observation of a massive explosion of the number of free trade agreements in the last twenty years, which resulted in a system of overlapping free trade agreements.

We have examined the evolution of the network structure focusing on density, degree distribution, degree assortativity and homophily by geographical region, and the intra and interregional density. We consider this measure to study the process of formation of free trade agreements, with the aim to test if FTAs network formation follows a path of globalisation or regionalisation, if this has changed over time, and if there is a preferential attachment process ensuring that well-connected countries will become even better connected over time. Our results show clear signs of preferential attachment process and a semi-globalised structure in which FTA agreements are mainly inside each region while only a few countries chose partners outside their region.

In the second part, we characterized the nodes in the network by analysing the different position of the countries in the FTA network. We consider the core-periphery structure of the network and the centrality of the actors involved checking if the most important countries have changed over time. Our empirical analysis underlines the important changes occurred in the free trade agreement system in recent years. For all the metrics considered in our analysis, the last sixteen years witnessed a dramatic change that has totally reshaped the general structure and the relative countries' positions.

The general hubness of the system has increased since the degree distribution started to fit a power law distribution and the important countries are becoming even more important and geographical proximity, a key factor to predict FTA formation, is losing importance.

In this scenario, new countries are emerging as key players. Unlike in the past, we do not have mainly European countries deeply involved in FTAs formation, but some middle-income countries are emerging as regional leaders in this process and are signing new agreements with partners outside their geographical region. Our results suggest that the evolution of the free trade agreements network is far from reaching an end-point and is likely to continue.

10.6 Appendix

Table 10. A1: Table of Acronyms

WTO	World Trade Organization
RTA	Regional Trade Agreement
FTA	Free Trade Agreement
EU	European Union
US	United States
NAFTA	Nord America Free Trade Agreement
EFTA	European Free Trade Association
ASEAN	Association of Southeast Asian Nations

10.7 References

Acharya, R., 2016. Regional trade agreements and the multilateral trading system. Cambridge University Press.

Albert, R., Barabási, A.-L., 2002. Statistical mechanics of complex networks. Reviews of modern physics 74, 47.

Baier, S.L., Bergstrand, J.H., 2004. Economic determinants of free trade agreements. Journal of International Economics 64, 29–63. doi:10.1016/S0022-1996(03)00079-5

Baier, S.L., Bergstrand, J.H., Mariutto, R., 2014. Economic Determinants of Free Trade Agreements Revisited: Distinguishing Sources of Interdependence. Review of International Economics 22, 31–58. doi:10.1111/roie.12095

Baldwin, R., 2006. Multilateralising Regionalism: Spaghetti Bowls as Building Blocs on the Path to Global Free Trade. The World Economy, 29(11):1451–1518.33

Baldwin, R., Jaimovich, D., 2012. Are Free Trade Agreements contagious? Journal of International Economics 88, 1–16. doi: 10.1016/j.jinteco.2012.03.009

Bhagwati, J., 2003. Free trade today. Princeton, NJ: Princeton University Press.

Bhagwati, J., Panagariya, A., 1996. The Theory of Preferential Trade Agreements: Historical Evolution and Current Trends. The American Economic Review 86, 82–87.

Bhattacharya, K., Mukherjee, G., Saramäki, J., Kaski, K., Manna, S.S., 2008. The International Trade Network: weighted network analysis and modelling. J. Stat. Mech. 2008, P02002. doi:10.1088/1742-5468/2008/02/P02002

Borgatti, S.P., Everett, M.G., 2000. Models of core/periphery structures. Social Networks 21, 375–395. doi:10.1016/S0378-8733(99)00019-2

Clauset, A., Shalizi, C. R., Newman, M.E., 2009. Power-law distributions in empirical data. SIAM review 51, 661–703.

De Benedictis, L., Nenci, S., Santoni, G., Tajoli, L., & Vicarelli, C. ,2014. Network Analysis of World Trade using the BACI-CEPII dataset. Global Economy Journal, 14(3-4), 287-343.

De Benedictis, L., & Tajoli, L. (2011). The world trade network. The World Economy, 34(8), 1417-1454;

De Melo, J., Panagariya, A., & Rodrik, D., 2015. The new regionalism: a country perspective. In Developing Countries in the World Economy (pp. 323-357).

Fagiolo, G., Reyes, J., Schiavo, S., 2010. The evolution of the world trade web: a weighted-network analysis. Journal of Evolutionary Economics 20, 479–514. doi:10.1007/s00191-009-0160-x

Fagiolo, G., Reyes, J., Schiavo, S., 2008. On the topological properties of the world trade web: A weighted network analysis. Physica A: Statistical Mechanics and its Applications, Applications of Physics in Financial Analysis Selected papers from the 6th International Conference 'Applications of Physics in Financial Analysis' (APFA6), Lisbon, Portugal, 4–7 July 2007Applications of Physics in Financial Analysis 387, 3868–3873. doi:10.1016/j.physa.2008.01.050

Frankel, J.A., Stein, E., Wei, S.-J., 1997. Regional Trading Blocs in the World Economic System. Peterson Institute.

Freeman, L. C., 1977. A set of measures of centrality based on betweenness. Sociometry, 35-41.

Furusawa, T., Konishi, H., 2007. Free trade networks. Journal of International Economics 72, 310–335. doi:10.1016/j.jinteco.2006.08.003

Garlaschelli, D., Loffredo, M.I., 2005. Structure and evolution of the world trade network. Physica A: Statistical Mechanics and its Applications 355, 138–144. doi:10.1016/j.physa.2005.02.075

Ghemawat, P., 2003. The Forgotten Strategy [WWW Document]. Harvard Business Review. URL https://hbr.org/2003/11/the-forgotten-strategy (accessed 11.16.16).

Goyal, S., Joshi, S., 2006. Bilateralism and free trade. International Economic Review 47, 749–778.

Hummels, D., 2007. Transportation costs and international trade in the second era of globalisation. The Journal of Economic Perspectives 21, 131–154.

Hur, J., Alba, J. D., & Park, D., 2010. Effects of hub-and-spoke free trade agreements on trade: A panel data analysis. World Development, 38(8), 1105–1113. https://doi.org/10.1016/j.worlddev.2010.02.009

Kleinberg, J. M., 1999. Hubs, authorities, and communities. ACM computing surveys (CSUR), 31(4es), 5.

Krugman, P., 1991. The move toward free trade zones. Economic Review 5–25.

Lee, S., 2012. Creating a Region? The Evolution of Free Trade Agreement Networks in East Asia. EAI 1–32.

Lee, T., Bai, B.-I., 2013. Network Analysis of Free Trade Agreements: Homophily and Transitivity. The Korean Journal of International Studies 11, 263–293.

Lloyd, P.J., Maclaren, D., 2004. Gains and Losses from Regional Trading Agreements: A Survey*. Economic Record 80, 445–467. doi:10.1111/j.1475-4932.2004.00202.x

Maggi, G., Rodríguez-Clare, A., 2007. A Political-Economy Theory of Trade Agreements. American Economic Review 97, 1374–1406. doi:10.1257/aer.97.4.1374

Manger, M.S., Pickup, M.A., Snijders, T.A.B., 2012. A Hierarchy of Preferences A Longitudinal Network Analysis Approach to PTA Formation. Journal of Conflict Resolution 56, 853–878. doi:10.1177/0022002712438351

Martin, P., Mayer T., Thoenig, M., 2008. Make Trade not war?. Review of Economic Studies, 75(3):865-900.

Nitsch, V., 1996. Do Three Trade Blocs Minimize World Welfare? Review of International Economics 4, 355–363. doi:10.1111/j.1467-9396.1996.tb00109.x

Reyes, J., Fagiolo, G., Schiavo, S.,2008. Using a complex weighted-network approach to assess the evolution of international economic integration: The cases of East Asia and Latin America. Laboratory of Economics and Management (LEM), Sant'Anna School of Advanced Studies, Pisa, Italy.

Rombach, M., Porter, M., Fowler, J., Mucha, P., 2014. Core-Periphery Structure in Networks. SIAM J. Appl. Math. 74, 167–190. doi:10.1137/120881683

Serrano, M.Á., Boguñá, M., 2003. Topology of the world trade web. Phys. Rev. E 68, 15101. doi:10.1103/PhysRevE.68.015101

Smith, D.A., White, D. R., 1992. Structure and Dynamics of the Global Economy: Network Analysis of International Trade 1965–1980. Social Forces 70, 857–893. doi:10.1093/sf/70.4.857

Squartini, T., Fagiolo, G., & Garlaschelli, D., 2011. Randomizing world trade. I. A binary network analysis. Physical Review E, 84(4), 046117.

Squartini, T., Fagiolo, G., & Garlaschelli, D., 2011. Randomizing world trade. II. A weighted network analysis. Physical Review E, 84(4), 046118.

Teteryatnikova, M., 2015. R&D in the Network of Trade: The Role of Asymmetry.

Tornell, A., Esquivel, G., 1995. The Political Economy of Mexico's Entry to NAFTA (Working Paper No. 5322). National Bureau of Economic Research.

11.

Moving people: network analysis of international migration

Valerio Leone Sciabolazza

Data: International migration data from Abel and Sander (2014), which was derived from the Global Migration Tables published by the United Nations
Software: R (igraph, ggplot2, circus, ggnetwork)

11.1 Introduction

This chapter outlines a set of methods and visualization strategies to explore, describe and synthetize migratory processes from a network standpoint. The study of international migration is a natural field of application for Social Network Analysis (SNA). In fact, the set of interpersonal ties that connect migrants in origin and destination areas generate a network where each node indicates a place, and one edge connecting two nodes registers the number of people moving from one place to another.

My starting point - that motivates the use of network analysis - is analogous to the one of recent literature on gravity models of international migration (see Beine et al., 2015, for a comprehensive review of this approach), especially the one that gives relevance not only to the bilateral costs of moving from one country to the other, the so called bilateral resistance to migration (i.e. the one exclusively related to the characteristics of country *i* and country *j* involved in the migration flow), but also and primarily to the implicit cost of potential alternative destinations, the so called multilateral resistance to migration (Bertoli and Moraga, 2013). The reason why the attractiveness of other destinations represents a source of concern for the literature on migration can be intuitively explained by extending the thought experiment proposed by Krugman (1995) to the case of migration: if we imagine moving two European countries to Mars while keeping their characteristics unchanged, the migration flows between them would definitely increase, as a result of the reduction in the accessibility of alternative destinations. The study of the network dimension in which a migration flow is embedded is, therefore, crucial to understand how migrants sort themselves.

The interdependence of migration flows, generalized in this paper through the use of SNA, has a number of practical implications for understanding migration decisions and outcomes. First, it helps to explain the role played by transnational relations in the formation of the prospective immigrant's set of information and preferences. As a matter of facts, diasporas have long been shown to alter the context within which migration decisions are made: by providing information about opportunities in a location, and a source of help and support in the host society, they may encourage relocation decisions even when wage differential or recruitment policies cease to exist (Mytna Kurekova, 2010). In addition to this, recent literature suggests that these "diaspora externalities" (Rapoport, 2016) contribute to bilateral migration flows, much in the way they appear to contribute to bilateral trade (Pedersen et al., 2008; Mayda, 2010). The reason is that migrant communities create international business and social relations that bridges information between countries, facilitating cross-border transactions and promoting the consumption of foreign goods (Rauch, 2001; Wagner et al., 2002).[1] Second, the issue of interdependence sheds light on the negative externalities that may arise in the International Migration Network (IMN), as a result of the alteration determined by migratory processes in the composition of the host society. In fact, an increase in the size of a migrant flow at destination can have significant consequences for other migrant communities in that place: e.g., a growing competition for foreign workers in the local labour market (Borjas, 1987a), or a generalized increase of discrimination and prejudicial attitudes in the native population, who can perceive the inflows of new migrants as undermining their cultural, economic and social institutions (Card et al. 2012). As a result, a change in one flow may determine a reallocation of migrants along other routes. Third, the degree of interdependence between IMN flows affects the responsiveness of prospective migrants to policies coordinated at a supranational level. This is the case of the visa waiver granted in 2001 by the European Council (EC), where the effect of the migration policy change in one country was mitigated by the simultaneous change implemented by the other members of the EC (Bertoli and Moraga, 2013): i.e., the force of attractiveness of one country would have been stronger if no other policy change occurred.

[1] Consequently, it is not surprising that the complex web of corridors generated by the movements of people and goods are strongly correlated with each other (Fagiolo and Mastrorillo, 2014). As a matter of facts, they represent two layers of a network registering cross-country interaction channels.

The analysis of the dataset by Abel and Sander (2014)[2], which was derived from the Global Migration Tables published by the United Nations, will walk the reader through the discussion, and it will provide the fundamentals to approach international migration as a global network. Following the lesson of the literature on gravity models, the focus will be put on the role of interdependence in its interplay with the most important time-invariant bilateral components of migration costs, namely geographical distance, differences in economic conditions, colonial links, and linguistic proximity. My approach, however, is distinct from the one of gravity models on several grounds. First, the gravity approach is interested in identifying ex-post the determinants of bilateral migration flows, while here the emphasis is on the description and quantification of the topological properties of the IMN, and on the exploration of the multiple levels of interdependence generating of such network. Second, the way the gravity approach deals with the issue of multilateral resistance is through the operational assumption that interdependence is limited to the structure of error term in a linear longitudinal model (Pesaran, 2006; Pesaran and Tosetti, 2011). Graham (2015), using a statistical approach related to this model, demonstrates that this assumption does a reasonably good job in explaining the structure of interdependence in cross-sectional data,[3] but a more complex procedure is required when dealing with longitudinal observations. By contrast, I undertake a descriptive approach to explore how cultural, economic and geographical proximity may shape multiple structures of interdependence over time. Third, the role of geography on migration flows is captured by the (log)linear effect of distance in the gravity model, implicitly assuming that the friction of distance has an unvarying effect across spatial units; while I focus on the role of geography, in its interplay with dyadic interdependence, using the procedure developed in Abbate et al. (2012): generating from the (weighted) adjacency matrix of migrations flows a series of ten sub-matrices corresponding to the ten deciles of the distribution of bilateral distance between countries. Observing, for every five-year period included in the Abel and Sander (2014) database, the different topological properties of the ten different subnetworks, from the one of very short distance migration (in the first decile) from very long-distance migration (in the eighth, ninth and tenth decile), I am able to describe with a substantial degree of precision the role of geography in the network structure of migration flows. Moreover, by filtering the different push and pull factors of

---

[2] Available at
http://science.sciencemag.org/content/suppl/2014/03/27/343.6178.1520.DC1

[3] The reader interested in the application of this method to gravity models can refer to Charbonneau (2014).

migration movements at different distances, I can uncover important insights regarding the interactions of migration with the social and economic sectors.

It is worth emphasizing that the concepts and methods provided in this chapter focus on the role played by countries in the IMN. However, a number of studies have been already dedicated to investigating the structural and statistical properties of the IMN as a whole. This strand of research has consistently shown that the IMN architecture can be described by a hierarchical structure (Fagiolo and Mastrorillo, 2013, Tranos et al. 2015), where the largest part of international migration is directed towards few countries (hubs) offering better labour market conditions. The persistent difference in salary structures with these countries, and the presence of diasporas, maintained the stability of IMN architecture throughout the years. Most of the changes in migration patterns affected the intensive margin of the network rather than the extensive one (Fagiolo and Mastrorillo 2013; Peres et al. 2016). Perhaps unsurprisingly, new human corridors often originated in developing countries (Davis et al. 2013; Peres et al. 2016). Complementing with existing literature, Davis et al. (2013), Fagiolo and Mastrorillo (2014) and Peres et al. (2016) found also that proximity, linguistic and religious factors, and a common colonial history are fundamental drivers of the process underlying the formation of the IMN. Consistent with these findings, the results of my inquiry will show that the IMN is characterized by a strongly persistent hierarchical architecture, similar to the one reproduced in figure 11.1, regardless the spatial granularity of the data. Few countries, both at the local and at the global level, control the whole connectivity of the network, with a prevalence of star-like structures. Their force of attractiveness, conditional on distance, is directed to countries with same colonial heritage (i.e., cultural homophily) and, contrary to what Abbate et al. (2012) find for the World Trade Network, different in terms of GDP (i.e., economic disassortativity). The persistence of this topological structure over time is consistent with a well-established finding in literature (see, e.g., Pedersen et al. 2008; Fagiolo and Santoni 2015; Munshi 2016), and it provides additional evidence for the existence of "diaspora externalities" reinforcing the processes on the intensive margin of the IMN: i.e., an increase in the size of a migrant network at destination enhances the attractiveness of that place.

This chapter has three contributions. First, it acquaints the reader in a self-contained manner of a number of analytical tools provided by SNA that are particularly suited to explore the externalities generated by the interconnected nature of migration flows. Second, it provides an empirical framework to confirm and further extend our knowledge of the factors determining a decision to move from one place (push factors) to another (pull factors). Third, it shows how the level of embeddedness of one country in the IMN represents a powerful source of information on local processes of migrants' sorting and self-selection.

The remainder of this chapter is organized as follows. Section 11.2 presents a number of methods and visual representations to analyse migration flow data employing a network viewpoint. In section 11.3 is reported an extensive inquiry of the IMN at different geographical, institutional and economic levels, with a particular emphasis on how the network topology is changing in time and space. The results and implications of this investigation are discussed in the last and conclusive section of this chapter.

Figure 11.1: The structural features of the IMN – a toy example

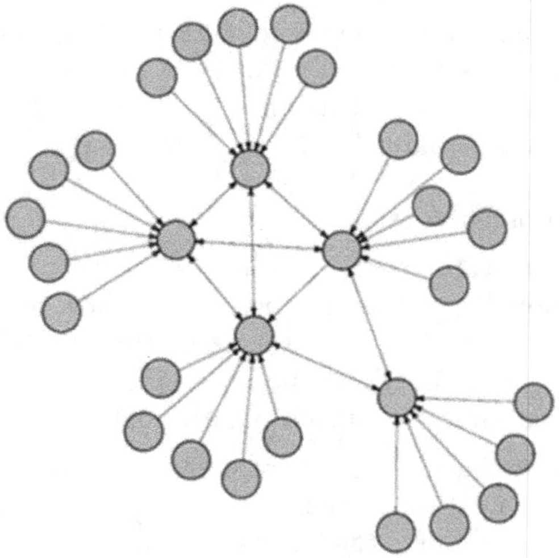

Color images of figures can be downloaded at the book's page [URL: https://vernonpress.com/book/96]

Note: Each node represents a country. An edge connecting two nodes indicates the presence and the direction of a migratory movement between two countries. Figure created with the R package "igraph."

11.2 Data and Methodology

In spite of the early works on national and international migration by Ravenstein (1885, 1889) and Zipf (1946), the empirical research on the movement of people at the bilateral level, using dyadic data, has been severely limited by the lack of data availability. However, in the last ten years, new data sets have been developed by scholars to assess the magnitude of some specific phenomena, such as skilled and female migration (Dumont and Lemaître, 2005; Docquier and Rapoport, 2012; Artuç et al., 2015). More recently, also international institutions, such as the World Bank, through the Bilateral Migration Matrix (Özden et al., 2011), or the United Nations, with the Global Migration database (UNDESA, 2013), began to provide new data on migration available to researchers.

Among the possible alternatives, I select the dataset by Abel and Sander (2014), which was derived from the Global Migration Tables published by the United Nations, and it provides a comparable set of global migration flows between 196 countries. Even though this data lack of information on important dimensions of international migration (e.g., education and gender), the country coverage (196 countries) and the considerable temporal dimension (four waves of data: 1990-1995, 1995-2000, 2000-2005, 2005-2010) suit well the requirements of temporal network analysis (i.e., the panel is balanced, and the boundaries of the network cover the large majority of world countries). However, it should be noted that the analysis will be focused only on 167 countries, namely those that other data sources were available for and that will be introduced at the end of this section.

11.2.1 Social network metrics

The bilateral data provided by Abel and Sander (2014) are used to create four networks corresponding to four instances of the IMN, one for each wave considered: 1990-1995, 1995-2000, 2000-2005, 2005-2010. In each network, one node represents a country, and one edge connecting two nodes registers the number of people moving from one place to another.

SNA provides a number of metrics to quantify the level of embeddedness of one country in each instance of the IMN (see Jackson (2010) for an introduction and detailed description). These measures rely on the idea that phenomena like visibility, involvement, and power are inherently relational, and they can be investigated looking at country's centrality in the space described by the network. In this chapter, I consider four among the most commonly used measures of centrality, in order to endogenously rank country's position in the IMN according to its relations inside and outside its geographical region and draw useful information on its role in the IMN. The first measure considered is referred to as indegree, and it counts the number of incoming flows of one country. Tranos et al. (2015) suggest using this measure as an indication of a country's cosmopolitan character since it documents the number of foreign communities that moved from their countries to one destination. The second measure is specular to the first, and it is called outdegree. It counts the number of outcoming flows of one country, and it can be interpreted as a measure of population mobility. The third metric considered is betweenness centrality, and it assesses how crucial is the presence of one country for brokering human movements between different countries in the IMN, assigning a higher score to nodes playing the role of hub in the network. Intuitively, it can be interpreted as a measure of the migratory pressure faced by one country because of its direct and indirect connections within the IMN. Finally, the fourth metric is local clustering coefficient, which measures the extent to which the countries connected to country *i* are also connected with each other. Consequently, it can be interpreted as the degree of similarity in the composition of the migrant population in country *i* and its connected neighbours.

These metrics can be formalized in the following way. Let $N = \{1,2, \ldots, n\}$ be the set of countries (nodes) in the IMN. For two nodes $i, j \in N$, define $g_t(i,j)$ as the relation (link) between them at time t, where the function g counts the number of migrants moving from i to j at a given time. The collection of nodes (N) and links between them, registered in the IMN at time t, represents the network G_t. Now, let $N_{i\to}(G)$ be the set of links for which $g_t(i,j) > 0$, and $N_{\to i}(G)$ be the set of links for which $g_t(j,i) > 0$. The number of links in $N_{\to i}(G)$ and $N_{i\to}(G)$ is referred to as respectively the *outdegree* and the *indegree* of node *i* in network G, and the sum of out and indegree is defined generically as *degree*. Moreover, say that it exists a *path* from *i* to *j* either if $g_t(i,j) + g_t(j,i) > 0$, or it exists a set of intermediate nodes $j_1, j_2, \ldots, j_n$ such that $\{g_t(i,j_1), \ldots, g_t(i,j_n)\} > 0$. The shortest combination of links connecting i to j is referred to as *shortest path.* The fraction of shortest paths in G passing through node *i* is defined the *betweenness centrality* of node *i* in network G. Finally, define as *triplet* a combination of three links, e.g. $g_t(i,j), g_t(j,k), g_t(k,i)$, and say that a triplet is *closed* if $\{g_t(i,j), g_t(j,k), g_t(k,i)\} > 0$, and that a triplet is *open* if one of the links considered is equal to zero. Now, consider the set of triplets in which *i* is embedded: the fraction of closed triplets over the total number of triplets in this set is referred to as the *local clustering coefficient* of *i*.

The study of the distribution and correlations between centrality measures will be used to single out the role of countries in the IMN, and characterize higher-order moments of the distribution of migration flows: e.g., the likelihood that strongly connected nodes are linked to weakly connected nodes (disassortativity), or the likelihood that countries sharing the same migration pressure also share the same composition of foreign citizens. It is worth emphasizing that this exercise may also provide a better understanding of the negative externalities resulting from the propagation of a shock: e.g., the likelihood that a restrictive immigration policy adopted by a congested hub of the network, will shift the preferences of prospective migrants towards countries playing the same role in the IMN, and facing a similar migratory pressure.

11.2.2 Data description and visualization

The four networks derived by Abel and Sander (2014) are summarized in table 11.1. The table shows an increase of almost 20% in the number of people leaving their country during the time interval considered, but no significant changes in the set of countries involved in the IMN (both as senders and receivers), and in the number of human corridors connecting them, supporting the hypothesis that the transformation of the IMN occurred mostly on its intensive margin. The stability of the IMN structure is also confirmed by the fact that the number of flows involving the largest portions of emigration (e.g., top 1 and 10% flows) remained almost constant over the years. Note, however, that the set of countries sending the largest number of migrants (e.g., those making up 50% or 90% of total emigration) reduced over time, hinting to a concentration of human movements in few major origin areas. On the contrary, the number of top destinations (e.g., those receiving 50% or 90% of total migration) has constantly grown, probably motivated by the rising attractiveness of new emerging economies (e.g., the four Asian tigers or the BRICs).

Table 11.1: Four waves of migration flows: 1990 – 2010

	I wave (1990-1995)	II wave (1995-2000)	III wave (2000-2005)	IV wave (2005-2010)
Countries reporting migration flows	169	169	169	169
Countries reporting migration flows (sender)	164	163	161	164
Countries reporting migration flows (receiver)	164	163	166	166
Total number of flows (# edges)	9,583	10,319	9,503	9,697
Density	0.675	0.7269	0.6694	0.6831
Total number of migrants (flows)	32,080,174	29,977,037	35,031,384	38,116,858
# countries making up to 50% of world migration (sender)	15	18	12	10
# countries making up to 50% of world migration (receiver)	8	7	7	8

# flows making up to 50% of world migration	54	65	72	75
# countries making up to 90% of world migration (sender)	62	70	65	62
# countries making up to 90% of world migration (receiver)	41	48	47	64
# flows making up to 90% of world migration	570	670	671	660
% of world migration accounted for by the top 10% flows (# links)	0.95 (959)	0.94 (1032)	0.93 (951)	0.94 (970)
% of world migration accounted for by the top 1% flows (# links)	0.61 (96)	0.59 (104)	0.56 (96)	0.55 (97)
# destination countries	40	36	64	36
# origin countries	57	62	51	44
Correlation between tot. immigration flows and # of in-flows by country	0.59	0.50	0.55	0.56
Correlation between tot. emigration flows and # of out-flows by country	0.34	0.28	0.33	0.32

A snapshot of the complex and dynamic nature of this network is given by figure 11.2, where migration flows in four different waves (1990-1995, 1995-2000, 2000-2005, 2005-2010) are represented. In this plot, the position and the colour of each country is related to the continent it belongs to (i.e., blue hues represent African countries, green hues represent American countries, red hues represent Asian countries, magenta hues represent European countries, cyan hues represent Oceania). The length of the curvilinear external coloured bands associated with each country's ISO3 code represents the total number of migrants, in 100k units, leaving (coloured part, internal band) or entering (white part, internal band) the country. The thickness of the links represents the number of people migrating, and the colour of the link corresponds to the one of the sending country.

Figure 11.2(a): Global International Migration flows – 1990-1995

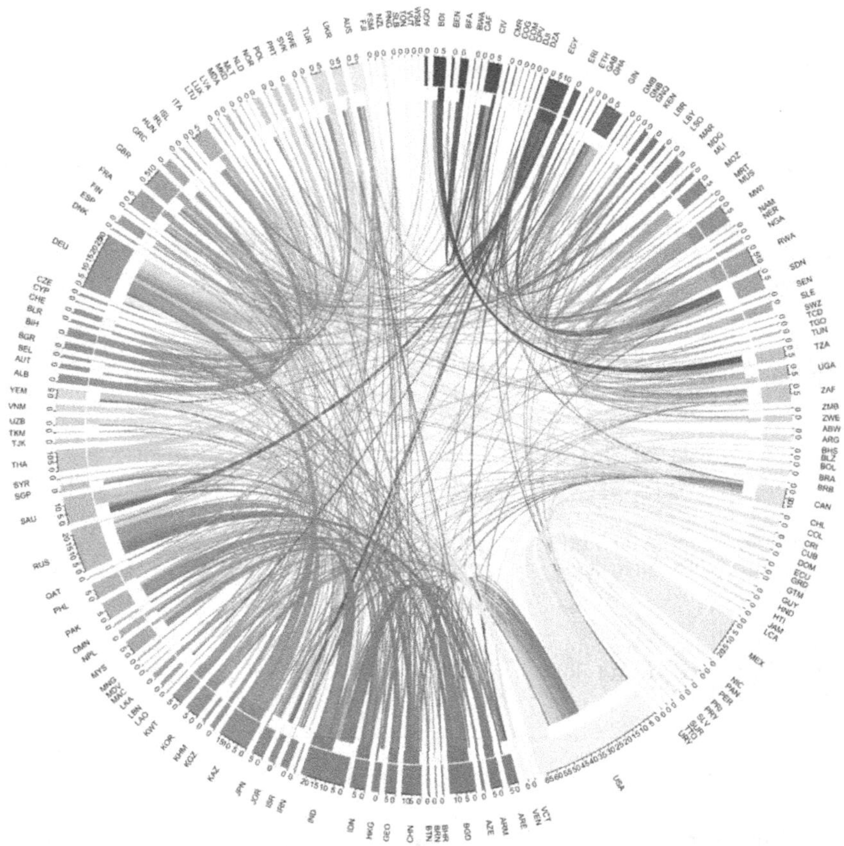

Color images of figures can be downloaded at the book's page
[URL: https://vernonpress.com/book/96]

Figure 11.2(b): Global International Migration flows – 1995-00

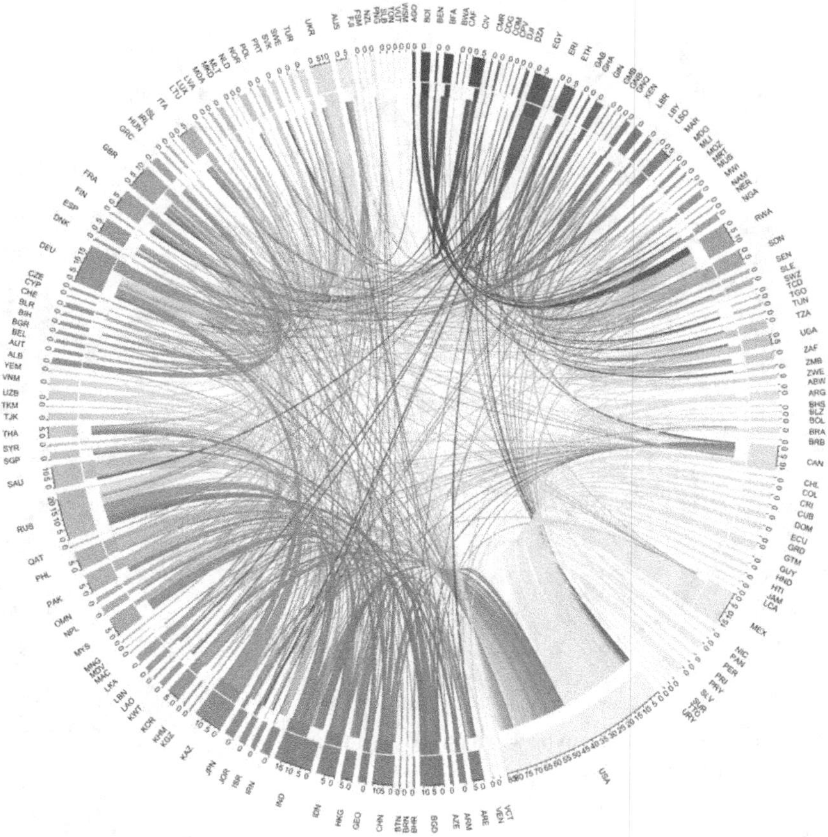

Color images of figures can be downloaded at the book's page [URL: https://vernonpress.com/book/96]

Figure 11.2(c): Global International Migration flows – 2000-05

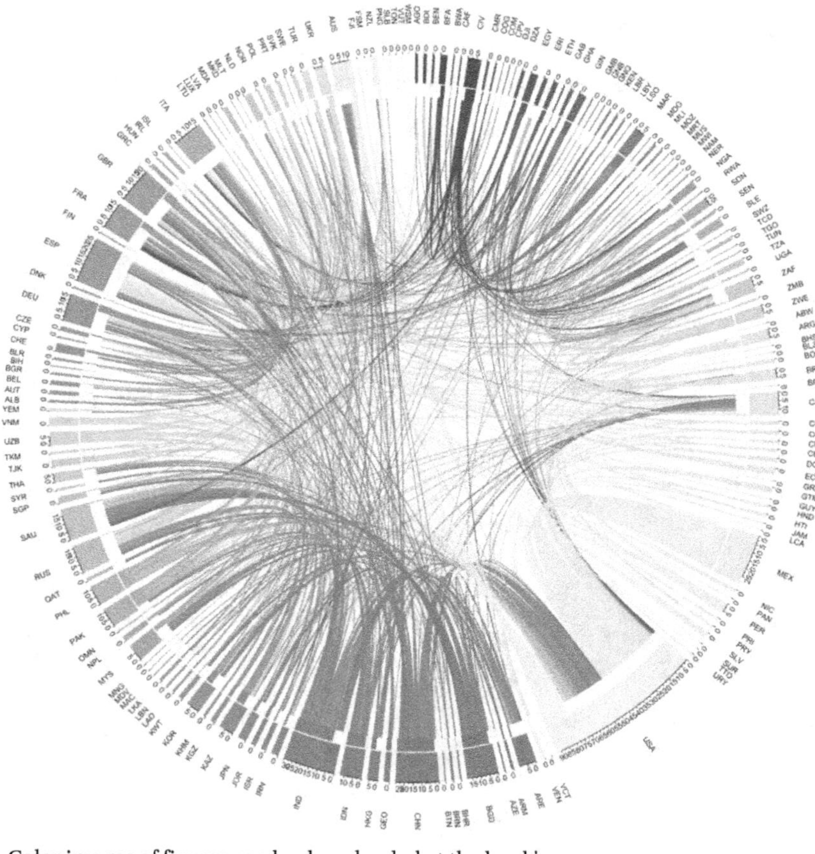

Color images of figures can be downloaded at the book's page
[URL: https://vernonpress.com/book/96]

Figure 11.2(d): Global International Migration flows – 2005-10

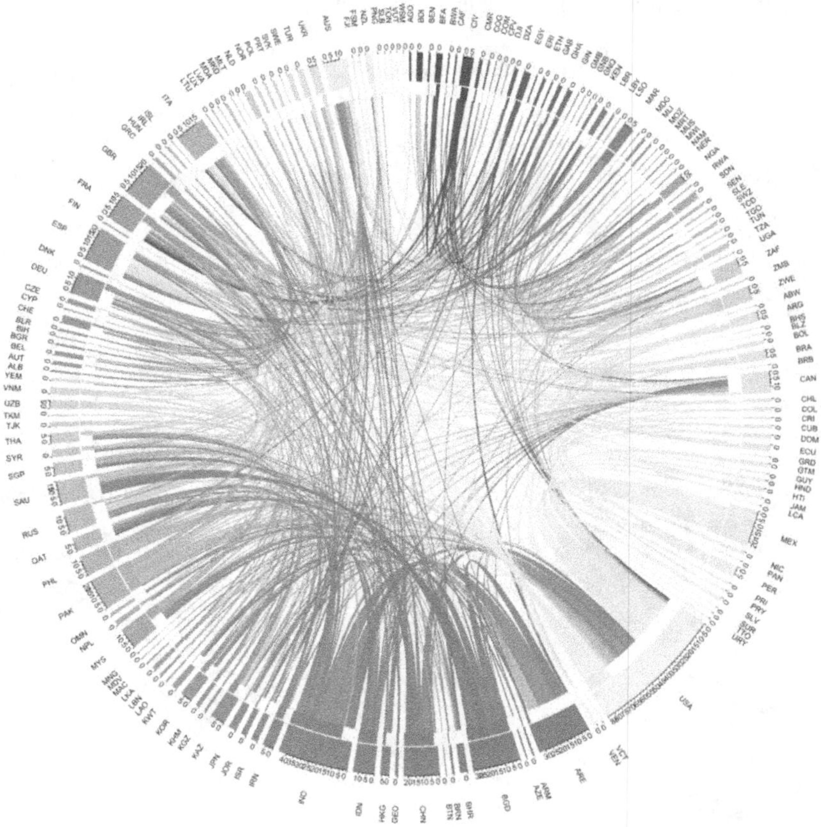

Color images of figures can be downloaded at the book's page
[URL: https://vernonpress.com/book/96]

Note: the origins and destinations of migration corridors are represented by the circle's segments. The direction of the flow is encoded both by the origin colour and by the gap between link and circle segment at the destination. The number of emigrants is indicated by the width of the link at its bases and can be read using the tick marks (in thousands) on the outside of the circle's segments. The size of the segments indicates the total amount of immigrants and emigrants of one country. Figure created with the R package "circus."

As an example, let's focus on US-Mexico migration flows between 1990 and 1995 (figure 11.3). As shown by the reference numbers, the total number of moving people from and to Mexico is above 2 million, while in the US is 7 million. The large majority of Mexican emigrants go to the US, while the US is receiving immigrants from Mexico, but also from other Central, North, and South American countries, as well as from Asian countries and, on a certain extent from the rest of the world. Emigrants from the US go to other American countries and Europe, in particular, Germany.

Figure 11.3: Global International Migration flows – 1990-95 – Zooming in (US – Mexico)

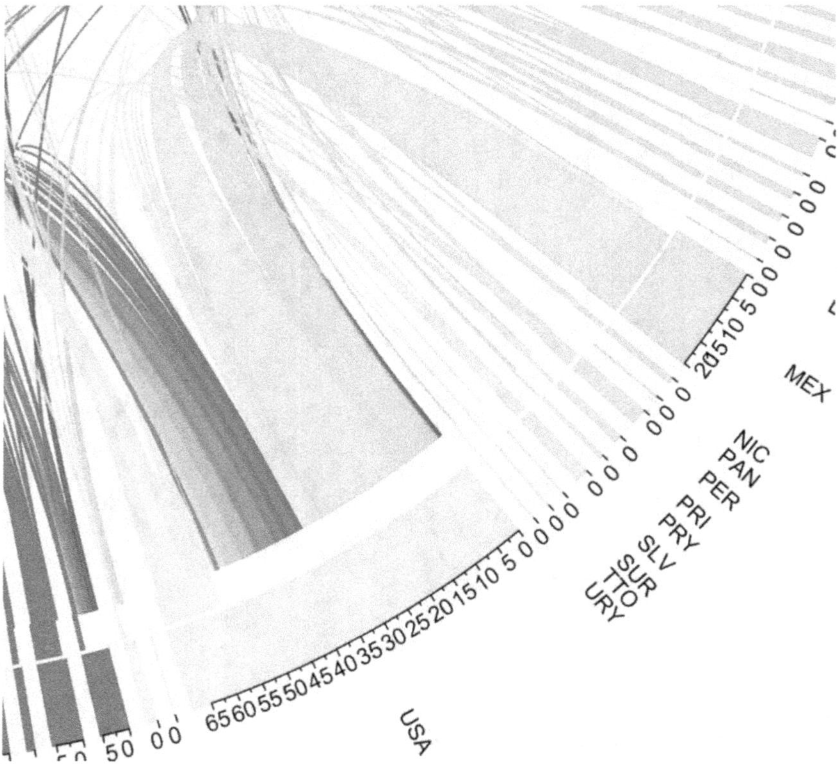

Color images of figures can be downloaded at the book's page
[URL: https://vernonpress.com/book/96]

Note: the origins and destinations of migration corridors are represented by the circle's segments. The direction of the flow is encoded both by the origin colour and by the gap between link and circle segment at the destination. The number of emigrants is indicated by the width of the link at its bases and can be read using the tick marks (in thousands) on the outside of the circle's segments. The size of the segments indicates the total amount of immigrants and emigrants of one country.

Now we can zoom-out and observe migration flows from a wider perspective. According to figure 11.2, a bird-eye view of the IMN reveals a stable intensity of global migration but some distinct features in the direction of movements. Most of the flows occur within the same arc of the circle, revealing that intra-continental flows are the most relevant share of world migration. In addition to that, we notice a decreasing trend in the number of flows passing through the centre of the circle, meaning that on average long radius distance flows are reducing over time. However, this phenomenon seems not to affect Asian countries. Moreover, if we compare the dimension of each segment in one circle, we find some large disparities in the level of the total immigration and emigration flows within continents: e.g., North America receiving and South America sending, Eastern Asia receiving and Southern Asia sending, Western Europe receiving and Eastern Europe sending. This evidence shows the constant presence of some leading countries in the network in terms of both degree and flow strength (i.e., number of migrants).

11.3 Descriptive analysis

11.3.1 Network topology features

The first network metric analysed to investigate the local and global properties of the IMN is degree centrality. To this purpose, figure 11.4 and 11.5 report the simple and cumulative distribution of this measure. This exercise reveals that the IMN is characterized by asymmetric interactions between nodes (disassortativity): i.e., weakly connected countries (i.e., low degree nodes) tend to connect to nodes with a high degree centrality, generating a degree distribution characterized by a positive skewness and a high heterogeneity, similar to those generated by a power-law. This finding, already documented by Fagiolo and Mastrorillo (2013), is consistent with a well-known process of network generation, that is a preferential attachment (Barabási and Albert, 1999). According to this model, high-degree countries are expected to get new connections at a higher rate of low-degree countries, and consequently, changes in the extensive margin of the IMN are more likely to involve countries already playing a major role in the network (e.g., world's largest economies).

Figure 11.4: In-Out Degree Distribution of the IMN – 1990-95

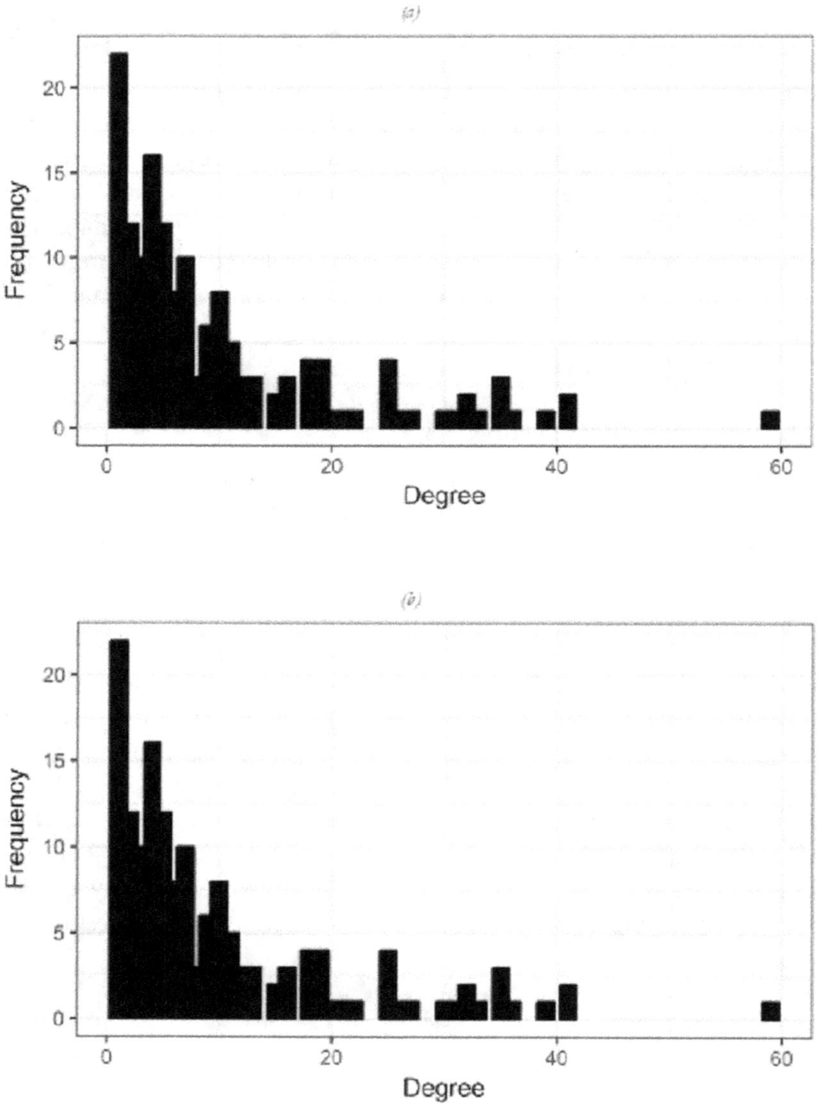

Color images of figures can be downloaded at the book's page
[URL: https://vernonpress.com/book/96]

Note: In Panel (a) and (b) is reported respectively the in and out degree distribution of the IMN. Figures created with the R package "ggplot2".

Figure 11.5: The cumulated degree distribution of the IMN

a)

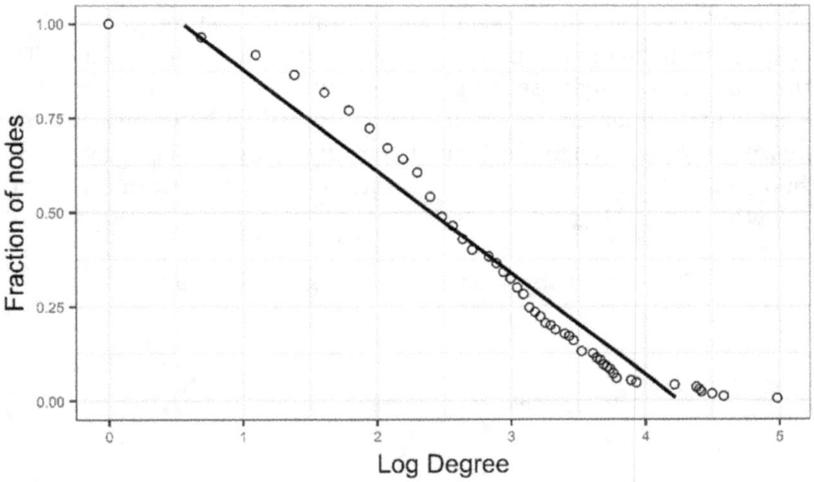

b)

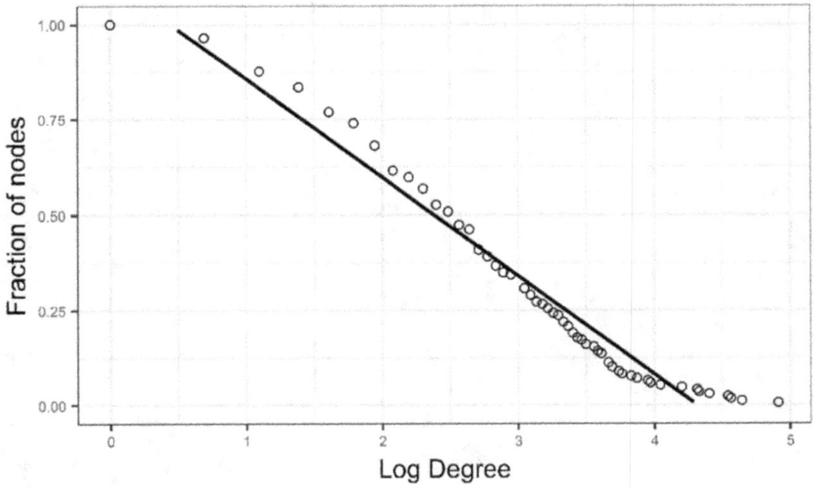

Color images of figures can be downloaded at the book's page
[URL: https://vernonpress.com/book/96]

Note: In Panel (a) and (b) is reported the cumulated degree distribution of the IMN respectively for the first and fourth wave of data. Figures created with the R package "ggplot2".

Seaquist et al. (2014) showed that the analysis of the degree in its interplay with betweenness and closeness centrality can be useful to gather additional evidence on network behaviours. Consistent with this approach, in figure 11.6 is plotted the correlation between degree centrality and respectively local clustering (panel a and b) and betweenness centrality (panel c and d). The figure shows that an increase in the degree centrality is correlated with a decrease of the former measure and an increase in the latter one. In other words, nodes connected to a high number of migration corridors play the role of hub (i.e., high betweenness) for countries not connected with each other (i.e., low local clustering).

Figure 11.6: Correlations in network centrality measures

a)

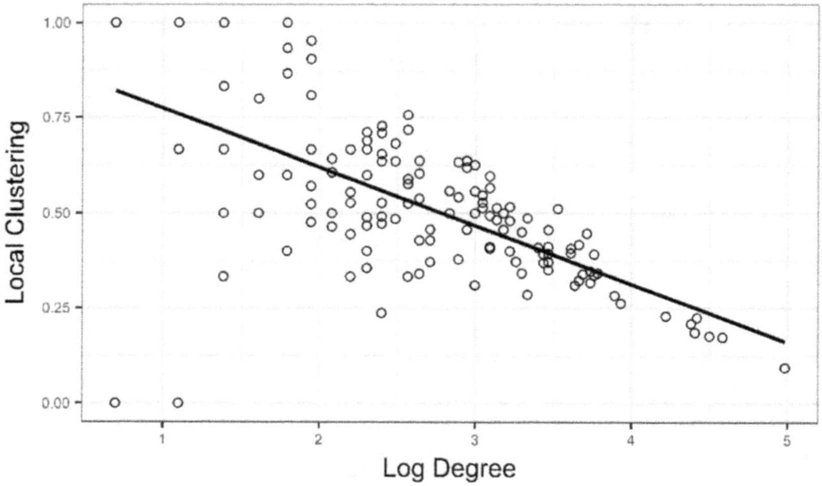

b)

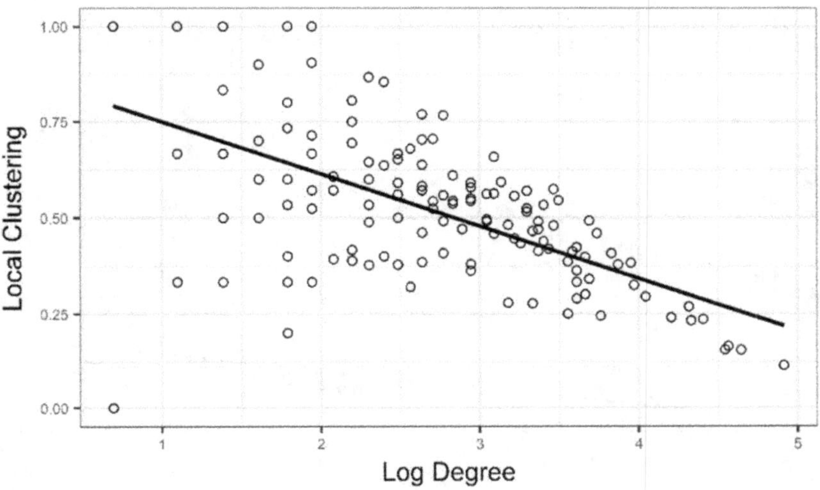
Local Clustering
1.00
0.75
0.50
0.25
0.00
1
2
3
4
5
Log Degree

c)

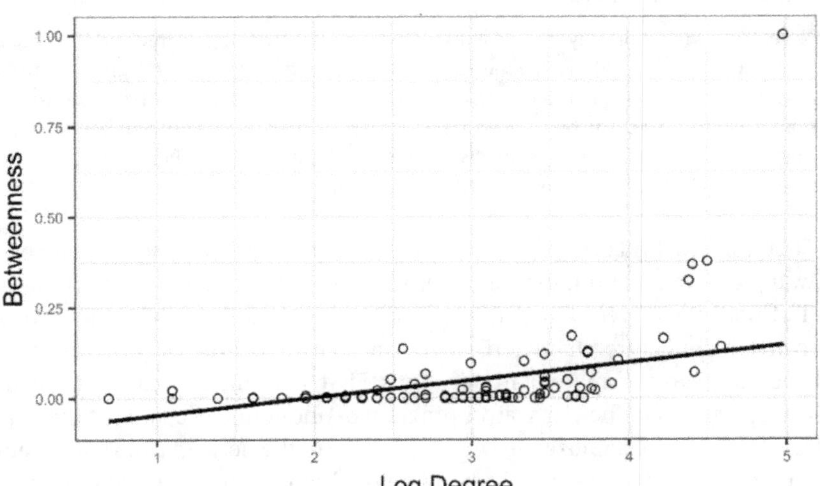
Betweenness
1.00
0.75
0.50
0.25
0.00
1
2
3
4
5
Log Degree

d)

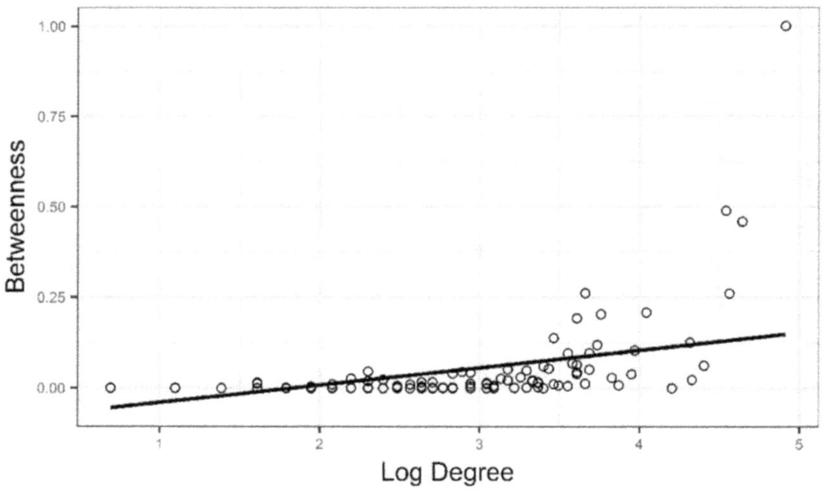

Color images of figures can be downloaded at the book's page
[URL: https://vernonpress.com/book/96]

Note: Panels (a, b) display the correlation between country's log degree and their local clustering. Panels (c, d) display the correlation between country's log degree and their betweenness. Panels (a,c) refer to the first wave of data, and panels (b,d) refer to the fourth wave of data. The black line represents the fit of an OLS regression between the (log) degree centrality and respectively the local clustering coefficient and the betweenness. Figures created with the R package "ggplot2".

Therefore, we find evidence that the IMN is characterized by the presence of few, but a significant number of nodes with many connections, and a trailing tail of nodes with very few connections. The result is the configuration of a peculiar architecture characterized by star-like structures as in figure 11.1. This finding has a number of implications. First, in terms of policy this means that a restriction in the visa waiver program of one country located at the core of the IMN may destabilize the whole structure of the network, and consistent with the disassortativity hypothesis, increase dramatically the migration pressure on other major hubs. Second, it suggests that the countries located at the core of the IMN architecture attract migrants from different peripheral areas, probably as a result of factors such as cultural and language proximity, and at the same time, they are able to affect each other's migration patterns, sorting migrants from one another. However, note that if the argument used to explain core-periphery connections (i.e., cultural and language proximity) is applied to explain the movements within the core of the network, we would observe the same composition of foreign population in all the major players of the IMN: e.g., core-nodes would be connected to the same set of peripheral nodes. This is clearly in contradiction with our findings, especially the one on the negative correlation between degree and local clustering. For this reason, under the plausible assumption that core-countries are represented by world's largest economies, I hypothesize a different mechanism of connection, that is economic proximity and skilled labour migration.

In order to test these hypotheses, the next section analyses migration flows looking at the spatial, cultural and economic features of the countries connected by them. To this purpose, the dataset by Abel and Sander (2014) is matched with the World Bank data on country GDP (World Bank, 2012) and the GeoDist CEPII dataset on bilateral distances, colonial and linguistic differences among countries (Mayer and Zignago, 2011).

11.3.2 Network configuration in space

We now turn attention to the effect of distance in shaping the global and local features of the IMN. The role played by this factor on human movements is well-known in migration literature, and it is open to a range of interpretations and measurements. Broadly speaking, bilateral geographical distance can be considered as a measure of travel time and costs, and a proxy of social, institutional, organizational proximity between two countries. As a result, it acts as a deterrent to population movements, and affect the extent of the search space considered in migration decision making.

To properly account for this effect, following Abbate et al. (2012), I create a geographical distance matrix D_t, where the generic element $d_t(i,j)$ is equal to the distance between the capitals of i and j, if they are connected in G_t, and 0 otherwise. Figure 11.7 (a) and (b) plots a kernel-density estimation for the distribution of the values of this matrix in the first and fourth wave of the data. It is easy to see that the distribution is skewed to the left and presents a peak at large distance, and that most of the migration corridors connect countries that are located at minimum 3000 kilometers from each other. The level of connectivity of the IMN as distance changes is shown in figure 11.7 (c) and (d), where it is represented respectively the simple and cumulated distribution of the percentage of connected country pairs in each kilometer. The figures show that majority of the flows occurs at short distances (i.e., between 3000 and 8000 kilometers), and there is a clear decay distribution of links as the gravity model suggests. Moreover, comparing the first and the last wave of migration, one can observe that this structural feature of the IMN has remained constant over time, even though it increased the preference for short routes.

Figure 11.7: Spatial analysis of the IMN

a)

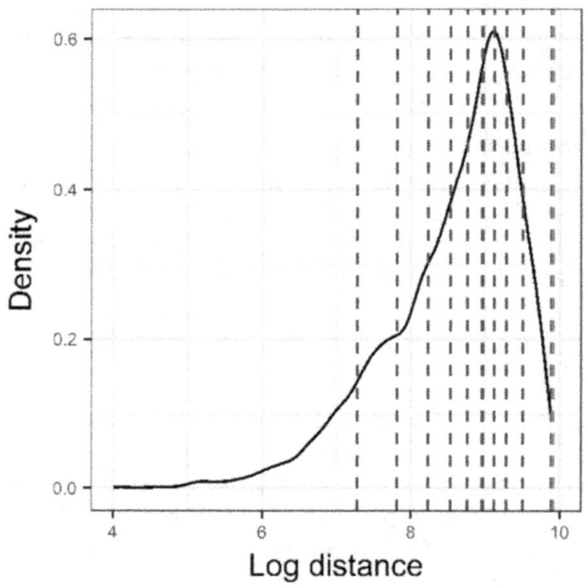

b)

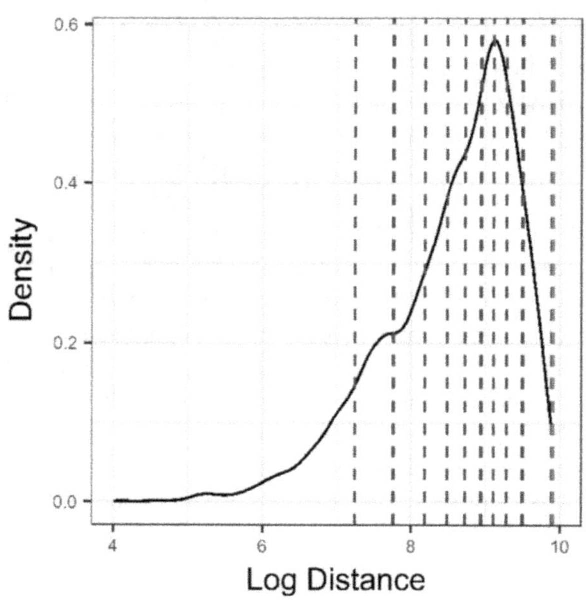

c)

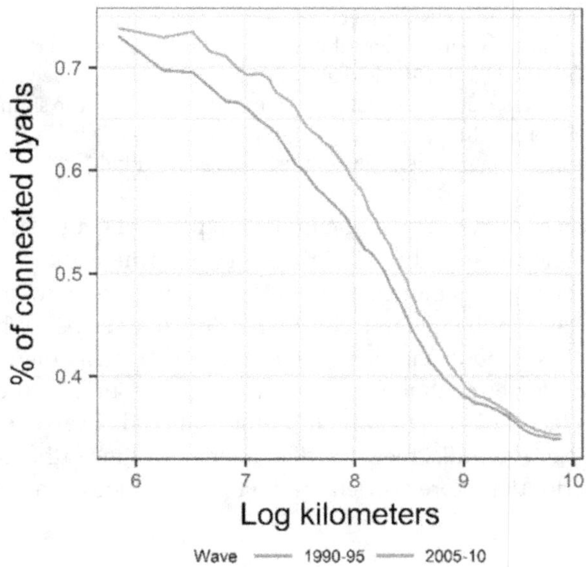

d)

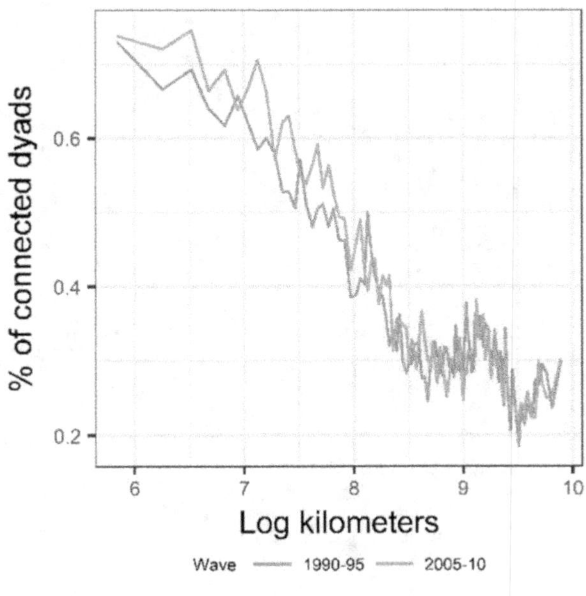

Color images of figures can be downloaded at the book's page [URL: https://vernonpress.com/book/96]

Note: Panel (a) and (b) shows, respectively, for the first and the fourth wave of the data the distribution of country pairs at different distances using a kernel density function (bandwidth = 0.09947751). Red and blue lines refer respectively to Equator distance and decile distribution. Panel (c) and (d) are respectively the simple and cumulated distribution of the percentage of connected country pairs in the IMN conditional on distance. Figures created with the R package "ggplot2".

The ten deciles of the distribution in the top panel of figure 11.7 are used to create ten subnetworks of the IMN in a given wave, where each link is equal to the number of migrants moving from i to j if the distance between two countries is smaller than the quantile considered, and 0 otherwise. When splitting the network based on distance, an interesting connectivity metric is the dispersion of the degree centrality in the network as measured by the Gini index. This value is reported in figure 11.8 (a), where one can observe that the index increases in each quantile, meaning that at larger distances the IMN presents a degree distribution more skewed on the right, configuring again a star-like structure.

Figure 11.8: Spatial and cultural features of the IMN

a)

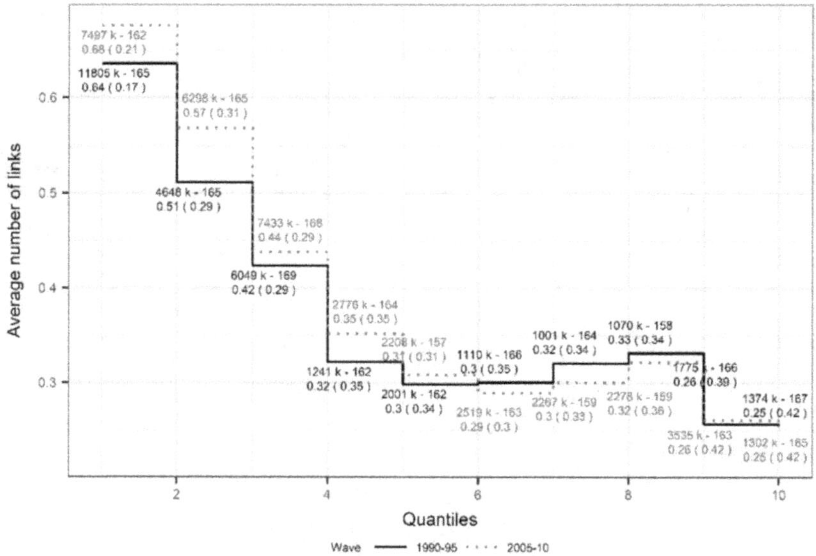

b)

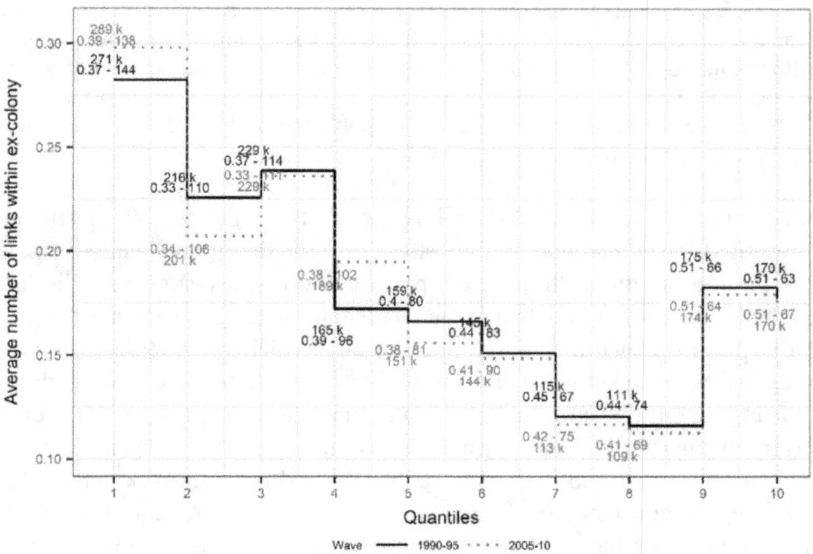

c)

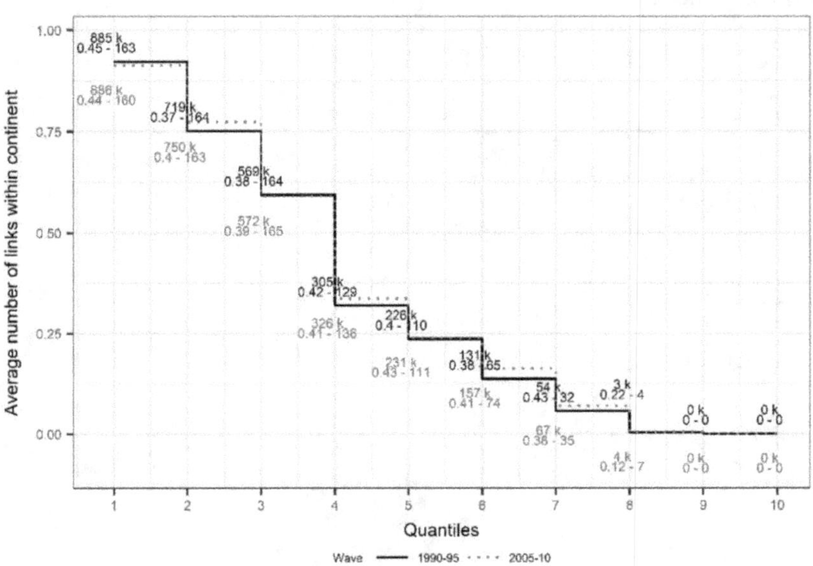

Color images of figures can be downloaded at the book's page
[URL: https://vernonpress.com/book/96]

Note: For each quantile is reported the average number of connected country pairs in the whole IMN (Panel a), within the set of countries located in the same continent (Panel b) or sharing a colonial heritage (Panel c). Each point in the plot is labelled with the number of people migrating (in thousands), the number of countries connected, and the average number of migrants passing through a migratory corridor within a quantile. Panel (a) also reports the GINI index of the degree distribution of the IMN in each quantile. Figures created with the R package "ggplot2".

An illustrative example of this finding is provided in figure 11.9, in which is represented the subnetwork of the IMN within the first (panel a and d), sixth (panel b and e) and tenth quantile (panel c and f), for respectively the first and the fourth wave of the data. In panel (a) and (d), the network is composed of a number of unconnected components, in which members are densely connected to each other. These components represent migration corridors occurring within the same continent, and perhaps unsurprisingly, the countries more engaged in these migration movements are the European ones. As the distance considered increases - panel (b) and (e) - network density becomes higher and connectivity is driven by two major hubs: one in North America, which is particularly relevant; one in Europe, where one can also observe an increased relevance of Eastern Europe, namely the Russian Federation and the Scandinavian countries. Finally, the plot of the tenth decile subnetwork shows a clear star topology, where Oceania is in the middle of world-wide flows.

Figure 11.9: The structure of the IMN at various distances

a)

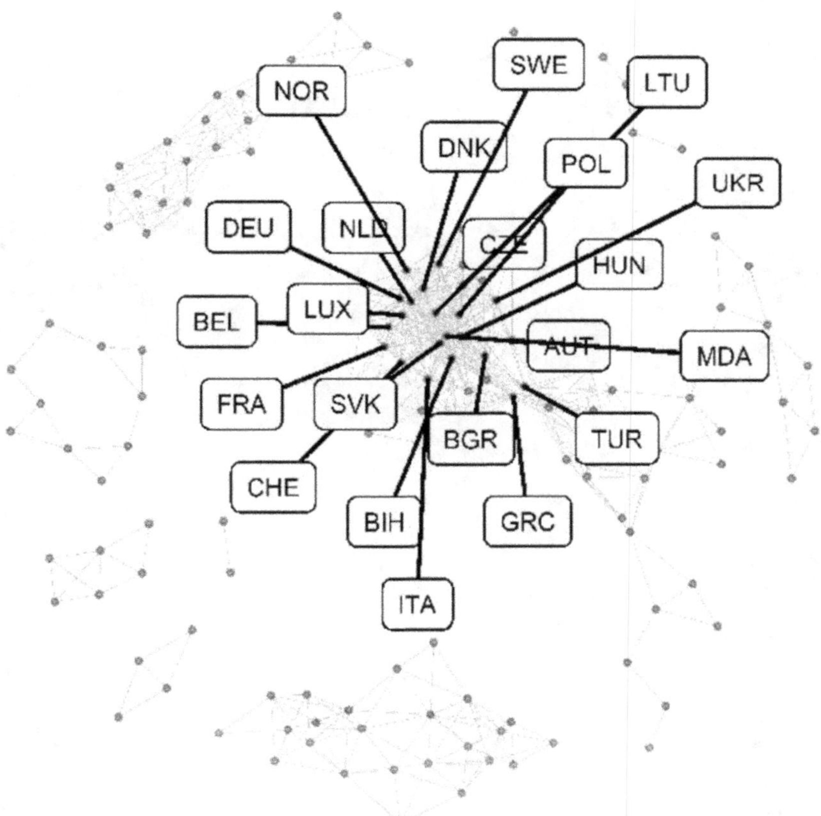

b)

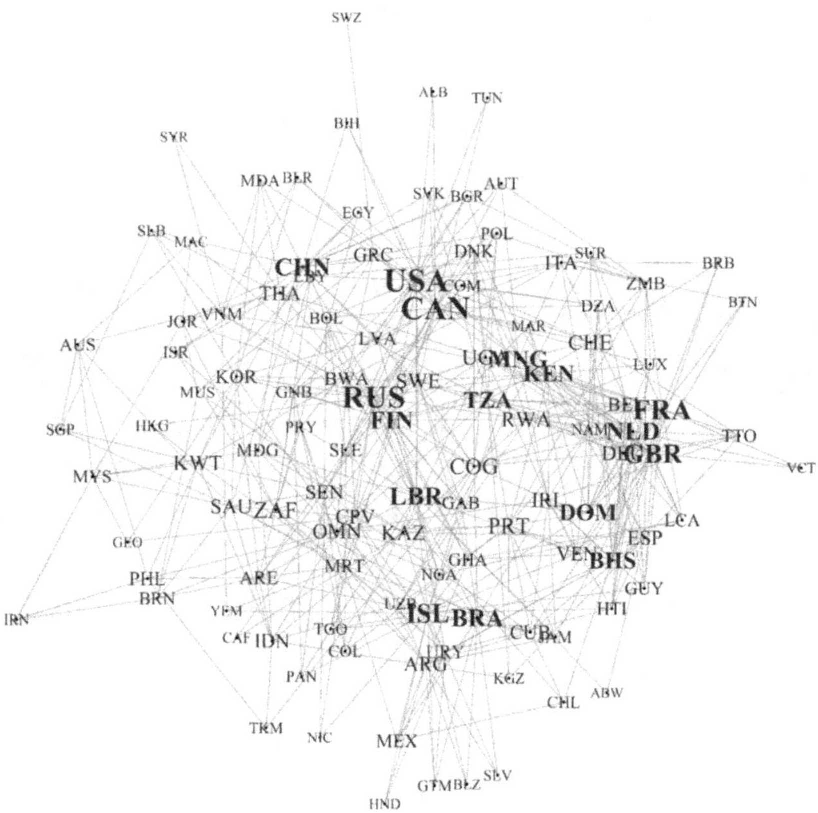
SWZ
ALB
TUN
BIH
SYR
MDA
BLR
AUT
SVK
BGR
EGY
SLB
MAC
POL
GRC
DNK
CHN
USA
CAN
ITA
SUR
BRB
THA
ZMB
DZA
BTN
JOR
VNM
BOL
MAR
AUS
LVA
CHE
ISR
LUX
KOR
BWA
SWE
KEN
MUS
GNB
RUS
TZA
FRA
SGP
HKG
PRY
FIN
RWA
NLD
TTO
MDG
GBR
KWT
COG
VCT
MYS
SEN
LBR
GAB
SAU
ZAF
CPV
DOM
LCA
OMN
KAZ
PRT
GEO
ESP
VEN
BHS
MRT
GHA
PHL
ARE
NGA
GUY
BRN
IRN
YEM
ISL
BRA
HTI
CAF
IDN
TGO
COL
ARG
PAN
KGZ
CHL
ABW
TKM
NIC
MEX
SLV
HND

c)

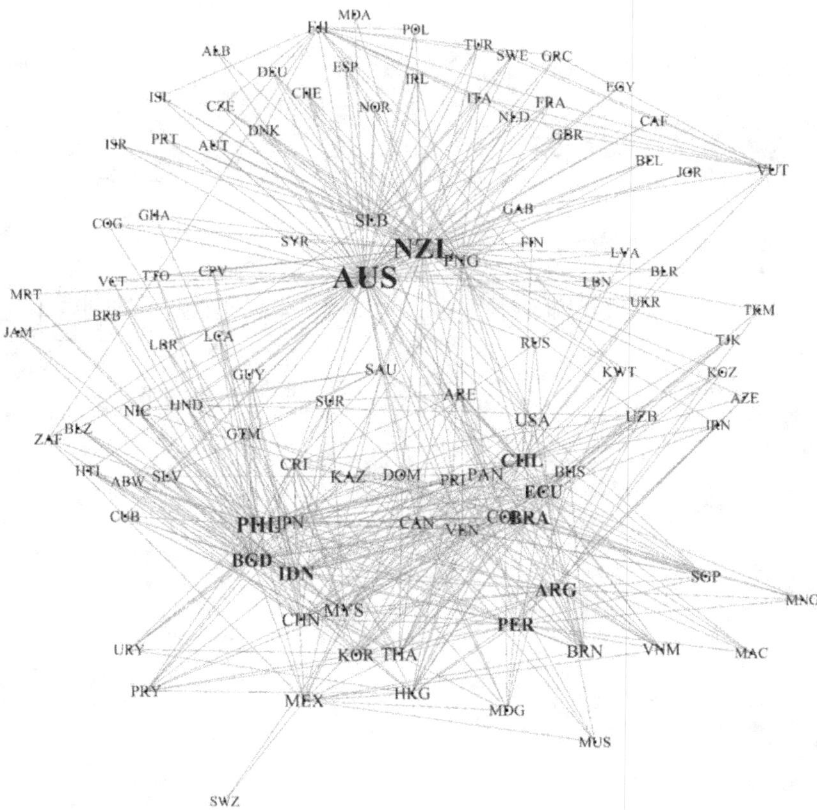

MDA
FJI
POL
ALB
TUR
SWE
GRC
DEU
ESP
IRL
ISL
CHE
EGY
CZE
NOR
ITA
FRA
NLD
CAF
DNK
GBR
ISR
PRT
AUT
BEL
JOR
VUT
GAB
COG
GHA
SEB
SYR
NZL
PNG
FIN
LVA
MRT
VCT
TTO
CPV
AUS
LBN
BLR
BRB
UKR
TKM
JAM
LBR
LCA
RUS
TJK
GUY
SAU
KWT
KGZ
SUR
ARE
AZE
NIC
HND
USA
UZB
ZAF
BLZ
IRN
GTM
CHL
CRI
HTI
ABW
SLV
KAZ
DOM
PRI
PAN
BHS
ECU
CUB
PHL
JPN
CAN
VEN
COL
BRA
BGD
IDN
SGP
ARG
MNG
CHN
MYS
PER
URY
KOR
THA
BRN
VNM
MAC
PRY
MEX
HKG
MDG
MUS
SWZ

d)

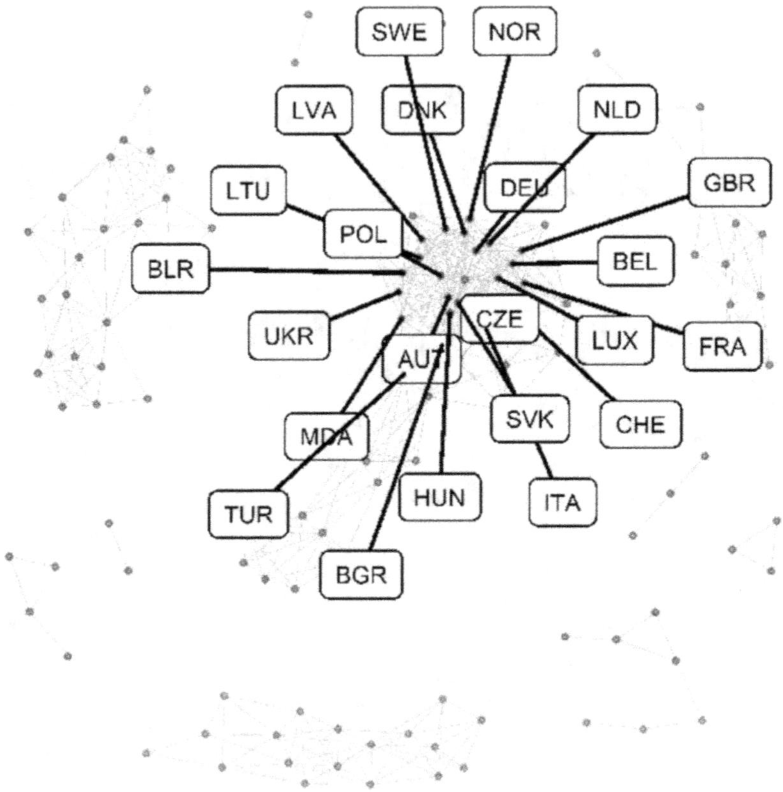
SWE
NOR
LVA
DNK
NLD
LTU
DEU
GBR
POL
BLR
BEL
UKR
CZE
LUX
FRA
AUT
SVK
CHE
MDA
TUR
HUN
ITA
BGR

e)

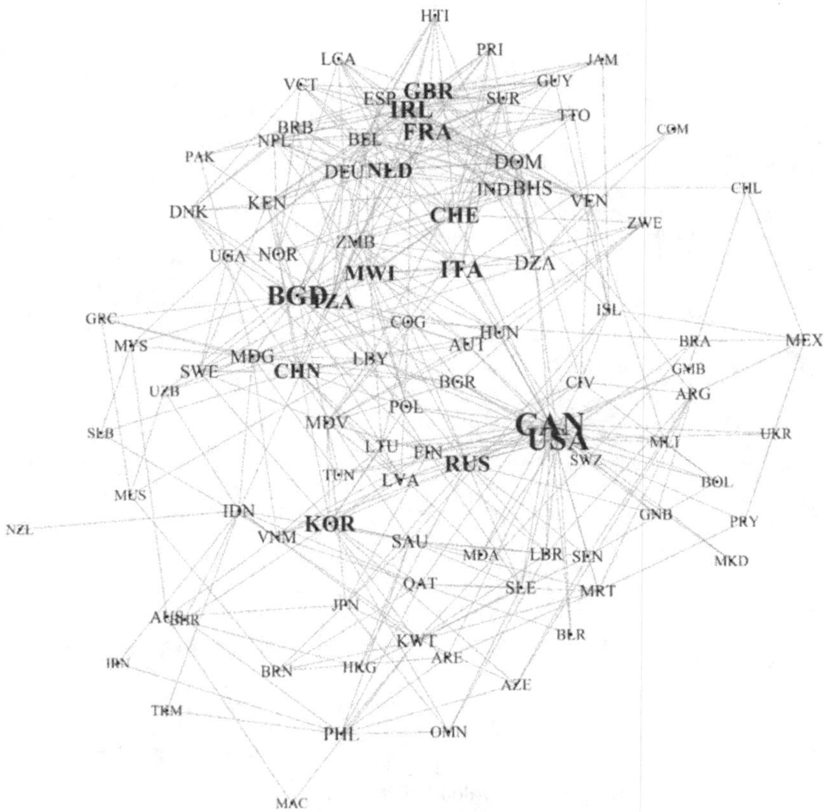
HTI
PRI
LCA
JAM
VCT
GUY
ESP
GBR
SUR
IRL
TTO
BRB
FRA
COM
NPL
BEL
PAK
DOM
DEU
NLD
IND
BHS
CHL
DNK
KEN
VEN
CHE
ZWE
ZMB
UGA
NOR
MWI
ITA
DZA
BGD
ZA
GRC
COG
ISL
MYS
HUN
AUT
BRA
MEX
MDG
SWE
CHN
LBY
GMB
UZB
BGR
CIV
ARG
POL
SLB
MDV
CAN
USA
UKR
LTU
FIN
MLI
RUS
SWZ
TUN
LVA
BOL
MUS
IDN
GNB
PRY
NZL
KOR
VNM
SAU
MDA
LBR
SEN
MKD
QAT
SLE
MRT
JPN
BLR
KWT
IRN
BRN
HKG
ARE
AZE
TKM
PHL
OMN
MAC

f)

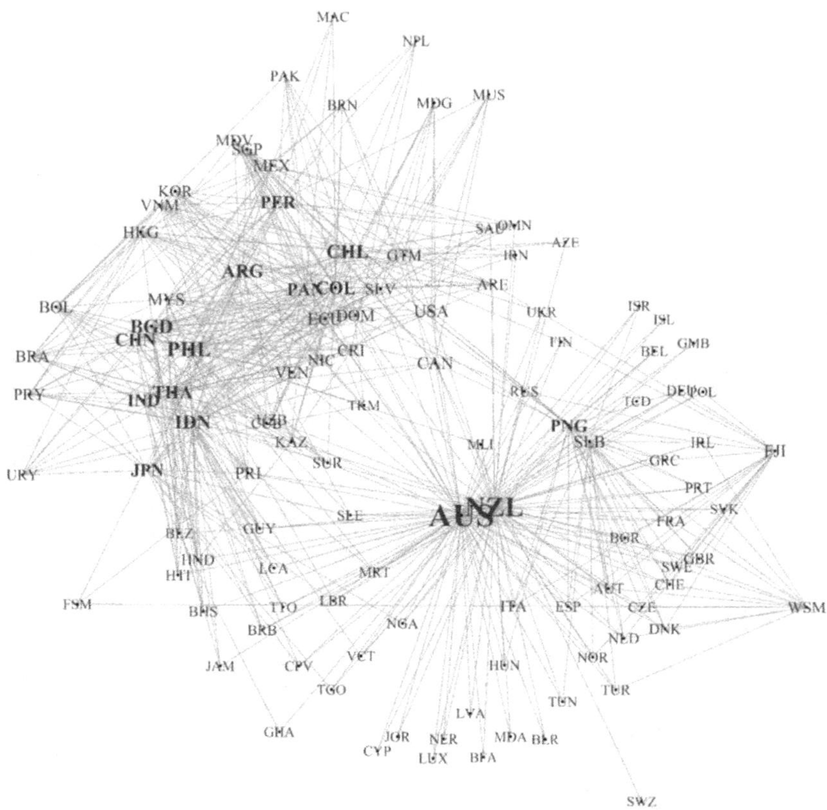

Color images of figures can be downloaded at the book's page
[URL: https://vernonpress.com/book/96]

Note: In each network, a node represents a country, and one edge connecting two nodes indicates the presence of a migratory movement between two countries within the first (panels a,d), sixth (panels b and e) and tenth (panels c and f) quantile. In Panel (a) and (d), only the 10-topmost degree countries are labelled. In the other panels, all countries are labelled, and the size of the labels is proportional to the degree centrality of the country. Labels corresponds to country's ISO3 code. Top and bottom panel represents respectively the first and fourth wave of data. *Figures created with the R packages "ggnetwork" and "igraph".*).

This exercise, by comparing countries' attractiveness and distance decay effects, provides an interesting insight into the way geography affects the formation process of the IMN. Specifically, complementing existing literature, the evidence suggests that prospective migrants discount countries' pull factors by distance, constraining the selection of potential destinations to those able to counteract distance decay effects. As a result, short distance routes tend to be homogenously distributed in a specific geographical region, while longer migration corridors tend to concentrate in specific areas, motivating the emergence of more organized star-like structures. Accordingly, we find evidence for the existence of local major players - with a high degree centrality - managing the connectivity of the network within a geographical region. However, when distance increases, few nodes remain central. To be more precise, African countries are not relevant anymore, major senders are concentrated in America and Asia, and major receivers are in Europe, North America and Australia.

11.3.3 Network cultural features

Apart from economic concerns, immigrants also seem to care about localised social interaction in the receiving areas (Wang et al., 2016). For this reason, it is common in literature to consider as a key migration driver the social, institutional and organizational proximity between two places. Consistent with this approach, in this section, I explore the IMN corridors that are likely to proxy connections between countries sharing a similarity of values and traditions. Specifically, I assume that perceived cultural proximity is stronger within a set of countries located in the same continent or sharing a common colonial heritage, as they are likely to have similar institutions or belong to the same linguistic community, and I investigate the structure of migration patterns within these areas of cultural proximity.

The average number of connected pairs in each subnetwork is reported respectively in figure 11.8 (b) and (c). The evidence from these figures shows that within the first and fourth quantile (c.a. 10,000 kilometers), a strong homophily effect is in action: more than 50% of the flows are intra-continental, and 25% of flows are directed within the same colonial community. Interestingly, this effect is almost doubled when considering only the flows making up the highest 10% of migration movements, as reported in table 11.2, column 3 and 4, meaning that a large portion of migrants is involved in this process. However, in this case, we observe a decay effect as we consider larger distance radius. In the case of intra-continental migration, this is clearly motivated by geographical reasons (i.e., the likelihood that two countries are located within the same continent decreases as distance increases). While in the case of migration between countries sharing a similar colonial past, it is likely that pull factors from other countries interfere as distance increases. As noted by Girma and Yu (2002) and Kugler et al. (2017), these migration flows connecting different cultural areas are of particular interest for the literature on trade and finance, and future research should address this topic. In fact, it is well-known that migrants facilitate cross-border transactions. Hence, they are likely to have a stronger impact on trade and financial flows for country pairs exhibiting higher informational frictions because of their cultural distance.

Finally, it should be noted that the Gini index of the degree distribution in each quantile fluctuates between 0.3 and 0.5, suggesting that stars characterize also the topology of all the subnetworks considered. In the case where only colonial linkages are considered, the hubs of these stars are most likely the ruling countries of former empires, such as Great Britain and France.

Table 11.2: Direction of top migration flows per quantile

Wave	Quantile	% of links within continent	% of links within the same colonial/linguistic area	% of links directed to countries with higher GDP
1990-95	1	88%	44%	70%
2005-10	1	88%	40%	37%
1990-95	2	69%	61%	73%
2005-10	2	92%	50%	69%
1990-95	3	87%	52%	82%
2005-10	3	92%	56%	80%
1990-95	4	55%	35%	60%
2005-10	4	52%	39%	65%
1990-95	5	12%	18%	41%
2005-10	5	10%	40%	70%
1990-95	6	26%	26%	84%
2005-10	6	30%	30%	50%
1990-95	7	0%	37%	56%
2005-10	7	10%	42%	68%
1990-95	8	0%	55%	83%
2005-10	8	0%	55%	70%
1990-95	9	0%	53%	86%
2005-10	9	0%	50%	100%
1990-95	10	0%	50%	71%
2005-10	10	0%	46%	73%

Note: The table reports the direction of the topmost flows in each quantile. Flows are selected from the highest decile of the distribution of link weights in the subnetwork of the IMN in each considered quantile.

11.3.4 Network economic features

This last section analyses the most relevant destination and origin countries and their ranking in the worldwide GDP classification. To this purpose, in table 11.2, column 5, is reported the direction of the flows making up the highest 10% of migration movements. In addition, in table 11.3 are listed the topmost relevant destinations and origins in each quantile, their in- and out-degree in the related subnetwork, and GDP rank.

As expected, despite some fluctuations, the majority of migration corridors are directed towards countries with a higher GDP (within a range of 50 to 80%), and topmost relevant countries of destination are characterized by a high GDP (i.e., USA, UK) or rising economies (Latin American countries and Asian tigers in the 90's, BRICs in the next decade), a finding consistent with Peres et al. (2016). This evidence, therefore, substantiates the hypothesis that economics is the key driver of the structure of the IMN.

More surprisingly, the richest destinations are also relevant origin countries, and many of them are located close to each other (e.g., European countries). The correlation between in and out degree measures and GDP, presented in figure 11.10, clearly shows that countries with a high number of both incoming and outcoming flows are mostly the members of the OECD or the BRICs.

Interestingly, when looking at the three topmost migration flows in each subnetwork, as in table 11.4, the majority of the senders are large developing nations, mostly located in Asia (e.g., Pakistan and Bangladesh), where the local economies have become more and more globalised in the last 20 years. A finding consistent with UNDP (2009).

Table 11.3: Top 1 Origin and Destination countries per quantile

		Topmost Relevant Destination				Topmost Relevant Origin			
Wave	Quantile	Country	Out Degree	In Degree	GDP Rank	Country	Out Degree	In Degree	GDP Rank
1990-95	1	India	3	4	16	Rwanda	5	0	131
1990-95	2	Egypt	22	10	47	Russian Federation	20	11	9
1990-95	3	Mexico	9	7	12	USA	15	18	1
1990-95	4	Colombia	6	5	40	Germany	7	17	3
1990-95	5	USA	18	16	1	Germany	10	14	3

1990-95	6	Philip-pines	5	11	42	USA	28	23	1
1990-95	7	USA	17	14	1	Germany	2	16	3
1990-95	8	Great Britain	12	13	6	Canada	13	22	7
1990-95	9	Korea	8	10	13	USA	26	27	1
1990-95	10	Thailand	30	1	29	USA	12	15	1
2005-10	1	Singapore	1	4	39	France	17	16	4
2005-10	2	United Arab Emirates	2	10	38	India	4	2	16
2005-10	3	USA	17	16	1	Mexico	9	9	12
2005-10	4	United Arab Emirates	15	9	38	Bangla-desh	10	2	52
2005-10	5	United Kingdom	11	21	6	USA	13	12	1
2005-10	6	Italy	3	16	5	USA	28	17	1
2005-10	7	Spain	2	19	8	China	14	6	11
2005-10	8	Spain	0	13	8	China	9	3	11
2005-10	9	USA	21	27	1	India	6	0	16
2005-10	10	USA	12	14	1	Philip-pines	31	20	42

Note: The table reports the top 1 origins and destinations of the IMN in each quantile. The value out (in) degree counts the number of out (in) flows connected to the country within the considered quantile. GDP rank reports country's ranking in terms of GDP in the considered temporal interval.

Table 11.4: Top 3 migration flows per quantile

1990-95		2005-10	
1th quantile			
Bangladesh	India	Malaysia	Singapore
India	Pakistan	Indonesia	Malaysia
Malawi	Mozambique	Tanzania	Burundi
2nd quantile			
Armenia	Russia	India	United Arab Emirates
Turkey	Germany	Bangladesh	India
Egypt	Saudi Arabia	Zimbabwe	South Africa
3rd quantile			
Mexico	USA	Mexico	USA
Kazakhstan	Russia	Kazakhstan	Russia
Guatemala	USA	Uzbekistan	Russia
4th quantile			
Colombia	USA	Bangladesh	United Arab Emirates
Bangladesh	Saudi Arabia	Bangladesh	Saudi Arabia
Kyrgyzstan	Germany	Bangladesh	Qatar
5th quantile			
Kazakhstan	Germany	Peru	USA
USA	Germany	USA	Spain
Peru	USA	Pakistan	Great Britain
6th quantile			
Philippines	Saudi Arabia	USA	Italy
Thailand	Australia	India	Great Britain

Bosnia and Herzegovina	USA	Indonesia	United Arab States
	7th quantile		
USA	Greece	Ecuador	Spain
Thailand	Germany	China	Australia
Egypt	USA	Zimbabwe	Great Britain
	8th quantile		
Great Britain	South Africa	India	Australia
China	Canada	China	Canada
Thailand	France	Argentina	Spain
	9th quantile		
Korea	USA	India	USA
China	USA	China	USA
India	USA	India	Canada
	10th quantile		
Thailand	USA	Philippines	USA
Philippines	USA	Great Britain	Australia
Brazil	Japan	Thailand	USA

Note: For each quantile are reported the three-topmost migration flows.

The evidence for star-like structures in the IMN, combined with that of a positive correlation between GDP and in and out degree, may indicate that the set of destinations for an origin country is a proxy of the skill composition of its labour force: e.g., unskilled workers from developing nations move towards richer countries to exploit higher salaries and a smaller variance in the distribution of the economic inequality (see, e.g., Borjas 1987b), determining a disassortative network process (i.e., star-like structures); on the contrary, the citizens of developed nations have a larger set of choices, since they represent a source of skilled workers or investments in each destination, and consequently they are more evenly distributed on a larger number of corridors, including the ones within the core of the network. To test this hypothesis, the scatterplots in figure 11.11 report the correlation between country's

GDP and respectively indegree (panel a and c) and outdegree (panel b and d). It is easy to observe a positive correlation between these metrics, and that the most relevant sources and destinations in the IMN are represented by the members of the OECD, China and the Russian Federation, a finding consistent with (Tranos et al., 2015).

Figure 11.10: Correlation between in and out degree

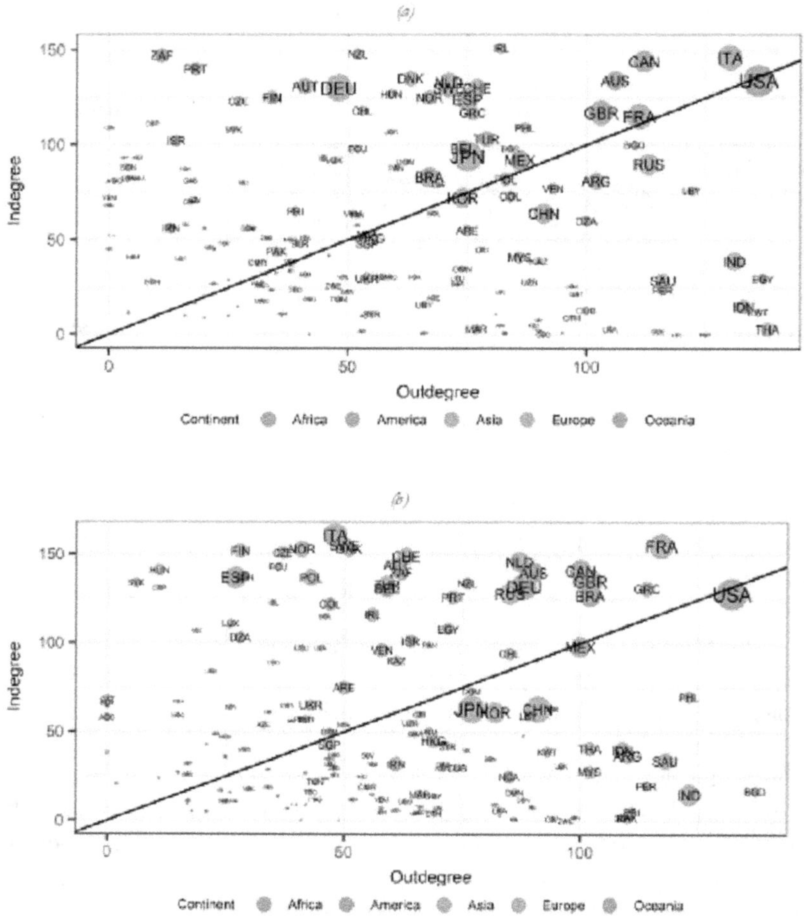

Color images of figures can be downloaded at the book's page
[URL: https://vernonpress.com/book/96]

Note: Panel (a) and (b) represents respectively the first and fourth wave of the data. The size and the label of each dot are proportional to country's GDP. The 45-degree line represents the region where in and out degree overlap. Figures created with the R package "ggplot2".

Figure 11.11: Correlation between In-(Out) degree and GDP

a)

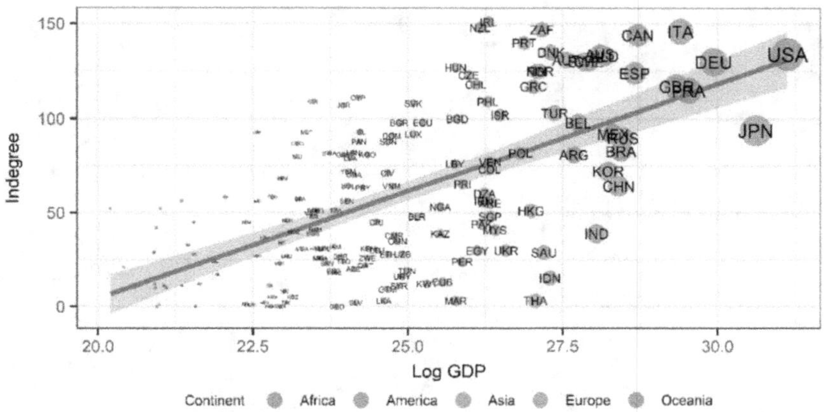

b)

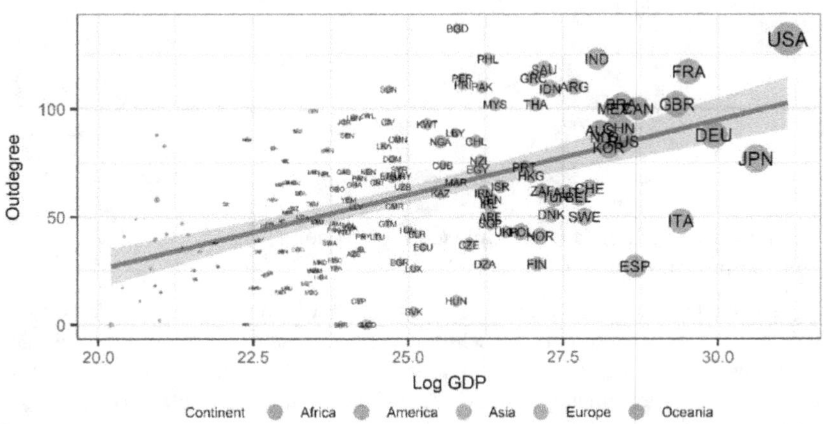

c)

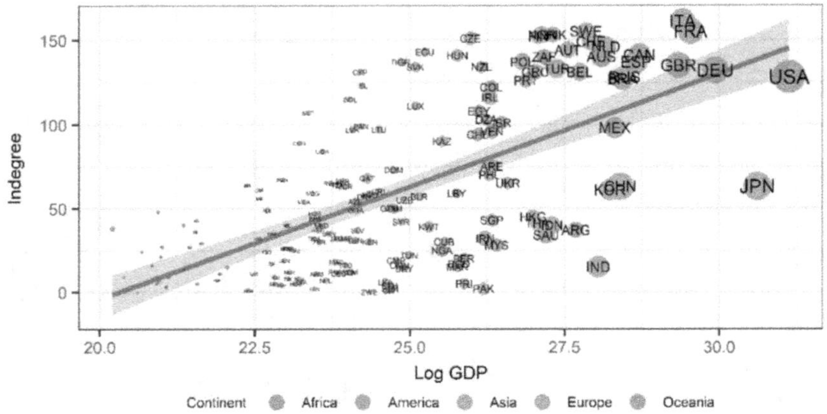

d)

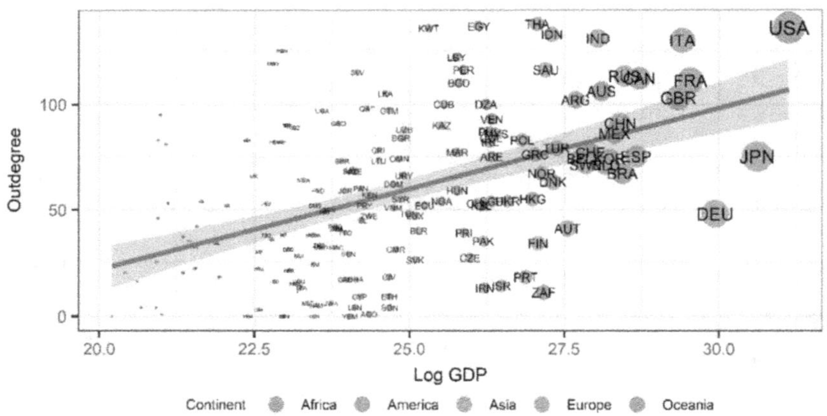

Color images of figures can be downloaded at the book's page
[URL: https://vernonpress.com/book/96]

Note: Panel (a) and (b) represents the correlation between respectively in and out degree in the first wave of data. Panel (c) and (d) represents the correlation between respectively in and out degree in the fourth wave of data. The size and the label of each dot are proportional to country's GDP. The blue line represents the fit of an OLS regression between In (out) degree and log GDP. Figures created with the R package "ggplot2".

The conjecture of a correlation between out-degree centrality and skill labour composition might point out future directions of research. A rising literature on the link between trade and migration (Lopez and Schiff, 1998; Docquier and Lodigiani, 2010; Aubry et al., 2012; Campaniello, 2014) found that the movement of people and goods are complementary in the case of skilled labour migration, and substitute when considering the mobility of unskilled workers. The implication is that opening markets in a specific area might slow down migratory movements originating from the core of the IMN (skilled workers) and promote inflows from the periphery of the network (unskilled workers), worsening the skill composition of foreign workers in that region. Consequently, the study of country's centrality in the IMN may provide interesting insights to orientate trade policies and evaluate their impact on migratory processes.

11.4 Conclusions

A thorough understanding of international migration dynamics is essential to fully realize the prospective benefits determined by this phenomenon while mitigating any adverse consequences (Davis et al., 2013). In this chapter, I introduce a number of methods and visualization strategies borrowed from the framework of the SNA, in the attempt to acquaint the reader of a set of available tools for an innovative approach to the investigation of human movements that explicitly consider the externalities generated by the multilateral resistance to migration. Drawing from the lessons of the literature on gravity models of international migration, and the one on the network analysis of the international trade network, this framework employs geographical and cultural distances between countries in order to filter the different push and pull factors of migration movements in the IMN and uncover important insights regarding the interactions of migration with the social and economic sectors.

Through an extensive characterization of the IMN over the last 20 years (1990-2010), I establish a basis with which to examine potential drivers of migration, namely geographical, cultural and economic distances, and how the relations between migration and these factors changed over the years. Consistent with existing literature, my main result is that geography matters also from a network perspective. The probability of observing the creation of a human corridor in the IMN decreases when considering larger distance radius. In addition to that, the analysis suggests that within the set of destinations available within a certain space, migrants do not choose at random: they prefer moving to countries sharing their linguistic-colonial heritage and with higher welfare. Moreover, comparing the GDP of the topmost sender and receiving countries at various distances, I have found that the outdegree of one country might proxy the skill composition of its labour force: while unskilled workers from developing countries move in large numbers through few human corridors, skilled migrants from developed nations are sparsely located in a higher number of links.

Comparing the results over time, I have found an increase in the number of topmost destinations in the IMN, largely resulting from an increasing involvement of developing countries as they are assimilated into the globalisation process. However, the analysis shows that the major modifications of the IMN occurred in the intensive margin of the network, meaning that the architecture of international migration has remained stable. This result is consistent with the hypothesis of a self-reinforcing process on the intensive margin of the network, and it indicates that the persistent difference in the economic sizes of the countries still explains most of the human movements, also from far-away countries.

The intrinsic heterogeneity of the different sources of migration, determined by the combination of all the factors discussed so far, can be adequately described by a persistent hierarchical architecture, with a prevalence of star-like structures, where few specific countries work as hubs of the system. I hypothesized that the mechanism underlying this process is that hubs receive unskilled migration from countries with similar cultural characteristics (e.g., language), and send skilled labour migration to other hubs similar to them. As a result, the level of embeddedness of one country in the IMN appears as a powerful source of information to improve and further unfold the dynamics underlying migratory processes and its multilateral resistances. With this respect, SNA provides an appropriate theoretical framework of analysis that can be used to extend this study in many innovative ways. In particular, I have stressed two potential direction of research: the study of the impact of different migration flows on informational frictions and the investigation of the mechanism through which trade policies affect the intensive margin of the IMN.

The major limitation of this study lies in the lack of a consistent methodology to precisely use SNA for modelling choices, in order to obtain a better assessment of the impact of migration drivers in determining the IMN structure. A natural framework for this analysis would seem the one provided by exponential random graph models. The main feature of ERGMs is the ability to model the structural generation of networks based on both endogenous and exogenous factors, providing an insight into the main drivers of relational phenomena without reducing their heterogeneous nature. However, the application of this method to the investigation of the IMN presents two major challenges at the moment. First, ERGMs provide consistent parameter estimates when the model is sufficiently sparse, so the extremely dense nature of the IMN is likely to generate problems of computation tractability. Second, a correct analysis of the link generation process of the IMN requires a consideration of the historical path dependence affecting the evolution of the network and the different intensities of migratory corridors. However, the state-of-the-art techniques allow ERGMs to model either the formation of the intensive margin in one temporal instance, disregarding the effect of "diaspora externalities" and changes in the extensive margin across time, or the temporal evolution of the IMN structure, assuming the same intensity in all migration flows. Further research is therefore required to provide an appropriate framework for an inferential analysis of the IMN.

11.5 References

Abbate, A., De Benedictis, L., Fagiolo, G. and Tajoli, L. (2012) 'The international trade network in space and time', LEM Papers Series, 17.

Abel, G. J. and Sander, N. (2014) 'Quantifying global international migration flows', Science, 343(6178), pp. 1520–1522.

Artuç, E., Docquier, F., Özden, Ç. and Parsons, C. (2015) 'A global assessment of human capital mobility: the role of non-OECD destinations', World Development, 65, pp. 6–26.

Aubry, A., Kugler, M. and Rapoport, H. (2012) 'Migration, FDI and the Margins of Trade', Boston: Center for International Development, Harvard University.

Barabási, A.-L. and Albert, R. (1999) 'Emergence of scaling in random networks', Science, 286(5439), pp. 509–512.

Beine, M., Bertoli, S. and Fernandez-Hueras Moraga, J. (2015) 'A practitioners' guide to gravity models of international migration', The World Economy, 39(4), pp. 496–512.

Bertoli, S. and Moraga, J. F.-H. (2013) 'Multilateral resistance to migration', Journal of Development Economics. Elsevier, 102(May), pp. 79–100.

Borjas, G. J. (1987a) 'Immigrants, minorities, and labor market competition', ILR Review, 40(3), pp. 382–392.

Borjas, G. J. (1987b) 'Self-selection and the earnings of immigrants', National Bureau of Economic Research.

Campaniello, N. (2014) 'The causal effect of trade on migration: Evidence from countries of the Euro-Mediterranean partnership', Labour Economics, 30, pp. 223–233.

Card, D., Dustmann, C. and Preston, I. (2012) 'Immigration, wages, and compositional amenities', Journal of the European Economic Association, 10(1), pp. 78–119.

Charbonneau, K. B. (2014) 'Multiple fixed effects in binary response panel data models', The Econometrics Journal.

Davis, K. F., D'Odorico, P., Laio, F. and Ridolfi, L. (2013) 'Global spatio-temporal patterns in human migration: a complex network perspective', PloS one, 8(1).

Docquier, F. and Lodigiani, E. (2010) 'Skilled migration and business networks', Open Economies Review, 21(4), pp. 565–588.

Docquier, F. and Rapoport, H. (2012) 'Globalisation, brain drain, and development', Journal of Economic Literature, 50(3), pp. 681–730.

Dumont, J.-C. and Lemaître, G. (2005) Counting immigrants and expatriates in OECD countries. OECD Publishing.

Fagiolo, G. and Mastrorillo, M. (2013) 'International migration network: Topology and modeling', Physical Review E, 88(1), p. 12812.

Fagiolo, G. and Mastrorillo, M. (2014) 'Does human migration affect international trade? A complex-network perspective', PloS one, 9(5), p. e97331.

Fagiolo, G. and Santoni, G. (2015) 'Human-Mobility Networks, Country Income, and Labor Productivity', Network Science, 3(3), pp. 377–407.

Girma, S. and Yu, Z. (2002) 'The link between immigration and trade: Evidence from the United Kingdom', Weltwirtschaftliches Archiv, 138(1), pp. 115–130.

Graham, B. S. (2015) 'Methods of identification in social networks', Annual Review of Economics, 7, pp. 465–485.

Jackson, M. O. (2010) Social and economic networks. Princeton: Princeton University Press.

Krugman, P. (1995) 'Increasing returns, imperfect competition and the positive theory of international trade', Handbook of international economics. Elsevier, 3, pp. 1243–1277.

Kugler, M., Levintal, O. and Rapoport, H. (2017) 'Migration and cross-border financial flows', The World Bank Economic Review, p. lhx007.

Lopez, R. and Schiff, M. (1998) 'Migration and the skill composition of the labour force: the impact of trade liberalization in LDCs', Canadian Journal of Economics, pp. 318–336.

Mayda, A. M. (2010) 'International migration: A panel data analysis of the determinants of bilateral flows', Journal of Population Economics, 23(4), pp. 1249–1274.

Mayer, T. and Zignago, S. (2011) 'Notes on CEPIIs distances measures: the GeoDist Database', CEPII Working Paper, (25).

Munshi, K. (2016) 'Community networks and migration', The Oxford Handbook of the Economics of Networks. Oxford University Press New York, NY, pp. 630–648.

Mytna Kurekova, L. (2010) Theories of migration: Conceptual review and empirical testing in the context of the EU East- West flows, CARIM AS 2010/44, Robert Schuman Centre for Advanced Studies, European University Institute.

Özden, Ç., Parsons, C. R., Schiff, M. and Walmsley, T. L. (2011) 'Where on earth is everybody? The evolution of global bilateral migration 1960--2000', The World Bank Economic Review, 25(1), pp. 12–56.

Pedersen, P. J., Pytlikova, M. and Smith, N. (2008) 'Selection and network effects-Migration flows into OECD countries 1990-2000', European Economic Review, 52(7), pp. 1160–1186.

Peres, M., Xu, H. and Wu, G. (2016) 'Community Evolution in International Migration Top1 Networks', PloS one, 11(2), p. e0148615.

Pesaran, M. H. (2006) 'Estimation and inference in large heterogeneous panels with a multifactor error structure', Econometrica. Wiley Online Library, 74(4), pp. 967–1012.

Pesaran, M. H. and Tosetti, E. (2011) 'Large panels with common factors and spatial correlation', Journal of Econometrics, 161(2), pp. 182–202.

Rapoport, H. (2016) 'Migration and globalisation: what's in it for developing countries?', International Journal of Manpower, 37(7), pp. 1209–1226.

Rauch, J. E. (2001) 'Business and social networks in international trade', Journal of economic literature, pp. 1177–1203.

Ravenstein, E. G. (1885) 'The laws of migration', Journal of the Statistical Society of London, 48(2), pp. 241–305.

Ravenstein, E. G. (1889) 'The laws of migration', Journal of the Royal Statistical Society, 52(2), pp. 241–305.

Seaquist, J. W., Johansson, E. L. and Nicholas, K. A. (2014) 'Architecture of the global land acquisition system: applying the tools of network science to identify key vulnerabilities', Environmental Research Letters, 9(11), p. 114006.

Tranos, E., Gheasi, M. and Nijkamp, P. (2015) 'International migration: a global complex network', Environment and Planning B: Planning and Design, 42(1), pp. 4–22.

UNDESA (2013) 'Trends in International Migrant Stock: Migrants by Destination and Origin', United Nations database, 2013.

United Nations Development Program (2009), Overcoming barriers: human mobility and development.

Wagner, D., Head, K. and Ries, J. (2002) 'Immigration and the Trade of Provinces', Scottish Journal of Political Economy, 49(5), pp. 507–525.

Wang, Z., De Graaff, T. and Nijkamp, P. (2016) 'Cultural diversity and cultural distance as choice determinants of migration destination', Spatial Economic Analysis, 11(2), pp. 176–200.

World Bank (2012) 'World development indicators 2012', World Bank database. World Bank Publications.

Zipf, G. K. (1946) 'The P1 P2/D hypothesis: On the intercity movement of persons', American sociological review, pp. 677–686.

Conclusion

This book is a collection of chapters authored by some of the most knowledgeable scholars working on the application of network analysis to international economics issues. Among these issues, many refer specifically to the study of international trade, the single most covered topic in this field. The chapters of this book explore broad questions that have been left partly understudied by the more traditional empirical literature. All of them relate to the general concern of better understanding the nature and features of the global economy, international economic integration and the more likely scenarios for the evolution of the various flows that link countries to one another, namely trade, investment, migration, international trade agreements, international production networks.

While the number of publications on network analysis to economics has significantly grown in recent years, this is the first book that specifically refers to the application of network analysis to international trade and investment, with the aim of providing a starting point and state of the art (through examples) that will aid interested readers in the exploration of this literature and help them make sense of the inter-disciplinary nature of the work that applies network analysis to international trade and investment.

This is why we believe it was important in the first chapter to provide a discussion of the origins of social network analysis and network science – the two main perspectives taken in this book – in a way that helps explain their differences and similarities. Despite the almost opposite take of these two approaches – with SNA emphasising the importance of theory and idiosyncrasies; while NS takes a theory-free and context-free approach aiming at identifying universal features across very different complex networks – we believe that they can complement each other and be used to answer different questions in the area of international trade and investment. While SNA can be used to test theories in specific settings, NS can provide insights about universal features across different networks that can help explain their structure.

Overall, the chapters in this book show that network analysis can be much more than a nice alternative or a useful complement to traditional methods ignoring the network structure of economic relations, but rather an essential approach and methodological toolkit to disentangle some of the inconclusive debates in the literature. For example, the analysis of the long-term evolution of global economic interdependence through a new generation of gravity models that can reproduce both the existence and the intensity of interactions can provide a comprehensive explanation to the idea that distance is not dead, despite the decreasing costs of covering that distance, and that the world is not flat, but hyperbolic.

Moreover, globalisation is an evolutionary process that develops through subsequent waves to which individual or groups of countries contribute, such as in the case of emerging economies. These countries can be considered an outcome of the so-called second wave of globalisation running from the 1960s until the 1990s, and at the same time a major driver behind the evolution from the second to the following wave, i.e., from a pattern of international interaction of all countries with one another regardless of any form of distance (globalisation), to a hub and spoke structure that prevails nowadays.

Unlike macro issues related to the international trade network, network analysis applied to the study of micro issues in international trade, such as the web of linkages among firms participating to the same value chain, is less frequent, due to the greater difficulty in collecting the necessary data. Identifying the complex micro-level network structure underlying the international trade network is challenging due to data availability but provides an area of promising future research.

Among the non-trade issues explored in this book, namely international investment, free trade agreements, and migration - there seems to be more scope for future research avenues for two main reasons. Firstly, they have somehow been underexplored so far due to data limitations. Secondly, international investment, international migration, international free trade agreements are all related to international trade in several ways that deserve further research efforts. As an example, the intensive margin of the international migration network can be affected by trade policies, while at the same time it is widely acknowledged in the literature that migration affects the pattern of international trade. This means there are mutual interactions between those two networks – the world trade network and the international migration network – which can be usefully studied with network methods.

Index

A

B

C

D

E

F

G

H

I

J

K

L

M

N

O

P

Q

R

S

T

U

V

W

www.ingramcontent.com/pod-product-compliance
Lightning Source LLC
LaVergne TN
LVHW010722210926
848485LV00007B/1422/J
9781622730650